Voyages and Beaches

Voyages and Beaches

Pacific Encounters, 1769–1840

edited by

Alex Calder, Jonathan Lamb, and Bridget Orr

University of Hawai'i Press

Honolulu

Library of Congress Cataloging-in-Publication Data
Voyages and beaches : Pacific encounters, 1769–1840 / edited by Alex
   Calder, Jonathan Lamb, Bridget Orr.
     p. cm.
   Papers presented at the 9th David Nichol Smith Memorial Seminar,
University of Auckland, 1993.
   Includes bibliographical references and index.
   ISBN 0-8248-2039-8 (alk. paper)
   1. Oceania—Discovery and exploration—Congresses. I. Calder,
Alex. II. Lamb, Jonathan, 1945–   . III. Orr, Bridget. IV. David
Nichol Smith Memorial Seminar (9th : 1993 : University of Auckland)
DU20.V69   1999
995—dc21   98-42426
                                                                CIP

University of Hawai'i Press books are printed on acid-free paper and meet the
guidelines for permanence and durability of the Council on Library Resources.

Designed by Jennifer Lum
Printed by the Maple-Vail Book Manufacturing Group

CONTENTS

ILLUSTRATIONS

1

INTRODUCTION

Postcoloniality and the Pacific

Alex Calder, Jonathan Lamb, and Bridget Orr

The essays collected in this volume originated as papers delivered to the ninth David Nichol Smith Memorial Seminar, convened at the University of Auckland in 1993.[1] The organizers of that event hoped its location, squarely in the South Pacific, might provide an opportunity for a more even-handed discussion of contact between Polynesians and Europeans than has been common in accounts and critiques of eighteenth- and early-nineteenth-century voyages of so-called discovery. It was hoped that the continuity of South Pacific cultures, despite the large scale of European intervention after the eighteenth century, might be manifest not just as the theme but also as the climate and condition of Oceanic history. Samoan, Fijian, Tongan, and Maori scholars agreed to collaborate with their colleagues from the other side of the beach to produce a joint investigation of a shared past. The conference was welcomed by Albert Wendt, the renowned Samoan novelist who holds the chair of English at Auckland University, and it was formally invited onto the *marae* of the University by Ranginui Walker, the chair of Maori studies.[2] In the first session, Professor Walker outlined a conspectus of Maori myth; in the last, the Niuean writer and painter John Pule told the story of a recent journey home. This helped to anchor the terms of the conference in the South Seas, promoting the sort of dialogue called in Maori *"korero,"* where the exchange of views constitutes a political reality as well as a search for truth—where something is done as well as known. The extent to which the gathering responded to this challenge the following selection of papers will tell; but even as an idea, it registered a new departure in arraying and judging the stories of voyages and exchanges in the Pacific region. So often limited to a chronicle of violence and exploitation, disguised as a civilizing mission and involving the unlimited aggressive entry of an alien power upon indigenous societies, it was hoped that the joint enterprise of *korero* might disclose the analogies, overlaps, and to-ings and fro-ings that entangle the Polynesian and European senses of the past.

It need hardly be said that written histories of Pacific voyaging have been partial. J. C. Beaglehole's encyclopedic editions of the journals of Captain James Cook and Sir Joseph Banks (1956–1967), which remain the best source for documents ancillary to Cook's three voyages in the Pacific between 1768 and 1779, are nevertheless organized from a point of view celebratory of a great feat of European navigation, not from a perspective of an equal Pacific history. John Dunmore's *Who's Who in Pacific Navigation* (1991), while acknowledging the skills of Chinese, Polynesian, and Melanesian sailors, limits its entries to Europeans on the grounds that the myths of Kupe, Maui, and Hotumatua, for example, "do not provide sufficient data for adequate biographies in the historical sense of the term."[3] The most recent history of Europeans in the South Seas is concerned with tracing the effects of novelty solely in terms of the categories and tastes of the voyaging culture: "As the Marquesan question was the nature of the savage, so the Tahitian question was the nature of the civilized savage—thus of civilization itself."[4] It remains a theoretical task of magnitude to find a mode of ethnographizing European voyages on the one hand, and on the other of reciting local histories in their own terms, without falling foul of the very categories that make the reversal necessary in the first place. Notable attempts have been made: Greg Dening's *Islands and Beaches: Discourse on a Silent Land* (1980) remains the starting point for historical reflections on what can be known of cultures in moments of contact that are not our own; Marshall Sahlins has theorized the "structure of the conjuncture" of encounter in several innovative and controversial works whose reception we discuss below. The inspiration of Dening and Sahlins is a thread that leads or unravels through most of the contributions to this collection in ways they might not have foreseen but that we acknowledge with gratitude.

The privileging of the written record of the Pacific has involved such a radically binary idea of difference that it is difficult to articulate any cultural relation between voyagers and indigenes without its becoming starker. Political history in Europe begins with the distinction between the civilizing contract and the savage state of nature; and depending on the bent of each political philosopher, either the benefits of contract are so plain as to make the alternative unthinkable (Thomas Hobbes, Edmund Burke), or civil society has entailed corruption on such a scale that the state of nature must be mourned as a lost paradise (Rousseau, Adam Ferguson). Depending on the school of thought, savagery has worn either the extreme face of unrestrained violence and pernicious ignorance, producing infamous instances of cannibalism, infanticide, and lewdness, or the no less extreme aspect of primordial innocence, where food comes without work and sexual pleasure without penalty.[5]

William Ellis' book *Polynesian Researches in the South Sea Islands* (1829) provides a compendium of the first sort of savagery, comprising a list (drawn up in remarkable detail) of the idolatries and enormities the first missionaries encountered and then set themselves the task of eradicating. Conventionally, Denis Diderot's *Supplement au voyage de Bougainville* (1773), which exploits the French explorer's reaction to Tahiti as "New Cythera," a pastoral idyll equal to François Boucher's landscapes, is regarded as the amplest testimony to the nobility of the savage; but in fact the discovery of Tahiti by Europeans simply confirmed what they had known since Thomas More published his *Utopia* (1516), namely, that if the perfect state (eutopia) was not a figment with no location (outopia), then it was to be found in the South Seas. Various scientific, erotic, and political commonwealths were set there, culminating in Jonathan Swift's coalition of the genres of utopian romance and modern maritime journalism, *Gulliver's Travels* (1726).[6] In *The Great Map of Mankind* (1982), P. J. Marshall and Glyndwr Williams have traced the appropriation of Oceanic cultures to similar Arcadian and Theocritan idylls. On the basis of Richard Walter's enthusiastic account of Commodore Anson's voyages along the western seaboard of South America, Horace Walpole, for example, compares Juan Fernández (Alexander Selkirk and Robinson Crusoe's island) with the garden of Alcinous in the *Odyssey*.[7] The fashion for Gothicizing or Hellenizing the adjuncts of Polynesian life, comparing their practice of warfare with ancient models of patriotic valor, such as Lord Kames' treatment of the Maori in his *Sketches of the History of Man* (1774), was reinforced by the efforts of Cook's artists, especially William Hodges on the second voyage and John Webber on the third, whose predetermined ways of seeing the primitive as the past made present, have been well chronicled by Bernard Smith in *European Vision and the South Pacific* (1960) and *Imagining the Pacific* (1992).

Perhaps there are worse fates than to be made the alibi of European political history, the vivid instance of what civility is not, its prehistory cast in the form of geographical remoteness and simple manners, but it is extremely hard to escape from. The harsh injustices visited by Europeans on the inhabitants they found—the enslavement of Easter Islanders, the massacre of Australian Aboriginals, the alienation of Maori land, the dismantling of religions—joined with the epidemics of venereal disease, smallpox, tuberculosis, and influenza that threatened the extirpation of whole populations, are some of its grimmest consequences. Others are to be observed, paradoxically, in the very modes chosen to lament these enormities. By casting the European role in the Pacific as a contribution to a concerted global program of exploitation, whether cognitively or economically conceived (the "writ of rationality" or the "penetration of the marketplace"), the rehearsal of the "fatal-impact" thesis reinforces the very binary distinction between a civil or corrupt society and an evil or innocent tribal culture upon which the whole enterprise was originally founded. To reverse the terms of ignoble and noble savagery does nothing theoretically to remove the burden borne by those representing the starting point of Western history; for one way or another their loss defines and vindicates this history by presenting its subject (European consciousness) with its other (what it cannot or will not know).[8] Whether it is Ellis' horror at idolatry or Diderot's nostalgia for sexual spontaneity, history streams on uninterrupted, validating a subject position for which that history is the indispensable predicate, and for which savage existence is the preterite. Even as it valorizes the so-called authentic voice of a local culture, the fatal-impact narrative deploys a *taste* for the primitive in order to place the voice out of hearing—and therefore to call its silence "prehistoric" as well as tragic—as effectively as the most assiduous missionary.[9] The value of savagery lies thereafter in the unfathomable enigmas proposed by its muteness—in short, in its titillation of subjectivity.

Authenticity and total loss reinforce each other in this globalizing equation, where the degree to which a culture is irrecoverable is the sure index of the fineness of the consciousness that registers it, whether to celebrate or deplore its disappearance. Greg Dening calls this "the zero point of ethnohistory,"[10] the result (as Jacques Derrida points out in his essay on Levi-Strauss) of the inescapable Eurocentricity of the anti-Eurocentric gesture.[11] It is a paradox expanded by Jonathan Friedman, when he represents the anthropological *prise de conscience* as operating with one's back to the center while fixing one's gaze "innocently upon a captive and already classified periphery."[12] It really does no service to local culture to say that in changing it becomes less than it was, because it leaves the victims of change the options either of vanishing into the long night of authenticity or of applying for subject status in the only history on offer. Yet this is the theme, and these are the terms, of that branch of postcolonial thought deriving from the Subaltern Studies group, led by the Indian Marxist Ranajit Guha and now, especially in the work of Gayatri Spivak and Homi Bhabha, drawing on a wider theoretical base, and influential in the Anglo-American academy. In this argument, subalternity is the surplus of a worldwide colonial design, the waste created by a supremacist plot so extensive that the only exit is via its network of repressive agencies. Only by means of a hybridization of the subject position, achieved by methods cognate with the deconstructive turn in poststructuralist thought, such as interpellation (in respect of ideology), transference (in respect of the unconscious), or textualization (in respect of the signified), the subaltern acquires a portion of the consciousness, language, and agency used for the plot.[13]

Questions concerning who has the right to represent the subaltern as speechless in the first place, or to redeem him and her from hegemony by mandarin feats of analysis, or to introduce the essentialist difference between subjectivity and alterity as the precondition for deconstructing it, or to suppose the Western subject delineates the horizon of all emergent or "insurgent" narratives and histories, have been defended vigorously enough.[14] But it is clear that subaltern studies and postcolonial discourse theory, while insisting on representing their clients in the global terms of the subject/other binarism, maintain an agenda peculiar to specific economic and political regions, chiefly postcolonial India, the Middle East, and the former slave economies of the Caribbean and the Americas, where the question of alienation involves the elements of a sophisticated market, such as labor, class, commoditization, and feminism, rather than land or culture in its pre-civil state. Indigenous cultures in the Pacific that have survived colonialism, such as those in Fiji, Vanuatu, Samoa, Tonga, and Aotearoa–New Zealand, are anomalous to this way of thinking, and sometimes quite repugnant to its political assumptions, and have attracted relatively little attention from its representatives. So far as this debate has reached them, it has been inflected by two discourses tangential to the theorization of the subaltern: those of feminism and cultural nationalism. The same repressive violence that constructs subalternity also constructs gender, thus providing a global correlate for metropolitan feminists by means of aligning the form of the feminine and its gender markings to specific cultural practices in Oceania, such as tattooing.[15] Locally, indeed, the resemblance between the politics of gender and the insignia of cultural difference have contributed to the discovery of powerful female voices, yet it remains an issue whether the specificity of the ethnographic datum—for example, the use of tattoos precisely to distinguish male from female—does not get lost in the process. Cultural nationalism in its various forms conspires with settler guilt to narrate a history of violent entry and land seizure as an overture to postcolonial accommodation with subalternity that confirms a new joint nationhood. To trade the confession of wrongdoing, or even the outrage of indigenous victims, for an endowment in a place that can be called "home" ("the promise that the subject will once again be able to appropriate all those things that are kept at a distance by difference, and find them again in what might be called his abode")[16] is an act of atonement, or accusation, which sentimentalizes the savageries of the past to guarantee a future and proves once again that the *primitive,* being essentially a temporal concept, is a category, not an object, of Western thought."[17] It is merely an extension of the missionary position, exhibiting the sin of despoliation in the best light, and proffering itself at once as a rape and a benediction, like Diderot's chaplain in Tahiti who cries out, "But my religion! But my holy orders!" as he copulates with Orou's daughter. The most corrupting myth to have entered the Pacific, perhaps, was the myth of innocence. There can be no more notorious instance than the French decision to resume nuclear testing at Mururoa Atoll in 1995: The same nation that discovered a paradise on these islands resolved, with all the insolence of power, to complete their transformation into a hell on the grounds that the inhabitants were hybridized citizens of the French republic, their rights intact and unabused. It is among the intellectual salons of the same nation that postcoloniality is awarded a ticket of leave in order to pursue the critique of imperialism.[18]

In awareness of what it costs to posit an accurately observing and judging subject, anthropology has been ahead of the game that postcolonial discourse theory and cultural nationalism only hesitantly play in the South Pacific. As well as being properly cautious about the gaze they turn to the periphery, anthropologists make no generalizations about hegemony, or about the coherence of European designs upon Oceania. "The prospects that normally attracted Europeans—the acquisition of land and territory for settlement, the extension of trade and the discovery of gold and silver—here played only a minor role."[19] The scientific enterprises of the British and French explorers of the Pacific were notable for diversity and digression rather than tabulation and taxonomy, as David Mackay points out below; and even when curiosity gave way to exploitation, conversion, and colonization, the projects were as likely as not to fail or to provoke an outcome very distant from the intention.[20] The pragmatic and uncertain tendency of the process seems to have encouraged an extraordinary attentiveness to detail, or what ethnographers term, after Clifford Geertz, "thick description," and what the earliest journalists apologized for as "minute particulars" or "little circumstances."[21] Well before B. K. Malinowski compiled the details of the Kula ring, the revolving protocol of exchange in the Trobriand Islands (*Argonauts of the Western Pacific*, 1922), such missionaries as William Ellis paid scrupulous attention even to those ceremonies they were most keen to see abolished.[22] Ellis wrote Polynesian ethnography in spite of himself, noting, for example, the seven levels of the Arioi, the group of libertine, aristocratic vagrants who circulated among the Tahitian Islands, together with the names and designs of the seven different tattoos appropriate to each class.[23] There has been plenty of local information, and local informants have not disappeared. By knowing that they had their backs to a center while facing, not so innocently, a constructed periphery, anthropologists have recorded minutely and (as far as they could) without prejudice Polynesian practices of self-representation and cultural reproduction that conspiracies of European ignorance, hostility, guilt, and piety have not succeeded in interrupting or eradicating. The puzzled fascination with which Europeans such as Joseph Banks and William Ellis greeted tattoos has not resulted in the loss of the art, nor in the obstruction of the social and political purposes tattooing serves, although the historical "truth" of such a practice — requiring a judgment concerning the determinate relation of an aesthetic phenomenon to the material circumstances of its production at a given moment in time — may never be known. A recent book on the topic suggests that the Maori, from before Cook's arrival up to the extraordinary ritualization of violence in the film of Alan Duff's novel *Once Were Warriors,* have used tattoos to signal and to adjust their relation to power.[24] As a legatee of this tradition of particularizing anthropology, Nicholas Thomas warns against the danger of importing the globalizing tendency of postcolonial discourse theory into the analysis of Oceanic data. He argues that European explorations and settlements within the Pacific have generated a mass of information that is various and local, to be understood not in terms of class and category but in terms of moments of cultural entanglement.[25]

The diffidence shared by anthropologists of the Pacific about garnering and arranging information, and their hesitancy in offering totalizing accounts of postcolonial circumstances, have a cost. If history is not global but local, and if it is not simply the series of recited genealogies, what law of change does it observe and what discontinuities can it sustain? How does time work in a Polynesian narrative? And who tells the story? Marshall Sahlins and Valerio Valeri have put these questions frequently and ingeniously; and in collaboration with Patrick Kirch, Sahlins has attempted a history of Hawai'i based on the evidence of archaeology, archives, genealogies, chants, and myths.[26] It is the culmination of a lifetime's work in the Pacific, during which he has become convinced that its history is best summed up in the paradox "Usurpation itself is the principle of legitimacy."[27] Between the descent from the gods articulated in genealogy and the ambitions of individual chiefs expressed in various acts of mayhem, there is a perpetual conflict partly disguised by the *mana* of the victor, which he acquires by virtue of a sacrilege cashable as a divine imprimatur. As for the narrative of this history, *mana* has a lot to do with it too, for another axiom of Polynesian history, according to Sahlins, is that "an action that fails for want of *mana* is a lie."[28] The legitimate form of such a narrative ought to be performed in that extension of the first person singular that Sahlins, after J. P. Johansen, calls "the kinship I," where the pronoun encloses the experience not of one individual but the whole tribe.[29] If the paradox of legitimation by usurpation is to retain its force, however, there must be a moment of pronominal egoism that precedes and flavors the kinship I and must issue—at least for a moment—as a singular and specific challenge from one I to another I.

Sahlins' work has met with a good deal of skepticism, principally because his structuralist account of cultures that reproduce themselves by means of violent interruptions seemed to pre-systematize historical change, and to trap it in a pattern of synchronic correspondences. Nicholas Thomas has argued that Sahlins has not produced a theory of indigenous change that can account for the transformation of Hawaiian and Western Polynesian societies along different lines.[30] To take Sahlins' own instance, why did Hawaiians make themselves into the food of gods by human sacrifice, while Maori used ritual cannibalism to eat like gods?[31] As for the kinship I, and its hovering between the points of egoistic challenge and tribal representation, Johannes Fabian has suggested that the inherently autobiographic nature of anthropological reporting, disguised by the obstinate use of the third person, is another version of this problem, where the challenge comes "marked as discourse/commentary pronounced by an I, first person singular."[32] This may help to explain the challenges and counterchallenges recently exchanged on this very topic of usurpation between Gananath Obeyesekere and Marshall Sahlins, in the course of which they have hashed and rehashed the circumstances surrounding Cook's death at Kealakekua Bay in Hawai'i, in 1779. In two pieces of historical anthropology, *Historical Metaphors and Mythical Realities* (1981) and *Islands of History* (1985), Sahlins suggested that the death of Cook was a consequence of his making an unlucky entry into the ritual display of usurpation in the Hawaiian calendar, the Makahiki festival, and, in being mistaken for Lono, the god of fertility, who is fated to die, of embarking on a sequence that would lead to an equally fatal conclusion. By constituting the very usurpation that the ritual represented, Cook provoked the descent from mythic generality to eventful particularity on which Hawaiian history depends. In the specifically usurpational terms that constitute both the modes of cultural renewal among Hawaiians and also their sense of genealogy as history, he made something happen that would be remembered: "The generic version of the theory of usurpation was working in Hawaiian politic-ritual practice down to, and including, the advent of Captain James Cook."[33] It was an interruption both foreseen and contingent, preserving the descent of Hawaiian history from myth to event by means of unique interruptions that actualize general phenomena.[34]

In an argument that is in some ways exemplary of a subaltern studies position, Obeyesekere accused Sahlins of ornamenting and perpetuating a British imperial myth by resting his case on the assumption that Hawaiians would be so naïve and impractical to mistake Cook for a god. That is the sort of mistake, contended Obeyesekere, that the British imperialist flatters himself the indigenous person always makes because he is so overawed by the self-command and the power of the white invader. He may well be right about the illusions of the British, and even perhaps of Cook, who seems to have entered willingly enough into the role of Lono, but he was not right about Sahlins, who was doing his best to explain and prove the power of local history to absorb contingencies, and to exploit for its own ends the actions of the famous explorer. Sahlins has always aimed to show how Hawaiian history overrode, and can still override, exotic historical narratives by usurping in their turn the usurpations they threaten. To give any color to his case that Sahlins was doing the opposite, Obeyesekere was obliged to literalize the claim for Cook's place in the Makahiki (Cook really was Lono, not the "icon of an icon," as Sahlins says) and then to base his rebuttal on the facts of the matter and the common sense, the "practical rationality," of the Hawaiians. Of course, these facts are difficult to come by, as he went on to point out, since they are retailed for the most part by interested British sailors, or at a later date by Hawaiians already corrupted by missionaries. The postcolonial drift of the exercise becomes clearer in the argument as Obeyesekere first desiderates the authentic account ("there is much in [these native histories] that is hidden, waiting to be brought to the surface") [35] and then, apropos the mysterious coconut offered to Cook shortly before he was killed, despairs of its ever being brought to light: "My own guess is that we will never know why this offering was made jointly to Cook and Kalani'opu'u, and any number of hypotheses are possible and plausible." [36] Obeyesekere sacrifices all real knowledge of the culture's history for a virtual authenticity whose guarantee of purity is that it cannot be known, his own purity of motive being ensured by his knowing that nothing can be known for certain of pre-European Hawaiian culture. At the same time, the knowledge gained by practical rationality—the empirical encounter with reality—is the only knowledge he values. As Sahlins said in his rejoinder, the refusal to consider an encounter between two cultures as historically valuable, a meeting moreover where the nature of usurpation, change, time, and pronouns are all so critically at stake, simply because of the fear of contaminating an unknowable truth leaves Hawaiians destitute of "any specific cultural or historical knowledge." [37]

There is a terrifying obscurantism in Obeyesekere's brand of skepticism. "Myth and commonsense answer different questions," as Greg Dening says as he rehearses the events surrounding Cook's death in *Mr. Bligh's*

Bad Language, a book largely defensive of Sahlins' brand of anthropology. The events resulting from the collision or overlap of two cultures are construed, he argues, by means of "wink upon wink upon wink," an obliquity of view that thrusts meaning into spirals of "never-ending amplification" not to nurture an assumption that facts can never be known or judged in such a situation, but specifically so that deeds, even the most shocking, can be observed to take their place as tokens of what is already believed to be the case.[38] This is how the question of *mana* brushes the edge of European history and, with its mixture of egoistic sacrilege and legitimating success, challenges the subject of that history to tell the credible story of a power shift. After the death of Cook, this is precisely what the British witnesses of the event were unable to do, being hopelessly divided in their first-person accounts. At that particular conjuncture in Kealakekua Bay, power and credibility happened to fall entirely into the hands of the Hawaiians, as they demonstrated with their prompt institution of the cult of the dead Cook, a feat of idolatry the British could only manage to imitate once they were home.

We have dwelt upon this dispute over Cook's death because it touches directly on some of the issues raised in this collection of essays. Futa Helu, Malama Meleisea, and Okusitino Māhina each develops an argument about the relation of myth to history, and of myth to political power, that accommodates Sahlins' theory of usurpational legitimacy, as opposed to Obeyesekere's belief that abrupt discontinuity and cultural amnesia are the inevitable accompaniments of contact and imperial design. The argument requires a resituation of the narrative I from world history to the narratives of local change. Rather than constructing the European eyewitness as the subject who encounters a noncognizable Other, and who is so comfortable with the facts of novelty that he can write, according to John Dunmore, "adequate biographies in the historical sense of the term," a singular ego, challenging yet at risk, is to be located first among the sharks who went by water and land, the Polynesian chiefs, male and female, hungry for power and territory, whose deeds are recorded in myth and song, and then in the stories of the Europeans, the new sharks eager to make their depredations plausible. Helu argues that in its general outline, the history of Europeans in Oceania repeats the cycle of Maui myths, which record the Polynesian navigations and settlements of the Western Pacific. He does not attempt, as Sahlins does, to chart a descent from a general mytheme to a particular event, but he emphasizes that myth is not the congealing of a prehistoric stability but a powerful concurrent factor in eventual history: "Canons of myths do present a clear picture of cultural transformation," he says. "Myths can give us a picture of how communities have changed."

Meleisea emphasizes the specifically prophetic function in the rela-tion of myth to history: It not only is repeatable, it declares the mode in which it will be repeated. Thus the mass conversion to Christianity on Samoa between 1830 and 1869 completes the delegation of political power decreed by the goddess Nafanua in respect of the great chief Malietoa, and its aftermath is the fulfillment of this intention. Like the various Ringatu prophets in New Zealand, of whom the most famous was the Messiah (Mihaia) Rua, there is an element here of simple counter-appropriation—an indigenization or adaptation of a Christian structure to a local political crisis. But as far as the conversion is the second in a se-ries of usurpations, it belongs to the dynamic of genealogical descent out-lined by Sahlins, and it involves a politics of swift change and counter-change that constitutes much of the data, as well as the continuity, of Pacific history. Unstable situations are genealogized so that they may de-clare simultaneously the contingency and necessity of the same event. How myth mediates between genealogical and historical or personal claims is the theme of Māhina's essay. Queen Sālote solves the problem of her widowed state, and a rank so high it forbids a second marriage, by songs that marry her difficulties with those of Samoa, when the Samoans were under the dominion of the Tongans. The turtle-shell Sangone illus-trates the necessity of disturbing settled power relations, and disobeying the peremptory rules of succession and alliance, by celebrating the inter-marriage of Samoan and Tongan dynasties.

The implications of these three arguments are strange and unsettling be-cause of the light they throw on power shifts, and on the way they are rep-resented, in the Pacific. The European sense of such political instability can take many forms, some of them quite contradictory. David Mackay suggests that the most dominant reaction was the urge to classify and tab-ulate, and that Linnaeus stands as the tutelar genius of this effort to fix and define the fluidities of Oceanic experience. But he mentions too the intercalary states of mind that afflicted travelers and disturbed the global reach of their lucubrations, such as the weird raptures of the botanist Commerson, Cook's fits of wrath, the dreamy abandonment of Bougainville, the growing obsession of Banks and Bligh with the poten-tial of the breadfruit tree—all indicative of how stubbornly myth and mythic speculation drive out the tabulated datum. The aesthetics of such moments belong to the sublime, as Greg Dening suggests,[39] and so do the politics because, according to Longinus, it is in that exalted or abject mood of incalculable intensity that the power is transferred in the fastest and most violent ways. Like Don Quixote's dreams of romance, which rest on his biographer's extravagant claims to be writing punctual and impartial historiography, so the voyager numbers up particulars and circumstances only to be deceived, or to deceive. Stranded between the points of credulity and credibility, where the difference between history and fiction is determined solely by the force of an assertion delivered in the first person singular, eyewitnessing is transformed into the egoistic challenge of autopsy, as Anthony Pagden reminds us.[40]

John Pocock, Stephen Turner, and Paul McHugh tackle one of the most crucial concepts imported by Europeans into the Pacific, namely that of civil society and the various rights, contracts, exchanges, properties, and providences associated with it. Pocock traces the course of the ambivalence with which agents of civil society viewed the state of nature. On the one hand it is the precontractual, precommercial condition that is noble, because it is free of custom and self-interest. The establishment of rights over property, land, and other people—the hegemonic moment—introduces customs of voyaging and consuming that are as ignoble as they are unnatural. The innocent victim of this corrupt expansion of commerce is the noble savage, actuated by nothing but honor and hymned by Adam Ferguson as the purest emanation of the patriot spirit: "Hence the obstinate attachment of a savage to his unsettled and defenseless tribe . . . hence the devoted patriotism of an early Roman. Let those examples be compared with the spirit which reigns in a commercial state."[41] And no more need be said! But it does, and it gets said, for the representative of civil society is also the representative of progress and of the providence that superintends all its feats, even the self-interest of the merchant. The same providence ensured the escape of Cook's *Endeavour* from the coral of Australia's Great Barrier Reef, and John Hawkesworth made a great mistake publicly to doubt it. As far as the savage is the theme of that providential history he is less than perfect: The ignoble savage is natural man historized. Here the ground of the conflict between the general history of civilization and the other history of local cultures—myth— takes shape. But at the same time, history unsettles itself, for it detects the principles of change in the stages of savage culture (where cannibalism comes to indicate a mark of advancement on the line of progress, for example) and reads its own doom in the record. When Lord Kames looked at Hawkesworth's *Account,* for example, he found it difficult to condemn the violence of Maori warriors in the same idiom he used to commend their contempt for luxury. What was best about them was also worst, and in that equivocal state they most resembled the English (not the British— he reserves himself that margin of certainty): "Nations the most remarkable for patriotism are equally remarkable for aversion to strangers. . . . Patriotism, a vigorous principle among the English, makes them extremely averse to naturalize foreigners. The inhabitants of New Zealand, both men and women . . . treat one another with affection, but are implacable to their enemies, and never give quarter."[42] As Pocock points out, the test of voyaging and of claiming a property over others is the test not only of the acuity of one's historical self-consciousness but also of the *sangfroid* needed to confront the existential difficulties that make history writing unique to European culture. A conflict erupts between the Herderian "one big eye" of Christian providence and the I that observes the views of that larger eye and makes calculations as to their narratability: "It follows," argues Pocock, "that there is a real sense in which the most important encounter made by Europeans in the age of Enlightenment was the encounter with themselves, with their pasts and their own historicity."

According to Stephen Turner, this encounter is still unresolved in New Zealand, where a settler culture has claimed a property and lost its identity, whether identity is considered in the desiderative discourse of *propreté de soi* proposed by cultural nationalism or in the terms of standing place and honor (*turangawaewae* and *mana*) of the indigenes whom they dispossessed, and whose nobility they have lately had to acknowledge, or reacknowledge. The uncertainty of the *pakeha* when faced with a history heavily inscribed with the contests between a civil society and a precommercial local culture, a history moreover in which the rights to property seem to have been usurped rather than legally or contractually assumed, is owing to its continuity with a dynamic of historical transformation that had been thought to have been superseded. In short, the *pakeha* find themselves in a state of nature, without *mana* and without *turangawaewae*, destitute of cultural capital no matter how well endowed with acquired goods. In the absence of an independent authority to govern the question of right and the entitlement to power, politics has adapted itself to the sort of forceful rhetoric first heard by Captain Cook as the *haka* of the warriors who greeted him in their war canoes with a challenge, paying him the compliment of an invitation to fight and boasting how soon he would succumb to their weapons. This is the politics (and the prophecy as it turned out) of *utu*, of the debt of honor and of retaliation; and once again the implications of such a politics are unsettling, while at the same time being inexplicably exciting. Under the reactivated provisions of the Treaty of Waitangi (1840), the irenic possibilities of seeing "eye to eye"— and I to I—over the issues of local history, in the spirit of *korero*, are blended with the agonistic alternative of *utu*, of taking an eye for an eye, an I for an I.

The Treaty exists in two versions: one in English cedes Maori sovereignty to that of the Crown, extends the rights and privileges of British subjects to Maori, while reserving for Maori "the full exclusive and undisturbed possession of their Lands and Estates Forests Fisheries and other properties." The Maori version cedes *"kawanatanga"* but reserves *"rangatiratanga."* The former is a loan word from English—intended to mean "governance"—and the second is a Maori word, which among its possible meanings are not only all the less-tangible aspects of chiefly authority and responsibility but also, arguably, the notion of sovereignty itself. But in the positivist legal practice of the late nineteenth century, which regarded Maori of 1840 as a community beyond the community of law, the Treaty was retrospectively regarded as a simple nullity, a contract made with those who, by circular definition, could not enter into contract. For those who believed they had, the Treaty was and has remained the focus of attempts to redress the manifold injustices of the past hundred and fifty or so years. Yet the positivist legal tradition, dominating legal thinking from the mid-nineteenth century to the present, casts a long shadow. The innovations and successes of the Waitangi Tribunal notwithstanding, the government is legally bound to follow statute; other matters are, shall we say, morally binding, which is also to say that the government is by no means obliged to follow Tribunal recommendations. One response to this *différend* has been to find positive law immanent in the tendency of the versions of the treaty: to use such words as *partnership, fiduciary responsibility,* and so on, which, as Paul McHugh notes, are likely to have been somewhat remote from the intentions of the Treaty framers and signers. His essay is an examination of the common law's relation to its past, a past that scarcely exists apart from the claims of the present. He argues that legal understanding of legal history can be broader than the ahistorical reservoir of case law and statute assumed by positivist practice. While much of the Tribunal's business has of course involved research into Maori understandings of the past, an understanding of the European legal past has on the whole (such is positivist practice) been taken for granted. McHugh, however, finds that the common law of the early modern period worked with different assumptions—involving notions of custom and immemoriality, of redress rather than rights—which favored community-minded results not dependent on the foresight of statute. A more historicized approach to common-law method (as opposed merely to doctrine) is calculated to widen the moves available to contemporary players.[43]

Greg Dening has written, "If I were asked what ethnographic history may ultimately be, I would answer that it is an attempt to represent the past as it was actually experienced in such a way that we understand both its ordered and its disordered natures."[44] The remark has a bearing on how those who continue in Dening's wake have posited the relation of Pacific ethnohistory to its archives of evidence, to its theory of culture and of cultures in contact, and to its understanding of violence. In the past, attitudes to these matters—of evidence, culture, violence—have tended to go hand in hand, and this remains a feature of the more detailed studies of contact in this collection, all of which attempt to understand the ordered and disordered nature of the experience of encounter.

It is no longer possible to write about early cultural contact between Europe and the Pacific without also negotiating a complex set of positions on the nature of the surviving documentary evidence. We have been taught to be suspicious of imperial designs, to beware not to replicate the assumptions of Eurocentrism, and therefore not to take these documents at face value. The Pacific journals of explorers, scientists, missionaries, and others can no longer be viewed unsuspiciously, but they can be read for the telltale signs of ideological loading, for their propensity to project European fears, hopes, or expectations in the place of the native, and for the contribution they make to the formation of indigenous peoples as colonized subjects. Yet the critique of ethnographic authority, however necessary and well taken, soon reaches limit points, many of which, we have argued, are indicated by an unintended repetition of hegemonic gestures and the anxious manufacture of positions of moralizing authenticity. That said, the ethnographic historian still must work with a compromised archive, with documents whose claims to adequately represent their object of ethnographic inquiry are unsustainable. But what is to be done with contaminated evidence? It is important to remember that it is not the only record of early contact that is involved in this problem: Oral archives have been variably preserved, local knowledges have been maintained, but it is almost always the case in the Pacific that the archive of European incursion forms the greater part of the evidence. Perhaps this written archive is like a barrel of ship biscuit: When the historian dips into it, it may be with the expectation that weevil-like ideological impurities might be rattled out and discarded, leaving behind some portion of an original substance. We incline to the view that there is no getting rid of the weevils. The archive of European exploration and settlement is regarded neither without suspicion nor in an effort to rehabilitate past interpretative deficiencies, but as a more or less reliable eyewitness of the disordered "actual experience" of one people's contact with another.

This may explain why such scrupulous attention has been paid to the textual record of European discovery in two of the essays that investigate episodes on Cook's voyages of discovery: Nicholas Thomas' study of "cruelty-to-parents" among Maori in Queen Charlotte Sound, and Ian Barber's account of the killing and eating of the *Adventure*'s boat crew at Grass Cove. Like Shakespearean textual scholars, these anthropologists examine variants, emend the corrupt memory of actors, and explore other versions of the "same" story. Out of these possible readings, they reconstruct the ragged *ur*-text of contact, a patchwork of investigation and inference that is assessed finally on how adequately it represents the interactive complexities of encounter. For Barber, this is a standard the European journals not surprisingly fail to meet, for their occasional insight into their own responsibility for conflict does little to modify long-established notions of the ignobility of "savage violence." But the journals also make Barber's revisionary understanding possible, offering evidence that a misunderstanding over trade, and the reciprocal misrecognition of each other's concept of exchange, led to the killing of the boat crew at Grass Cove. Thomas' essay is a contrasting study: Where Barber considers an event experienced by the voyagers as a catastrophe, Thomas is concerned with events that presented no discernible sign of emergency. Yet the Dusky Bay encounter was "replete with difficulties and ironies that were peculiarly difficult for Europeans to comprehend," uncertainties, he argues, that are "paraded rather than disavowed in their texts." Rather than rectify those European uncertainties—they wondered whether these Maori were a family, and if so, what relations between them might say about the advancement of local civilization—Thomas aims to unfold their doubts and hesitations further, tracing them back to contradictory valuations of progress in the writers of the Scottish Enlightenment, such as Kames and Ferguson. Where an earlier tradition of interpretation would tend to highlight the monolithic bias of Eurocentric interpretation, Thomas underlines the range of uncertainties and possibilities that early encounters contained, and does so to keep sight of "the creative strategies of accommodation, appropriation, and resistance that *tangata whenua* employed, at the time and ever since," and as a reminder that "if other things easily could have happened, it is perhaps easier to imagine that other things might happen now."

Fatal impact scenarios have often been criticized for a tendency to postulate a dynamic European culture in contact with a vulnerable and unadaptive indigenous one. Pat Hohepa, writing as a *kaumatua* (elder) on a *marae* might speak, redresses the balance from his own Ngapuhi side of the beach. His essay offers a background to the calamitous Musket Wars that devastated much of Aotearoa–New Zealand in the early part of the nineteenth century. When he suggests that the acquisition of muskets and missionaries was fueled by the pursuit of *mana,* and that the ensuing destructive arms race opened a window of opportunity for the Treaty of Waitangi, it is not with the funereal tones of one who laments the fatal contact of an indigenous society with the West, nor with the cool appreciation of irony that may characterize some more-recent approaches, but with a strong sense of the continuity and vigor of Maori resistance to colonialism. For other contributors, the demise of fatal-impact theory has led not only to the realization that, in the drama of contact, indigenous populations followed agendas as complex and various as the voyagers who encountered them, but also that access to the culture of early modern Europe cannot be taken for granted.

But the revision of fatal-impact scenarios need not always involve producing more-equitable applications of the predicates of "being a culture." Indeed, once we purge the term of the tautologies and reifications that bedevil our use of it, once we have deconstructed and historicized the organicist origins of "culture," what are we left with? In James Clifford's words: "Culture is a deeply compromised idea I cannot yet do without."[45] Nicholas Thomas' study of contradictions internal to Johann and George Forster's notion of civil society, which disarrange their perceptions of ethnographic similarity and difference, indicate that versions of this bind are as old as the early modern experience of contact and (as J.G.A. Pocock suggests) may even be said to characterize it. Alternatively, recalling the terms of Dening's definition once again, we might say that the more ordered we suppose people's experience of the past to have been, the more readily we talk of culture; and the more disordered the experience, the more our talk of culture seems redundant or vestigial, as if the once proud noun of anthropological grammar had forsaken all but the humbler duties of an adjective.

Dening's definition also reminds us that ethnographic history bears a necessary and complex relation to violence. On one hand, the subtle and routine violence of disciplinary regimes contributes to the ordered nature of experience; on the other, various contingencies may challenge or elude control and contribute to the sometimes ordinary, sometimes aberrant disorder of experience. Indeed, violence inhabits all the various borders people draw and have drawn between ship and shore. It anxiously patrols every border between an "us" and a "them." Violence is the very essence of what belongs on the far side of borders—one reason why violence is integral to perceptions of the other (Islander or European) as savage and warlike; why the sublimities of violence in the literature of discovery are so prone to excite and defeat representation. Alongside essays patently concerned with the violence of contact—the Musket Wars, killings, and cannibalism at Grass Cove, what it means to hit one's mother—is an essay by Paul Turnbull that, in examining the rationale for the scientific collection of Aboriginal skeletal remains, also records an ongoing institutional violence and the history of Aboriginal resistance to that violence. The protagonists of his essay, the anatomists John Hunter and Johann Friedrich Blumenbach, were voyagers only by proxy. They

were omnivorous readers of voyages and ethnographies, however, and assiduous dispatchers of instructions and requests to sea captains, ships'
surgeons, and a network of agents in the colonies. This, too, is a story of
contact that seeks to contextualize the role of violence in the production
of Enlightenment.

We have said that some essays in the collection consider the extent
to which traditional European ideas about organizing and legitimating
claims to territory and power, through the political and legal discourses
of exchange, contract, property, and right, were invoked and problema-
tized in the South Pacific; others, focusing on a series of "actual" as well
as conceptual encounters, record the violence endemic in such scenes.
Although issues of power are clearly to the fore in both accounts, neither
bears witness to an unproblematic European success, ideologically or materially, in the scientific and political projects of an expansive colonialism
with which the voyages of exploration are now popularly associated. Indigenous resistance, combined sometimes with indifference toward European incursions, as well as a capacity to absorb and transform their impact, is matched by a record of Western observation and action as notable
for its ambivalence and confusion as its single-minded pursuit of cultural,
religious, and political hegemony. Another cluster of essays—those dealing with representations of encounter and the specifically aesthetic discourses with which early travelers and settlers attempted to make sense of
the Pacific in the aftermath of "discovery"—reveals a similar degree of
ambivalence and division in the arts of writing and painting. We find that
what colonial discourse analysis dignifies as the representational work of
imperial subjects is really much more heterogeneous. The texts discussed
here suggest that while a properly postcolonial suspicion of travelers, missionaries, translators, and illustrators will reveal predictable blind spots
and partialities in the colonial gaze, the stare of supreme assumptions is
turned and modified by what it fails to notice.[46] Informed by recent work
on the colonial discourses employed elsewhere in the "New World," these
essays locate local differences that not only emphasize the ambiguities
and incoherence of colonial modes of representation in their moment of
production but also trace the degrees to which the power that was assumed to be authorizing them was dispersed and transferred.

Rod Edmond's comparison of two missionary narratives, Ellis' *Polynesian Researches* and Williams' *Narrative of a Missionary Enterprise*—titles that
neatly encapsulate all the suspect terms of ethnographic inquiry, commerce, and conversion—reveals that despite the transparently instru-
mental purposes of these accounts, curiosity and contradiction keep
breaking in. Ellis' text is defined by Edmond in terms proposed by Mary-
Louise Pratt as an "anti-conquest" narrative,[47] shifting between the reg-

isters of scientific inquiry (with its tendency to naturalize the non-European subject) and the sentimental evocation of scenes of human reciprocity, the two working together to mystify the exploitation inherent in colonial relationships. Edmond localizes this argument in Ellis through reference to contradictions in missionary narratives, where particularity overrules the demands of order, and he concludes by emphasizing the peculiarity of the attempt in *Polynesian Researches* to seal up irreconcilable views of Tahitians in a fond fantasy of a ubiquitous island domesticity. The adoption of such a solution to the conflict between notions of Polynesians as savagely "cultureless" and complexly socialized is as meretricious—but as culturally imperative, Edmond argues—as the contemporary novelistic drive to conclude depictions of social conflict and alienation in Victorian fiction with a vision of hearth and home.

Leonard Bell's essay also invokes Mary-Louise Pratt, but while he accepts as a general principle the interpenetration of scenes of exotic landscape and the colonial project that she identifies in much nineteenth-century art, his account of Augustus Earle's *The Meeting of the Artist and the Wounded Chief Hongi* is concerned as much with Earle's violations of the tropes of exotic representation as with his adherence to them. Bell emphasizes that Earle, very unusually, shows himself at work within the painting. This results in an image that is far from the predictably detached and controlling view adopted by a comparable artist, such as Louis de Sainson. By foregrounding the process of representation as a cautiously friendly encounter between individuals, the painting suggests the possibility of cross-cultural relations enacted as dialogue, or *korero,* rather than the one-sided gaze of dominion. Bell does not romanticize Earle as a noble exception to a dismal imperialist rule—a gesture that would simply underline the predominance of sovereign views—but he points out that the artist's practice was probably a result of his visiting New Zealand in the period before full-scale colonization began. The conditions of possibility for infractions of an imperialist aesthetic and its associated norms of behavior would not last long, he suggests, but their promise remains in the texts produced under such auspices, redeemed in part by careful reading, such as Bell's.

Sarah Treadwell's essay examines the confounding of European doxa by *hakari* (feast structures) and reed *whare* (dwellings), both forms of woven architecture. Her readings of early reports of the *hakari* convey a sense both of the complex social functions and the extraordinary combination of delicacy and grandeur in these structures. This account-from-refraction is notable for its ability to illuminate the particular and limiting assumptions with which Europeans "on the ground" arrived, while also drawing attention to the creatively deconstructive readings of woven architecture developed simultaneously by metropolitan theorists, such as Gottfried Semper. The implicit argument here, conducted as much through the resolutely deconstructive method as by the scrupulous canvassing of a variety of historical constructions of *hakari* and reeded *whare,* is that relations between Pacific and European aesthetic practice and theory can be construed as dialectical.

Simon During's essay analyzes the way late-eighteenth-century metropolitan literary discourses such as primitivism and pastoral both facilitated the process of Australasian colonization and revealed the limits of such aesthetic transplantation. During argues that Thomas Warton's official primitivism not only provided a local genealogy for Britain's martial and imperial role but valorized the settler colonist's life of brutal isolation and material deprivation by emphasizing the simple virtue of such existence. Tracking the effects of various literary discourses in the settler colonies of Australasia, however, During notes that their inherent contradictions were thrown into relief by the presence of indigenous peoples and the intractability of material conditions. While primitivism might celebrate both Maori and pioneer alike, unlike Georgic, it was not a mode that could legitimate the wholesale appropriation of Maori land by European settlers. During further points up the sheer inefficacy, in the colonies, of metropolitan literary discourses whose mode of consumption required the material support of institutions like theaters, periodicals, and presses, which would take decades to establish. The early colonial experience of diminished and destabilized modes of literary authority thus gave rise to the partial adoption of indigenous culture, a process that is by no means complete.

Mark Houlahan also frames his discussion of cultural translation in terms that emphasize the importance of exchange, rather than domination, in Pacific encounters. This may seem surprising in the context of his subject, the lifework of Henry Kemp, colonial subject par excellence: translator of the Treaty of Waitangi, translator (at government request) of *Robinson Crusoe* and *Pilgrim's Progress,* and (notoriously) chief government agent in the largest land purchase from Maori, when the bulk of the South Island was obtained from the Ngai Tahu people. It would be difficult to find a figure who better exemplifies the twin thrusts of the colonial desire to appropriate territory and inculcate civility. And yet, as Houlahan's careful excavation of the heroic banalities of this early settler biography reveals, Kemp's career offers little comfort to postcolonial pieties: "A mimic man in a contact zone," he figures, perhaps too closely for contemporary academic comfort, the awkward position of the publicly paid man of letters purveying metropolitan culture to the locals.

The concluding essay reframes Kemp again, and in no uncertain terms. Margaret Mutu's account of the Maori land tenure system, which he, like the other members of the Land Purchases Department would not or could not understand, returns us to the large themes of the collection. *Tuku whenua,* a Maori version of leasehold land tenure, could not be comprehended through the notions of property brought by the early voyagers. Violence accompanied the clash of conceptual systems governing on the one hand the desire to retain ownership of land and on the other the desire to appropriate it as freehold. The essay explains as well as joins a debate as old as "New Zealand." It is a debate about the emergence of Europeans in Oceania, an emergence dogged from the beginning by an extravagance of mind and action—mutiny, fantasy, homicide, and delirium—which has always thwarted the symmetry of a simple appropriation. It is a debate that has never ceased, although its modulations frequently have been changed. It is in the spirit of the principle of modulation that this collection celebrates its continuity.

The editors wish to acknowledge the support of the following people and institutions: Jane Sanders and Michael Shephard (the artist) for the "Motu Paradiso" painting on the cover; Laura Sayre for helping with the preparation of the manuscript; the Council for Research in the Humanities and Social Sciences, Princeton University; and the University of Auckland Research Committee.

NOTES

1. See also the selection of Papers from the Ninth David Nichol Smith Memorial Seminar in *Eighteenth Century Life* 18 n.s., 3 (1994).
2. A *marae* is a ceremonial plaza, outside a meetinghouse, onto which visitors and the dead are ritually welcomed. Until recently, it would have been unusual for universities to have *marae*. As this word would not normally be translated or italicized in a local publication, we would like to clarify the conventions governing our use of Polynesian words in this volume. We have written in standard American English, and all "foreign" words, including those Maori or Polynesian words (such as *marae*) that have become part of English in the Pacific, are in italics. As for the reefs and shoals of Polynesian spelling, we have not attempted to set standards where there are none, but have generally followed contributors' preferences over the use of macrons, double

vowels, or "Englished" spellings. Thus, the same word may appear as *hapu, hâpû,* or *haapuu.* A few regularly used words (such as *pakeha*) appear in a standard form throughout.

3. John Dunmore, *Who's Who in Pacific Navigation* (Honolulu: University of Hawai'i Press, 1991), xiii.

4. Neil Rennie, *Far-Fetched Facts: The Literature of Travel and the Idea of the South Seas* (Oxford: Clarendon Press, 1995), 201.

5. The history of this primitivist line of thought, together with the theory of the stadial development of civil society that it eventually produced, is told by Ronald Meek in *Social Science and the Ignoble Savage* (Cambridge: Cambridge University Press, 1976).

6. David Fausett, *Writing the New World: Imaginary Voyages and Utopias of the Great Southern Land* (Syracuse: University of Syracuse Press, 1993).

7. Horace Walpole, *On Modern Gardening* (New York: Young, 1931), 4.

8. Michel Foucault, *Archeology of Knowledge,* trans. A. M. Sheridan Smith (New York: Pantheon, 1972), 12.

9. Renato Rosaldo, *Culture and Truth: The Remaking of Social Analysis* (Boston: Beacon Press, 1989).

10. Greg Dening, *Islands and Beaches* (Honolulu: University of Hawai'i Press, 1980), 37.

11. Jacques Derrida, *Writing and Difference,* trans. Alan Bass (Chicago: University of Chicago Press, 1978), 282.

12. Jonathan Friedman, *Cultural Identity and Global Process* (London: Sage, 1994), 3.

13. Gyan Prakash, *After Colonialism: Imperial Histories and Postcolonial Displacements* (Princeton: Princeton University Press, 1995), 3–6.

14. Gayatri Spivak, "Subaltern Studies: Deconstructing Historiography," in *In Other Worlds* (London: Methuen, 1987), 197–221; "Can the Subaltern Speak," in *Colonial Discourse and Post-Colonial Theory,* ed. Patrick Williams and Laura Chrisman (London: Harvester/Wheatsheaf, 1994), 66–111.

15. Harriet Guest, "Curiously Marked: Tattooing, Masculinity, and Nationality in Eighteenth-Century British Perceptions of the South Pacific," in *Painting and the Politics of Culture,* ed. John Barrell (Oxford: Oxford University Press, 1992), 101–134.

16. Foucault, *Archeology of Knowledge,* 12.

17. Johannes Fabian, *Time and the Other* (New York: Columbia University Press, 1983), 18.

18. "Situated within the current academic theater of cultural imperialism, with a certain *carte d'entrée* into the elite theoretical *ateliers* in France, I bring news of power-lines within the palace." Spivak, "Subaltern Studies: Deconstructing Historiography," 221.

19. Urs Bitterli, *Cultures in Conflict: Encounters between European and Non-European Cultures, 1492–1800,* trans. Ritchie Robertson (Cambridge: Polity Press, 1989), 155.

20. Nicholas Thomas, *Colonialism's Cultures* (Princeton: Princeton University Press, 1994), 100, 167.

21. Jonathan Lamb, "Minute Particulars and the Representation of South Pacific Discovery," *Eighteenth-Century Studies* 28(3) (1995): 281–294.

22. Christopher Herbert, *Culture and Anomie: Ethnographic Imagination of the Nineteenth Century* (Chicago: University of Chicago Press, 1991), 163, 165.

23. *Polynesian Researches,* 2d ed., 4 vols. (London: Fisher, Son & Jackson, 1832–1836), 1:320.

24. Alfred Gell, *Wrapping in Images: Tattooing in Polynesia* (Oxford: Clarendon Press, 1993), 242–253.

25. Nicholas Thomas, *Entangled Objects: Exchange, Material Culture, and Colonialism in the Pacific* (Cambridge: Harvard University Press, 1991), 130–131.

26. Valerio Valeri, "Constitutive History: Genealogy and Narrative in the Legitimation of Hawaiian Kingship," in *Culture through Time,* ed. Emiko Ohnuki-Tierney (Stanford: Stanford University Press, 1990), 154–192; Patrick V. Kirch and Marshall Sahlins, *Anahulu: The Anthropology of History in the Kingdom of Hawaii,* 2 vols. (Chicago: University of Chicago Press, 1993).

27. Marshall Sahlins, *Islands of History* (Chicago: University of Chicago Press, 1985), 80.

28. Sahlins, *Islands,* 28.

29. J. Prytz Johansen, *The Maori and His Religion* (Copenhagen: Munksgaard, 1954); Marshall Sahlins, *Historical Metaphors and Mythical Realities* (Ann Arbor: University of Michigan Press, 1981), 13–14.

30. Nicholas Thomas, *Out of Time: History and Evolution in Anthropological Discourse* (Cambridge: Cambridge University Press, 1989), 109.

31. Marshall Sahlins, "Hierarchy and Humanity in Polynesia," in Memoir 45, *Transformations of Polynesian Culture,* ed. Antony Hooper and Judith Huntsman (Auckland: Polynesian Society, 1985), 215.

32. Fabian, *Time and the Other,* 84.

33. Sahlins, *Historical Metaphors,* 17.

34. Sahlins, *Islands,* vii.

35. Gananath Obeyesekere, *The Apotheosis of Captain Cook* (Princeton: Princeton University Press, 1992), 168.

36. Ibid., 180.

37. Marshall Sahlins, *How "Natives" Think: About Captain Cook, for Example* (Chicago: University of Chicago, 1995), 101, 105, 116.

38. Greg Dening, *Mr. Bligh's Bad Language* (Cambridge: Cambridge University Press, 1992), 199.

39. Ibid., 248–250.

40. Anthony Pagden, *European Encounters with the New World* (New Haven: Yale University Press, 1993), 82.

41. *Essay on the History of Civil Society* (Edinburgh: Edinburgh University Press, 1966), 28.

42. *Sketches of the History of Man,* 2 vols. (Edinburgh: W. Creech, 1774), 1:371.

43. The literature on the Treaty of Waitangi is vast. Some starting points are I. H. Kawharu, ed., *Waitangi: Maori and Pakeha Perspectives of the Treaty of Waitangi* (Auckland: Oxford University Press, 1989); W. H. Oliver, *Claims to the Waitangi Tribunal* (Wellington: Department of Justice, 1991); Claudia Orange, *The Treaty of Waitangi* (Wellington: Allen and Unwin, 1987); William Renwick, ed., *Sovereignty and Indigenous Rights* (Wellington: Victoria University Press, 1991); Andrew Sharp, *Justice and the Maori* (Auckland: Oxford University Press, 1990); and Ranginui Walker, *Ka Whawhai Tonu Matou/Struggle Without End* (Auckland: Penguin, 1990).

44. Dening, *Mr. Bligh's Bad Language,* 5.

45. *The Predicament of Culture* (Cambridge: Harvard University Press, 1988), 10.

46. See Alex Calder, "Maning's Tapu: Colonialism and Ethnography in Old New Zealand," *Social Analysis* 39 (1996): 3–26.

47. *Imperial Eyes: Travel Writing and Transculturation* (London and New York: Routledge, 1992).

2

NATURE AND HISTORY, SELF AND OTHER

European Perceptions of World History
in the Age of Encounter

J.G.A. Pocock

I intend in this essay to give some account of three topics: the perception of history taking shape in the Europe that made the encounters; the diversity of the kinds of encounter Europeans made, among which encounters on beaches at the ends of voyages were deeply important though not the only kind; and the ways in which they tried, or failed, or did not try—all three happened—to integrate the peoples they encountered into the history they made out of their understanding of themselves. It will be a Eurocentric essay in the sense that it is concerned with Eurocentricity, but I shall try to show that this characteristic was the product not of cultural arrogance only, not of bewilderment in the face of the Other only, but also of the circumstance that Europeans' awareness of themselves as historical beings was growing in several senses more critical in that sector of the age of encounter that we know by the name of Enlightenment. I shall speak only of the first half of the period this anthology covers: that ending with the French Revolution, after which evangelism, empire, and positivism brought great changes. Within those limits, however, there is a vast difference—a change by land and sea—between Valerie Flint's world of Christopher Columbus[1] and Anne Salmond's world of James Cook and Marion du Fresne;[2] and part of this difference is that people in the later world found it hard to incorporate others in history as they understood it, not only because their idea of history was simple and self-serving, but also because it was advanced, secular, complex, and self-critical. I shall pursue Enlightenment at a level of high culture, where a few writers produced ambitious works of history and social philosophy—not only because I think there is much to be learned by seeing what they devised, but also because there are occasions, like Cook's first and second voyages, where the ideas have worked their way into the world of practical men and we do see Enlightenment on the beaches. In exploring this matter I shall make something of the differences between encounters with peoples—like the Chinese—who possessed an ancient literature in which they projected and criticized an image of their history, which Europeans might translate and interpret, and encounters with peoples—like the Tahitians and many others in the Pacific and the Americas—who did not possess that particular resource and could too easily be said to have no history, and to live instead in an ahistorical condition known as nature or a prehistorical condition known as savagery. I shall argue also that both these conditions had been and still were part of Europeans' perception of themselves and their history, and this may help me arrive at a point where I can pose some questions not merely about the encounter of Self with Other but about the concept of such an encounter: a concept that is itself historical and contingent, and should therefore be our instrument and not our master. I have begun by using the term *Europeans*, and because the word *Europe* is elastic, indeterminate, and easy to distort and exploit, we should begin by reminding ourselves what sort of "Europeans" these *pakeha* or *tau iwi* were when they made the encounters. For the most part they were French or British, Dutch or Spanish, Scandinavian or German, voyagers, officers, sailors, and—to single out those who interpreted the encounters without always having made them—intellectuals, *philosophes*, and *gens de lettres*. For the most part, then, they came from the Atlantic extremities of the European peninsula, where the ending of wars of religion between Catholics and Protestants and the expansion of a global commerce existed in a complex relationship; we are not yet obliged to take account of the history of German or Central "Europe." But expansion and encounter of another kind was going on in the Eurasian lands that lie east of whatever we mean by "Europe," and this needs to be taken into account. This expansion was produced by the decline of the Ottoman Empire south and east of the central Danube, and the reorganization of the Hapsburg and Romanov Empires that accompanied this decline; it was produced also by the "Europeanization" of the Russian state and its expansion in the form of an empire across Turco-Mongol Central Asia and the Siberian regions farther north, at which point—remarked the historian Voltaire—the distinction between Europe and Asia lost all meaning and it might be well to adopt another terminology.[3] He proposed the term *Terre arctique* as a kind of counterpart to *Terra australis incognita*. In the arctic or subpolar north, encounters were made with peoples remote enough in their culture to qualify as Others and be thought of as natural men or as savages; but there were encounters also with outliers of literate civilizations, Islamic or Chinese, linked in the long run with encounters between maritime Atlantic Europeans (including Americans) and the civilizations of India, China, Japan, and Indonesia. There were encounters with literate peoples and encounters with those who were not; there were encounters with voyagers on beaches and encounters with overlanders: travelers, soldiers, and officials.

The Atlantic "Europe" that made the maritime encounters—and looked upon Peter the Great's Russia as recruited to its culture—had centers of literary production ranging from Edinburgh to Naples, in which the intellectual currents we know as Enlightenment took shape. This Europe remembered itself as having very lately escaped from an age of wars of religion and wars about the concurrent danger of a Spanish or French universal monarchy or empire. It saw itself as having overcome these dangers in two ways: first, by the reorganization of "Europe" as a republic or confederation of civilized sovereign states, held together by the ties of commerce, capable of settled government over societies increasingly commercial, and capable of regulating the wars that still occurred by the advanced military and financial technology, which warfare, and civil society in general, acquired in an age of commerce. The concept of commerce took on such an importance that it was in many ways fetishized; certainly, we cannot understand the European perception of history in the age of encounter without constantly placing it at the very center and climax. Second, the danger of religious war had been reduced by the systematic lessening of all claims that Christian obedience or inspiration might make against the authority of civil society; whether the danger arose from the authority of the clergy or the rebelliousness of the laity, and whether the authority of society was described in absolutist or liberal terms, were important but secondary questions. This lessening of the danger from religion entailed the construction of versions of religious belief increasingly deprived of the concept that divine spirit acted independently in the material world; there was launched a steady erosion of the cardinal and traditional doctrines of the Trinity and the Incarnation, the Atonement and the Gift of Tongues. Beyond this reduction of Christian beliefs to those necessary for the support of a civil religion lay the possibility of a philosophical deism, a natural religion accessible to all, whether Christian or not. And beyond that lay the more dangerous possibility of a religion of nature, an acceptance of the universe as spirit and matter in one, a monistic pantheism that was the commonest form in which either materialism or atheism occurred in the Age of Enlightenment and Encounter, and was of importance when it came to assessing the religion of Other cultures (whether Chinese or Tahitian).

These two strategies—let us label them the commercial and the deist—came together at the point where it was suggested that the inhabitants of commercial societies were peculiarly fitted to recognize that they had only opinions, and never knowledge, of the structure of either god-

head or universe, and could do no better than arrange their opinions in
tentative and experimental bodies of doctrine, tolerant and respectful of
one another. Here we encounter the very interesting suggestion that it is
precisely commerce that shapes the mind in this way; defined as the constant interchange of goods, words, ideas, and emotions, commerce presents both the world perceived and the mind perceiving as transactional,
so that the knower apprehends both the world and himself as they pass
from one set of hands to another. Appearing soon after 1700, this perception crowned the much older thesis that the human being was rendered sociable—and therefore human—by the possession of property
and the laws regulating his encounters with other proprietors; it anticipated later materialism by depicting the personality as shaped in a universe of moveable goods. An outcome might be that it was possible to
know no more of God than by knowing how the human mind found itself
generating and coordinating ideas concerning God; and when encounters occurred with forms of religious belief quite startlingly Other, it was
possible to evaluate these by setting up hypotheses concerning the condition of property and society in cultures that had produced them. But we
shall not understand the social and historical theories being generated in
this Europe at the outset of Enlightenment if we do not understand that
they were profoundly contestable. Not only were they vigorously contested between contending groups of theorists; each contained the idea
of a transformation of values that might be evaluated in more ways than
one. We find at this period what has been termed *la crise de la conscience
européenne,*[4] a term that includes the appearance of a vigorous consciousness of modernity. This Europe was acutely aware that it had emerged
from the wars of religion by acquiring characteristics that made it no
longer feudal, no longer Christian either in the Reformation or the medieval sense, no longer ancient or classical in the Greco-Roman sense that
had preceded the medieval; and while this sequence of emergences or
transformations could be depicted as a process of progressive enlightenment, values from each and every one of these pasts were sufficiently
alive, vehement, and demanding to ensure that a quarrel between ancients and moderns went on in every case, not only between contending
groups of advocates but within the *conscience* of every literate person. History was beginning to look like a sequence of moral and cultural transformations, concerning each one of which the consciousness must reach
contestable judgments because the consciousness was itself historically
generated. Europeans became possessed, by the eighteenth century, of
an extremely complex history of themselves, in which the classical narratives of things done by kings and cities merged with a new narrative of
changing states of law, language, and religion, and a further narrative of

conflicts between encoded values and states of civilization: Greeks and Romans, Israel and Christianity, ancients and moderns, Goths and Romans, virtue and corruption, barbarism and enlightenment. It would not be easy for them to write similar structural narratives of the history of other civilizations, and they may not have been altogether wrong in supposing that other civilizations did not write this sort of history of themselves. It follows that there is a real sense in which the most important encounter made by Europeans in the Age of Enlightenment was the encounter with themselves, with their pasts and with their own historicity, so that it was into these highly sophisticated and even self-critical schemes of historiography that they sought to integrate, or gave up trying to integrate, the cultures with which they came in contact. The Others found all the problems of European history dumped upon them, in short, without much prior information as to what these were or where they came from; and this is true even at the points where European critical sophistication had reached a level at which the whole of European history seemed a corruption of humanity's original nature. (I think this was not far from the mindset of Marion du Fresne.) A time came when Europeans claimed that even this empowered and entitled them to rule over Others; they lived in history, they said, with all its moral and existential ambivalences, and Others did not.

Social theorists in the mid-seventeenth century, the climax of the wars of religion, had found it necessary to explain how man, the social animal, was capable of such homicidal brutality against his fellows and, conversely, how so feral and violent a creature had been capable of society in the first place. They had taken up the already ancient vocabulary of natural jurisprudence, and had imagined a condition in which humans were without society, in order to imagine them acquiring it—a move that permitted theorists to imagine nature as dynamic as well as static, a becoming as well as a being. What was called "the state of nature" became differentiated into two stages. In the first, a Hobbesian state of war, humans had wandered, as individuals or in very small procreative groups, on the face of an earth altogether uncultivated, or wilderness, in violent and immediate conflict with any Other whom they encountered. Hobbes had suggested that this was the condition of what he called "savage" hunters in America, and Aristotle had said that it was the condition of Cyclopes, like Polyphemus in the *Odyssey,* a figure who needs more attention. It was already possible to use this theoretical construct as a description of actual human groups, thus using nature to explain history as the emergence from nature. The second stage was that of society, the Lockean or Pufendorfian state of nature, arrived at through rationality and the acquisition of property. As humans began to cultivate the earth and appropriate it, they discovered the need of language, norms, and laws to regulate their relations with their fellow proprietors; and even Amerindian hunters came to know the need of lawful right to the game they killed, if not yet to the land over which they hunted it. Tillage, the mixture of one's labor with the land, produced true property and society; but Locke still calls this a "state of nature" in the pre-historic sense. It may entail the growth of civil government possessing authority to enter into treaties with neighbors and make grants of power and even authority; but "extensive" or "enormous" government becomes necessary, and civil history begins, only with the advent of money, which extends human interactions over spaces and times more extensive than the interactions can control without the introduction of artifice. Where commerce begins, humans leave the state of nature; but it is their nature to do so, since art is their nature. So far, then, nature and history are perfectly compatible, but unlike some other contemporaries, Locke did not attempt to write the history of commercial societies, in which it was beginning to be a question, by the time of his death, whether human nature persisted or was changed, corrupted, or even destroyed.

That theme will recur when we come to close encounters with the remoter kind of Other, the kind not organized in extensive empires or previously known to exist. These, first met with by the Spaniards in the Caribbean, were of course found in the eighteenth-century Pacific but were also encountered in subarctic regions in the course of the Russian expansion toward the Bering Strait. Lapps, Samoyeds, Ostiaks, Buryats, Yakuts, and Chukchi appear in the reports of German surveyors and botanists in the Russian service, and a work by the late Gloria Flaherty, *Shamanism and the Eighteenth Century,* helps us to see how they were integrated into Enlightened understandings of the history of religion.[5] When these groups were associated with the Inuit described by Jesuits in northern Canada, it became possible to form the idea of a subpolar chain, or rather, circle, of arctic cultures, and this interacted with the already ancient but rapidly changing problem of the population of the Americas or New World. Rather than dealing with this, however, we need to look at that contact with a literate and imperial Other that meant most to the writers of the Enlightenment. Voltaire's history of Peter the Great (already cited) begins with a survey of Russia's human geography, including the arctic hunting cultures,[6] but has as one of its climactic points the Treaty of Nerchinsk on the Amur River, signed in 1689 between emissaries of the tzar and the K'ang-hsi emperor.[7] Voltaire, who sees Peter's achievement as the bringing of previously barbarous Russia into the European fellowship of commercial states, presents his treaty with China in the same light. For the first time, he says, the Chinese civilization ac-

knowledged the existence of an equal and entered into treaty relationships with it according to the universally acknowledged laws of the *jus gentium;* the purpose of the treaty included the furtherance of commerce.
Voltaire's optimism was not to be borne out by the failure of Lord Macartney's mission, though he might have known whom to blame if he had
lived to hear of that. The immediate point is that he attributes the presence of the language of *jus gentium* in the Chinese text of the 1719 treaty
to the two Jesuits who served as interpreters (as missionaries sometimes
did in treaties of this kind). He is doubtless right to do so; but when he
further notes the presence of language in which both Russians and Chinese acknowledge the authority of an undenominational God, he does
not give the Jesuits credit for this, though they fairly certainly deserve it.
Voltaire was a deist and used his deism to discredit Christian missionaries,
but he knew more about the Jesuit role in China than he was prepared to
admit.

The last chapter of the *Siècle de Louis XIV,* Voltaire's other history of a
great king's triumph over barbarism, deals with the Rites Controversy and
the ejection of Christian missionaries by the same K'ang-hsi emperor.
Matteo Ricci, the greatest scholar of the Jesuit mission, had confronted
the nontheist monism of neo-Confucian metaphysics, the ruling paradigm of Ming and Ch'ing government, and had written a work in Chinese
that attempted to show that the founders of Chinese philosophy had recognized the presence of a T'ien-chu in T'ien, a Lord in Heaven, a personal god behind the indwelling principle, the *li* and *ch'i,* which was all
the Neo-Confucians recognized. It is possible to trace how Chinese and
Korean[8] philosophers dealt with Ricci's book, conflating it with the Moh-
ist and Buddhist heterodoxies with which they were already acquainted.
From the European standpoint, however, it is clear that Ricci was appealing to natural rather than revealed religion, and to the Old Dispensation
rather than the New, thinking presumably that the Chinese needed to be
acquainted with God the Father before they were introduced to the saving merits of his Son. This is why the theistic language of the Treaty of
Nerchinsk is likely to be Jesuit in origin; but at this point Voltaire may be
imagined as intervening to call a halt, to impose a deistic closure on the
Jesuit enterprise. Nor would he have equated the common father of all
nations with the God of Israel. We know that from his *Essai sur les Mœurs,*
where the ancient Jews are as despicable as the modern, and the type of
natural monotheism is not Israel but Islam. The Arabs, conquering everywhere to make Allah known to all men, are noble as the self-seeking Jews,
hugging their God to themselves, are not; "Et ce sont nos pères," exclaims
Voltaire; the biblical origins of Christianity do it no credit. For this reason,
the Jesuits get no credit for the deist language of the 1689 treaty; and the

account of the Rites Controversy, in which Voltaire might have shown some sympathy for the Jesuit position, closes with an impartial condemnation of all Christian missions for being in China at all.[9] He cites the K'ang-hsi emperor's remark that Chinese do not travel to Europe and impose their doctrinal disputes there (though in Korea and Japan it might be held that they did); and we seem to meet for the first time with the implication that voyaging and encounter are an original sin and that individuals should stay at home in their own cultures instead of traveling great distances to impose themselves on others. It is an aspect of Enlightened thought that we shall meet again, and it needs to be reconciled in some way with Voltaire's insistence that the role of Petrine Russia was to open up both Eurasia and specifically China to the civilizing effects of global commerce. Would he have blamed the failure of Macartney's mission on Ch'ing memories of the Rites Controversy? It seems possible.

In the *Essai sur les Mœurs,* which purports to be a survey of the history of *l'esprit humain* at large, Voltaire's initial chapters are devoted to China, India, Iran, and Islam, in that order, before fixing his starting point in Europe at the reign of Charlemagne. But the sole purpose he pursues is that of using these civilizations, and the rational deism ascribed to China in particular, to unseat the traditional Christian image of universal history, with the Old and New Dispensations at its center and all Gentiles, other than the Greeks and Romans, relegated to the margins. And having used the Chinese to decenter the Jews and deconstruct the Christian scheme, Voltaire has no further need of them; he does not narrate their history (though he does that of the Mongols) in narrating the history of Europe as that of Christian barbarism followed by commercial enlightenment, and the other civilizations of the globe are described only when the history of Europe impinges upon them, or they (Mongols and Turks) upon it, until finally the whole *Essai* is summed up as a prelude to the glorious *Siècle de Louis XIV.*[10] Enlightened historiography was no longer Christocentric, but had in no way ceased to be Eurocentric, and if there is a world history here, it exists only with the global commerce of the eighteenth century, in creating which Peter the Great stands beside Louis XIV and his Dutch and English enemies. Voltaire is constantly urging Europeans not to see themselves as unique; but they appear to be unique in possessing enough Enlightenment to see themselves as historically specific. No one else is enlightened; no one else writes history. And indeed, no one in Ch'ing China or Tokugawa Japan, as far as I am aware, wrote a history of Europe; was it only cultural aggressiveness that made Europeans write as they did? And how—in the last analysis—are we to write a history along post-Copernican lines, one that does not have a center at all?

What Europeans needed and constructed was a history of themselves, designed to show how they had reached their present condition, what its problems were, and how these might be coped with. Such a history need not necessarily be complacent; or to put the same point more negatively, we have to understand how it became possible for them to be self-critical and complacent at the same time. Nor was its primary motive that of justifying European domination over others, though it did of course serve that purpose as the need arose; but the justification of empire in this sense, and the counterattack on its justification, are themes that arise late, and in a most important sense marginally, in the historiographical literature of the age. When Europeans—even Spaniards—thought of "empire," they thought of it as something they had eliminated from their own lives: the domination of Europe by a single power, internal or external in its origin. Pope Boniface VIII and Genghis Khan, Mehmed the Conqueror and the emperor Charles V, were gone and would not return; Europe the republic of independent states had proved stronger than they were (and would in the end prove stronger than the revolutionary emperor Napoleon). The question whether commercial society was itself corrupting the natures of Europeans had to be confronted and became part of their understanding of history; but the fact that the postimperial states of Europe were establishing empire in the sense of hegemony over others required a new definition of such terms as *empire* and *colony, imperialism* and *colonialism.* It was not on the agenda of European historiography before the 1770s and 1780s, when Denis Diderot and G.T.F. Raynal set out to place it there;[11] and even they treated colonialism as something marginal and harmful in European history, and the colonies of Europeans settled beyond seas as marginal to Europe—an attitude that persisted and is of some importance to *tau iwi* everywhere.

Therefore, the history of Others was integrated in, as well as being excluded from, the history that Europeans were constructing of themselves; and if this is a colonialist phenomenon, it was produced not simply by the need to dominate others but also by the sheer fact that Europeans were writing history to which Others were marginal, while Others were not writing history in which Europeans were included. And it is possible that we should have to alter the meaning of the word "history" before we could say that Others were constructing histories of themselves. The only culture outside Europe of which we can say with confidence that it was reassessing its own texts and its own history is Tokugawa Japan, where it was not yet a matter of responding to European culture but to Chinese and Buddhist components in its own; and on the beaches of the Pacific, we have to do with peoples who did not write history because they did not "write" at all, and must therefore be said—and said by whom?—to have assessed their "history" in other terms.

We have watched Voltaire's limited incorporation of China into the history he understands, its paradigms being international law, interstate commerce, and enlightened deism. A debate about China went on through the remainder of the prerevolutionary period, its themes being the appropriateness of Chinese agriculture to the developing European discourse of political economy, and the issue of whether the Chinese monarchy was to be admired as absolutist and enlightened or condemned as despotic. Clearly, much of this turned on the conflicting attitudes of Europeans toward their own absolute monarchies, and much of the rhetoric about "Oriental despotism" is oblique satire aimed at Versailles; this is why Voltaire, who deeply admired the monarchy of Louis XIV, would not accept it. On the whole, however, the Ch'ing emperors escaped inclusion in this trope in its commonest form; the often exaggerated image Europeans entertained of the uniformity and unchanging nature of Confucian rule impelled them to believe that it was "a despotism of manners" (a highly Enlightened phrase) and to see Chinese history as static and cyclical, but not to impose on the dynasties the melodramatic picture of "Oriental despotism" as violent, sensual, and exercised within the palace, or to depict the social structure as despotic in the sense that the individual's property was subject to the ruler's arbitrary and self-indulgent will.

It was in this last sense that Europeans constructed their self-image in terms of a property, a liberty, and a security under law that "Orientals" did not enjoy and that might explain Europe's development of the commerce now girdling the globe and sending out voyagers; but though China's nonparticipation in this commerce needed increasingly to be constructed and explained, it was as French and then British commercial empire expanded in India that the paradigm of "Oriental despotism" became central and controversial. The Europeans in India found themselves heirs to the Mughal emperors, and it was a temptation to say that these had been despots, and that their agrarian subjects, having never enjoyed security of property or liberty under law, were servile by nature, or by the effects of their history, and could only be governed despotically. But it was a truism that if despotic rule oppressed and degraded the subject, it also corrupted the ruler; and the French and British in India found reason to fear what finding themselves "Oriental despots" might do to their own history. With this mixture of motives, therefore, the French scholar A. H. Anquetil-Duperron[12]—a man whose independence of mind attained a kind of saintliness—set out in a treatise *De la Législation orientale* (1778) to attack the "Orientalist" paradigm by showing that Indian and Islamic land tenure was protected by a thick texture of laws and customs, and that the rulers of these societies were not "despots" in the full and perhaps fictitious sense. As a survivor of the last days of French India, Anquetil sometimes wrote in an anglophobic tone, and this produced an equally francophobe response from the usually mild-mannered William Jones, the British scholar whose studies of Hindu law were themselves to displace the despotic paradigm and lead to the far-reaching discovery that Sanskrit was an ancient language akin to the languages of Europe.[13] The Indo-Europeans, and more ominously the Caucasians and the Aryans, began to populate the historical imagination and vocabulary; more immediately, however, the chief British opponent of "Oriental despotism" as a paradigm was not Jones but, of all people, Edmund Burke, who spent much of the seven years of his impeachment of Warren Hastings demonstrating that the peoples of India were acquainted with law and should not be governed despotically.[14]

The Bengal land settlement carried out under Lord Cornwallis embodied an attempt to understand Indian land tenures and integrate them with those found in Western medieval history in forms that the British understood and could operate to their own advantage.[15] Once again, it was the model of European history that remained paramount and was imposed on others, but this was being both modified and developed as it was enlarged into a broader understanding of the history of Eurasia. The most energetic opponent of the "static and unchanging" reading of Chinese history was the French scholar Joseph de Guignes, who had learned to read the great collections of documents sent to Paris by the Jesuit missionaries in Peking. The Chinese were a warlike and imperial people, he said, whose history contained as many revolutions as that of Europe; but de Guignes had learned this through writing a history not of the Chinese dynasties but of the nomad peoples of Central Asia, recorded in Arabic and Roman as well as Chinese sources, from which he constructed a great study of the continental interactions between the Desert and the Sown.[16] De Guignes encountered the furious jealousy of Voltaire, for whom this was a mere history of "wolves and tigers" (though he had need of it in the *Essai sur les Mœurs* when providing the history behind the Mongol invasion of Europe and Syria in the thirteenth century).[17] There was a deeper issue between the two historians: de Guignes had attacked Voltaire for destroying the unity of the history of the human race—itself an Enlightenment value—and had proposed restoring it by regarding the most ancient Chinese as a colony sent out from Egypt.[18] This enabled Voltaire to caricature de Guignes as a slave of Christian and Jewish mythology, retreating into the history of the Old Testament. The point was, however, that Voltaire, having used China to destroy the Mosaic chronology and the Noachic genealogies, had nothing to put in their place and had abandoned all idea of humanity's descent from an original pair. Instead, he regarded the human as an animal species—in which he had the support of naturalist Buffon—and went on to suggest its differentiation in a number of subspecies. Repeatedly, he declared that the Lapps, and other Arctic peoples, were genetically distinct from their Scandinavian and Russian neighbors and must be thought of as evolving independently in interaction with their peculiar environment—autochthonous, in short, aboriginal or *tangata whenua* in the literal rather than the metaphorical sense of those terms. We detect scientific racism in this, as a child of Enlightenment, and our suspicions are confirmed when we find Voltaire insisting that the sensory organs of Chinese are differently formed from those of Europeans, and that this is why they can initiate the fine arts but never carry them to perfection.[19] (In the Walters Art Gallery in Baltimore there is a collection of Ming and Ch'ing ceramics encrusted with gold by Dutch and French artificers, and this, I fear, is what Voltaire had in mind.)

But though it is right to see scientific racism as a consequence of the Enlightened deconstruction of the Bible, there is another implication of the quarrel between de Guignes and Voltaire. The latter's polygeneticism led him to envisage diverse human populations evolving in different and spatially constant environments, and so to privilege the idea of relatively stationary societies, whereas de Guignes' diffusionism, the product like his residual Biblicism of his desire to maintain the human race's unity, privileged the idea of a dynamically expanding human population, and so the idea of the voyage, over land or sea (he thought that shipborne Egypto-Chinese had gone on to the settlement of the Americas). The antithesis between the stationary and the mobile is central to the concept of the voyage and the encounter, central also to Enlightened accounts of the evolution of society and the morality of colonization. In centering the role of nomad pastoralism in the history of the Eurasian landmass, de Guignes was emphasizing and advancing the importance of shepherd society in the schemes of human evolution that were beginning to appear. We begin now to inspect that scheme of four stages developed by French and Scottish theorists and restored to modern attention by Ronald Meek.[20]

This scheme, of various and complex design, became a historization of the seventeenth-century juristic model of the two states of nature in which humans had discovered their natural sociability—a model having as its goal the realization of that commercial condition in which Enlightenment situated Europe after the wars of religion. In one of its earlier formulations, *De l'Origine des Loix, des Arts, et des Sciences,* the work of Parisian jurist Antoine-Yves Goguet,[21] the starting point is still biblical, the Dispersion of the Peoples following the Confusion of Tongues and the Fall of the Tower of Babel (a potent series of sociological myths). From the plain of Shinar (the Olduvai Gorge of Christian anthropology), the peoples set out on a series of wanderings that ends in the population of the earth but the near-loss of their humanity; for the farther they travel the less they conserve, remember, or understand, until in Patagonia, and other uttermost parts of the earth, they reach the point where they have almost forgotten language and have so far forgotten their human nature as to eat one another. From antiquity there comes to mind the figure of Polyphemus, shepherd, cave-dweller, and cannibal, his language so far truncated that he must call Odysseus "Nobody"; we wonder what encounters by archaic Aegean seafarers lie behind this powerful representation, and we realize that part of the trouble in Queen Charlotte Sound and at Grassy Cove was that anthropophagy was being practiced not by miserable cave-dwellers but by people in an advanced state of sociability; this made it harder to bear. The greater James Cook's achievement, then, in declaring that it was not evidence of dehumanization but simply a custom. From more modern thinking appears the image of the orangutan or anthropoid as not a prehuman but a degenerate man, who can perhaps interbreed with races on their way down to his level.

The process of dehumanization, the product of the vagrant condition, is reversed in Goguet's scheme as the hominids rediscover the arts that once made them human. From hunting their fellow inhabitants of the earth, they learn to domesticate them and become herdsmen and horsemen; from gathering the fruits of the earth, they relearn to cultivate them and become agriculturalists and proprietors. This is the decisive recovery, for it renders them once more sedentary; cultivating and occupying fixed points on the earth, they transmit them to their heirs and begin developing the arts of social memory; and the sedentary settlements constitute a social space, across which goods, words, songs, laws, and information begin to pass in a pattern of movement, not vagrancy but exchange. Agriculture and commerce, the ploughland and the city, appear simultaneously, and the recovery of human nature is accomplished. Though Goguet's system recognizes the four arts—hunting, herding, farming, and trading—it contains only two stages, a vagrant and a sedentary. The shepherd is not decisively removed from the "savage," the *selvaggio* or forest food-gatherer—we recall that Polyphemus was shepherd and cave-dweller at the same time—and the agrarian engaging in trade with the next village has not reached the point where his land is a commodity exchangeable for cash. This could be called the Waitangian moment, at which Glenelg, Secretary of State for the Colonies, could declare that the Maori were "not New Zealand savages living by the chase" but had the capacity to apportion lands among themselves; and history is a commentary on just how precarious it was, when used as a means of ascribing culture to Others.[22]

It is not easy to see how theorists moved from Goguet's system, in which the shepherd condition was a mere prolongation of the savage, to Adam Smith's, in which it is a decisive rupture and creative breakthrough; perhaps European history had something to do with it. The purely nomadic Huns were needed to push the pastoral but black-soil Goths and the forest Germans on to the great estates of the Romans, where their interactions somehow produced the free tenures protected by law that made Europeans capable of liberty and commerce; and de Guignes' pioneer account of the "empire of the steppe" placed pastoral nomadism at the center of Eurasian history, leaving open the question of Europe's uniqueness. The savage was now needed as the starting point, the presocial and all but prehuman condition of feral individualism from which all human progress had been made. His characteristics—I use this pronoun because his capacities for gender and even sexual relationships were held to be as undeveloped as the rest of him—were the consequence not merely of his failure to appropriate, but of his vagrant hunter-gatherer condition. Formally, he represented human nature as it was when none of its potentialities had yet been realized; empirically, there existed a copious literature describing the culture he had when in this condition.

It will be remembered that the historiography of Enlightenment included a history of religion as well as of property and commerce. The four-stage scheme explained the religion of the savage food-gatherer as a religion of animism; as he passed from one encounter to another his imagination located a spirit in every rock and tree, in the haunts of every ancestor, and so polytheism was invented. The shepherd, following his flocks across the enormous spaces of Arabia or Eurasia, might perhaps reach the point of contemplating the starry heavens without and the moral law within; but in the great cities of Mesopotamia, Egypt, and India, the sages of Oriental antiquity—what we term the Axial Age—had coordinated polytheism into great systems of allegory, appearance, and representation, in which everything that was appeared an allegory or emanation of some primordial substance that might even be termed *nonbeing* (as in so many Eastern languages it was). This was the worship of the cosmos itself, from which nothing was separate and in which everything had its place, the worship we so gladly attribute to indigenous peoples as the antithesis of our restless selves. It is visibly like the Maori world picture described by Ranginui Walker; but the philosophers and theologians of Europe could not imagine it being generated among a people of hunters and gatherers—still less among what they had hardly begun to imagine, a maritime people of fishers and voyagers. They located it in agricultural and urban Asia, among cities, sages, priesthoods, and law-givers; and Christian theists and Enlightened deists joined in condemning it by the name of "enthusiasm" and in sharply separating themselves from its history. They narrated how ancient Hebrews and relatively modern Muslims had isolated the One God as separate from the universe he had created, and how free Greek and Roman citizens had reflected on their own moral and social nature, and set about deducing the probability of the One God from that. This distinguished Hebraic and Hellenic Europe from the Oriental world, though disastrous survivals of the latter, like Neo-Platonism and Catholic theology, continued to plague the former.[23] It was not the deists and skeptics of European Enlightenment but the handful of genuine atheists—followers of Spinoza in refusing to separate God from the universe or spirit from matter—who sometimes upheld the monism of the Neo-Confucians against Jesuits and deists alike.

The four-stages scheme was an Old World construction, the product of European encounters with Asian pastoralists and agriculturalists and of Europe's reflections on its own character—including that basic encounter between Romans and invading barbarians from which Europe itself was derived. There are two major points to be noted about it. In the first place, it presupposed that the human was a land-dwelling species, whether sedentary or migratory, and contained little account of its capacity for travel by sea. And is this not a presumption made even among specialists in the history of oceanic peoples? Is it not easy to assume that the whole imposing cosmogony of the Polynesian peoples was devised for no other purpose than to justify a unity with the land, and even claims to it, and was carried down the vast distances of the Pacific simply to fertilize one tiny *whenua* after another? But is this really so? Did so great a people of navigators in fact subordinate the *waka* to the *whenua*, and marginalize Tangaroa to his brother Tane, so completely as to make themselves people of the land and not the sea? I do not presume to know, but if they did, the circumstance is worth remarking on.

Second, the four-stages scheme did not fit well in any of the world new to Europeans. In America, where there was no large-scale herding of beasts, and maize agriculture had not sustained cities beyond those destroyed in the Spanish Conquest, it was easiest to relegate all native peoples to the category of hunter and savage. The Pacific was an even less tractable problem, since the shortage of land mammals meant that the human populations were fishers instead of hunters, gardeners instead of herdsmen or ploughmen. Whether there is literature in which Enlightened anthropologists were trying to devise new schemes to fit this situation I do not know; but here it is desirable to recall that encounter does not stop at the beach. In the continental spaces of Australia there were highly mobile gatherer cultures, and the model of the vagrant and possibly degenerate savage could be restored in full strength. The islands of Aotearoa, it seems worth saying, are large and diverse enough to count as small continents; one leaves the beach to venture inland, among grasslands, bush, mountains, and *te wai pounamu,* and the problem of occupancy and appropriation becomes as crucial as it was by 1840. But the beach—especially when it lacks a four-stages hinterland—is the *locus classicus* of encounter with the Other: the human culture for which one has no interpretative paradigm; and here clearly is a point at which the stereotype of the savage can reassert itself.

What the history of Oceanic encounter in the European theoretical mind tells us is that the image of the savage was still split two ways by the tension between nature and history. The noble savage, still very much part of the story, is the natural man uncorrupted by history, knowing by innate rationality what it is natural for humans to know. Diderot's Tahitians in the *Supplément au voyage de Bougainville* are noble savages in this sense: The wise elders are interested only in morality, the spontaneous women are interested only in fertility, and everything is as it ought to be. They are not Tahitians at all, in the sense that they are not products of a system of culture and custom that they have generated for themselves. Diderot knew perfectly well that he was not writing about real Tahitians, and he knew that if he had understood their culture, he would have found that it was not natural or noble, according to the standards of enlightened sentimentality. The function of natural man is to criticize historical culture, and the idealized Tahitians are there only to criticize French culture, itself stereotyped not in the person of the *philosophe* Bougainville, but in the person of his Christian chaplain—who has to be fictionalized as a monk, so that Diderot can use Tahitian sexual liberty to criticize the dreadful Christian customs of monogamy, celibacy, and repression. These Tahitians have no *tapu;* only Europeans have them, and they are all malignant. Nature is being used to criticize history; the Other exists to decenter the Self but not to find a center or a self of its own. Consequently, Diderot the critic of history can attribute history only to Europeans; the Tahitians have none and are supposed to be happier without it. History is the war between nature and custom, waged within every human.

When Diderot alludes to Bougainville himself, it is to raise the radical question whether there ought to be voyages at all.[24] If the civilized Parisian is content with his own culture, why should he leave it to intrude on another's? If he leaves it because he is dissatisfied with it, what will he learn from another's? To enter the world of natural man is to deconstruct one's own culture, but it will equally deconstruct the Other's once that is seen as historically specific. The cosmopolitan intellectual believes that everyone else should stay at home, happily enclosed within one's own community; yet he knows that it is a community of custom, not of nature. Diderot and Rousseau were honest enough to know that the stationary ideal was out of reach, but that for them was the tragedy of history; the wanderings of feral and vagrant man had been replaced by the restless and predatory curiosity of European voyagers and settlers. We echo this view when we become disturbed by the phenomena of tourism. The tourist comes not to exploit us but to appropriate and consume us by the sheer weight of his anxious or incurious gaze; has he a history, and will he leave us one?

But did it not occur to Diderot that Tahitians must have been voyagers themselves to have reached the happy islands at all? By the time Cook, Banks, and Tupaia—a curious explorer in his own right—reached Queen Charlotte Sound, they knew that Polynesians were a diffused and voyaging people, with a common language but a diversity of locally generated customs. One of these, anthropophagy, Tupaia is said to have disliked as much as the English did; it was Cook who said it was a custom and not a degeneration from nature, though he thought it a custom that might be unmade. But for Diderot, as for Rousseau, all customs were a departure from nature, though a departure that could not be avoided; and this left it possible to take a step that Diderot was not concerned to take, and to characterize Polynesians (or any peoples encountered) as savages rather ignoble than noble. The ignoble savage is the natural man historized, a figure in a system where nature must have a history to develop in; his nature is undeveloped—he is social man not yet socialized. Primitive rather than degenerate, he and she are trapped in the hunter-gatherer culture that is all they have, in whatever customs that condition has permitted them to invent. It was only too easy to convert the noble into the ignoble savage in a single move whenever a shock, like the death of Marion or Cook, or a greed for land, labor, or converts impelled one to do so. Diderot was better placed to denounce this rhetoric than to resist it; he was not trying to supply Tahitians with customs or a history of their own, only with using them to make Europeans unsure of themselves. As long as the Other is used to deconstruct the Self, the Other has no history; and a history involved with an encounter between Selves requires that there should be two Selves, neither one nor none. There have been and there are critical intellectuals who regard it as their business to deconstruct Selves wherever they meet them, and for whom in consequence all the world is their Other. These are of little use to Others trying to reassert their identity as Selves; and because there is one of them lurking in every one of us, we need to look cautiously at our use of the idiom of Self and Other. It can prove a cyclical trap, though it describes a condition from which we would like to escape.

But what I have been calling "history," which Enlightened theorists still opposed to the idea of nature, is very much the memory of the Self, a self-reinforcement even when it is a self-criticism. Europeans believed themselves to be a profoundly dynamic people precisely because they possessed an identity that they had always contested deeply among themselves. They had developed by the age of encounter a complex narrative of that history, carried to the present when the commerce that was its culmination was encircling the globe. They could include others in it, or they could exclude others from it; they could use the excluded Others as the image of a nature used to criticize their own history or even history itself; but their history as they understood it went on (and has gone on) happening, and they have continued writing it. The sometime Others, therefore, need to speak and write themselves into articulate existence, and may seem to need a history of their own. But they do not need a history of themselves written in exclusively European terms, and they have a case for holding that the very notion of history, as so far presented, is *pakeha* ideology. They may choose to present themselves in their own version of the opposition between nature and history: to present themselves as the *pakeha* are sometimes willing to see them, as noble shamans in direct succession to the noble savage, wholly at one with the Spinozist cosmos as the latter was wholly at one with natural law; and they are often able to make a strong and convincing case for doing so. But this is a strategy that has a *pakeha* history of its own; the first anticolonialist ideology was that of German romantic nationalism resisting the cosmopolitanism of Enlightenment and Revolution, where the *tangata whenua* appeared in the form of the *Volk* close to the *Erde,* generating themselves out of it by means of folk songs, ancestral memories, and linguistic forms uniquely their own and sometimes incommunicable to others. The opposition of nature to history leads straight to the question whether cultures should make contact with one another, and what happens when they cannot be kept out of it. It can never, of course, solve the problem of what is to be done when contact has irrevocably happened; and we appear to be proceeding on the assumption that at this point both parties to the original contact must write history, that the *tangata whenua* cannot retreat into *te po* and that the *tau iwi* cannot write history on no other foundation than that of their own guilt. Both now have memories of change and must inscribe these more deeply and fully; but the memories, and the history, of each people are their own—except that they now remember each other and must write each other's history. What we find ourselves talking about, then, is not the possibility of a new Enlightenment—though, in the degenerate form of a universal and vulgarized disenchantment, that seems to be what we are getting—so much as the possibility of reconstituting distinctive voices that can speak to each other across very divergent concepts, some of them not yet formulated, of what history, and the relation between nature and history, are all about. It is a daunting prospect; but the image of a *marae*, where challenges are converted into greetings and Others into Selves, is a valuable starting point.

NOTES

1. Valerie Flint, *The Imaginative Landscape of Christopher Columbus* (Princeton: Princeton University Press, 1992).

2. Anne Salmond, *Two Worlds: First Meetings between Maori and Europeans, 1642–1772* (New York: Viking, 1992).

3. Voltaire, *Histoire de la Russie sous Pierre le Grand* (1760), cited in chap. 1, *Oeuvres Historiques,* ed. René Pomeau (Paris: Plèiade, 1962), 368.

4. Paul Hasard, *La Crise de la Conscience Européene, 1680–1715* (Paris: Boivin, 1935).

5. Princeton University Press, 1992.

6. Voltaire, *Oeuvres Historiques,* 359–361, 369–376.

7. Ibid., 409–411.

8. Chong Son Yu, "Confucius, Chu Hsi, and the Doctrine of T'ien-chu: Political Thought of the Korean Catholics, 1614–1801," Ph.D. diss., Johns Hopkins University, 1992.

9. Voltaire, *Oeuvres Historiques,* 1101–1109.

10. "Chap. 197. Resumé de toute cette Histoire jusqu'au temps ou commence le beau siècle de Louis XIV."

11. In Raynal's *Histoire philosophique et politique des établissements et du commerce des Européens dans les deux Indes* (1770–1790), to which Diderot made many contributions. These, and the *Supplement au Voyage de Bougainville* (1772), are translated in John Hope Mason and Robert Wokler, eds., *Diderot: Political Writings* (Cambridge: Cambridge University Press, 1992).

12. There is a recent study of him in Jean-Luc Kieffer, *Anquetil-Duperron: L'Inde en France au XVIII*^{e} *Siècle* (Paris: Société d'édition "Les Belles Lettres," 1983). See also the edition of his *Considérations Philosophiques, Historiques et Géographiques sur les Deux Mondes* (1780–1804) by Guido Abbatista (Pisa: Scuola Normale Superiore, 1993) with an important introduction.

13. S. N. Mukherji, *Sir William Jones and British Attitudes towards India* (Cambridge: Cambridge University Press, 1968); Garland Cannon, *The Life and Mind of Oriental Jones: Sir William Jones, the Father of Modern Linguistics* (Cambridge: Cambridge University Press, 1990).

14. P. J. Marshall, ed., *India, Madras, and Bengal, 1774–1785,* and *India: The Launching of the Hastings Impeachment, 1786–1788,* vols. 5 and 6 of *The Writings and Speeches of Edmund Burke,* general ed. Paul Langford (Oxford: Clarendon Press, 1981, 1991); Frederick G. Whelan, *Edmund Burke and India: Political Morality and Empire* (Pittsburg: Pittsburg University Press, 1996).

15. Rolando Minuti, "Proprietà della Terra e Dispotismo Orientale: Aspetti di un dibattito sull'India nella seconda metà del settecento," in *Materiali per una storia della cultura giuridica,* VIII, 2 (Bologna, 1978): 29–176.

16. Joseph de Guignes, *Histoire Générale des Huns, des Turcs, des Mogols, et des autres peuples tartares occidentaux* (Paris: n.p., 1756–1758).

17. Voltaire, *Essai sur les Mœurs,* chap. 60: "De l'Orient et de Gengis-khan." See Rolando Minuti, *Oriente Barbarico e storiografia settecentesco rappresentazioni della storia dei Tartari nella cultura francese del XVIII secolo* (Venice: Marsilio, 1994).

18. See S.A.M. Adshead, "China a Colony of Egypt: An Eighteenth-Century Controversy," *Asian Profile,* 12(2) (1984): 113–127.

19. Voltaire, *Histoire de Russie* (n. 3 above); for the concealed attack on de Guignes, see 359–360 (Lapps); *Essai sur les Mœurs,* chap. 1 (Paris: n.p., 1835), 1: 26; Chinese as a separate species, chap. 119 (3: 10–11; Lapps likewise).

20. Ronald L. Meek, *Social Science and the Ignoble Savage* (Cambridge: Cambridge University Press, 1975).

21. Paris, 1758; an English translation appeared in Edinburgh in 1761.

22. See further J.G.A. Pocock, "Tangata Whenua and Enlightenment Anthropology," *New Zealand Journal of History* 27(1) (1992): 28–53, and *Law, Sovereignty, and History: The Case of New Zealand and the Treaty of Waitangi* (Lancaster, England: Lancaster University, 1992).

23. The best source for this is Jakob Brucker, *Historia Critica Philosophiae* (Leipzig, n.p., 1742–1744), vol. 1.

24. For this see Anthony Pagden, *European Encounters with the New World* (New Haven: Yale University Press, 1993), chap. 5.

3

SOUTH PACIFIC MYTHOLOGY

'I. F. Helu

My old teacher John Anderson, of Sydney University, maintained that if there is anything that mythical thought cannot handle it is the inevitability of social change. Arguing that punishment is society's way of restoring the network of relationships between institutions and the integrity of social boundaries that have been injured by unauthorized behavior, Anderson asserted that it would still be impossible to "maintain boundaries and avoid encroachment," "that there will always be forces opposed to it, that there will always be social conflict." He summarizes his position in the following way:

> While primitive thought dimly realises this (as in stories of wars among the gods) and tries to counter it (as in the conception of Moira, or proper apportionment which "governs even the gods"), it cannot really grapple with what this implies—the inevitability of social change, the impossibility of the indefinite continuance of the forms of social (tribal) activity in existence at any given time.[1]

When later I came to look at mythology myself, and especially Polynesian mythology, I thought an insight could still be added to the Andersonian thesis; namely, that canons of myths do present a clear picture of cultural transformation even though this dimension of the mythical sequences may have escaped recognition by (or interest of) the ancient peoples. I wish to illustrate this point by relating a Polynesian corpus of myths about the exploits of one of our demigods.

But I want to take Anderson's view together with a theory of Marshall Sahlins'—at least as it relates to Hawaiian myths—and briefly examine them for what they are worth in terms of my own interpretation. Sahlins, in his account of the Lono myth, implies that myths have a predictive value or fulfillment effect and that the fulfillment of myth is what we call "history."[2] Of course, there can be other possible readings of the Lono series. For example, it can simply be taken to be a standardized excuse for behavior that otherwise would be intolerable in terms of the ethics of the wider society.

The Maui Canon

Maui is a pan-Polynesian culture hero or demigod. Polynesian mythology admits of a distinction similar to the classicist's between epichoric (local) myths and pan-Hellenic (pan-Polynesian) myths. The level of conflict, however, between the local and the overarching mythologies is much higher in the case of the classical corpus than in the Polynesian.[3]

The Maui canon is represented in most Polynesian island groups, but it seems to me to be fullest in the Maori versions.[4] It is a series of myths that chronicles the exploits of a trickster or a demigod. If we take myth in Giambattista Vico's sense,[5] that is, as about society, then we must regard Maui as a popular hero, a champion of the people much like Prometheus in Greek mythology.

1. The earliest Maui tale depicts him as a miraculous fisherman who fished up not fish but islands. In the Tongan version, Maui fished up with hook and line the islands of 'Atā, 'Eua, and Eueiki (Havaiki?). The 'Uveans have a myth in which Maui caught and pulled up in his fishing net most islands in their group, and the Maori story divides the two main islands of New Zealand into different parts—head, mouth, tail, fins, and so on—of *Te Ika a Maui,* the Fish of Maui. All the above can be references to original settlements or founding of communities—this is the agreed meaning for tales of wandering and travel—but all couched in the symbolism of a marine culture and economy (fishhooks, canoes, nets, islands, the sea, etc.).

2. The next myth shows Maui stealing fire from the Underworld and giving it to man. He narrowly escaped being caught by his pursuers, whose wrath would have had fatal consequences if they had caught him. The traditional method of producing fire by rubbing two dry sticks together derived from Maui's heroic act. Maui then was the father of technology and civilization, and Levi-Strauss' *le cru et le cuit* (the techno-culinary mode) also is echoed here. The moral aspect of this myth is of great interest also and confirms the relativistic character of moral values. An act of a clearly unethical character is offset by another act of the highest level of humanism.[6]

3. The third group of myths recounts Maui's struggle against and triumph over man-eating plants and animals. Maui thus appears as the originator of agriculture and animal husbandry. The plant and beast specifically mentioned as having been domesticated by our hero were a man-eating plant, *hiapo*, the mulberry tree from whose bark *tapa* cloth is made, and a man-devouring *nifo*, or wild boar.

4. The next story has Maui snaring the Sun with his fishing net. The tale says that until then the Sun shot across the sky in no time, leaving people and the Earth always in darkness and bitter cold. Maui, with the assistance of friends, managed to catch the Sun with his net, and while it was thus captive set to beating the Sun with his war club. When at last Maui released the Sun again, the latter was already decrepit and weak and had to crawl across the sky at the much slower rate that we now know. It is possible that this legend may be carrying the memories of the relocations of settlers from semipolar regions to places in the tropics or mid-latitudes.

5. The last tale in the Tongan Maui canon presents the hero as a prosaic taro farmer on the island of 'Eau, one of the lands Maui fished up from the bottom of the ocean. One day he got into a fit (being sick of the humdrum existence he was leading), and he smote the dry earth with his digging stick so vehemently that the hole thus created went all the way underneath the land and connected with the deep waters of the encircling sea, creating a most impressive natural bridge, the Matalanga-'a-Maui (the planting-hole-of-Maui). This is how this demigod ends his career in the Tongan rendition of the canon. According to Tongan mythology, then, Maui started as a navigator-discoverer of islands, as the founder of communities. He is next shown as the originator of civilization and creator of the principal departments of culture, and finally ended his days in routine horticulture and farming. This sequence of myths is surely the epic of the evolution of Tongan society—the metamorphosis of a culture that was oriented to the sea and a marine economy into one based on farming and animal husbandry.

6. One Maui myth found in the Maori series is conspicuously absent from the Tongan traditions. In this story, Maui attempted to obtain the secret of immortality from the Great Mother Goddess, Hine-nui-te-Po (Great-Lady-of-the-Night), by entering her enormous body (while she slept) through a rear hole and coming out through her mouth. The goddess awoke before Maui was completely out of her huge frame, and she dismembered him with great fury. It is usual to regard this type of myth (see also Orpheus and Eurydice and the Gil-

gamesh myths) as "speculation" on the impossibility of immortality for man.[7] Yet the insights of Mary Douglas in her work on body symbolism[8] and Victor Turner's on rituals[9] may offer means of opening up the complex of meaning packed into this myth. It then becomes possible to read this story as a depiction of the body politic and the way in which rebellious spirits who attempt a transmutation of values[10] (represented by the reversal of direction of natural processes in Maui's act) achieve their apotheoses through being sacrificed at the altar of social integrity and permanence. In fact, all the myths that epitomize the transformation of Maui (Tongan society) declare that culture is invariably the product of resolute but perilous enterprise— lands are torn from their original moorings, creatures are subdued and made captive, fire is stolen on pain of death, and so on.

Mythical versus Historical Discoverers

If we take Maui to represent the ancient seafarers who first entered that part of the Pacific known as the Polynesian triangle, we can make very general comparisons of them with the modern discoverers who came in the early period of European contact. This would be another way of using the same Maui canon to measure the validity of the Andersonian and Sahlinsian theses, as well as to test them for any light they may throw on the writing of the history of the Pacific Islands:

1. Mythical discoverers came for land; modern discoverers came for markets or raw materials. 2. Mythical discoverers became indigenous peoples;[11] modern discoverers became colonial administrators. 3. Mythical discoverers domesticated man-eating plants and animals; modern discoverers domesticated cannibals and savages. 4. Mythical discoverers invented fire (Stone Age technology); modern discoverers introduced new fire (metal and modern technology).[12] 5. Mythical discoverers introduced subsistence agriculture; modern discoverers introduced the capitalist market. 6. Mythical discoverers created social systems in which the individual is held down at every point by social taboos; modern discoverers introduced the ideas of liberty and rights with which the individual can wear down the rigidity of traditional conventions.

We are now in a position to make general observations, in the light of the above analysis, regarding the views advanced by Anderson and Sahlins. With regard to Anderson, we can add to his insight the recognition that myths can give us a picture of how communities have changed. This is easier with a series of myths—a canon, like the Maui corpus— than with single tales. In the case of Sahlins' view, we can see that although history can never exactly reproduce mythology, instructive parallels can be drawn. In other words, myth and history have a general fit between them, never a specific one.[13]

History of the Pacific Islands

It is now becoming common to isolate three types of histories for the Pacific Islands. In the first place we have the standard histories written by foreigners. Most of these were based on the diaries, reports, and correspondences of explorers, colonial personnel, and missionaries, themselves foreigners. By and large, island histories by foreigners have been quite useful and provided primary and secondary sources on which later histories were to be built. Still, they were far from being entirely satisfactory. The charge of ethnocentrism is valid enough in these cases, but there are other matters that require notice. One of these is the tendency of foreign historians either to bypass or overstate the negative side of island cultures. One is tempted to recognize a principle here: The negative aspects of a culture are never fully available to foreigners.

There is then a need to complement the first type of history by one written by native or local historians. And I am delighted to see Islanders themselves—an example is my fellow contributor to this volume, Professor Malama Meleisea—producing fine histories of their own communities. Most of our historians are trained professionals who have learned every trick of the trade. But there is another twist to this approach: to adopt entirely the indigenous perspective and refuse to employ any part of the traditional standpoint of scientific historiography. This has yet to come in the case of the Islands, but for the Americas it is exemplified by Nathan Wachtel's *La Vision des Vaincus*.[14]

The third type of history possible for the Islands is one based on hypotheses taken from the study of myth and oral traditions. It is true that what we learn from ethnohistory is more often general characters and principles of social systems than specific, concrete facts— thus, mythology is more useful to sociology than to history. Still, we can engage the said hypotheses not only as a control for our studies but also to suggest innovative strategies for a more exact knowledge of our prehistory. Some of the best studies in this area have been done by Dr. 'O. Māhina, who is also a contributor to this volume.[15]

What is important in all this is method—scientific method—because, I maintain, there is no logical difference in status between the three types of history (though procedural details can be very different), since the factuality of the propositions enunciated in any of them are all on the same logical footing. This in fact is so with all sciences, natural or social—they differ only in subject matter. Thus all histories, assuming they employ scientific method, can be brought under the rubric of studies of social complexes. Contrast this with an art, which is the effective presentation of some material. Although both psychology and literature deal with a psychological complex, the former is a scientific study of personality, while the latter is an artistic presentation of neurotic personalities.[16]

We conclude this essay with a brief discussion of the nature of myth and its relation to history (both in the general and the academic sense of the term). We may, first of all, divide myth into two main classes, both derived from ideas found in Vico: (1) creation myths, and (2) "historical" myths.

The relation to Vichian ideas is as follows. In his theory of the origin of language, Vico presents a graphic picture of how the original human inhabitants of the earth paired natural sounds (thunder, etc.) with emotions inside man's bosom, and who regarded the sky as (or containing) a manlike being but infinitely superior in power and in every respect.[17] Adapting this view we can take creation or origin myths (that is, origins of parts of nature and the natural environment but excluding origins of society and the built environment) as attempts to explain natural phenomena in terms of human interest and social organization.

There is nothing wrong with this type of primitive curiosity, an instinctive itch for explanations of striking and fearsome natural events. For that purpose, however, early man had no other resources but human character and practice. The question here is whether the cosmos has a human content. Obviously, the answer is No. This does not mean that we cannot use this type of myth in ways we like—we do this all the time. The point is, creation myths offer nothing to science (history) because nature and its parts have their own ways of working, which are independent of human or social interest. Hence, any reliable explanation of natural phenomena must be in their own terms.

Certain types of human activities (such as farming) or important historic events (such as wars of conquest) often correspond exactly in their formal structures to important natural or cosmic events, especially natural or cosmic cycles. When a pair of this sort is identified by people, they are often united to form a single myth with the historical event imposed on the basic form afforded by the natural or cosmic event. Because of the recurrent character of those events, the social component of the combination is reinforced by being brought back to memory in this cyclical and rhythmic manner for as long as that cultural dispensation retains its identity. In fact, both myth and religion aim at perpetuating a certain way of life.[18]

Something like this seems to be involved in the Lono myth that Sahlins expounds in *Islands in History*.[19] It is possible that the Lono myth denotes folk-memory of a momentous and historic event in the immemorial past of East Polynesians—the conquest of their territory by "foreigners" (God/Lono) and subsequent accommodation with the "locals" (King/Warriors?)—or other events of such stupendous significance for their social development. And to keep society reminded of the special contribution the "foreign" invaders made to the local culture, the past event was grafted onto the recurring seasonal changes, which bring with them their unique boons without which the continuity of human society and institutions cannot be maintained. Thus, a historical event is transformed into a repeating occasion by being "mounted" on the form of a natural cycle. The product is myth, which from time to time becomes the social present. The purpose of this type of myth, then, is the reproduction of a particular kind of society, or the maintenance of a certain way of life. With the Lono cycle, the Hawaiians were conditioned to preserve a type of society that originated in the "politics of encounter" of the distant past.

With regard to the second category of myths, the "historical" myths, we propose the following hypothesis. In preliterate societies, epoch-making events stay with the "collective memory" and in the process of transmission, orality—whose principal power is "elaboration" in the literal sense of the term—goes to work on the historical material until a stage is reached where the originally spatio-temporal events take on surreal and miraculous aspects and they become myth. The scientist's problem therefore is this: to devise a method by which we can reverse the process or demythologize, peeling off the mythical overlay to get down to the factual core that is history. It must be added that the oral process is always harnessed by political passion to establish in myth a political program.

We must also recognize that in purely oral transmission the desire for novelty, for distinction in presentation, becomes compulsive and takes precedence over accuracy. This opens the door for distortion, and actual occurrences begin to transcend the boundaries of possibility to become fantastic and magical. The required methodology therefore would essentially consist of (a) elimination of events or characteristics that are logically impossible; (b) elimination of purely oral effects, for example, literary devices that are merely cosmetic but have no structural connection to the myth; and (c) identification and elimination of any superimposed political agenda in the myth.

For an example of a historical myth, we may take any one from the Maui sequence referred to at the beginning of this essay. The first story in the series relates to a "voyage of discovery" in which Maui "fished up" most of the Polynesian islands. We are bound, therefore, to reject any idea of literal truth attached to "islands being pulled up from the bottom of the sea by fishhooks" and think of the story as relating to chance landfalls made in the course of pursuing a maritime way of life and economy.

Thus, we can represent the "historical" kernel of this myth by the following statement, which we may assume, for the sake of argument, to be true: A "fishing expedition" led by Maui (or the Maui?) was the first voyage to land on such-and-such an island.

So these voyagers were the first to have ventured beyond a certain familiar orbit, to have hit upon new islands, and to have returned home to tell people of their discovery, firing the imagination of the home folks and causing an exodus to the new lands. The feat was repeated again and again, until the whole of the Polynesian islands were discovered and settled. The earliest heroes remained in the folk memory, however, and they eventually became gods; their deeds, after passing through the prism of orality and the cauldron of political sentiment, became miraculous. Folk gods then were originators of dispensations or new "civilizations." Their deeds form the content of "historical" myths.

Myth has no use for dating. This most important item in the historian's arsenal is, for people who are busy creating or servicing a way of life, only a nicety at best and even unnecessary dross. Such people care about subsistence, security, permanence, and perpetuity and little else. Yet it is still possible to determine approximate dates not only by logical examination of "internal" evidence but also through "external" evidence afforded by the sister sciences—archaeology, philology, anthropology, ethnobotany, and so on. The gradual change, for example, from a marine to an agricultural economy (which the myth of the Matalanga-'a-Maui embodies) can now be given a rough date by archaeology for Tonga (late sixth century A.D.). The analysis can be carried further for a higher refinement of this value. And that would give us a reference point for throwing backwards our yardstick in search of the approximate dates for the other myths in the Maui corpus.

Even if we believe that my argument falls short of defining history in the scientific sense, the proposition enunciated at the beginning—namely, that myths can be sources of hypotheses about history—seems well enough defended. If that claim is to be denied, however, we are left only with the conclusion that beyond the writings of explorers and missionaries there is a veil that can never be lifted.

NOTES

1. From *Psychological Moralism*, a review of J. D. Flugel's *Man, Morals, and Society: A Psycho-Analytic Study*, which Anderson wrote in 1959 and published in the

collection of papers *Studies in Empirical Philosophy* (Sydney: Angus and Robertson, 1962), 363–374.

2. See Marshall Sahlins, *Islands of History* (Chicago: Chicago University Press, 1985), 103–135.

3. See the introduction to D. C. Pozzi and J. M. Wickersham, eds., *Myth and the Polis* (Ithaca: Cornell University Press, 1991).

4. Although it cannot be taken to be a law, we can regard it as a rough rule of thumb that the community giving the fullest and most detailed version of a myth, legend, or tradition has the best claim to be its originator.

5. This is the whole argument of Book 1 *(Establishment of Principles)* and Book II *(Poetic Wisdom)*—that when the "expressiveness" of myth is peeled off, we are left with historical events, or, as I should put it, myth is about society. See also D. Bidney, "Vico's New Science of Myth," in *Giambattista Vico: An International Symposium,* ed. G. Tagliacozzo and H. V. White (Baltimore: Johns Hopkins Press, 1969).

6. The myth states the ethical problem nicely. Stealing is an antivalue only when it operates *within* the group. When practiced on other groups (or "orders of being") for the benefit of our group or humanity, thieving transforms into a moral value. Yet humanity is not a universal solvent for ethical problems. For then we are confronted with the opposition humanity/cosmos, and in this sense, care of Nature is of a "higher" ethical value than regard for mankind, just as love of humanity is morally higher than care for our group ("inferred" from the group/humanity dichotomy).

7. Although all mythologies conclude that immortality is ruled out for mankind, Americans and Christians maintain the hope that death will one day be defeated.

8. Mary Douglas, *Purity and Danger: An Analysis of the Concepts of Pollution and Taboo* (London: Routledge and Kegan Paul, 1966), 128.

9. Victor Turner, *The Forest of Symbols: Aspects of Ndembu Ritual* (Ithaca: Cornell University Press, 1967), 88–91, 107.

10. The Hine-nui-te-po myth parallels at many points the account in *Also Sprach Zarathustra* of the dragon that lies across the path of the child and on whose every scale are written the words "Thou Shalt Not." Both the child and Maui aim at "reversing the tables," i.e., at creating a new morality and therefore a new type of social formation.

11. At the end of the oral presentation of this paper, historian John Pocock commented that he could not see the force of the distinction between "settlers and colonists" (my original formulation). The point is well taken and I have recast the opposition as "natives and colonial administrators," which, after all, was my original meaning.

12. Efficiency is the king of technology: No matter how popular a particular technology is at any given time, it is rendered obsolete as soon as more

efficient technologies are developed for the same application. Reviving an obsolete technology can be effected in two ways: by replacing use-value with an exchange-value, or by turning it into a social symbol.

13. It is difficult to adapt Sahlins' thesis, for Tonga at least. Many navigators, sailors, and missionaries met their deaths at the hands of islanders, but with Tonga, it was always the lure of the higher technology (the new fire) and trade goods that was the main motive. In fact, it is alleged that Tongan chiefs plotted to kill Captain Cook at the same time as they lavishly entertained him (which also prompted Cook to call these islands the Friendly Isles). But here the motive was again the acquisition of superior technology and firearms. The Tongans could not carry out their plan for lack of unanimity. Also, history never repeats itself exactly. For every event has unique features, as well as features that it has in common with every other event; so history can be said to repeat itself only "partly." Alternatively put, every historical event is both universal *and* particular.

14. N. Wachtel, *La Vision des Vaincus* (Paris: Gallimard, 1970). Wachtel is so devoted to his methodology that he refuses to use any of the foreign names for the Americas.

15. See 'O. Māhina's Ph.D. dissertation, submitted to the History Department, Australian National University, 1992.

16. This is the case with the classics of European literature. Starting with Achilles in the *Iliad* and going through the Hamlets and Lady Macbeths, down to the Rashkolnikovs, the Karamozovs, the Tartuffes, and the Ahabs, we can see the centrality of the concern with "peculiar" people, who have some aspect of their psyche much more emphasized than the rest, i.e., people with pronounced neuroses. This can be used to distinguish literature as traditionally understood from all the stuff that passes as literature today.

17. Feuerbach's thesis that God is simply Man (minus his imperfections) conceptually blown up to infinite proportions largely follows Vico. Alternatively put, Man is prior to God, i.e., God, and the idea of God, could not have been part of the fabric of the world if there were no Man.

18. The classic expression of this fundamental purpose of religious ritual is Jesus' injunction at the Last Supper, "Do this in remembrance of me." Rituals are pieces of social theater that teach a lesson and aim at reinforcing the supremacy of a certain type of social organization.

19. Gananath Obeyesekere, *The Apotheosis of Captain Cook: European Mythmaking in the Pacific* (Princeton: Princeton University Press, 1992) delivers a devastating critique of Sahlins' exegesis of the mixture of myth and history regarding Captain Cook's death in Hawai'i.

4

The Postmodern Legacy of a Premodern Warrior Goddess in Modern Samoa

Malama Meleisea

As I understand it, the postmodernist position is one that accepts the notion of multiple "truths," communities with common understandings communicating within the framework of their assumptions and beliefs about reality. In this sense, the Samoans were postmodernists before they became modern. "Truth" in Samoa is established by the telling of events that cannot be convincingly refuted, even while all the listeners know that other truths exist:

> Samoan traditions were subject to a large amount of local colouring and genealogies were even revised to fit in with the ascendancy or decline of the leading families. . . . The custodian of these traditions, however, is well aware of . . . weak points in the genealogy of the chief, and this knowledge is used by him, at times, almost to the extent of blackmail.[1]

The conversion of Samoans to Christianity between 1830 and 1869, resulting from the efforts of a small band of London Missionary Society evangelists from London, Tahiti, and Rarotonga, is usually interpreted historically by Samoans, as well as by foreign historians, as the beginning of a new ideological era in which there was a massive transformation of the Samoan moral and political order. A discourse has developed over the past century, however, that gives these events continuity with the past and claims they were predestined by Samoan gods, thus removing any concern Samoans may feel, in contemplating their past, that in the nineteenth century they were more subjects than actors.

The crucial link between the old and the new religious systems is a narrative about the pre-Christian war goddess Nafanua, now seen as a prophet by devout Christian Samoans, who foretold the coming of the Gospel several generations before the event.

Nafanua had ambiguous origins, the daughter of the union between Saveasiuleo (a spirit who ruled the underworld, Pulotu) and Tilafaiga, the daughter of Saveasiuleo's brother, a connection culturally defined as incestuous in Samoa. Nafanua was born as a "clot of blood"[2] but later emerged from where she had been hidden in the earth near Falealupo, which is located at the extreme westerly point of the island of Savai'i, the jumping-off place for the spirits of the dead on their way through the *fafa* rocks offshore, which leads to the underworld, Pulotu. Emerging from her hiding place as a fully grown woman possessed of awesome supernatural powers and extreme ferocity, Nafanua played a crucial role in the civil wars between the districts of eastern and western Savai'i. There is a place there still, "the meeting ground of shame," named for the day when the defeated army discovered that the fierce warrior leading the victors was female when her cloak blew back, revealing her breasts. Having led her side to victory, Nafanua lent her powers of conquest to the ruling dynasty of the district of A'ana. With her assistance, A'ana defeated all its rival chiefdoms and became the *malo*, the ruling coalition of districts. In return, Nafanua was given the highest chiefly titles of A'ana and Atua.

Going back sixteen generations of chiefly successions, the political order of Samoa appears to have been an archipelago with common language and customs divided into distinct, rival, district chiefdoms (as was the case until the nineteenth century) but each possessing its own hierarchy, like small states, and several of these served as outposts of chiefs from Tonga. Traditions recorded in the nineteenth century, however, agree that political unity in the form of a nationally recognized, central locus of paramount rank, if not political authority, was first established in the lifetime of Salamasina, a female chief whom Kramer records as having being the twenty-first Tui A'ana. A new political order was established, resting on the recognition of a paramount chief of all Samoa as the holder of four royal titles: Tui A'ana, Tui Atua, Gatoaitele, and Tamasoali'i. Salamasina combined in her ancestry all the aristocratic lineages of Samoa, as well as those of Fiji and Tonga. The four titles were given by Nafanua to her descendant Levalasi So'oa'emalelagi, but this lady declined the honors and gave them to the daughter of her mother's sister's son, whom she had taken as a foster child. This child was named Salamasina.[3]

Nafanua is associated in Samoan history with periods of great political and ideological transformation, the first some five hundred years ago. According to the Samoan traditional historian, the late Gatoloaifaana Peseta Sio (whose point of view was that of the district of Safotulafai in Savai'i), after the war of A'ana, the orators and chiefs of A'ana removed Nafanua's house to the *malae* of Falealupo, for which service Nafanua gave them new titles, all recorded today in the *fa'alupega* (constitution) of Leu-lumoega, the principal village of A'ana (e.g., Lepou, Liufau, Agilau, Lau-vao, Tupuola, and Leoli).

Nafanua also established the historic role of the Alataua of Tufutafoe, Neiafu, and Falelima of Savai'i as warriors with the duty of mediating be-tween fighting factions, a role they are still recognized as having today. She gave the village of Sataua and its principal families their historical role as caretakers of the forest on Savai'i.[4] She established the political or-der of Falealupo still reflected in its constitutional *fa'alupega:*[5]

TULOUNA LE FALEFA A LE TAPUA'IGA	Greeting the house of the four, pleading for good fortune	*Refers to Tonumaipe'a and Nafanua's inter-cession*
TULOUNA LAU AFIOGA AUVA'A O LE VA'A FAATAU O NAFANUA	Greeting your high-ness, Nafanua's war-ship (high priest)	*Auva'a became Nafa-nua's priest, through whom she spoke.*
TULOUNA SOLIA-MA FOA'IMEA O LE MA'AUPU O NAFANUA	Greeting Soliama and Foa'imea, Nafanua's chiefly family	*Descendants of Nafanua*

The other titles of the Falealupo are also associated with roles defined for them by Nafanua (Fuiono, Taofinu'u, Soifua, and Silialei). Nafanua put to the test the chiefs of A'ana, who had come to pay their respects to her, by competing with them to see who could stay underwater longest. When she won by remaining underwater for longer than any human be-ing could, some of the chiefs complained that she was taking advantage of her supernatural powers. Those who did so were demoted in rank, whereas those who did not—Aiono of Fasito'outa, Misa of Falelatai, Vaili of Samatau, and Tanuvasa of Nofoali'i (all in the district of A'ana)—had their status increased as pillars of the new political order. She warned the *ali'i* of A'ana that although they were the leaders of the *malo,* she would one day come and lead the *malo* at Maauga and Nuuausala (also in A'ana), saying, "Be prepared for my arrival or you will not achieve the *malo* for which you came. I will stay here to pray for the successful estab-lishment of the *malo* in days to come."[6] For some thirteen generations af-ter Salamasina, A'ana allied with Atua appears to have been the dominant district in Samoa and head of the *malo,* as Nafanua had decreed, at least according to the traditions of A'ana.[7]

After the chiefs of A'ana had departed, Malietoa arrived, having heard that positions of power were being reallocated, to seek a place in the new order. When he reached Falealupo, Nafanua told him that she had already given away the "head" and "body" of the *malo,* and that only the "tail" was left for him, which he was to take with him and await a "head" for his *malo* to come from heaven.[8]

In 1830, pioneer evangelist John Williams arrived on the shores of Samoa in his ship *Messenger of Peace,* which he had handcrafted for himself in Rarotonga. He had sailed to Samoa via Tonga, where he had collected a passenger, the chief Fauea of Manono, who directed him to anchor in Samoa at Malietoa's village of Sapapali'i. The news greeted Williams there that Malietoa's coalition of districts had won a great victory in their war against A'ana.[9] According to tradition, Nafanua had also played a role in this power shift from A'ana to Savai'i. Before Malietoa's accession, she had traveled by canoe from Falealupo to Leulumoega in fulfillment of her promise to establish herself at Maauga and Nuuausala, but when she arrived she was not received with honor. Hot and tired from her journey, she called on some village girls to bring her water to drink, but the girls rudely declined. So, Nafanua turned her canoe around for the journey back to Savai'i. While crossing the strait between Upolu and Savai'i she encountered a chief, Leiataua Lelologa, out fishing, who presented her with his catch. Gratified, she possessed him and gave him her powers. His son, Tamafaiga, apparently inheriting these powers, became a cruel, greatly feared warrior-priest who conquered A'ana. Some years later, this chief was put to death as an act of revenge for taking a village maiden. The obligation then fell upon Malietoa, his kinsman, to seek revenge against A'ana, and this led to the war that Malietoa had won just before John Williams arrived in Samoa. By defying Nafanua's injunction to be prepared for her arrival, A'ana lost the *malo* and Malietoa gained it. Malietoa now stood at the head of the *malo,* having gained control of the royal chiefly titles of Samoa.

Williams' arrival was seen as a fulfillment of Nafanua's prophesy, and Malietoa became a powerful patron and sponsor of the Christian church in Samoa. When he died, a decade later, believing God's Kingdom was at hand, and impressed by the missionaries' efforts to establish Christian peace, he made a will that dispersed the ruling titles back to the districts from which they had originated, instead of passing them to his heir along with the certainty of another war of succession. Malietoa is firmly established in the minds of Samoans as having first established Christianity in Samoa, and associated with the origins of the dominant Congregational Church of Samoa founded by the London Missionary Society. But among his many chiefly rivals and enemies, some refused to become Christian or continued to adhere to syncretic sects established in earlier years by run-away sailors and Samoan prophets, until many decades afterward. Others sponsored rival Christian churches, such as Tonumaipea Talavou, who first established the Wesleyan Church by welcoming Methodist mission-aries to Manono, and Tuala Talipope, who first established the Catholic Church by welcoming Marist missionaries to Lealatele.

This narrative confirms Samoan popular beliefs that there was no dis-continuity involved in the mass conversion to Christianity that followed Williams' arrival in 1830. After all, if Nafanua had decreed the major po-litical institutions and power structure of Samoa, many of which exist to-day, then could she not also have been Jehovah's prophet? The logic of this belief may seem strange to outsiders, since Nafanua, a pagan woman with awesome supernatural powers who behaved with extreme ferocity, was a type much disapproved of in Christian Scriptures, even the Old Tes-tament. But this theory fitted in with the modern Samoan characteriza-tion of their pre-Christian and Christian eras as times of darkness *(o aso pouliuli)* and enlightenment *(o aso malamalama)*, with Nafanua predicting not only a new religious and social order but her own end. That is the way in which Samoans have come to see it, but dozens of foreigners have seen it differently and have subjected Samoan legends to all kinds of theo-retical scrutiny—theological, historical, psychological, structuralist, sym-bolic, and even Marxist—although as far as I am aware they have not yet been systematically deconstructed. As Samoans see it, it was not foreign-ers who inspired their religious transformation but Samoa's own gods, who decreed that this must happen, and had undoubtedly inspired the events in England that led to the rise of missionary evangelism, as well as the prior history of the Christian church, and had ultimately guided John Williams to Samoa to fulfill their purpose.

NOTES

1. Taisi O. F. Nelson, "Legends of Samoa" (an address to the Samoa Research Society, 30 November 1923), *Journal of the Polynesian Society* 34:124–145.

2. *Alualutoto; alulu* is a jellyfish; *toto* is blood. In Samoan oral traditions, such births are often attributed to the result of incest and the birth of a super-natural being.

3. Augustin Kramer, *The Samoa Islands* (1902), trans. Theodore E. Verhaaren, 2 vols. (Auckland: Polynesian Press, 1995), I:13.

4. Gatoloaifaana Peseta S. Sio, *Tapasa o Folauga i aso afa: Compass of Sailing in*

a Storm (Western Samoa: University of the South Pacific Centre, 1984), 110–116.

5. Every Samoan polity *(nu'u)* has its *fa'alupega,* which states the order of precedence of its principal chiefs and orators in the form of a set formal greeting, each with a specific historical allusion to the origin of the title. The example given is a portion of the *fa'alupega* of Falealopu, where Nafanua originated (Kramer, *Samoa Islands,* I:103).

6. Sio, *Tapasa o Folauga i aso afa,* 110–116.

7. This was Kramer's opinion and that of Steubel and Hermann, whose work Kramer had studied along with his Samoan sources. Sio disagrees, however, insisting that only three people in history united Samoa by holding the four titles; these were Salamasian, Fonoti, and Malietoa Vaiinupo.

8. Sio, *Tapasa o Folauga i aso afa,* 110–116.

9. See Kramer, *Samoa Islands,* I:8–19.

5

Myth and History

'Okusitino Māhina

The formal relationships between myth and history may be examined in relation to the Tongan concept *tala-e-fonua,* which literally means "telling-of-the-land/people" (*fonua* means both land, *kelekele* and people, *kakai*). *Tala-e-fonua* is a kind of spiritual unity binding land and people together—a vernacular ecology-centered mode of cultural and historical ordering. In considering these distinct but connected human phenomena, the aim in this essay is to observe the complementarity and opposition between myth and history. The connection between myth and history is explored on two levels: first, myth and history are formal expressions of the interplay of human demands within a social context; and second, the opposition between myth and history is expressed by a practice that divides the mythical from the historical, the symbolic from the actual, or human illusions from reality.[1]

Myth, of course, has been observed and defined in a variety of ways. The structuralist and the functionalist, for example, have respectively explored the socioeconomic and pragmatic bases of myth, emphasizing its *ex post facto* expression of common needs and desires, which remain constant over time. These accounts set aside the agency of myth in defining the conflicts within communities between rival modes of social and political reproduction. I shall be emphasizing this constitutive, rather than the expressive, role of myth.

Myth is a social and psychological phenomenon, constituting the attitudes of human beings both to one another and to their environment. As far as myth is a sociopsychological reality, it is a historical fact. Within this anthropo-ecological dimension, myth not only expresses but also activates social, mental, and material energies. Thus, myth may be regarded as an attempt by people to explain natural and social phenomena that myth itself constitutes and sacralizes, as it triggers marvels and heroic deeds that it then naturalizes in terms of human interests and social organization. Both natural and social events are, thus, wrapped up in the same mythic fold, and through oral transmission the historical fact of myth puts on a miraculous character.

Myth not only reflects the outlook of a people, it also constitutes the historical kernel of events themselves. This joint aspect of myth affords us a synchronic view of the past in which myth expresses a social reality; it also affords a diachronic view of historical process, in which myth acts and reacts with definite social situations in order to produce new outcomes. While there is a need to observe the structural and functional aspects of myth, the more important issue is to examine what people attempt to see through it. We are always bound to come back to some kind of human arrangement.

Myth of the political kind is both synchronic and diachronic in character; it reflects conflict at a particular point in time as it sustains order through time.[2] Not only is it significant how myth, by structurally legitimizing dominance, arises in society in the first place, but it is also interesting how its function as a political charter varies in order to accommodate historical change. Both synchronic and diachronic aspects of myth are about power, whether it is concerned with hegemony, which appeals to myth for authority, or counterhegemony, whose challenge brings about a new order. In this context, myth may function in the interests of the dominant order; but equally it may encourage usurpation.

There are two senses of history to correspond with these two tendencies of myth.[3] First, history is a product of the interplay of human demands in a social context. The sum of events makes up the historical account. Second, history is a discourse, emerging from a dialectic between the object and the subject in which both terms are mutually modified. When history is regarded as the outcome of the sum total of events, then myth and history are complementary. But when history involves the subject in a dialectic with the object, where the question of truth and illusion bears directly on the political outcome of this dialectic, then it is a case of tala-e-fonua, where continuity and change are at stake in the shifting relation of the symbolic and the historical. Myth, in this process, is opposed to history as the sum of events. The tension between myth and history in this narrower sense is a dialectic between modes of domination and possibilities of liberation.

The relationship between myth and history can be examined in the context of two Tongan myths, the Turtle Sangone and the Double-Canoe, featured in two lakalaka poems entitled "Sangone" and "Nailasikau," by Queen Sālote. Synchronically speaking, the two myths represent actual political events surrounding the historical Tuʻi Tonga; diachronically, they are linked with the present, embodied by the respective rise of the new Hau, Tuʻi Haʻatakalaua and Tuʻi Kanokupolu. The diachronic use of the myths, their retelling in the poems, in this case, may be seen as a reaffirmation of the specific connections between Tuʻi Tonga and Tuʻi Haʻatakalaua and Tuʻi Kanokupolu, and, generally, of a dynamic tension in the continuity between past and present (see figs 5.1 and 5.2).

The past can play an influential role in the present, provided it is loosened from summary history. If it is approached as a time that was as real and uncertain as the present, then the present order, though actually based on sanctioned models, is subjected to the oppositional pull of counterhegemonic impulses.

The myth of the Turtle Sangone is associated with the eleventh Tuʻi Tonga, Tuʻitātui, who, in about A.D. 1200, began the Tuʻi Tonga imperial expansion beyond Tonga.[4] Initially, this imperial expansion seems to have started with Fiji, represented here by Pulotu[5] (see fig. 5.1), and Samoa, particularly the westernmost island of Savaiʻi.[6] Such Tuʻi Tonga imperial activities, by linking center and periphery, involved the extensive extraction of socioeconomic resources through conquest.

The theme of the myth, as interpreted within the ecology-centered cultural and historical mode, is structured on the oppressive nature of the Tuʻi Tonga imperial rule, symbolized by the winds (matangi) blowing from Tonga.[7] The Tuʻi Tonga's oppression was allegorized by Lekapai's[8] confrontation with the winds, and the killing and eating of Sangone and the burying of its shell.[9] This was then followed by a period of intense diplomacy and alliance formation through treaty, symbolized by Fasiʻapule's visit and the exchange of fine mats.

The first talatupuʻa, the Turtle Sangone,[10] told and translated by the author, is as follows:

THE TURTLE SANGONE

One day a Pulotu maiden, Hinahengi, landed in Tonga with her mother, Sangone, a turtle. But in Samoa, Lekapai had been troubled by the south winds destroying his yearly crops. Angered and frustrated by the mishaps, he set out in a canoe to find the winds, blowing from Tonga, and their source, and to wage war against them. On arrival in Tonga, Lekapai found Hinahengi sleeping and drying herself in the sun; her hair was tangled in nearby bushes. Undoing her hair, they then cohabited. Learning that the winds and their source

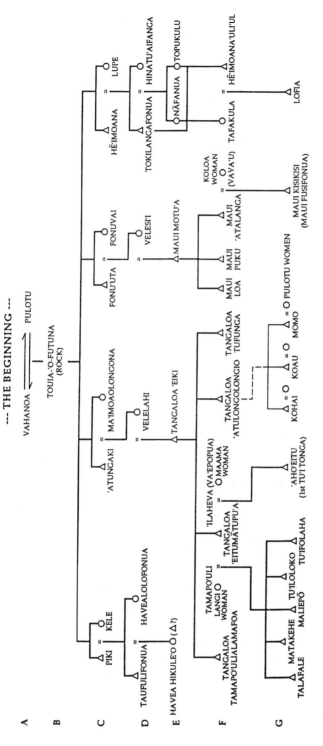

Fig. 5.1   The Tongan creation myth, or *talatupu'a*, traced through a genealogy (*hohoko*) connecting a mythical but historical past to the present: *A*, known beginning, characterized by tensions between Vahanoa, the immensely unknown ocean, and Pulotu, the Tongan afterworld; *B*, rise of presumed island, Touia-'o-Futuna, the rock; *C*, incestuous union of mythical beings; *D*, incestuous procreation between Taufulifonua and his sister, Havealolofonua, and classificatory half-sisters, Velelahi and Velesi'i, and between Tokilangafonua and his sister, Hinatu'aifanga; segmentation of He'imoana-Lupe in Tokilangafonua, ruler of 'Eua; *E*, rise of three principal deities, Havea Hikule'o, Tangaloa 'Eiki, and Maui Motu'a, connected with possible eastern Polynesian influences via Samoa; Hikule'o and her parents divided Tongamama'o between them, while she retained Pulotu, assigning Langi and Lofofonua (or Maama) to Tangaloa and Maui, respectively; *F*, creation of lands by Tangaloa and his children, then fishing up of islands by Maui and his children by Maui Kisikisi, bitter conflicts between 'Aho'eitu and his Langi brothers, which saw him emerge as the first Tu'i Tonga.

were, respectively, Hinahengi's children and father, Lekapai confronted them. His attempt was fruitless, so he gave up. He then asked Hinahengi if he could return to Samoa. By agreeing, Hinahengi made way for Sangone to take him back. Hinahengi instructed Lekapai that, in dropping him in Samoa, she

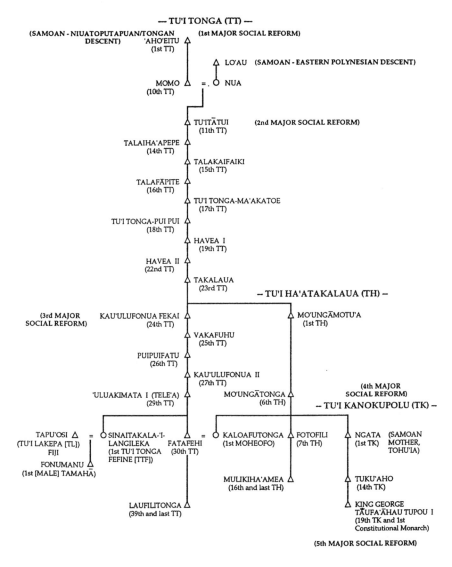

Fig. 5.2 The rise of the Tuʻi Tonga and the collateral segmentation of the Tuʻi Haʻatakalaua and Tuʻi Kanokupolu, associated with influential figures, resulting in the emergence of major social institutions of great economic and political significance.

had to safely return home to Tonga, bringing back with her a bunch of coconuts and a coconut-leaf mat for her. None of the instructions, however, was honored. Instead, the people in Savai'i killed and ate Sangone, then buried her shell. Among the witnesses were Lo'au, in Samoa searching for the sun, and a young boy named Lafai. Lo'au put his hands on Lafai, saying that he, by growing stunted, was not to die until Sangone's shell was found. Since then his name was changed to Lafaipana.

On returning to Tonga, Lo'au reported the matter to Tu'i Tonga Tu'itātui. This prompted Tu'itātui to send his half-brother, Fasi'apule, to Samoa to recover the shell. When arriving in Samoa, they were received in a kava ceremony; Fasi'apule took charge of kava distribution and food allocation. Fasi'apule, by engaging in the task, made an esoteric speech. The aims were to locate Lafaipana, who, because of his age, would be the only person to understand them, and who, of course, knew of the shell. Symbolic fragments of his speech included *fūfū mo kokohu* (lit., clap-and-fume, i.e., kava roots); *kau pongia 'i vao* (lit., a bunch of wilted-in-the-bush, i.e., a second-generation bunch of plantains); *lou tangia mo kokī* (lit., leaves of cry-and-parrot, i.e., young taro leaves); *kapakau tatangi* (lit., wings-of-high-pitch, i.e., a wild chicken); and *ngulungulu mo tokoto* (lit., grunt-and-lie-down, i.e., a huge pig). These items were brought as *fono* for the ceremony.

The Samoans were initially troubled each time Fasi'apule made a *kisu kava,* with each one skillfully interpreted. Lafaipana, who explained them, was identified. He took the Tongans to the burial site, where they exhumed Sangone's shell. Having found the shell, Lafaipana then collapsed and died. Fasi'apule and his party afterward returned to Tonga, taking with them the shell and the two fine mats, Hau-'o-Momo and Laumata-'o-Fainga'a, given by the Samoan chiefs for presentation to the Tu'i Tonga.

The *lakalaka* poem, itself entitled "Sangone," was composed by Queen Sālote and performed by the Lomipeau group and the Mu'a people, probably to celebrate the removal of Sangone's shell and the fine mat, Hau-'o-Momo, from the queen's palace to the Toloa Museum. The poetry was put to music by the famous Mu'a poet Vili Pusiaki, who also choreographed it. It is not known when the event took place, but Queen Sālote is believed to have composed "Sangone" around 1948.[11]

Queen Sālote has been hailed as the greatest contemporary poet that

Tonga has ever produced.[12] Her literary works are mainly featured in two of the Tongan poetic genres, *lakalaka* (lit. walk-walk, i.e., to walk at a faster pace; rhythmic walk; topical poetry of places) and *hiva kakala* (lit. song-[of]-[sweet-smelling]-flowers; love lyrics). The literary forte of Queen Sālote is seen in the way she structures her theme, utilizing several poetical modes, such as *fetau* (rivalry), *lau'eiki* (*lau-'eiki;* lit. enumeration-[of]-chiefs), *laumātanga* (*lau-mātanga;* lit. enumerating-[of]-beautiful spots; pride in locality, the Tongan Nature poetry), and *viki (viki)'eiki* (praising of chiefs).[13]

Queen Sālote's detailed knowledge of *tala-e-fonua,* as reflected in her literary works, was intimately imparted to her through close association with notable ceremonial spokesmen *matāpule* and her adoptive mother, Rachael (Lesieli) Tonga, a well-educated woman remarkably well-versed in *tala-e-fonua.*[14] It is believed that the number of tragedies in her life—the death of her mother, in 1902, when she was only two years old; the death of her father, Tāufa'āhau Tupou II, in 1918, when she became queen; the death of her unmarried half-sister, Fusipala, in 1933; the tragic death of her second son, William (Viliami) Tuku'aho, in 1936; and the untimely death of her husband, in 1941—deepened her literary perceptions.

Specifically, the constraints arising from the death of her husband, given her feelings as a human being, on the one hand, and her social position relative to her direct Tu'i Tonga descent and her being a Tu'i Kanokupolu, on the other, tend to surface in her works from time to time. Thus, Queen Sālote was confronted with real-life contradictions on two levels, the personal and the social. Queen Sālote handles the former in her *hiva kakala* poetry, while she addresses the latter in her *lakalaka* works.

On the personal level, Queen Sālote was prevented by her high office from remarrying after her husband's death. But on the sociopolitical level, Queen Sālote incessantly struggled to reconcile real-life constraints between her Tu'i Tonga descent and herself being a Tu'i Kanokupolu. By way of title-ranking, the Tu'i Tonga is the only *'eiki* (chiefly status) of the three royal titles; the other two kingly titles, Tu'i Ha'atakalaua and Tu'i Kanokupolu, are, by the Tu'i Tongan standard, formally *tu'a* (commoner status). Accordingly, Queen Sālote, via her mother, Lavinia Veiongo, a direct descendent of the Tu'i Tonga (see fig. 5.3), assumes an *'eiki* position, but she is, by theory, *tu'a* as a Tu'i Kanokupolu.[15]

Even Queen Sālote's attempt, through her marriage to Tungī Maile-fihi, to combine the three royal titles in her children, while it politically reinforced their social position, still situated them in a *tu'a* space in relation to the *'eiki* Tu'i Tonga (see fig. 5.3). But the structure of *'eiki* is at risk through practice, which modifies it, giving *'eiki* a new structural and func-

tional meaning, especially in a manner that serves the present order.[16]
Against these actual genealogical and political constraints, poetry provided Queen Sālote with a psychological outlet, her works being characterized by an ability to bind emotional intensities to landscapes and
specific localities once connected with her own ancestors.

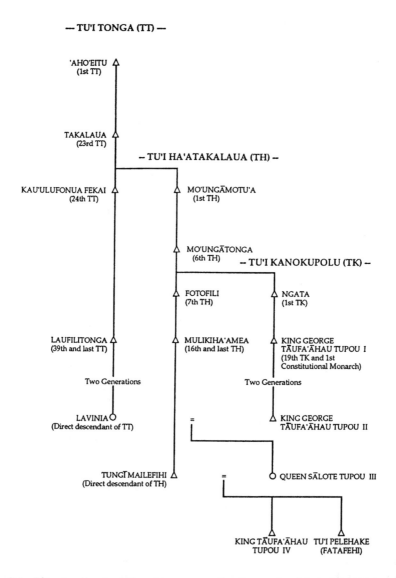

Fig. 5.3   The structural relationships among the three related but competing royal
titles, Tuʻi Tonga, Tuʻi Haʻatakalaua, and Tuʻi Kanokupolu, showing how Queen
Sālote's children, Taufaʻahau Tupou IV and Fatafehi Tuʻi Pelehake, combined the
three bloodlines in their persons.

The first poem, "Sangone," translated by the author, is as follows:

SANGONE

Neʻineʻi hako mei he tonga	No wonder the winds blew from the south
Tapa e ʻuhila mei lulunga	And flashed with lightning from the northwest
He naʻe mana e Feingakotone	Struck with thunder at Feingakotone [17]
Fakahake e ʻuno ʻo Sangone	At the lifting of the shell of Sangone
Lafaipana e peʻi ke mohe ā	Lafaipana, rest on in your sleep
Kae tuku mai siʻota faiva	But pass on to me your skills
Te u lau folahaka he ʻaho ni	Let me talk by dancing today
Ke meʻite ai e muʻa taloni	To entertain the front of the throne [18]
Holo pē ʻa e nofo ʻa muʻa ni	Make comfortable seaters of the front
Mo ha sola ʻoku taka ʻi Pangai	And any strangers roaming in Pangai [19]
Kau fola siʻi Hau-ʻo-Momo	I now unfold the valued Hau-ʻo-Momo
He ko e takafi ʻe tau nofo	As the outer cover of our living
He maaʻimoa fai ʻi Heketā	Being a chiefly undertaking at Heketa
Naʻe ʻaokai mei Haʻamea	That was wooed from Haʻamea [20]
ʻIseʻisa! Naʻe fena pē ka ko Nua	Alas! Though wrinkle yet it was Nua
Penepena e ngatuvai fakula	A hair mixture for the old *fākula* [21]
ʻE Fasiʻapule haʻu ke ta o	Fasiʻapule, come let us sojourn

'O tala ho 'uhinga ki he 'afio	And tell your mind to the king
Ke hā ai e finangalo na'e toi	Revealing the secret that was hidden 22
'O sivi e 'ofa 'oku mo'oni	And measure the love that is real
Na'e 'aikona pē 'o 'omai	That was carried in the waist and brought
He na'e 'ikai fa'a hua'aki	As it was hard to be mentioned
'E Ulamoleka! poto 'i he lau	Oh, Ulamoleka! Skilled in talking 23
Hono 'ikai ke mālie kia au	Had it not been pleased to me
Ho'o tala 'a e vaha mama'o	Your forecast of distant oceans
Kuo vaofi hotau 'aho	We've been drawn closer in our day
Kakala talā kakala mo'oni	Utmost kakala genuine kakala 24
'Oku faifio 'o toki manongi	They intermingle, emitting sweet-scent
Kisu kava e mei Ha'amoa	Secrets of kava from Samoa
Na'e tali hapo e me'a kotoa	It hastily revealed everything
Kisu e fūfū mo kokohu	Secrets of clap-and-fume 25
'A e kau pōngia 'i vao	A bunch of wilted-in-the-bush 26
'A e lou tāngia mo kokī	Leaves of cry-and-parrot 27
Pea mo e kapakau tatangi	And also a wing-of-high-pitch 28
Kau ai e ngulungulu mo tokoto	Including a grunt-and-lie-down 29
Mo e vahe taumafa 'o e fono	And allocation of king's food of fono
Pea toki 'ilo ai e koloa	Then the finding of the treasure 30

Ko e kānokato e tala 'o Tonga	The all-embracing traditions of Tonga
Talu ai pe hono fakaili	Which was since dearly nurtured
Ko e fakama'u 'o hou'eiki	As a symbol for the chiefs
'Oku 'ilo 'e ha taha kuo anga	Someone knows but with experience [31]
'A e ola 'o e Taka-i-pomana	The outcome relating to Taka-i-pomana [32]
He kalia 'o e vahamohe	The *kalia* that sailed the pacific-ocean
He kalia na'e tau ki 'One	Hence the canoe that arrived at 'One [33]
Fakalele ki he Makahokovalu	Hurriedly I depart for Makahokovalu [34]
Pakimangamanga 'i he Siangahu	Perform bonito-fishing sport at Siangahu [35]
Ko e ika moana si'ene fotu	Where the deep-sea fish appears
Fakahakehake 'i Fonuamotu	Landed in abundance at Fonuamotu [36]
Longolongo ma'anu 'i Hakautapu	Calmly it surfaced at Hakautapu [37]
No'o 'i Havelu mo e Kokatapu	Berthed at Havelu and the Sacred-*koka* [38]
Ko e ola e 'oku ou lau	The result of which I say
Fai'anga ia 'o e fetau	It is place of rivalry and pride [39]
Tau tui falahola 'ene hopo	Let us string ripen *falahola* [40]
He kuo kakai e Vaha'akolo	For it has been crowded at Vaha'akolo [41]

In the poem "Sangone," Queen Sālote evades the salutation (*faka-tapu; faka-tapu;* lit., in-the-style-[of-the]-sacred), notable in her other compositions, by going straight into the myth. She acknowledges the imperial links between Tonga and Samoa (lines 1–5) where the Samoans were subjected to the Tu'i Tonga, symbolized by the south wind (line 1). The exhumation of the shell of Sangone in Samoa (line 3), as a kind of Samoa counterhegemony, is symbolized by lightning (line 2). With the lightning in Samoa, it struck the Tu'i Tonga, symbolized as Feingakotone (line 4), thus putting his rule at risk. Queen Sālote goes on to recognize the political ingenuity of Lafaipana (lines 5–6), as a tool for her quest to legitimate her power (line 6), and by way of paying homage to the Tu'i Tonga (line 7), she then lowers herself by dancing, for she is, by title, *tu'a* or inferior in status to the Tu'i Tonga, the most chiefly of all titles (lines 8–9). Queen Sālote, representing the Tu'i Kanokupolu title symbolized by Pangai, is aware in her own mind of this situation, although it may not be known to the uninformed, or those ill-informed about traditions (line 10).

Lines 11–16 also refer to the superiority, as the most *'eiki* title, of the Tu'i Tonga. This is represented by the Hau-'o-Momo, one of the Samoan fine mats *(kie Tonga),* which was also a symbol of the power of Momo (line 11), whose reign witnessed the laying down (lines 14–16) of the Tu'i Tonga imperial foundation (line 13). Queen Sālote, in lines 11–16, refers to the political marriage between Nua (line 15) and Momo (line 16), representing Lo'au symbolized by Ha'amea (line 14), from which Tu'itātui (line 13) further emerged with power, regionally consolidating the Tu'i Tonga empire beyond Tonga. She recognizes the pragmatic value of the notion of *'eiki,* though by way of appearance (line 12), it nevertheless sustained order in the society. There is, then, a sense of history and culture incorporated in this line, where conflicts, masked by complicity, are nevertheless present.

Queen Sālote reverts to the myth (line 17), not only to accompany Fasi'apule in his reunion with his kingly half-brother, Tu'itātui (line 18), but to liken it to her own striving for the desired *'eiki* or sacred substance. She stresses how Tu'itātui, by keeping his blood relation to Fasi'apule a secret (line 19), simply treasured it with burning love in his heart (line 20). Their feeling for each other is referred here to Fasi'apule carrying a basket, in which he placed items/objects to express symbolically his mutual attachment to, and love for, Tu'itātui (line 21).[42] It was an emotional reunion that is hard to describe (line 22).

Now Queen Sālote changes course, making reference to Ulamoleka. She admires (line 24) the poet and navigator, Ulamoleka, who combined

Tu'i Tonga and Tu'i Kanokupolu in his genealogy, for his skills in conversing and voyaging (lines 23, 25). Queen Sālote, who also united in herself the two titles (line 26), likens herself to Ulamoleka, who, Queen Sālote thinks, had prophesied her destiny. In other words, the union of the major titles, Tu'i Tonga and Tu'i Kanokupolu, in her person (line 27) had given rise to her high status (line 28; see fig. 5.3).

Once again, Queen Sālote resorts to the myth, concentrating on Fasi'apule's voyage to Samoa (lines 29–37). She takes the shell of Sangone to be a symbol, by way of valued traditions *(koloa)*, of Tongan culture (line 37). Reference is made here to the social exchange of women, by means of *koloa* or material goods, such as fine mats *(kie Tonga)*, undertaken between the Samoan and Tongan elite families.[43] It is a form of encompassment, a kind of totality (line 38). Nurturing the *koloa*, given the tension between culture and history, suggests it to be a risky business (line 39). This *koloa*, by encompassing the aristocratic interests, remains a bastion for the chiefs (line 40).

The knowledge of traditions, which is thought to be a prerogative of the chiefs, preserved in the esoteric mode and known only to a privileged few, points to the political dimension of Tongan history (line 41). Queen Sālote refers here to heroic history, particularly the political relationships (line 51) between the major chiefly titles, Tu'i Tonga, Tu'i Ha'atakalaua, and Tu'i Kanokupolu (lines 42–54).[44] She points to the *kalia* Taka-i-pomana, which brought a Samoan woman as bedmaid for the Tu'i Tonga (lines 42–43); it landed first at 'Onevai before going on to 'Olotele, Mu'a (line 44). Queen Sālote alludes here to the Tu'i Tonga links with 'Uiha (a village in Ha'apai), symbolized by Makahokovalu, which was associated with Ngana'eiki, the older of the two sons of Tatafu'eikimeimu'a, the twentieth Tu'i Tonga. Ngana'eiki unsuccessfully courted a beautiful Samoan princess, Hina (line 45), who instead fell in love with his handsome younger brother, Nganatatafu, residing at Ha'ano (a village in Ha'apai).

Queen Sālote then moves on to mention Siangahu, a symbol for Tungua (a village in Ha'apai), the residence of the Tamahā (Tu'i Tonga's sister's child), also deriving from the Tu'i Tonga (line 46). She now refers to the pervading *'eiki* of the Tu'i Tonga, through the exchange of women between the elite families of Tonga and Samoa, likening it to an appearance *(fotu)* of a deep-sea fish (line 47). This chiefly position persisted, engulfing the Tu'i Ha'atakalaua, symbolized by Fonuamotu (line 48). This continues in force to encompass the Tu'i Kanokupolu, represented by Hakautapu, Havelu, and Kokatapu (lines 49–50). After recounting her position in this genealogy (line 51), Queen Sālote acknowledges her pride in it, especially its usefulness for her quest for power (line 52; see fig. 5.3). But let the Tu'i Kanokupolu take the honor, she says (line 53), for it had won the battle, symbolized by Vaha'akolo (line 54).

The second myth, the Double-Canoe, is connected with the imperial activities of 'Uluakimata or Tele'a, the twenty-ninth Tu'i Tonga, about A.D. 1600.[45] By this date, the declining Tu'i Tonga dynasty, after being subjected to continuing challenges, appears to have become concerned with local and regional alliance formation. The formation of regional alliance, in the form of slave labor, as reflected by the symbolic Fijian and 'Uvean connections with Tonga, was specifically utilized for the consolidation of the local power of the Tu'i Tonga.[46] Though the Tu'i Tonga power declined during this period, the exchange of women and material resources between center and periphery, based on the social principle of *'eiki,* continued to sustain his imperial rule.

The theme of the myth, symbolically and socially defined by *lahi* (huge, great size), and structured on the ongoing Tu'i Tonga imperialism through locally and regionally generated systems of support, reflects this Tu'i Tonga political position. In fact, the idiomatic use of *lahi* as a notion in Tonga is associated with great social deeds generally, and in particular with power.[47] It can be said that the Tu'i Tonga's power, on the historical level, is manifested in the central role played by Fijians and 'Uveans in the building of the huge double-canoe, together with its ingeniously heroic launching, the fitting of the two high islands between the two hulls, and the creation of Mo'unu Island.[48]

The second *talatupu'a,* told and translated by the author, follows:

THE DOUBLE-CANOE, *Kalia,* LOMIPEAU

Once upon a time, a huge *kalia* was built in 'Uvea for a child, Tahitala, who went crying to Lauliki, his mother's brother, after having been beaten by Peautau for damaging his canoe berthed at sea. Annoyed by the incident, Lauliki approached boatbuilders Ngavele and Lavamutu to build one for Lauliki. They built the canoe in Muliutu, with *fehi* wood from Ilfilaupakola. On its completion, the canoe, named Lomipeau because it was so huge, could not be launched by the combined people of Tonga and 'Uvea, so huge that, when it sailed to Tonga, the high islands of Kao and Tofua were fit between the two hulls. A Fijian demigod, though, Nailasikau, was summoned by the Tu'i Tonga for the task. Standing on the gunwales, Nailasikau urinated from there down, slowly moving the

boat to sea. It is reported that the canoe was used for transporting stones from 'Uvea for the construction of the Tu'i
Tonga's royal tombs in Lapaha at Mu'a. The Fijians loaded and
unloaded the stones, crafted by 'Uveans and Futunans. On top
of the hulls was built the deck (*fungavaka*), where the deck-
house (*falevaka*), oven (*tālafu*), and compass (*'olovaha*), placed
in the prow, were constructed. The Tongan navigators directed
navigation from the *falevaka*, the sea residence of the Tu'i
Tonga and his Falefā. Cooking was done in the *tālafu*. Nailasikau is said not to have eaten meat, but it often happened that
the crew's meat disappeared without trace. The Falefā later
found out that, when the crews had gone to sleep, Nailasikau
would rotate the circular *tālafu*, open the crew's oven, and de-
vour the meat. Nailasikau was punished and ordered to unload
the stones on his own. It is also said that the *tālafu* was so huge
that when the ashes were tipped to sea, it formed the island of
Mo'unu.

The second *lakalaka* poem, "Nailasikau," named after one of the protagonists in the myth, was composed by Queen Sālote about 1934 or 1935
and performed by the Lomipeau group and people from Lapaha in Mu'a
on Tongatapu.[49] Again, Vili Pusiaki created the accompanying music and
dance. It is believed that this *lakalaka* was composed for the celebration
of the birthday either of Viliami Tuku'aho, who died in 1936, or Sione
Ngū, now Fatafehi Tu'i Pelehake, two of Queen Sālote's three sons, in
1934 or 1935.[50]

The text of the *lakalaka*, "Nailasikau," translated by the author, is as
follows:

NAILASIKAU

Fakatapu mo e taloni 'o Tonga	My obeisance to the throne of Tonga[51]
Pea tapu mo e kakala hingoa	And sacred be the esteemed flowers[52]
He mo si'i lupe kei manoa	Beloved dove still tamely tethered[53]
Kae tui e papai falahola	While a necklace of *fakula* is strung[54]
Aofaki atu e ha'a kotoa	Sacred be the lineages in all

Kae fakaha'ia hoku 'ofa	I wish to express my love
Ki he 'aho 'oku ta fakahokoa	For this day we commemorate
Hopo ai e fakahalafononga	With sunset stars rising
'Isa 'e ngalo ange 'ia au	And lest I do not recollect
He ko e 'aho ni 'e tukufolau	That today will pass away
Ka 'oku ou fie talanoa atu	But let me relate to you
Ki he anga si'omau vakatapu	This tale of our sacred ship
He fai'anga 'o e fakatalutalu	The source of honor and pride
'O fakafeangasi mo Lo'au	A tradition accompanying that of Lo'au
He vaka ni ko e fakatangitama	The ship was built for her petitioning-child[55]
He kia Lauliki 'a Tahitala	Made to Lauliki by Tahitala
Fa'u 'e Ngavele mo Lavamutu	Crafted by Ngavele and Lavamutu
'O fakatoukatea 'ene tu'u	Being double-hulled in its standing
'O tu'u he fanga he ko Muliutu	It stood in the shore of Muliutu
Si'i fehi 'o Ifilaupakola	Dear *fehi* wood of Ifilaupakola
He fanāfotu ia ne 'iloa	Her mast visible from afar
Pea to e fai ki ai e tala	And also mentioned in traditions
Nailasikau 'i he telekanga	About Nailasikau upon the gunwales[56]
'Avea 'a e vaka ki moana	Launching the ship into deep sea
Si'oto loloma he uta ko ia	My amazement at that load

'A e makakafu e 'otu langi na	For the flat-stone-lid of the royal tombs
Pea ko e lau he te ke 'iloa?	Though mentioned, had you ever known?
Ne tala 'e hai kiate koe?	And whoever did tell you?
Ke ke 'eve'eva he Paepae	To take a stroll at the Paepae [57]
'O mamata ai he makaofe	And witness its L-shape cornerstones [58]
Ofo'anga e kau pasese	Being a wonder for the tourists
Lau na'e lingi e tālafu	As stated they emptied the ship's oven
Tu'u ai e motu ko Mo'unu	Creating the islet of Mo'unu
'Oku fakaholo si'ete nofo	It gladdens my life evermore
Pea fakanonga ki hoku loto	Thus rendering peace to my heart
'A e uta maka 'i ono'aho	Once a load of masonry in ancient days [59]
Kae uta ha'a 'i onopō	But a boat full of clans in modern times [60]
Pe'i mou laka mai 'o mamata	Come ye along and wonder
He teunga 'o e loto falevaka	The attire of the inner deckhouse
He 'otu pupunga e sotiaka	There are the constellations of the zodiac [61]
'Oku tu'utonu mālie e La'ā	The Sun is high noon [62]
Tu'u kātoa e Māhina	And it is also full Moon [63]

'Alotolu mo e Tuingaika	'Alotolu and Tuingaika [64]
Fine'utuvai mo Sipitangata	The Fine'utuvai and Sipitangata [65]
Me'afua mo e Tangatafana	Me'afua and the Tangatafana [66]
'A Ma'afulele mo e Toloa	The Ma'afulele and Toloa [67]
'A e Humu mo e Ma'afutoka	Humu and the Ma'afutoka [68]
Takitaha tauhi hono hala	Each one keeps to its orbital route
He kuo lava si'eta talave	It has been over for our conversation
Kau li atu ka mou puke	I throw it to you to hold
Pea nofo e kakala mo'onia	Remain as you are genuine *kakala* [69]
He kuo ha'u e fekau kia kita	For an order has come to me
Ke u foku ki he Faka'otusia	That I return to Faka'otusia [70]
Ko hoku Naite 'o Patilika	It is my Knight of St. Patrick [71]
Ko si'oto 'enisaine tupu'a	It's my beloved eternal ensign [72]
'Oku fusi mei he Futukovuna	It is hoisted from Futukovuna [73]
Hono lanu ko e fo'i fākula	Its color is a blood-red pandanus fruit [74]
Ko e faka'ilonga 'o e ikuna	Being a mark of victory
Holo pē nofo e hau'atea	Make comfortable my wearied audience
Kau tuli e hua he laulea	But let me strive for joy conversed
Ko e fakaholo e ha'ofanga	In entertaining the social circle
Ko hai 'e tuhu ki he 'umata?	Who dares point to the rainbow?

In the second composition, "Nailasikau," Queen Sālote continues to tussle with politics, reaffirming her position in history. She begins with the *fakatapu*, the introduction of the *lakalaka* (lines 1–8). She salutes the existing order, the Tuʻi Kanokupolu title (line 1), represented by herself, being a female monarch (line 3). Queen Sālote regards her role as the reigning monarch to be a guardian of traditions (line 4). The obeisance is thus extended to the high chiefs, most probably the Tuʻi Tonga (line 2) and all the chiefly lineages (line 5). Queen Sālote, by excusing herself, sets out to express her views (line 6) on the celebrated occasion (line 7). It is about her opinions of the new social and political order, represented by the evening star, which is the Tuʻi Kanokupolu (line 8).

Besides the progress of time, and the fact that the occasion would soon be over (line 10), she takes it as an opportunity to promote her social cause, and, in this case, her political course (lines 11–12). Again, she cannot help but feature the Tuʻi Tonga, using his *ʻeiki* status as a tool, symbolized by the *vakatapu*, Lomipeau (line 12). The mention of Loʻau, the reputed craftsman of the land *(tufunga fonua)*, is a tribute to his great achievements (line 14).[75] Queen Sālote then recounts the myth of the Lomipeau (lines 12–24). She highlights the power of the Tuʻi Tonga, likens his sacred-secular attributes to the two hulls (line 18), affirming that his reputation, as mentioned in traditions (line 22), stands out like a mast (line 21). She also notes that it was by way of the imperial links with ʻUvea (lines 15–17) and Fiji (lines 24–25) that such reputed power was upheld.

Queen Sālote is naturally attached to the political cause/course set for the Lomipeau (line 25), which transported the stones for the construction of the royal tombs, another expression of power (line 26). She continues playing politics, and by differentiating social boundaries, particularly the *tuʻa* classes (lines 27–28), she sings of the glory of the Tuʻi Tonga (lines 29–33). She refers here to the beauty of the Langi Paepae-ʻo-Teleʻa (line 29), especially the great craftsmanship with which the stones were carved (line 30), which raises the tourists' eyebrows (line 31), and the enormity of the ship's oven (line 32), whose ashes formed Moʻunu Island (line 33). It is this praise that Queen Sālote strives for (line 34), which, by its political usefulness, sustained her position (line 35). It is the load of stones from which the power of the Tuʻi Tonga was transcended in the past (line 36), but for Queen Sālote, in her quest for grace in the present, this is her justification for her rule among the lineages (line 37).

She then invites her audience for a tour (line 38) to witness for themselves the paraphernalia of the *falevaka* (line 39), symbolizing the Tuʻi

Tonga. Queen Sālote, by offering an aristocentric view of society, likens the *falevaka* to the universe, whose trappings are made up of the constellations of the zodiac (lines 40–48). This universe, which is Tongan society, for Queen Sālote, is a social one, where at the helm sits the Tuʻi Tonga. Descending in order of rank, by way of the different characters of the celestial bodies (lines 41–47), are the different lineages, ranging from the lesser kingly lines to those at the bottom of the social pyramid. She ingeniously likens the gravitational force that holds the heavenly bodies[76] in orbit to the social boundaries *(kau ʻā)*[77] that, by maintaining the existing social structure, cement the different classes in Tongan society together (line 48).[78] Just as the universe is doomed for destruction if the gravitational force fails, in Queen Sālote's view, Tongan society, should the *kau ʻā* collapse, will also disintegrate.

Queen Sālote now bids farewell (line 49). She exerts herself even more by demanding her audience to observe traditions (line 50).[79] Once more she excuses herself, paying her tribute to the Tuʻi Tonga (line 51). She acknowledges the pragmatic value of the *ʻeiki* status of the Tuʻi Tonga, which she aims for, by way of exchange through marriage, in her political struggle (line 52). It is precisely for those reasons that she, in the form of an order (line 52), had to return to the *faka ʻotusia,* one of the two most *ʻeiki kakala,* symbolizing the Tuʻi Tonga. She likens the *faka ʻotusia* to the highest of ranks (line 54), which she hoists as an eternal flag from Futukovuna, another symbol for the Tuʻi Tonga, in her quest for grace. Queen Sālote reminds her audience of the status of the Tuʻi Tonga (line 57), which she thinks to have been successfully united in her person (line 58; see fig. 5.3). Once again she assures her wearied audience (line 59) that she gets carried away with joy in conversing on her topic (line 60), and in entertaining them (line 61). In line 62, Queen Sālote again pays tribute by acknowledging the *toputapu* of the Tuʻi Tonga.

The formal relationships between myth and history, where they are complementary in some respects and opposed in others, have been explored. Not only is myth synchronic, as it arises out of hegemonic structures justifying a specific social demand or a definite hierarchy of interests, it is also diachronic, for it is counterhegemonically appropriated for political advantage. Thus, permanence and change are in constant dialogue, as has been shown by Queen Sālote's retelling of the two myths. But, more important, Queen Sālote, by recreating the ordered movement of people through a landscape and a history, altering the order and being altered in her turn, focuses our attention on the dialectic, where an appeal to the historical fact of myth has the power to challenge history.

NOTES

1. Related approaches include: I. Futa Helu, "Myth and Oral Tradition as History" (MS, paper presented at the Second Tongan History Conference, Auckland, 18–23 January 1988), and "Traditional History" (MS, lecture, Centre for Pacific Studies, Auckland University, 7 August 1990); Finau 'O. Kolo, "Historiography: The Myth of Indigenous Authenticity," and 'Okusitino Māhina, "Myths and History: Some Aspects of History in the Tu'i Tonga Myths," in Phyllis Herda, Jeniffer Terell, and Niel Gunson, eds., *Tongan Culture and History* (Canberra: Research School of Pacific Studies, Australian National University, 1990), 1–11, 30–45.

2. Christine Ward Gailey denies the synchronic dimension of myth, saying that while it reflects structural and experiential tensions, myth cannot be regarded as a manifestation of reality; she also adds that myth is only a possession of its present practitioners, who create and change it in their favor. See "'Our History is Written . . . in Our Mats': State Formation and Status of Women in Tonga" (Ph.D. diss., New School for Social Research, 1981). See also Marshall Sahlins, *Historical Metaphors and Mythical Realities* (Ann Arbor: University of Michigan Press, 1981), and *Islands of History* (Chicago: University of Chicago Press, 1985); and Ralph Piddington, "Synchronic and Diachronic Dimensions in the Study of Polynesian Cultures," *Journal of the Polynesian Society* 62 (2 and 3): 108–121.

3. See E. H. Carr, *What Is History?* (London: Macmillan, 1961); Greg Dening, "History in the Pacific," *The Contemporary Pacific: A Journal of Island Affairs* 1:134–139; Patrick Kirch and Roger Green, "History, Phylogeny, and Evolution in Polynesia," *Current Anthropology* 28 (4): 431–456.

4. See Edward Winslow Gifford, "Tongan Society," *B. P. Bishop Museum Bulletin* 8 (1929; reprint, New York 1971); and 'O. Māhina, "Religion, Politics, and the Tu'i Tonga Empire," Master's thesis, Auckland University, 1986.

5. The Pulotu/Fiji–Samoa/Langi–Tonga/Maama links suggest extraction of socioeconomic resources, whether in the form of exchange of women between the elite families or slave labor, most probably in the interest of the Tu'i Tonga. This is both implicit and explicit in the myth. Sangone, mother of Hinahengi, a maiden from Pulotu, was probably presented as a wife to the Tu'i Tonga, symbolized by the source of the wind, Hinahengi's father. But Hinahengi, daughter of the Tu'i Tonga, was, in turn, presented as a wife to the probably discontented Samoan chief Lekapai. It is said in Tongan traditions that Pulotu, the Tongan original land and afterworld, is believed to be an actual island situated to the northwest of Tonga, which, as supported by both archaeology and linguistics, is naturally Fiji.

6. It seems that at this time the possible traffic between eastern Polynesia, via

Samoa, and Tonga was at its peak. These assumed eastern Polynesian influences, which were formalized in the rule of the Tu'i Manu'a, had covered the whole of Samoa, from Manu'a in the east to Savai'i in the west, and included Fiji and Tonga. The localization of these probable eastern Polynesian influences in Tonga, associated with the appearance of the three principal deities, peaking in the counterhegemonic rise of the Tu'i Tonga in relation to the Tu'i Manu'a, and the succeeding Lo'au-Momo association, materialized in the rule of Tu'itātui, who is thought to have begun the Tu'i Tonga imperial expansion beyond Tonga. Tu'itātui, by utilizing his eastern Polynesian–Samoan connections via Lo'au and reversing the former trend, started with Fiji and Savai'i, where the rest of Samoa and beyond were colonized by later Tu'i Tonga.

7. The idiomatic use of the term *matangi* (wind) in Tonga symbolically refers to people, through extraction of material resources, burdened with *fatongia* (duties). This is literally reflected in the Tonga expression "Kuo hangē ne tō ha matangi (he fonua)" (It has been as if the wind has fallen [on the land and its people]), symbolically referring to people, including material extraction, exhausted from executing their *fatongia*.

8. The names Lekapai (*leka-pai;* lit., small-dwarfed), the plantation owner, and Lafaipana (Lafai-pana; lit., lafai-[the]-stunted), the keeper of traditions, are suggestive of servility. The terms *lekapai* and *pana* are used as idioms, referring to physical retardation due to being burdened with a life of service (*fatongia, kavenga*). Literally, such references are symbolic of exploitation and oppression. Doing people's *fatongia*, often the commoners, is alluded to as *fua kavenga* (lit., carrying burden [on one's back]), as the idiomatic expression goes "Kuo piko e tu'a e kakai he lahi e fua kavenga" (The people's backs have been bent from excessively carrying burdens [on their backs]).

9. Though killing *(tāmate)*, in its symbolic sense, is an extreme manifestation of social and physical revenge, the terms *kai* (eating) and *tanu* (burying) are its milder symbolic forms, as in the idiomatic expressions "Kai ho'o tamai!" (Eat your father!) and "Tanu ho'o 'ita!" (Bury your anger!). These literal references, because of oppression, were probably symbolic of Samoan opposition to the Tu'i Tonga rule.

10. The myth of the Turtle Sangone has been recorded in several contexts. See, for example, Kenneth Bain, *The Friendly Islanders: A Story of Queen Sālote and Her People* (London: Hodder and Stoughton, 1967), 145–149; E.E.V. Collocott, "King Taufa" (MS held in Records Room, Department of Pacific and Southeast Asian History, Australian National University, n.d.), 3–34; E. W. Gifford, *Tongan Myths and Tales* (*B. P. Bishop Museum Bulletin* 8, 1924; reprint New York, 1971), 49–55; Adrienne L. Kaeppler, "Folklore as Expressed in the Dance in Tonga," *Journal of American Folklore* 80 (1967): 160–168; Malu-

kava [Kavaefiafi], "Faiva: Taʻanga, Hiva mo e Haka," and Ula [Tāufanau], "Tala Faka-Fonua" (MS, Tongan Culture lectures, ʻAtenisi University, Tonga, 1973). In what follows, I also rely on interviews with Lehāʻuli, 1988; Mafimalanga, 1988; and Helu, 1988.

11. Kaeppler, "Folklore as Expressed in the Dance in Tonga," 161.

12. See *Faikava: A Tongan Literary Journal* (1978); F. Helu, MS, Tongan Culture Lectures (1972, 1989); A. H. Wood and E. Wood Ellem, "Queen Salote Tupou III," in *Friendly Islands: A History of Tonga*, ed. Noel Rutherford (Wellington: Oxford University Press, 1977), 190–209. For a biographical account of Queen Sālote, see Bain, *The Friendly Islanders*.

13. Helu, lectures, 1972, 1989. See also "Collection of Queen Sālote's Poetry," "Collection of Tongan Song Texts (Ancient, Traditional-Classical, and Modern)," and "Collection of Works by Tongan Poets," all undated MSS held by the author; and *Faikava: A Tongan Literary Journal* (1978, 1980).

14. Rachael Tonga's accounts of Tongan traditions can be found in Gifford, "Tongan Myths and Tales," and "Tongan Society," *B. P. Bishop Museum Bulletin* 61 (1929): 118.

15. Elizabeth Bott with the assistance of Tavi, *Tongan Society at the Time of Captain Cook's Visits: Discussions with Her Majesty Queen Sālote Tupou* (Wellington: Polynesia Society, 1982).

16. Cf. Sahlins, *Islands of History*.

17. *Feingakotone:* a *malaʻe* near ʻOlotele, the residence of the Tuʻi Tonga, where the *ʻinasi* ceremony was held, together with sports and entertainment, for the Tuʻi Tonga; a symbol for the Tuʻi Tonga.

18. *Muʻa:* a symbol for high chiefs.

19. *Pangai:* a symbol for the Tuʻi Kanokupolu.

20. *ʻAokai* (request for food): a symbolic reference to Momo, who, through his *matāpule* (spokesman), Lehāʻuli, requested Loʻau literally for yam seedlings to cultivate, where Momo, in social terms, actually proposed to marry Loʻau's daughter, Nua. *Haʻamea:* the residence of Loʻau in Central Tongatapu.

21. *Penepena* (to apply lime to one's hair): a chiefly word for the Tuʻi Tonga's application of a hair mixture made of lime on his hair (see Gifford, *Tongan Myths and Tales,* 121). Symbolically, it was also the name of a piece of bark cloth *(ngatu)* with which the Tuʻi Tonga literally covered himself in sleep (Helu, interview). But socially, it refers to sexual union via marriage, where Nua *(penepena)* was presented as wife to Momo, symbolized as *fākula* (line 16). *Ngatuvai fākula* (old/sweet-scented red pandanus fruits): *Ngatuvai,* a symbol for the outstanding *ʻeiki* status of the Tuʻi Tonga, the reputed *fākula.*

22. *Toi* (hidden): refers to the love Tuʻitātui had for his half-brother, Fasiʻapule, who, one day, came to present himself to the Tuʻi Tonga, carrying with him a basket of *foʻi kilitoto* (a fruit of *toto*), *foʻi uhoʻifusi* (an inside pith of banana

stem), *foʻi mamae* (a fruit of *mamae* plantain), and a *foʻi malala* (a piece of black charcoal). These were to be used as means of informing his kingly brother, Tuʻitātui, of their "blood" relation, and their "love" for each other.

23. Ulamoleka (*Ula-mo-leka/Leka;* lit., Ula-and-leka/Leka): He was a great poet, son of a daughter of Ula, the Tuʻi Kanokupolu's navigator, who married a son of Leka, the Tuʻi Tonga's navigator, thus uniting Kauhalaʻuta ('Uta) and Kauhalalalo (Lalo) in himself, hence, Ulamoleka. Ulamoleka is the author of *"Folau ʻa Ulamoleka ki Niua"* (The voyage of Ulamoleka to Niua), in which he refers to this union: *Ko e va ʻo 'Uta mo Lalo* (That distance between 'Uta and Lalo), *Ka puna ha manu pea tō* (If a sea bird flies [its length], it tires and falls), *Ka kuo vaofi ʻi hoku sino* (But, indeed, they ['Uta and Lalo] have been united in my person) (Helu, interview, 1988).

24. *Kakala talā* (lit., *kakala* [of-the] famous), *kakala moʻoni* (lit., *kakala* [of-the] genuine): a symbol for high chiefs.

25. *Fūfū mo kokohu:* a symbol for *kava* roots.

26. *Kau pongia ʻi vao:* a symbol for a second-generation bunch of plantains *(hopa).*

27. *Lou tangia mo kokī:* a symbol for young taro leaves.

28. *Kapakau tatangi:* a symbol for a wild chicken.

29. *Ngulungulu mo tokoto:* a symbol for a large pig.

30. *Koloa* (durables, such as bark cloth [*ngatu*] and fine mats [*kie Tonga*]): it refers to women's products, as opposed to men's products *(ngāue),* used for socioeconomic exchange between groups.

31. *Anga* (experienced): symbolic reference to an expert in traditions, i.e., in telling *(tala)* of esoteric/political traditions; reflects the classical character of *tala-e-fonua,* possessed only by a privileged few.

32. Taka-i-pomana: name of a *kalia,* which landed at 'One ('Onevai), Tuʻi Tonga's offshore island reserved for recreation, said to have brought a Samoan maiden to sleep with the Tuʻi Tonga; a symbol for sexual union (Helu, interview, 1988).

33. 'One: shortened name for the island 'Onevai, a Tuʻi Tonga island reserved for his pleasure trips.

34. Makahokovalu: symbolic name for the island of 'Uiha in Haʻapai, which is connected with the Tuʻi Tonga through the two brothers Nganaʻeiki and Nganatatafu.

35. *Pakimangamanga* (*paki-mangamanga;* lit., plucking-of-the-branches): a chiefly sport of bonito fishing, in which the bonito tails (*mangamanga,* symbolized by the V shape) are plucked *(paki),* and the rest of the fish is thrown into the sea. Whoever had the most tails was declared winner. *Siangahu:* a mound *(sia)* in Tungua, the residence of the Tamahā. Again, it is symbolic of the Tuʻi Tonga, and all the *ʻeiki* persons derived from him, such as Tamahā.

36. Fonuamotu (*Fonua-motu;* lit., Land-[of]-island; also known as Fonuatanu [*Fonua-tanu;* lit., land-filled-with-earth], an island connected to the mainland by a causeway): residence of the Tuʻi Haʻatakalaua, as opposed to ʻOlotele, the residence of the Tuʻi Tonga, respectively, symbolized by Kauhalalalo (*Kau-hala-lalo;* lit., Side-[of-the]-road-[in-the]-lower-[part]) and Kauhalaʻuta (*Kau-hala-ʻuta,* lit., Side-[of-the]-road-[in-the]-upper-[part]), spatially separated by the main road to Hahake, signifying the structural and functional relationships between Tuʻi Haʻatakalaua and Tuʻi Tonga.

37. Hakautapu (*Hakau-tapu;* lit., Reef-[of-the]-sacred): a reef off Hihifo, the residence of the Tuʻi Kanokupolu; a symbolic name for the Tuʻi Kanokupolu.

38. Havelu, a place in Hihifo, the residence of the Tuʻi Kanokupolu and the Kokatapu (*koka-tapu;* lit., *koka*-[of-the]-sacred]; a tree under which the investitures of Tuʻi Kanokupolu were done): symbolic names for the Tuʻi Kanokupolu.

39. *Fetau:* poetry of rivalry. Queen Sālote found this poetic genre convenient for her *lau ʻeiki* (lit., enumerating of chiefs in terms of the *ʻeiki-tuʻa* distinction relative to the Tongan social organizing principles). The notion of *lau ʻeiki,* in which Queen Sālote was an expert, involves tracing one's social position, especially the *houʻeiki* (chiefs), to the Tuʻi Tonga, or the high chiefs of Tonga. In her poetry, Queen Sālote does little but this.

40. *Falahola* (fine, red-blood pandanus fruits): a symbol for high chiefs.

41. Vahaʻakolo (*Vahaʻa-kolo;* lit., Bounds-[between]-villages): symbolic reference to the boundary between Kolomotuʻa (*Kolo-motuʻa;* lit., Village-[of]-old) and Kolofoʻou (*Kolo-foʻou;* lit., Village-[of]-new) associated with the Tuʻi Kanokupolu. Aleamotuʻa, the eighteenth Kanokupolu, lived in Kolomotuʻa, while Kolofoʻou was settled, after Tāufaʻāhau I rose to power, by the Tuʻi Kanokupolu chiefs from Vavaʻu and Haʻapai, symbolically known as the *tautahi* (*tau-tahi;* lit., warriors-[of-the]-sea, meaning the northerly groups of Vavaʻu and Haʻapai), literally making up Tāufaʻāhau I's army.

42. Examples of *tala-e-fonua.*

43. See Jonathan Friedman, "Notes on Structure and History in Oceania," *Folk* 23 (1981): 275–295; Adrienne Kaeppler, "Exchange Patterns in Goods and Spouses: Fiji, Tonga, and Samoa," *Mankind* 11 (1978): 246–252.

44. See J. W. Davidson, "Problems of Pacific History," *Journal of Pacific History* 1 (1966): 5–21; H. E. Maude, "Pacific History: Past, Present, and Future," *Journal of Pacific History* 6 (1971): 3–24.

45. Gifford, "Tongan Society," 56–57.

46. Ula, lectures, 1973; Helu, Lehāʻuli, and Mafimalanga, interviews, 1988.

47. As used idiomatically in Tonga in such expressions as *Tonga Lahi* (lit., Tonga-[the]-Huge/Great, i.e., huge in terms of *ʻeiki,* associated with the Tuʻi Tonga, residing there), *Vavaʻu Lahi* (lit., Vavaʻu-[the]-Huge/Great, i.e., huge warm-

heartedness and generosity), *Tangata Lahi* (lit., Man-[of-the]-Huge/Great, i.e., huge in power and prestige), *Loto Lahi* (lit., Heart-[of-the]-Huge, i.e., huge in bravery), and *'Eiki Lahi* (lit., Chief-[of-the]-Huge/Great, i.e., powerful chief); they all refer not to literal "hugeness" or "greatness" but symbolically to specific social and psychological attributes relating to power.

48. Mo'unu was the anchorage for the Tu'i Tonga imperial fleet; see Patrick V. Kirch, *The Evolution of the Polynesian Chiefdoms* (New York: Cambridge University Press, 1984).

49. A son of Ratu Edward Cakobau, half-brother of Queen Sālote, has been named Nailasikau; see *Faikava: A Tongan Literary Journal* (1978): 3–7.

50. Helu, interview.

51. *Fakatapu:* the introductory part of *lakalaka,* which involves the paying of respect to the king, in descending order of the social pyramid.

52. *Kakala hingoa* (lit., Flower-[of-the]-named): sweet-scented flowers, symbolizing chiefs.

53. *Lupe* (dove): poetic symbol for a female monarch; *mānoa* (tamely tethered): symbolically refers to a living female monarch.

54. *Falahola* (fine, sweet-smelling, red pandanus fruits): a symbol for high chiefs.

55. The term *fakatangitama* (*faka-tangi-tama;* lit., [In-the-style]-[of-the]-crying-child, i.e., the child that petitions) is symbolically defined within sister-brother relations in which requests for material and social support made by a sister's child (*'ilamutu*) to his or her mother's brother (*fa'etangata/tu'asina*) are socially regulated by the Fahu-'Ulumotu'a principles.

56. *Telekanga:* an archaic word for the gunwales of a *kalia.*

57. Paepae: shortened name for Langi Paepae-'o-Tele'a, connected with Tu'i Tonga 'Uluakimata I or Tele'a, and the Lomipeau.

58. *Makaofe* (*Maka-ofe;* lit., Stones-[that-are]-bent): a symbolic reference to the L-shape cornerstones of the Langi Paepae-'o-Tele'a; symbolic reference to the fine craftsmanship of the 'Uvean and Futuan stonemasons, reflecting the Tu'i Tonga glory.

59. *Ono'aho:* past.

60. *Onopō:* present.

61. *Sotiaka* (zodiac): symbolic for Tongan society.

62. *Tu'utonu mālie e la'ā* (sun directly overhead): symbolic of a male monarch in his prime, or a female one, as with Queen Sālote.

63. *Tu'u kātoa e māhina* (full moon): a reference to a female monarch at her prime.

64. *'Alotolu* (*'Alo-tolu;* lit., Rowers-[of]-three; also known as *Ha'amonga-'amaui* [*Ha'amo-('an)ga-'a-maui/Maui;* lit., Burden/Carrying-stick-(of)-maui/Maui]; the trilithon, Ha'amonga-'a-Maui, grand gateway to the Tu'i Tonga royal compound in Heketa, was probably named after this celestial

body): "the belt of Orion." *Tuingaika* (*Tuinga-ika;* lit., String-[of]-fish): Sirius. See Kik Velt, *Stars over Tonga: Ko e Ngaahi Fetuʻu ʻo Tonga* (Tonga: ʻAtenisi University, 1990).

65. *Fineʻutuvai* (*Fine-ʻutuvai;* lit., Woman-carrier-[of]-water): Aquarius. *Sipitangata* (*Sipi-tangata;* lit., Sheep-[the]-male; ram): the Ram.

66. *Meʻafua* (*Meʻa-fua;* lit., Thing-[that]-weighs; the Balance or Scale): Libra. *Tangatafana* (*Tangata-fana;* lit., Man-[the]-shooter): Saggitarius.

67. *Maʻafulele* (*Maʻafu-lele;* Maʻafu-[the]-runner): "the large Magellanic cloud." *Toloa* (Wild Duck): the Southern Cross. See Velt, *Stars over Tonga,* 100–101.

68. *Humu* (a kind of fish): Southern Fish; "the Coalsack, the well-known dark patch near *Toloa,* the Southern Cross;" *Maʻafutoka* (*Maʻafu-toka;* lit., Maʻafu-[the]-defeated: "the small Magellanic cloud" (Velt, *Stars over Tonga,* 100, 102).

69. *Kakala moʻonia* (*kakala-*[of-the]-genuine): a symbol for high chiefs.

70. *Fakaʻotusia* (*Faka-ʻotu-sia;* lit., Parading-[of]-row-[of]-mounds: "mound" is connected with chiefs, depicting hierarchy; a kind of chiefly *kakala;* a symbol for high chiefs.

71. Knight of St. Patrick, taken as a kind of medal, assumed to be symbolically worn by high chiefs in social rivalry among themselves.

72. *ʻEnisaine tupuʻa* (Eternal ensign): symbolic reference to *Fakaʻotusia* as a kind of flag for the Lomipeau, symbolized as the Tuʻi Tonga.

73. *Futukovuna:* this flag, a symbol for the Tuʻi Tonga, is hoisted from Futukovuna, another symbol for the Tuʻi Tonga. Queen Sālote refers here to the encompassing *ʻeiki* status of the Tuʻi Tonga, surpassing all others.

74. *Foʻi fākula* (a sweet-scented, blood-red pandanus fruit): a symbol for high chiefs. *Fākula* and *heilala* are the most *ʻeiki* of all *kakala,* which are symbols for the Tuʻi Tonga, including those socially derived from him, such as the Tamahā, Falefisi, Tuʻi Tonga Fefine. Queen Sālote, by symbolically referring to these objects, is talking about the politics of genealogies, where lineages are politically manipulated in terms of *ʻeiki.*

75. Bott; Lehāʻuli, Mafimalanga, Moala, interviews, 1988; Ula, interview, 1973.

76. See E.E.V. Collocott, "Tongan Astronomy and Calendar," (*B. P. Bishop Museum Occasional Papers* 8 (1922): 157–173; and Velt, *Stars over Tonga.*

77. Though Tongan society is rigidly multistrata, social mobility is nevertheless possible. This, as a kind of buffer, is formally facilitated by the accident of birth (*faʻeleʻi*), and by social, economic, and political antecedents such as *toʻa* (bravery in the form of a successful rebellion), *faʻa* (economic prowess), and *talavou/hoihoifua/fakaʻofoʻofa* (physical beauty). The Tongan idiomatic term for social mobility is *tanusia* (*tanu-sia;* lit., building-[one's]-mound; a chiefly symbol, as mounds were built only for the pleasure of chiefs), which is symbolic of one's improving one's social position, often from less powerful

groups, by marrying chiefs, tapping on the social substance of *'eiki*. The call for maintaining *kau'a*, social boundaries and associated privileges, is manifested in such idioms as *'Oua 'e hikihiki kau'ā* (Do not overstep your bounds).

78. An example of *tala-e-fonua* as an ecology-centered concept of cultural and historical ordering.

79. See Epeli Hau'ofa, "The New South Pacific Society: Integration and Independence," in Antony Hooper et al., eds., *Class and Culture in the South Pacific* (Auckland and Suva: Centre for Pacific Studies, University of Auckland; Institute of Pacific Studies, University of the South Pacific, 1987), for a discussion of how traditions are imposed on people, concealing the increasing gap between the rich and the poor brought about by capitalistic tendencies. Cf. Michael C. Howard, "Vanuatu: The Myth of the Melanesian Socialism," *Labour, Capital, and Society* 16 (1983): 176–203.

6

A History Lesson

Captain Cook Finds Himself
in the State of Nature

Stephen Turner

On 10 October 1769, at Poverty Bay, three days after Nicholas Young, the surgeon's boy, sighted the east coast of New Zealand from the *Endeavour,* Captain Cook became entangled in a conflict of his own making with the indigenous Maori. Since touching at New Zealand, Cook's relations with the local Maori had been punctuated by a number of violent episodes. To improve relations with the local people, Cook decided on the expedient of kidnapping some of them in the hope of making his good intentions known. But when his crew attempted to seize a group of seven Maori sailing into the bay off the newly named Young Nick's Head, they naturally resisted, throwing everything they had on board the canoe at their attackers. The English responded by firing at the group, and four were killed. The remaining three, all youths, including two brothers, were taken from the water and carried to the *Endeavour,* where, once assured of Cook's good intentions, or rather, once assured they would not be killed and eaten, they cheered up. Cook found it difficult to justify what had happened:

> I am aware that most humane men who have not experienced things of this nature will cencure my conduct in fireing upon the people in this boat nor do I my self think that the reason I had for seizing upon her will att all justify me, and had I thought that they would have made the least resistance I would not have come near them, but as they did I was not to stand still and suffer either my self or those that were with me to be knocked on the head.[1]

The Maori present Cook with a problem of right. Their behavior, which Cook did not anticipate, makes his own actions appear unjustified. Cook wrestles with his conscience but he cannot square his behavior with

his own notions of right. Cook finds himself in the "state of nature," supposedly the original condition of "mankind," and the basis of the classical theory of right. As it is defined by John Locke in The Second Treatise
of Government, "Where-ever any two Men are, who have no standing
Rule, and common Judge to Appeal to on Earth, for the determination of
Controversies of Right betwixt them, there they are still in the state of Nature."[2] This is the case with international heads of state, and with "primitive" peoples. Locke's examples include two men stranded on a desert island, or the meeting of a "swiss and an indian in the woods of america."
Cook and the Maori come into the latter category. The British, however,
thought that the Maori, certainly not themselves, were in the state of nature. In the early modern theory of right, those thought to be living in the
state of nature were generally culturally other—the American Indian
provided the usual example—but their difference was not conceived in
what we would today consider "cultural" terms; rather, it was thought that
they represented human society at an earlier stage in the development of
civilization as a whole. Locke famously remarks that "in the beginning all
the World was America."[3] The difference between primitive and civilized
peoples was not inherent—the basic unity of mankind was assumed—
but merely reflected the difference in their relative advancement. In the
eighteenth century, the theorists of the "progress of man" from the earliest stages had not yet developed a notion of "culture" with which to characterize human diversity.[4] The development of ethnological thinking was
greatly stimulated by Cook's voyages, but Cook himself had little notion
that the peoples he encountered might have been acting in a wholly different but internally coherent way. As a result, he could hardly begin to
comprehend the social premises underlying Maori behavior. In Poverty
Bay, the problem of right is inflected by the emergence in the late eighteenth century of "culture" as a new way of characterizing difference.
Cook's predicament suggests that cultural conflict, or the manifestation
of cultural difference as conflict, is the basis of the theory of right, and of
the social contract, in societies founded on settlement.

The problem of right as a cultural conflict is a legacy of voyages such
as Cook's. In New Zealand, it has been highlighted by Maori pressure on
white *(pakeha)* hegemony through claims under New Zealand's own "social contract," the Treaty of Waitangi, signed in 1840 by a number of
Maori chiefs from the North Island and a representative of the British
Crown, Captain William Hobson.[5] A historian of constitutional law, Paul
McHugh, claims that "the Treaty represents the application of the con-
tractual theory as the basis of the Crown's sovereignty over Maori tribes";[6]
but Locke remarks that "'tis not every Compact that puts an end to the
State of Nature between Men, but only this one of agreeing together mu-

tually to enter into one Community, and make one Body Politick; other Promises and Compacts, Men may make one with another, and yet still be in the State of Nature."[7] In retrospect, it is difficult to say that both parties to the Treaty "agreed together mutually to enter into one Community, and make one Body Politick." As a result, New Zealanders today find themselves in the position of Cook and the Maori, both constitutionally and culturally, living in the state of nature. For white New Zealanders, the problem of right is a problem of authority. To question the basis of right in New Zealand is to question the worldview on which it is based. The one is bound up with the other. If the Treaty of Waitangi is New Zealand's social contract, the encounter between Cook and the Maori suggests a state of nature in yet another sense: It constitutes the original condition of both parties to the contract. The notions of right that Cook brought to New Zealand, along with various animals, crops, and plants, have since become established there. Herein lies a lesson of colonialism, or settlement, an example of the transportation of ideas in voyages of exploration. The original encounter can tell us something about the conditions of this inheritance. This is to look at the theory of right in practice, in history, in the very state of nature it purports to describe. Returning to the history of encounter offers new ways of conceptualizing the relation between culture and justice. It is not just Maori who are able to think that the past is *nga raa o mua*, "the days in front," and that the future is *kei muri*, "behind."[8]

Not only did the British regard the Maori as living in a condition that was close to the state of nature, but they found themselves in a state of nature in relation to the Maori. They did not properly grasp this state of affairs because they could not have understood the way in which the Maori might be different. Where there is no settled agreement between individuals to regulate their relations, Locke says they are bound by the "Law of Nature" to refrain from invading each others' lives, liberty, and possessions.[9] In New Zealand, however, the law of nature is subsumed by the fact of cultural difference. The British found it difficult to anticipate or comprehend the behavior of the Maori. Instead of finding primitive peoples in a state of nature living according to the law of nature, the British found themselves, at first, in a state of war, which we can now understand as a cultural conflict. The problem of right is not due merely to the absence of a common authority but to the absence of a common basis on which a single authority might be established. In Maori New Zealand (now called "Aotearoa"), the law of nature was alien.

To the British, the behavior of the Maori was contradictory. Cook remarked that the Maori "would shake [their weapons] at us, at times they would dance the war dance, and other times they would trade with and

talk to us and answer such questions as were put to them with all the
Calmness imaginable.[10] The Maori appeared at once aggressive and sociable. It was difficult for the British to accommodate these different aspects of Maori behavior within their conception of the social personality.
The Maori *haka* (dance) seemed to be at once a greeting and a challenge.
Sir Joseph Banks remarked that "they seemd fond of using it upon all occasions whether in war or peace."[11] For local Maori, the *haka* was an act
of self-assertion, proclaiming the *mana* (authority, power, prestige) of
their tribe and its domain. It was a challenge to British authority, in
Banks' view a "Song of defiance." The British were no doubt expected to
reply in kind. Apart from the *haka* that greeted them around New
Zealand coasts, Banks and Cook noted the well-fortified villages *(paa)*
located on promontories, clearly constructed for defense. To Banks, the
Maori were a people "much given to war."[12] Their villages indicated
"the state of war in which they live, constantly in danger of being sur-
prizd when least upon their guard."[13] Along the East Coast, however, "the
people seemd free from apprehension and as in a state of Profound
peace"; Banks mistakenly believed this was "owing to their being joind together under one cheif or king."[14] He found it hard to imagine a peaceful society that was not governed by a single authority.

In the British tradition of the theory of right, the condition of peace
implied a single authority, or sovereign. In the absence of such an authority, New Zealand could only be a state of war. Dismissing the idea that
the East Coast Maori "were united under one head or chief," Cook says
that "whatever place we put in at or whatever people we spoke with upon
the Coast they generaly told us that those that were at a little distance
from them were their enimies; from which it appear'd to me that they
were very much divided into parties which make war one with another,
and all their actions and beheavour towards us tended to prove that they
are a brave and open warlike people and voide of treachery."[15] The warlike behavior of the Maori suggested Hobbes' "natural condition," a
"warre, as is of every man, against every man." The law of nature was contradicted, in particular, by the Maori practice of cannibalism. Banks "was
loth a long time to beleive that any human beings could have among
them so brutal a custom."[16] The Maori custom of eating human flesh was
a symbolic ingestion of the *mana* of their enemies and their enemies' ancestors. In place of the law of nature, and a political body empowered to
administer it, the world of the Maori was governed by concepts associated
with *mana,* primarily *tapu* (the sacred) and *utu* (compensation).

Mana is ultimately the power of the gods, which descends to men
through their common ancestry. In traditional Maori society, the individ-

uals most directly descended from the founding ancestors had the greatest *mana* and were extremely *tapu* individuals, surrounded by prohibitions. The power that *tapu* exercised over ordinary individuals may be explained as the appearance of the *mana* of the gods in the earthly realm. The structure of belief grounded by the presence of *mana* constituted an effective system of social control. *Mana, tapu, utu,* and associated spiritual beliefs formed a working cluster of assumptions, an ideological package. *Utu,* the law of compensation, or balance, could take violent forms in acts of retribution, and led the British to conceive the Maori in terms of the state of war. Hobbes' version of the state of nature provided a model. *Utu,* however, as an obligation associated with the *mana* of the tribe, entailed reciprocating friendly acts as well as seeking compensation for offensive acts.[17] It is a principle of equivalence. A perceived imbalance between kin and outsiders had to be redressed. Maori social relations thus presented a dual aspect to the British, at once sociable and warlike.

British social relations, conceived in marked contrast to those of primitive peoples, were governed by a different law. The theory of right is based on the conception of the individual in the state of nature. The state of nature, as the condition of the Maori seemed to prove, was sometimes peaceful, sometimes violent. For Locke it depended on whether individuals in the state of nature followed the law of nature, which dictates the right to the preservation of life, liberty, and estates encompassed by the general term, *property.* Many commentators, however, note that Locke often means by "property" simply "estates." The law of nature in eighteenth-century England was the law of property. And property, as Roy Porter remarks, was the "soul of eighteenth-century society, residing in anything from mere goods to rights . . . or persons."[18] The rule of property, supported by the most strict criminal code in Europe, had become official ideology in eighteenth-century England. The law had grown to accommodate the rapid development of trade, commerce, and industry, and an increasingly sophisticated credit economy. Property was expanding in many forms, and demanded protection. Locke was its oft-cited apologist. For him, notoriously, "Government has no other end but the preservation of Property," a claim that was accepted uncritically by most later writers, and not restricted to the extent of British society.[19] William Blackstone, the great constitutionalist, could speak about "that law of property, which nature herself has written upon the hearts of all mankind."[20] The law of property was not, however, written on the hearts of the Maori, and had to be impressed upon them. When the Maori attempted to steal from the British, or cheated at trade, the British started shooting at them. In Mercury Bay, one Lieutenant Gore, commanding the *Endeav-*

our while Cook was ashore, shot dead a man for refusing his side of a bargain. Cook did not reprimand Gore, though he "thought the punishment a little too severe for the Crime."[21] Banks agreed that the man's life was too hastily "forfeited to the laws of England."[22] In England at the time, one could be hanged for stealing a one-shilling handkerchief. The Maori did not respond with force because in their own terms the British act was *utu,* a payment for a wrong, and a satisfaction of honor. This did not satisfy an anonymous journalist on board for whom there "never were people more ignorant or regardless of the principles of natural justice."[23]

In the theory of right, the individual, and the basis of right, is defined in terms of property: "Every man has a *property* in his own *person:* this no body has any right to but himself. The *labour* of his body, and the *work* of his hands, we may say, are properly his."[24] The Maori "self," and the Maori notion of right, cannot be understood in these terms. When Banks visited a "family" of seventeen Maori in Queen Charlotte Sound, and understood that a child among them owned "the land about where we wooded," he says that this was "the only instance of property we have met with among these people."[25] This was because the Maori "self" is understood in terms of kinship affiliations, rather than individual property. Individual status is derived from the tribal group and is inconceivable outside this community. What the individual possesses is what the tribe possesses in the individual. This, ultimately, is the self-understanding of the tribe—its history, traditions, and practices. Right, or *tika,* depends on acting in accordance with the traditional practices of the tribe. Correct action involves re-creating the history of the tribe.[26] The British notion of right, depending on the attributes of the individual prior to the formation of civil society, could have no basis in traditional Maori society.

For the British, the law of nature was also the law of God, which demands the individual appropriation and cultivation of land. Locke says that God gave land "to the use of the Industrious and Rational (and *Labour* was to be his *Title* to it); not to the Fancy or Covetousness of the Quarrelsom and Contentious," that is, not to the Maori.[27] Private property succeeds individual industry as a matter of course: "God, by commanding to subdue, gave Authority so far to *appropriate.* And the Condition of Humane Life, which requires Labour and Materials to work on, necessarily introduces *private Possessions.*"[28] Cook, like Locke, could not conceive of collectively owned land, or collective labor: "Intrest is the great Spring which animates the hand of industry, few would toil themselves in cultivating and planting the land if he did not expect to injoy the fruits of his labour, if everything was in common the Industerous man would be upon a worse footing than the Idle Sluggard."[29] For Locke, the law of nature dictates *"the direction of a free and intelligent Agent* to his proper Interest," and its end is *"to preserve and enlarge Freedom."*[30] This is the essence of "utilitarian man," later stripped of his natural-law covering by Hume and Bentham. The Maori, in this tradition of thought, was not rational. The Maori organization of labor could not be accounted for in terms of the theory of property. The supra-individual network of *whanau* (immediate kin), *hapu* (extended kin), and *iwi* (tribe) exist as entities in relation to collectively held land. Collective labor is based on the collective relationship to the land of members of the kin group. Dominion over the land was not therefore a matter of asserting individual entitlement, but of asserting the territorial boundaries of the tribal domain, the area over which the tribe has established control, and which constitutes its standing and identity *(turangawaewae)*. Tribal affiliation and the tribal domain remain inseparable: Maori understand the tribe to be the *tangata whenua* or "people of the land." The fires *(ahi kaa)* that the British saw around New Zealand as they coasted its shoreline asserted the claim of local Maori, the *tangata whenua,* to the land.

The theory of right is implicated in the long history of conflict over the acquisition of land from the Maori by Europeans, because right inheres in property the occupation or cultivation of land-granted dominion. Land that was not directly occupied, or otherwise being used, was regarded by the British as waste. Thus, Cook felt able to assert British dominion over seemingly unoccupied and uncultivated land. In the South Island, he took formal possession of Queen Charlotte Sound, which he had just named, and the adjacent lands in the name of the British Crown. Cook also regarded the North Island, despite its greater population, as open to anyone prepared to appropriate its resources: "Was this Country settled by an Industrus people," he says, "they would very soon be supply'd not only with the necesarys but many of the luxuries of life."[31] The "best place for the first fixing of a Colony," he adds, "would be either in the River Thames or the Bay of Islands."[32] The perception of New Zealand as a state of nature made it naturally subject to British dominion. Cook is not so much prophetic as ideologically consistent. Those who were prepared to appropriate the land were the "industrious" and "rational" and were therefore entitled to it. The Maori also appeared "too much divided among themselves to unite in opposing, by which means and kind and gentle usuage the Colonists would be able to form strong parties among them."[33] New Zealand would be appropriated and cultivated in British interests. The theory of property anticipates Edward Gibbon Wakefield's mercantilist theory of "systematic" colonialism in the nineteenth century. The Maori would be paid with "civilization," as commerce with other peoples would bring them out of the state of nature (Banks was impressed with their "ingenuity," given that they had "had little or indeed no commerce with any others").[34] Civilization followed the progress of commerce. Cultural encounter, however, is more than a commercial exchange. It creates a debt that cannot be accounted for in terms of social relations predicated on a developing market economy.

In Locke's account, right is based on an originary individualism. The individual, living in the state of nature in accord with the law of nature, has a right to his life, liberty, and possessions, defined as his "property." But having property in your person, and in the products of your labor, does not tell you who you are. In contemporary New Zealand, given increasing respect for Maori custom *(tikanga)*, if you do not know who you are, you do not have a place to stand *(turangawaewae)*. The possessive individual implicit in the theory of right exists everywhere and nowhere, outside history and culture. This notion lies at the origin of the problem of right raised by Cook's encounter with the Maori. Right *(tika)*, for the Maori, involves acting in terms of the traditional practices of the tribe. The sense of identity gained from belonging to the tribe provides individual Maori with cultural capital, or in Maori terms, *mana*. White New Zealanders, by contrast, have economic and political capital but lack cultural capital: Neither European nor properly indigenous, they have a perceived problem of identity (books and articles on this topic constitute a local industry). On his grumpy travels in the South Pacific, Paul Theroux, an outsider, remarks that in New Zealand the Maori "were the only people who looked right at home."[35] The issue of identity complicates the simple definition of right in terms of property. When the Maori mixes labor with the land, it becomes the property of the tribe as much as the individual. It is the source of individual identity. It makes the Maori the *tangata whenua*. Whites may have largely appropriated the land, but Maori make them look like they are not at home.

These conflicting conceptions of the individual mean that the original encounter between the British and the Maori constitutes a state of nature. In the theory of right, the insecurity of the state of nature creates the need for political society. The theory of right, however, does not take into account cultural conflict; "culture," after all, is an object that postdates encounter. The theory of right could not therefore help Cook justify his actions. In the absence of an ethnological understanding of cultural difference, the state of nature appeared to be a state of war. The theory of right, understood in this historical context, suggests that the fact of cultural difference constitutes the need for political society in societies founded on settlement. This was recognized both by Europeans and

Maori in the 1830s with the increasing European presence in New Zealand. During this period, the British monarch was petitioned both by Maori chiefs and European settlers to secure order in New Zealand. The European perception of growing lawlessness, particularly in the Bay of Islands area of the upper North Island, led to Hobson's arrival in 1840 with instructions to negotiate a treaty with the Maori in order to establish a nominal government. If the state of nature presents a cultural conflict, as I have suggested, the purpose of constituting political society is not simply to protect "property," but, given the cultural inflections of this term, to mediate British and Maori differences. If political society does not acknowledge that it is founded in the fact of cultural difference, it has not been properly constituted, and New Zealanders, at least, are still living in the state of nature.

Rights, finally, are a product of history as much as of theory. The increasing cultural capital of the Maori in New Zealand has less to do with the limitations of the theory of right than the historical and cultural contradictions of the position of white New Zealanders. They remain a frontier culture, living on the edge of the Western world, culturally and geographically; hence, they are peculiarly vulnerable to the pressure placed by the indigenous culture on Western categories. The issue of identity suggests that non-Western cultures are implicated in Western thought, that the West is indebted to non-Western peoples for its self-conception. This may be widely acknowledged in critical theory, but for white New Zealanders living in the same cultural neighborhood as Maori, it is a matter of practice, of felt experience (the Maori word *"pakeha"* is the only term that properly describes whites within New Zealand). In the so-called West, the theory of right is being transformed as other peoples give voice to the name of the primitive. The return of the *mana motuhake* (special and distinctive *mana*) of the Maori exhibits the logic of *utu*. For Maori, the historical record—the erosion of Maori *mana* through Western influence—must be balanced. The lesson for white New Zealanders is that history is subject to double-entry bookkeeping. Maori, at least, have been keeping accounts. Like other settler societies challenged by indigenous peoples in their midst, whites are subject to the demand for "maorification" as the fact of Maori difference reveals the gap between the worldview they have inherited and the world they actually live in. Without acknowledging an originary cultural difference, the radical individualism of whites cannot explain their position in the society they have settled. There has been no real settlement. Cultural differences continue to "unsettle" settler societies, returning them to the state of nature. The problem is that right is a product of the vicissitudes of culture in history rather than a natural inheritance, simply the power that happens to be. The result is that societies founded on settlement are being forced to confront, and negotiate anew, the basis of authority.

NOTES

1. *The Journals of Captain James Cook,* ed. J. C. Beaglehole, 4 vols. (Cambridge: Published for the Hakluyt Society at the University Press, 1955–1967) 1:171.
2. John Locke, *Two Treatises of Government,* ed. Peter Laslett (Cambridge: Cambridge University Press, 1988), 326.
3. Ibid., 301.
4. George Stocking, in *Victorian Anthropology* (New York: Free Press, 1987), explains that Enlightenment thinkers did not yet understand "culture" in the modern anthropological sense of the term, defined as the "constituting medium of different thought-worlds" (19).
5. The circumstances of this event, the intent of the parties involved, and the validity of the document itself—there are competing versions in Maori and English—have more recently been placed under a cloud of historical revisionism. See in particular Claudia Orange, *The Treaty of Waitangi* (Wellington, N.Z.: Allen and Unwin, Port Nicholson Press, 1987).
6. "Constitutional Theory and Maori Claims," *Waitangi: Maori and Pakehaa Perspectives of the Treaty of Waitangi,* ed. I. H. Kawharu (Auckland: Oxford University Press, 1989), 30.
7. Locke, *Two Treatises,* 276–277.
8. Joan Metge, *The Maoris of New Zealand,* rev. ed. (London and Boston: Routledge and Kegan Paul, 1976), 70.
9. Locke, *Two Treatises,* 271.
10. Cook, *Journals,* 1:281.
11. *The Endeavour Journal of Joseph Banks, 1768–1771,* ed. J. C. Beaglehole, 2 vols. (Sydney: Angus and Robertson, 1962), 2:30.
12. Banks, *Endeavour Journal,* 1:424.
13. Ibid., 2:31.
14. Ibid., 2:32.
15. Cook, *Journals,* 1:281.
16. Banks, *Endeavour Journal,* 1:443.
17. Ranginui Walker, *Ka Whawhai Tonu Matou—Struggle Without End* (Harmondsworth: Penguin, 1990), 69.
18. Roy Porter, *English Society in the Eighteenth Century* (London: Allen Lane, 1982), 15.

19. Locke, *Two Treatises,* 329.

20. Quoted in Douglas Hay, "Property, Authority, and the Criminal Law," in *Albion's Fatal Tree: Crime and Society in Eighteenth-Century England,* ed. Douglas Hay, Peter Linebaugh, John G. Rule, E. P. Thompson, and Cal Winslow (Harmondsworth: Penguin, 1975), 19.

21. Cook, *Journals,* 1:196.

22. Banks, *Endeavour Journal,* 1:429.

23. Cook, *Journals,* 1:196.

24. Locke, *Two Treatises,* 27.

25. Banks, *Endeavour Journal,* 2:463–464.

26. See John Patterson, *Exploring Maori Values* (Palmerston North, N. Z.: Dunmore Press, 1992), 123.

27. Locke, *Two Treatises,* 291.

28. Ibid., 292.

29. Cook, *Journals,* 2:270.

30. Locke, *Two Treatises,* 305, 306.

31. Cook, *Journals,* 1:276.

32. Ibid., 1:278.

33. Ibid., 1:278.

34. Banks, *Endeavour Journal,* 1:138.

35. Paul Theroux, *The Happy Isles of Oceania: Paddling the Pacific* (Harmondsworth: Penguin, 1992), 11.

7

MYTH, SCIENCE, AND EXPERIENCE IN THE BRITISH CONSTRUCTION OF THE PACIFIC

David Mackay

In December 1785, James Strange, an East India Company employee from Madras, wrote to the eminent scientist Sir Joseph Banks seeking support for a voyage of discovery to the northwest coast of America. Two vessels were to be employed in the expedition. They were to be equipped to the highest possible standards, with the journals of previous voyages of discovery, navigational instruments, antiscorbutics, and all the paraphernalia regarded as *de rigueur* for voyages of discovery at that time. The commander was himself instructed to keep proper logs and journals with accurately recorded observations. The voyages of James Cook were held up as the model, and as homage to this noble tradition the ships were named the *Captain Cook* and the *Experiment.* In explaining why he sought Banks' advice, Strange disarmingly asserted, "I wished to avail myself of the Knowledge which in every Branch of Science, so Eminently distinguishes You, in that Station you hold with so much credit to yourself & Advantage to the Publick."[1]

Strange had approached the right person and touched the right bases: the president of the British Royal Society and the acknowledged patron of late-eighteenth-century science. As James King had said four years earlier, Banks was "the common Centre of we discoverers."[2] The entreaty had also been packaged in terms thoroughly appropriate to the age and likely to attract the sympathy of Banks. This was, we are told, a rational era, in which accurate observation, precise measurement, and controlled and repeatable experiment had superseded deductive reasoning and speculation. The irony in the case of James Strange was that the true purpose of the expedition was to trade for sea otter furs on the northwest coast of America, rather than to carry out scientific investigation, and far from being a model of scientific seamanship the voyage was from the outset an utter shambles.

Dozens of other supplicants petitioned Banks in similar ways, often with the customary homage to Cook, or perhaps Linnaeus—generally with obeisance to the deity of empirical science. Banks' correspondence is replete with accounts of investigations and experiments ranging from the most prosaic to the most bizarre, in many cases with the additional ca-chet of the greater good of humankind. The empirical and experimental method was synonymous with the notion of progress and improvement, and its triumph was seen as distinguishing European culture from that prevailing in more sultry climes.

It is convincing to argue that this ethos largely accounted for the great successes of the age of exploration, which began with Byron and reached its apogee with James Cook. The forty years before this had in terms of geographical knowledge been preoccupied with the debate about two of the remaining myths: the Northwest Passage to China and the location and character of *Terra australis incognita*. In its Pacific aspect, the latter showed a persistence in European consciousness out of all pro-portion to the supporting evidence for its existence brought back by ear-lier explorers, such as Mendaña, Quiros, Schouten, Le Maire, and even Tasman. Map representations of the Pacific between the middle and end of the eighteenth century display the manner in which these fabrications gave way to firmly placed dots and then lines, which rendered the ocean a surer and more accessible place in European eyes, and one now ready for economic exploitation.

In the view of many explorers, the reasons for this change could be traced to the application of measured, precise, and scientific practices in navigation that had exposed the follies of such armchair theorists as Harris, Campbell, de Brosses, and Dalrymple. The great French explorer Bougainville stated the position succinctly:

> I agree that it is difficult to imagine such a large number of low-lying islands and half-submerged pieces of land without as-suming the existence of a nearby continent. But geography is a science of facts; if one yields to the systematizing impulse while sitting in one's study, one risks falling into the greatest errors, which sometimes can be corrected at the cost of sailors' lives.[3]

The practice of seamanship and sailing had therefore been influ-enced by the changes in scientific method and knowledge. More accurate instruments, in the form of reflecting sextants, compasses and chro-nometers, and astronomical tables describing lunar distances, and com-manders with the skills and application to employ these aids, were vital to a more precise rendering of the Pacific. The historiography of James

Cook generally depicts him as the archetype of the dogged, systematic, meticulous seaman, laying down exact and particular geographical facts, inscribed in charts and views for the benefit of those who followed. He emerges as the true Gradgrind of navigators, although in fairness, some of his disciples—Bligh, Vancouver, and later Flinders—could lay stronger claims to such a title.

Even shipboard life and industrial relations could be brought under proper and systematic schemes of management that would benefit the discipline, and particularly the health, of crews. The vessel could be cleaned, smoked, and freed of foul bilge water. A strict diet could be enforced, with emphasis on fresh foods and a scientifically constructed regime of antiscorbutics. Cleanliness and adequate clothing would reduce the incidence of disease, as would the employment of reliable and properly trained surgeons. Cook, as an example, experimented with a wide range of antiscorbutic products and even presented a paper on the subject to the Royal Society, earning its Copley medal for his efforts. Thus equipped, an expedition could pursue more prolonged and less dangerous systematic discovery.

The century required, however, that not only coasts and harbors in the Pacific should be exactly known but that the lands themselves should be subject to precise scientific scrutiny. This could not be entrusted solely to mariners, and therefore the practice of carrying scientists on voyages of discovery began, first with Commerson and Véron on Bougainville's voyage, reaching through the Cook era to Vancouver, La Pérouse, and the more substantial parties accompanying both Baudin and Flinders. Their tasks were to thoroughly examine and evaluate new lands and peoples and return to Europe with observations and collections of interest to science. Infused with the proper Baconian spirit, the scientists were also to record products likely to be of use to the arts, manufacturers, and commerce of their home countries.

Among scholars and seafarers, Cook's second voyage has rightly acquired the status of being the most distinguished feat of maritime exploration of the century. It was the first voyage with Joseph Banks on the *Endeavour,* however, that captured the scientific imagination and established the minimum requirements for Enlightened expeditions. Even the Forsters, Johann and George, ruefully acknowledged this fact, although their own contributions to science were memorable and respected. With Banks and his party lay the advantage of novelty, which made their massive and exciting collections the talk of academies across Europe. The failure to publish the natural history results of the expedition—for which Banks has been castigated in this century—mattered less at the time because he had returned with a veritable museum of specimens that were freely available to serious researchers, and have generally been so ever since.

The intention here is not to enter into the discussion about the prime objectives of the *Endeavour* voyage—as to whether its aims were primarily scientific or strategic/commercial—for whatever the outcome of that debate, there can be no doubt that the ship was sent out with serious scientific objectives. The Royal Society itself prompted the expedition, and the observation of the transit of Venus was a global undertaking with strands in California, Norway, and Hudson Bay.[4] This objective—so improbable in the eyes of the Portuguese at Rio de Janeiro—symbolized the elevated place of science in the affairs of the nation. The Pacific component of this enterprise required the establishment of the precise location of Tahiti, and the use of precision instruments by persons competent to operate them.

The voyage was a benchmark in natural history, and because the botanist on board was to dominate the management of British science for the next half century, it became a model for the evaluation of new lands. New natural history phenomena were to be collected, described, measured, classified, graphically depicted, and preserved. Their habitat was also to be accounted for, including the soil and climatic regimes. Products likely to be of economic use were to be studied and gathered. The physiognomy, language, economy, government, religion, and culture of indigenous peoples were to be recorded. Detailed journals would be a necessary accompaniment to the natural history collections, with transactions and impressions of places and peoples recorded daily. Behind this process lay a confidence that an exact description and analysis of new lands was both possible and profitable.

All this is well enough known in the context of Cook's voyages and those of some subsequent discoverers. I doubt, however, that the pervasiveness of this global evaluative process is fully realized. In the fifty years after his return from the *Endeavour* voyage, Joseph Banks and Kew Gardens were part of a vast botanical imperium with the mercantilist aim of identifying and classifying species likely to be useful to an industrializing Britain. Thousands of plant and animal specimens flowed toward London, accompanied by the accurate descriptions of provenance and environment that the new empiricism required.

It is perhaps worth documenting the scale of this undertaking. From 1770 to Banks' death, in 1820, I have so far identified 126 collectors working in the non-European world who sent plant specimens to Banks and Kew Gardens. Many of these were botanists or gardeners with a good grasp of the Linnean taxonomy. Another large group were surgeons and physicians educated in a herbalist tradition and accustomed to the identification of useful plants for medicinal purposes. Many in this category were also students of Linnaeus. Even some of the military and naval officers and government officials, who formed the next largest group, were familiar with Linnean classifications.

The activities of these collectors varied enormously in scope and duration. A few were occasional correspondents in exotic lands who sent specimens to Banks—hopeful, no doubt, of a share of his patronage. Others were dedicated amateurs who maintained a lengthy and profitable correspondence. Some were sent out on specific collecting missions with written instructions from Banks.

Although agents were dispersed to all corners of the world, the greatest number of commissioned collectors were sent to the Pacific and Australasia. In the view of Banks, this region offered the most encouraging prospects of finding new and profitable species. Once described and classified, such products could be transshipped to climatically similar parts of the empire within a complex network of plant exchange. This process presented opportunities for rationalizing and enhancing colonial natural resources to the benefit of Britain. The infamous breadfruit expedition to Tahiti was emblematic of this process.[5]

The scientific context in which these collectors worked was most apparent in their instructions. Archibald Menzies, accompanying Vancouver, was directed to the minutest examination of geology, soil, climate, landform, and plant and animal life. Plants were to be accurately described and samples returned to England. He was to search for useful minerals in exposed strata and ensure that samples were collected for microscopic examination in England. The land was to be evaluated in terms of its potential for raising European crops and livestock. The customs, language, culture, religion, and manufactured goods of the indigenous inhabitants were to be inquired into. The whole enterprise required diligence, perseverance, discretion, and good sense.[6]

Implicit in this empirical process was the belief not only that the environment of new lands could be exactly described and understood but also that it could in a sense be reordered. Indigenous descriptions and categories did not fit usefully into European patterns, and therefore the whole of the natural world had to be systematized, analyzed, and rendered in European terms. This was a necessary preliminary to exploitation.

I have said little so far about analysis of the indigenous inhabitants of new lands, although explorers and scientists were generally asked to observe and describe them in similar terms to those contained in the instructions to Menzies. Categorizing them or drawing up precise guidelines for analysis was a little more difficult, although it was thought that the cultural interface could be regularized. Cook drew up five basic rules for guiding relations between his crew and the peoples of the Pacific. On his second breadfruit expedition, Bligh, perhaps understandably, extended this to seventeen. Again, perhaps understandably, the first rule was: "At the Society or Friendly Islands no seaman or officer is ever to speak of the Loss of the Bounty, or that Capt. Cook was killd by Indians."[7]

Although in Cook's era there was no ethnological blueprint issued to expeditions, there was an assumption that peoples could be subjected to the same empirical evaluative procedures applied to the rest of the natural world. While there were all sorts of enlightenment theories about the ordering of humankind, there was as yet no Linnaeus to produce an agreed-on classification; that was to come in the nineteenth century. Once in the Pacific, however, the voyagers not only observed and described, they attempted to classify, and almost two-thirds of Johann Forster's *Observations Made During a Voyage Round the World* is given over to a discussion of the peoples of the Pacific. This produced a classification into two main groups, corresponding to Polynesians and Melanesians, with an explanation of difference based largely on environmental factors.

By the end of the century, the rational scientific method was being carried over into the investigation of humankind. The Société des Observateurs de L'Homme was established by Louis François Jauffret in December 1799, with the objective of establishing guidelines for the systematic study of natural man in his natural habitat. Vain theories and rash speculations were to be abandoned in favor of studies that would comprehensively investigate the anatomy, physiology, hygiene, language, law, and history of humankind. Perhaps inevitably, and sadly, the physiological differences proved the easiest to categorize, and the members of the Society, which included Cuvier, Lamarck, Bougainville, and Degérando, concentrated on craniometry, skeletal structure, skin color, and muscular strength.

The Pacific significance of the Society was demonstrated by its part in briefing on the procedures for the evaluation of natural man for the benefit of the Baudin expedition to the Pacific. A seventy-page essay was drafted for the expedition by Degérando and became part of the instructions for François Péron. Degérando laid down the essential procedures to be followed and the problems inherent in assessing unknown tribes. He placed great emphasis on language and the role it played in shaping the world of ideas and the imagination. Suffused with an environmentalist understanding of the differences between peoples, the essay was an ambitious attempt to provide a comprehensive ethnology of non-Europeans.[8]

Through such means, the Pacific and its peoples could be rendered more exactly; all was now grist to the empirical mill. The information being taken back to Europe would break down the myths that had confounded a proper description of the ocean, accurately represent the natural world, and provide the basis for an objective analysis of the environment, resources, people, history, and culture of the region. The full advantages of the Pacific to Europe could then properly be considered.

Even in the eighteenth century, there were those who were less impressed by the outcomes of these great voyages. Horace Walpole's view was that "the Admiralty have dragged the whole ocean, and caught nothing but the fry of ungrown islands, which had slipped through the meshes of the Spaniard's net." He later noted that the *Endeavour* voyagers had "fetched blood of a great whale called Terra Australis incognita, but saw nothing but its tail."[9]

Dr. Johnson, inevitably, was even more cynical. At a dinner in May 1773, he held forth on the merits of Hawkesworth's *Voyages:*

> JOHNSON: "Sir, if you talk of it as a subject of commerce, it will be gainful; if as a book that is to increase human knowledge, I believe there will not be much of that. Hawkesworth can tell only what the voyagers have told him; and they have found very little, only one new animal, I think."
> BOSWELL: "But many insects Sir."
> JOHNSON: "Why, Sir, as to insects, Ray reckons of British insects twenty thousand species. They might have staid at home and discovered enough in that way."

While from a European perspective this may seem a harsh verdict, it is worth addressing the question of the extent to which the empirical process was shaped by, and shaped, constructions of the Pacific.

To some extent the analysis of eighteenth-century science presented here is something of a caricature, since it naturally focuses on those empirical processes of observation, classification, and collecting that were prime concerns on voyages of discovery. They were foraging missions in a geographical and scientific sense, and the emphasis of science as it related to British expansion in the period was taxonomic in focus rather than concerned with the shaping of systems, or explanations for patterns or changes in natural phenomena. It is true that with both Cook and Banks there is speculation about the origins of Polynesian peoples, the formation of ice at sea, and the occurrence of minerals. Nevertheless, it is significantly only with the Forsters that there were attempts to examine wider functional relationships between natural phenomena and an understanding of the causal unity in nature.

Eighteenth-century science contained many subjective elements, and as it moved into the romantic era, it also found a place for the sublime. Kant, Alexander von Humboldt, and even Humphry Davy rejected the limited and rather mechanistic emphasis of the Linnean taxonomy, in which "objects are merely put beside each other and ordered in sequence one after the other." They looked for connections, relationships, and agencies that bound the natural world. In pursuing this course, they believed the empirical process had to be harmonized with an aesthetic one, which recognized and understood the beauties of nature.

When reading the journals of Banks, and even more so of the Forsters, father and son, one is constantly aware of what at first seems an ambivalence in their accounts of people and places. On occasion, the apparently dispassionate scientists lose themselves in poetic descriptions of landscapes and inhabitants, and it seems that they are not altogether clear as to the appropriate idiom or voice in which to describe the novel and often luxuriant landscape. At one level, however, it can be argued that there was no real antithesis between the empirical sciences and aesthetic sensibility in the science of their day. The more one scrutinizes the journals of Johann Forster, the more one realizes the debt owed to him by Alexander von Humboldt. Both held the view that the appearance of landscape affected the customs, culture, and sensibility of a people, and Humboldt acknowledged that it was a Rhineland journey with George Forster in the 1790s that revealed to him the value of scientific voyaging. The subsequent expedition to the Americas and the accounts of the stratified environments of Mount Chimborazo confirmed the holistic vision of nature toward which Johann and George Forster had been feeling their way.[10]

Joseph Banks was certainly less clearly in line to this tradition, but in his *Endeavour Journal* and in some of his later writings on plant transfer, there are indications that perhaps in an unreflective way he too was moving in the direction of Humboldt's view that "nature is herself sublimely eloquent."[11]

Of course, in an empirical sense, precision was brought to the geographical knowledge of the Pacific in the second half of the eighteenth century. The great myths of *Terra australis* and the Northwest Passage were knocked on the head, although in both cases it required quite savage and well-aimed blows to complete the task. Elsewhere, I have argued that many of the expectations contained in these entities were vested in real places, often with frustrating consequences.[12] Outstanding navigational work located the principal island groups in the vast ocean, leaving a limited amount of tidying up work to be done by whalers, traders, and later exploring expeditions. In a taxonomic sense, the flora and fauna of the region were revealed in great and marvelous detail. The Pacific as an entity, however, and the character of its peoples, remained stubbornly prey to speculation and myth.

At one level this should not surprise us. There was a strong tradition of utopian travel writing in Europe in the seventeenth century, and the scientific revolution had changed its character rather than destroyed it.[13] Fictional utopian writing had purported to describe real places and invest them with real people and events. In the eighteenth century, some of this literary energy was diverted into speculative accounts of territories acknowledged to be as yet undiscovered. The more fantastical components were stripped away, and the lands became less places for reflection on the character of the mother country and more venues for commercial exploitation. Although *Terra australis* was one rich repository of such possibilities, the scope of such speculation was much broader than this, encompassing Africa, the North Pacific, and North America.

Voyages of discovery, even those of Cook, did not put an end to this process. Although he had been a midshipman on the *Endeavour* when it cruised the coasts of New South Wales, James Mario Matra did not feel inhibited in describing the region thirteen years later, when recommending it for settlement. This was a land that would support both temperate and tropical agriculture because of its fertility and range of climates. Cotton, tea, coffee, spices, sugar, and tobacco would all grow there, and the land was undoubtedly rich in precious minerals as well.[14] He believed that it united in one territory all the productions of the known world. His plan for settlement in many respects conformed to those for North America almost two centuries earlier.

Sciences and the empirical method therefore provided but one lens through which the ocean was viewed, and in the context of the voyages, scientists were prey to the considerable dualism or ambivalence that I have suggested was intrinsic to late-eighteenth-century science. It was also apparent that voyagers who could be true empiricists in one context, in another could let a priori judgments or even popular myths shape their perceptions. The most bizarre example of this was probably the botanist Commerson, whose paradisal accounts published in *Mercure de France* were merely the strange ramblings of a mind collapsed by some sort of sexual narcosis.

It was characteristic, for example, that when seeking explanations for the cultural development of Pacific peoples, observers generally took refuge in the environmentalist thought that was pervasive in the Enlightenment, informing Montesquieu's *Esprit des Lois,* as well as more populist British works, such as James Dunbar's *Essays on the History of Mankind* and William Robertson's *History of America.*[15] The difficulty with this tradition was that it could be used in the same context both to portray an edenic environment in which a people lived in harmony with each other and with nature, and a more primitive, lethargic, and static society, incapable of civilization. No place illustrated this tension better than Tahiti.

Both Banks and Johann Forster loosely applied this theory to the Tahitians. Thus, Banks wrote of the breadfruit:

> Not that the trees grow here spontaneously but if a man should in the course of his life time plant 10 such trees, which might take the labour of an hour or thereabouts, he would as compleatly fulfill his duty to his own as well as future generations as we natives of less temperate climates can do by toiling in the cold of winter to sow and in the heat of summer to reap the annual produce of our soil, which when once gatherd into the barn must be again resowd and re-reaped as often as the Colds of winter or the heats of Summer return to make such labour disagreable. O fortunati mimium sua bona norint.[16]

Later, the negative cultural consequences of this were drawn out:

> The great facility with which these people have always procurd the nescessaries of life may very reasonably be thought to have originaly sunk them into a kind of indolence which has as it were benumbd their inventions, and prevented their producing such a variety of Arts as might reasonably be expected from the approaches they have made in their manners to the politeness of Europeans. To this may be added a fault which is too frequent even among the politest nations, I mean an invincible attachment to the Customs which they learnt from their forefathers.[17]

The simple life of Australian Aborigines could in turn be traced to the barren environment that provided so little encouragement to agriculture and industry, much less to more refined arts.

Johann Forster was equally, if not more, captivated by the Tahiti landscape: "The Cascades & views are all romantic & the Scenery is every where fine & picturesque, & the valley spacious & fertile, in short a little Garden, planted *au hazard* by the Natives, & fostered by the most benevolent influence of Mother Nature."[18] Not surprisingly, Forster too concluded, "When men live in a genial climate, nature does everything to vigorously promote their happiness; in less favourable climates, happiness requires physical power and creative genius."[19] Even wilder connections were made, for in explaining the difference in skin color between Melanesians and Polynesians, Forster turned for explanation not only to the environment but to the fact that the Tahitians washed themselves more frequently.

As these examples illustrate, an environmentalist approach could accommodate both positive and negative views of Pacific peoples. This depended at least in part on the mood or prejudice of the observer but also on a perception of the tastes of a potential audience. Environmental thought was thus reassuringly elastic, and one would have thought antithetical to empirical analysis. Banks' and Johann Forster's views of the Tahitians corresponded to those of philosophers who argued that tropical climates, while heightening sensuality, depressed industry and therefore could not produce higher forms of civilization. In this respect the Tahitians found themselves in the good company of the peoples of India and China, who were assessed in the same terms during the eighteenth century. Banks found this line of argument sufficiently accommodating to embrace what could in some circumstances be viewed as a contradictory theory, that of the great chain of being, which he deployed to explain cannibalism in New Zealand.[20]

What has come down to us of British perceptions of the Pacific, of course, is largely the more rational material consigned to journals, accounts, and odd letters to the newspaper, such as those at the time of the controversy following publication of Hawkesworth's *Voyages*. This perspective no doubt differed from the more opinionated and subjective accounts that crossed the table at coffeehouses, clubs, and country house salons, where there was less concern for prevailing tastes and traditions. Arguably, the impressions conveyed in this less formal way, which antedated the published accounts, had just as much influence in shaping wider perceptions of the Pacific.

In this context, the scientists and educated officers provided only one source of information—and perhaps not the most plausible and pervasive. There is no way of knowing the extent to which the impressions of the much more numerous junior officers and seamen shaped public opinion or, alternatively, were influenced by prevailing myths and theories. The journals of such men as Robertson on Wallis' voyage, Gilbert, Burney, Samwell, Elliot, and Pickersgill on Cook's, or Tobin on Bligh's second breadfruit expedition were not readily accessible in their day, but no doubt the personal views of their authors circulated among seamen and their contemporaries. There are suggestions that such men had picked up some of the theorizing on the quarterdeck and great cabin in a rendered-down fashion. There is also an indication, however, of a more immediate or primal response to new environments, mediated by such basic factors as the harshness or duration of their time at sea.

Describing the return to Hawai'i from the cold and barren environment of the Arctic, midshipman George Gilbert noted:

> The joy that we experienced on our arrival here is only to be conceived by ourselves or people on like circumstances; for after suffering excess of hunger and a number of other hardships most severly felt by us for the space of near ten months, we had now come into a delightfull climate were [sic] we had almost everything we could wish for, in profusion; and this luxury heightened by our having been at a shorter allowance of provisions this last passage than ever we was at before.21

The crew of the *Dolphin*, wracked by scurvy and depressed by alternatively grueling and tedious months at sea, experienced similar sensations. The sick were even prepared to leave their beds if they could but spend one night ashore. William Wales, on Cook's second voyage, noted that Bougainville's descriptions of Tahiti were colored by long months at sea and in a rather prosaic tone noted than even England appeared beautiful to him after long voyages.22

A similar experience affected the young third mate, George Tobin, who accompanied Bligh on his second breadfruit expedition. His rapturous accounts of the island contrasted with Bligh's prosaic journal entries, and at the end of his first day in Tahiti he summed up the experience in a way that probably reflected the views of the majority of the crew: "As the sun declined, the Canoes returned on shore, leaving by far the most desirable part of their freight among our crews, which after the trying self-denial of a long voyage, shut out from the dearest solace life affords, could not but be truly acceptable."23 This feeling was captured in his delightful, naïve watercolors of the Society Islands.

It is appropriate to end with the breadfruit expeditions, as in one way they illustrate a broader point. For twenty years, it has frustrated me that the historiographical and popular focus of the voyage has been on the mutiny. This is even the case with Greg Dening's brilliant recent reconstruction.24 In all such accounts, the lure of Tahiti combined with a problem in shipboard management to produce an explosive situation. But the truly remarkable aspect of the voyage is the fact that long before the mutiny, the lure of Tahiti had operated on Sir Joseph Banks, West Indian planters, and members of the Pitt administration with such power that they were prepared to invest in the magnificently fanciful voyage. One could argue that the voyages were scientific enterprises conforming to Banks' theory about plants thriving in similar climatic regimes and therefore fitting into his schemes of plant interchange. But surely the idea was more related to his particular observations of Tahitian life than to any scientific information about the physiology or morphology of the plant itself. Behind the expeditions lay a mythical conception of a lifestyle attached to a luxuriant landscape, and a belief that this lifestyle could in a sense be transshipped with the plants. The irony that in such an enlightened age it would benefit slaves seems to have escaped the Bath Butterfly.

NOTES

1. Strange to Banks, 3 December 1785, Banks Correspondence, *Kew, B.C.* I, 215. The Instructions are in *India Office Library, Home Misc.* 494, 420–422, 1 December 1785.

2. King to Banks, October 1780, British Museum of Natural History, D.T.C I, 304.

3. From *Voyage autour du monde*, cited in Urs Bitterli, *Cultures in Conflict* (Cambridge: Polity, 1989), 159–160.

4. W. H. Roberston, "The Endeavour Voyage and Observations of the Transit of Venus," *Employ'd as a Discoverer*, ed. J.V.S. Megaw (Sydney: A. H. Reed and A. W. Reed, 1971), 114–116.

5. These collecting activities are described in David Mackay, "Agents of Empire: The Banksian Collectors and Evaluation of New Lands," in *Visions of Empire: Voyages, Botany, and Representations of Nature*, ed. Peter Reill and David Miller (New York: Cambridge University Press, 1996).

6. Instructions dated 22 February 1791, *Add. MSS* 33979, 75–78.

7. Douglas Oliver, *Return to Tahiti: Bligh's Second Breadfuit Voyage* (Carlton: Melbourne University Press, 1988), 34.

8. See Miranda Hughes, "Tall Tales or True Stories? Baudin, Péron, and the Tasmanians, 1802," in *Nature in Its Greatest Extent*, ed. Roy MacLeod and Philip F. Rehbock (Honolulu: University of Hawai'i Press, 1988), 65–86.

9. Cited in J. L. Abbott, *John Hawkesworth, Eighteenth-Century Man of Letters* (Madison: University of Wisconsin Press, 1982), 154.

10. Malcolm Nicolson, "Alexander von Humboldt and the Geography of Vegetation," in *Romanticism and the Sciences*, ed. Andrew Cunningham and Nicholas Jardine (New York: Cambridge University Press, 1990).

11. C. J. Glacken, *Traces on the Rhodian Shore: Nature and Culture in Western Thought from Ancient Times to the End of the Eighteenth Century* (Berkeley: University of California Press, 1967), 179.

12. David Mackay, "The Burden of Terra Australis: Experiences of Real and Imagined Lands," in *Maps and Metaphors,* ed. Hugh Johnston and Robin Fisher (Vancouver: University of British Columbia Press, 1995).

13. See David Fausett, *Writing the New World: Imaginary Voyages and Utopias of the Great Southern Land* (New York: Syracuse University Press, 1993).

14. J. M. Matra to Lord North, 23 August 1783, Colonial Office Papers, C.O. 201/1, 57–61.

15. This strand of thought is discussed in Glacken, *Traces on the Rhodian Shore.*

16. "Oh greatly happy, if they but knew their own happiness." *The Endeavour Journal of Joseph Banks,* ed. J. C. Beaglehole, 2 vols. (Sydney: Angus and Robertson, 1962) 1:341–342.

17. Ibid., 1:352.

18. *The Resolution Journal of Johann Reinhold Forster, 1772–1775,* ed. Michael E. Hoare, 4 vols. (London: Hakluyt Society, 1982) 3:505.

19. Glacken, *Traces on the Rhodian Shore,* 615.

20. Banks, *Endeavour Journal,* 2:20.

21. *Captain Cook's Final Voyage: The Journal of Midshipman George Gilbert,* ed. Christine Holmes (Horsham: Caliban Books, 1982), 99–100.

22. *The Journals of Captain James Cook on his voyages of discovery,* ed. J. C. Beaglehole, 4 vols. (Cambridge: Cambridge University Press, 1961) 2:795.

23. Cited in Oliver, *Return to Tahiti,* 51.

24. Greg Dening, *Mr. Bligh's Bad Language* (Cambridge: Cambridge University Press, 1992).

8

A TRIBAL ENCOUNTER

The Presence and Properties of Common-Law Language in the Discourse of Colonization in the Early Modern Period

P. G. McHugh

Through 1840, the indigenous Maori chiefs of New Zealand put their mark to a document that became known as the Treaty of Waitangi. This pact, in its Maori version—the one signed by the vast majority of tribal signatories—purported to cede the *kawanatanga* of the country, reserving the chiefly *rangatiratanga*. The English version described the chiefs as relinquishing their sovereignty in return for a guarantee of their property rights and the conferral of British subjecthood on Maori. The political history of Maori since then is largely a tale of tribal attempts to vindicate their Treaty rights from a position of growing subjection and, as the nineteenth century turns into the twentieth, increasing political and economic marginalization. Not surprisingly, such efforts have involved recourse to the colonizer's courts, as well as activity in other fora, including the theater of war. The purpose of this essay is to consider aspects of the common law's involvement in that tale of unwilling subjection and attempts at vindication.

So far as it is possible to reduce a complex historical process into a pithy encapsulation, it might be said that the history of the response of the Anglo-Commonwealth common law to tribal societies is one whereby a general discourse (of the period prior to the mid/late nineteenth century), which did not have tribal peoples at its center, turns into a more specific discourse. The emergence of this specific discourse was largely facilitated by the coincidence of the positivization of common-law practice with a certain phase of British colonial history. Initially, the newly positivized common law, now being required to take a more specific stand than previously, excluded tribal societies from its area of justiciable concern. Later, one finds this resistance seeping out of the case law, which eventually begins to take an increasingly responsive, less dismissive attitude toward the position of tribal societies under the Crown's governance.

There is a tremendous amount of history swirling in that encapsulation, but at the center of it is a conception of the common law as a language. For Anglo-Commonwealth lawyers, the common law has always been the language through and by which lawyers describe the world and imbue it with meaning. It is a language with its own possibilities and impossibilities. As a living language, the common law contains possibilities and meanings that may shift and change over time. The common law, P. Goodrich reminds us,

> has presented itself historically as a system of memories: the law is tradition and it is precedent but it is more than that, it is immemorial usage; it is practice reverting to "time out of mind," custom that language alone remembers. . . . The language of law is depicted as a language of record, a perfect language that harbors true reference, that corresponds to real events, that is itself a monument, a memorial, a vestige or a relic of previous wisdom and prior judgment. The inhabitants of the legal institution are thus custodians not only of a tradition of rules and of texts but also of linguistic forms and of techniques of interpretation that will unlock the memories of legal language. Within the tradition of the language the lawyer is supposed to uncover the forms of life and of ethical practice that the institution was established to record and repeat. The institution was not only to reproduce the memorials of an authorized life, the reliquary of which legal language was the register, but it was also, as a lived and living tradition, to produce, to create new forms.[1]

The concern of this essay is with the character of the general discourse of the common law in the period prior to the positivization of legal practice during the second half of the nineteenth century. From the mid-nineteenth century, transformations in the nature of Anglo-Commonwealth legal practice invited the formation of the more specific discourse that is familiar not only to lawyers but, these days, to most students of New Zealand history. That specific discourse characterizes and has come to be applied to New Zealand's colonial history from the foundation of British sovereignty in 1840. Yet, despite its currency, that recently excavated legal story depicts early New Zealand history in "revisionist" ways, which discomfort some historians.[2] This discomfort is in no small measure well placed and may be explained briefly by way of prelude to this essay.

It can be said from the outset that the "revisionist" legal account embodies features utterly typical of common-law language. It constructs a narrative that is both positivist and Whiggish. It is Whiggish because it deploys a technique that implants the present into the past, reconstructing what purports to be a historical report of legal doctrine by reference to the present.[3] The past is described in terms of its progression toward its present, if not perfect then certainly perfectible, doctrinal condition. Those actors who are seen retrospectively to have stood obstructively in this path—Chief Justice Prendergast of the late nineteenth century, for example—become part of the demonology. Heroes and villains—stylistic devices that are the stuff of myth, creation stories, and tales of secular redemption spun by the legal clerisy—abound. The legal narrative is organized around the situation of the present such that it is the present that makes the past possible.

The legal account is also positivist in that it views law as a code, as a set of commands that are retrieved from the records of the past.[4] These commands are embedded in what positivist memory regards as the exclusive reliquary of legal doctrine: case law and statute. The narrative is thus exhumed from these sources, as though some wider, overarching history were interred in these particularist texts.

Yet to describe the "revisionist" legal narrative as Whiggish and positivist is not to disparage its worth within the interpretive community[5] to which it is addressed—which is to say, a professionalized legal community. The difficulty, if that is the right term, arises when a report written within one interpretive community is transplanted into the discourse of another. When, for example, the Court of Appeal is required by statute to apply the "principles of the Treaty of Waitangi" to the resolution of claims relating to the corporatization of Crown assets, it is being invited to implant the present into the past—to see the past in terms of problems fixed squarely in the present. Small wonder, then, that an 1840 text finds itself associated with concepts such as "good faith," "fiduciary," and "partnership," terms that do not appear in the Treaty texts. The same can be said of the Waitangi Tribunal Reports, which make so much use of history yet which must deal with an agenda located in the demands of the present. The texts generated from such particular situations have considerable value in contemporary discursive practices, but these are not texts that go any way toward an interpretation of meaning.

Legal method has a routine grammar and vocabulary, which the legal clerisy deploys with ready facility, yet this language that lawyers use in describing the situation of tribal societies is a contemporary one. The legal and ostensibly historical account of Anglo-American settler states' relations with tribal societies takes no account of the history of the common law as a language. The accounts that are constructed and that purport to be historically founded use modern linguistic techniques to describe the past: It is a technique that assumes the collocability of "aboriginal rights" with "common law," as though the common law were always (and even today) a rights-based jurisprudence. That is a disputable supposition. It uses reconstructive materials (case law and statute), which today are regarded as the exclusive transmitters of legal memory, yet which might not have performed such a heavy-duty function in an earlier stage of common-law language. The legal imagination of previous generations may well dwell in texts beyond the narrow compass of relevance held these days. Notions of legal obligation—law as "command"—are brought to bear upon the historical record as though the actors of earlier times shared the same position as lawyers today. The question "Was the Crown *legally obliged* to enter into a treaty relations with Maori or the Iroquois Confederacy?" is a modern one, which we cannot safely assume would have been posed, or even made sense, a century and a half ago.

The History and Properties of the Common Law

Locke's treatise *Some Thoughts Concerning Education* (1693) advised young men to familiarize themselves with the language of the law: "It would be strange to suppose an English gentleman should be so ignorant of the law of his country. This, whatever station he is in, is so requisite that, from a justice of a peace to a minister of state, I know no place he can well fill without it." During the early seventeenth century, the common law was almost the exclusive language of political discourse; however, after the "crisis of the common law" prior to the Civil War, other languages of discourse emerged: languages of classical republicanism, social contract, and the proto-positivist. This public face of common-law utterance contrasted with the private, more ritualized sites of formal language use, but it signified the common law's presence in a polemicized context of *move* rather than *mentalité*. Relatedly, it should be recollected that governance in Britain and the colonies during the early modern period was mainly an adjudicative matter. While there existed a multiplicity of jurisdictions and, certainly in the colonial courts of the seventeenth century, a variety of types of law (such as the borough, manorial, and Mosaic), the common law asserted its own jurisdictional superjacency. It thus insisted upon its ultimate status as the law governing Englishmen and colonists.

The common law asserted its jurisdictional ascendance over realm and colony, most especially in matters of governance, as the common law was the source of the ancient constitution. So far as political discourse of the period was concerned, the common law represented a language embodying a certain method of reasoning (based on custom, immemoriality, and community) with an argumentative but, after the Civil War, by no means exclusive availability. In its ritualized fora, it remained largely a procedurally and remedially minded language, lacking any rights-based orientation. So much as the common law could be said to have had any conception of "rights," this lay mainly in the sense of the subject's entitlement to what might be termed "procedural justice," as opposed to Grotian and Lockean depictions of rights as inherent and substantive. In particular, this meant access to the common-law courts, wherein a lawyer's artificial reasoning could be deployed through the grid of pleadings and remedies to produce a "community-minded" result. Not being a "rights"-based or "command"-oriented language, talk of "legal obligation" would strike a common lawyer of the early modern period as rather strange. Indeed, the very concept of behavior being dictated by a perceived sense of its *legal* character is very much grounded in the positivist view of law as command with sanction. There is little to suggest that individuals in the early modern period distinguished "legal" from any other type of "obligation" in the way that is commonplace to us today, where we routinely separate "legal," "moral," and, say, "religious" obligations.

The common law, as the expression of immemorial custom, was seen as being grounded in community, without any rigid doctrine of precedent such as it emerged from the mid-nineteenth century. Thus, the common law's resolution of disputes hardly needed to focus on the sources used to justify decision. There were a multiplicity of what legal method today might construe as "sources" available to explain the results reached by common-law language. These sources, however, were not so much rules as a vocabulary of the reasoning process and are more accurately viewed in that light.[6] The common law itself, its immemorial and customary reasoning process, was inherently legitimate and needed no authority to justify its resolution of disputes, filtered as they were through the elaborate system of pleading and procedure. The common law conceded the pluralism that existed within the realm, but at least until the mid-eighteenth century, such noncentralized sites of adjudication and law were tolerated. The movement to stifle such pluralism, a project in pursuit of which the common lawyers successfully enlisted Parliamentary assistance during the mid-nineteenth-century legal reforms, was not in any effective condition until the end of the eighteenth century. As E. P. Thompson has reminded us, the community that the common law served through the early modern period was always associated with the Whig gentry.[7] This was the community that had been reared and educated in its tradition. The vindication of its jurisdictional ascendancy through the late eighteenth and into the early nineteenth century was a collusive byproduct of the Whig project and a precondition for the emergence of the imperial nation-state.

Tolerated diversity, community, immemoriality, custom, the present-minded use of the past, time without temporality, argument by analogy and example, a procedural and remedial preoccupation—these are the hallmarks of common-law language in its classical and transitional phases.

The Voyaging Common-Law Imagination and Tribal Societies

The cases of the prepositivist period that are used by contemporary positivism to construct the common-law narrative concerning tribal societies usually start with *Calvin's Case* (1606) and end with the judgments of the U.S. Supreme Court in the 1830s and the New Zealand case of *R v. Symonds* (1847). These cases span more than two centuries. Through this period, the language of judicial decision becomes, to the modern eye at least, less ornate and stylized. The vocabulary becomes less Latinate and less spiritually inflected. Residual medieval traces diminish through that period. In many respects, however, those changes in style and expression are no more than decorative. When they are put to one side, there is a remarkable similarity in the character of judicial argument. Reasoning proceeds by way of analogy rather than by obligatory (i.e., the positivist technician's) reference to sources from which derive fixed and largely inflexible rules. Although the intensity of this analogy-drawing tends to diminish, it remains central to the language through the period. The texture of the language undoubtedly changes, but nonetheless, even as late as the 1830s and 1840s there is a substantial consistency to the shape of judicial argument. Rules are used without apparent concern for their formal "source." To the extent that "sources" are calculatedly invoked, it is to display the long-established character of the rule. Hence, historical parallels and (what we would see as) anecdotal examples are routinely and nonhierarchically given alongside cases and references to such treatise writers as Bracton, St. Germain, Grotius, Baudin, and, toward the latter half of the period covered by the cases, Coke, Hale, Pufendorf, Selden, Locke, and Blackstone, as well as such American writers as Kent and Story. The historical parallels that the judges draw can be ancient, medieval, biblical, or involve non-English examples. The point of their technique is not to establish the authority of the various rules through the analogy. The analogy, in other words, is not the rule. Rather, the analogous reasoning highlights the deep-seated antiquity of any particular rule. The rule thus gets its binding element from its source in custom and/or usage legitimated by immemoriality. All judgments reveal what seems an instinctive necessity to give any proposition of law an unoriginable historical anchor. The point of the analogy is that it illustrates the ancientness without claiming to be the origination of the particular point at hand.

Besides this form of reasoning by analogy, the cases also reveal a concern with the common law as a procedurally oriented language. Where analogy is drawn through previous cases, the parallel is usually framed in terms of the writs and pleading of the earlier case. This is particularly so where the case is plainly being resolved at the first level of judgment (the pleadings stage) rather than at what may seem a substantive level beyond that. Relatedly, the envisualization of "rights" as importing procedural justice is continually encountered. In the cases of the eighteenth century—the transitional period—there is emergent talk of individuals possessing inherent, absolute (Lockean) rights in the sense that such rights might be understood today. The usual character of such "rights," however, is to require that a situation be achieved a particular way, through a particular procedure. This procedural orientation remains the case, despite occasional judicial resort to such rights-based writers as Grotius, Locke, and Pufendorf. By the early nineteenth century, the notion of rights as inherent has a strong and growing foothold in the language of the common law, but in many regards this is no more than a rhetorical presence, for, at the end of the day, the "rights" to which the courts' judgments give rise remain largely procedural in character. (This remains a feature of common-law language even today. The common law has never especially settled into a rights-based jurisprudence.)

This may be no more than to say that even as late as 1847 we are still dealing with a common law that retains central elements of its classical form. Nonetheless, that conclusion of itself has important implications for the way one views British relations with tribal societies during the early modern period.

Calvin's Case (1606)

Calvin's Case or *The Case of the Post-Nati* (1606) concerned the status in England of Scotsmen born after the accession of James I to the English throne. This case was argued in Exchequer Chamber[8] before the Lord Chancellor and twelve judges, including Sir Edward Coke, Chief Justice of the Common Pleas (who subsequently reported the case). It was resolved unanimously that a Scotsman born after the accession was not an alien in England and owed allegiance to James I as King of England so much as he was King of Scotland. Coke's report of the case condenses the argumentation and grounds for resolution. In the jurisprudence of aboriginal rights, this case is traditionally investigated for its comments on the effects of conquest and the status of infidel societies and their laws.

In reaching its conclusion, the report ranges freely through a variety of "authorities." These authorities are never characterized as determinative so much as illustrative of a legal proposition. Their citation is usually prefaced by the phrase "and it appeareth in. . . ." Such writers as Bracton, Fortescue, Aristotle, Virgil, St. Germain, and Fleta, to list some of the notable luminaries, are consulted and cited. Statutes, cases, and records of writs and court proceedings, as well as historical episodes, are also used. These "authorities" mingle freely with one another, without any evident sense that one is hierarchically superior to the other so long as they are establishing the venerability of the legal point at hand.

Somerset v. Stewart (1772)

This case concerned the status of slaves in England. The argument for the plaintiff invokes such writers as Grotius, Pufendorf, and Locke, all of whom by then were associated with the tradition of viewing individuals in a rights-bearing way. Yet the structure of the plaintiff's argument shows that this invocation is part of a rhetorical flourish that includes a hackneyed Whig metaphor:

> The humanity of modern times has mitigated this extreme rigour of slavery; shall an attempt to introduce perpetual servitude here to this island hope for countenance? Will not all the other mischiefs of mere utter servitude revive, if once the idea of absolute property, under the immediate sanction of the laws of this country, extend itself to those who have been brought over to a soil whose air is deemed too pure for slaves to breathe in it; but the laws, the genius and spirit of the constitution, forbid the approach of slavery.[9]

While rights-bearing talk has infiltrated common-law language by this time, as in the wider discursive practices of contemporaneous political discourse, it mingles with ancient constitutionalism.[10] A new conception of "right" appears. The right is inherent but it is now "substantive" in that it involves more than, yet, paradoxically, is also tied into, the procedural orientation of the common law. These substantive rights, now becoming styled as if they are as inherent as the entitlement to procedural justice, draw on the language of previous generations and claim origination from (among other sources) the common law's ancient constitution. In *Somerset v. Stewart*, the argumentative appropriability of rights-based talk has not displaced the basic conception of the common law as a language of pleadings and remedies grounded in immemorial custom. Having made the introductory allusions, counsel for the plaintiff then comes to the heart of his argument. The immemorial custom of the realm, he maintains, has never known slavery, the nearest to it being villeinage tenure. This question of villeinage (in gross) occupies much of the subsequent argumentation. All counsel are agreed that the tenure has been abolished, however their various positions on the question reveal how time and the past become manipulable through common-law language. The plaintiff's argument is that villeinage was disappearing and had no more than residual status at the time of the conquest because this element of slavery went against the grain of the common law. Indeed, its disappearance is attributed to operation of the common law, which, to the extent it is seen to have once condoned any such unregulated and arbitrary servitude, did so to a very circumscribed extent and prior to the threshold of immemoriality (i.e., 1189) at that. This shows how the language of the common law was able to deploy a style of rhetoric by which the present (antislavery sentiment) was used to portray the past. The defendant's response to that argument is to suspend temporality. The notion that the common law has rejected or expunged any element akin to slavery is countered by the notion that what the law has expunged, it may again revive. Where the plaintiff's argument places the present in the past, the defendant's puts the past (or at least its potential reenactability) into the present. By the defendant's account, the changes in the organization of English society, the process by which villeinage seeped out of common-law language, might never have happened. The inference is that the present is doing no more than keeping the past at bay. In common-law language, one senses the past and present becoming interchangeable.

Johnson v. M'Intosh (1823)

The U.S. Supreme Court considered the character of title to land purchased by settlers directly from the aboriginal Indian owners in *Johnson v. M'Intosh* (1823). This case and several subsequent cases became well known to colonial administrators and were available and read in the New Zealand colony during the 1840s. The status of direct purchases by settlers from tribal owners had been as controversial a question throughout the seventeenth and eighteenth centuries in North America as subsequently it became in the colony of New Zealand during the 1840s.

Johnson v. M'Intosh asserted the government's exclusive power to silence the tribal title by purchase, holding this "preemptive right" to be a rule of common law. This was not regarded as any impairment of the tribes' rights to their ancestral lands, except to the extent of this limitation on its alienability. On that basis, this case came to be regarded as a cornerstone to contemporary doctrines of aboriginal rights. I do not want to excavate that rather overworked seam in this essay, so much as consider features of the language by which Chief Justice John Marshall described the (American) common-law position. The Chief Justice's judgment opens with this significant passage:

> As the right of society to prescribe those rules by which property may be acquired and preserved is not, and cannot be drawn into question; as the title to lands, especially, is and must be admitted to depend entirely on the law of the nation in which they lie; it will be necessary, in pursuing this inquiry, to examine, not singly those principles of abstract justice, which the Creator of all things has impressed on the mind of his creature man, and which are admitted to regulate, in a great degree, the rights of civilized nations, whose perfect independence is acknowledged: but those principles also which our government has adopted in the particular case, and given us as the rule for our decision.[11]

This passage resonates with a Lockean hum.[12] It asserts the applicability of principles of natural law embodied in the *jus gentium,* or law of nations, which law is reflected in the practice of the European states. Also, it recognizes that these principles are applicable in that they have been adopted by the government of the United States. What then follows is an extended history of the formality of Anglo-American presence on the continent. Law is treated as immanent in the British Crown's formal behavior—its charters, proclamations, and various grants under the Royal Seal. This formality is outlined chronologically, but any sense of historical sequence or order is simply one of organizational convenience. It becomes plain that this is because the common-law doctrine of the government's "preemptive right" to silence aboriginal title is an ancient practice demonstrated by rather than arising from this pattern of formality. In the end, Chief Justice Marshall locates the "preemptive right" in the feudal theory of the British constitution, according to which the subject's title to land derives from some grant by the sovereign. The historical accounts Marshall provides simply demonstrate that ancient principle.

So far as Indian title to their land is concerned, by and large this case treats the property rights as procedural in character. Marshall does not go the whole Lockean hog to hold that the Indians have property only over those lands that they have reduced into arable use. Indeed, Marshall never makes a prolonged exploration of the Indian right of property. His occasional asides and a brusque statement toward the end of the judgment ("It has never been contended that the Indian title amounted to nothing") [13] presume the existence of a tribal property right. He clearly subscribes, however, to the Lockean position that the function of law in a civil society is to define and protect property rights. So it is that he expresses the means by which settlers acquire title to land in a colony: Title is gained through the settlers' own positive laws—positive in the sense of there being laws that ameliorate the natural law of property acquisition. These laws embody the feudal doctrine of tenures (Crown grants). Yet also he recognizes that the procedures of American law are available to protect the Indian title, as through an action for ejectment.[14] What is important, then, is not the property right (which is incontrovertible) so much as the means that the positive law provides for settlers to vindicate it. He does not say that those settlers who have purchased land directly from the Indians have no property rights. He speculates that those property rights are under the tribal protection and laws—the tribes' own system of positive laws, as it were. However, they are certainly not afforded any protection by the Anglo-American common law. The plaintiffs who have purchased land from the Indian chiefs, and who can show no Crown or government patent in support, do not "exhibit a title which can be sustained in the courts of the United States."[15]

R v. Symonds (1847)

The judgments of the New Zealand Supreme Court in *R v. Symonds* (1847) display similar characteristics redolent of classical common-law method. This case presented the same issue as that in the American case *Johnson v. M'Intosh,* namely, the status of direct land purchases by British subjects from tribal owners. In opening his renowned judgment, Justice Chapman provides a statement of "the principles upon which our conclusion is based."[16] This lengthy passage merits reproduction in full:

> The intercourse of civilized nations, and especially of Great Britain, with the aboriginal Natives of America and other countries, during the last two centuries, has gradually led to the adoption and affirmation by the Colonial Courts of certain established principles of law applicable to such intercourse. Although these principles may at times have been lost sight of, yet animated by the humane spirit of modern times, our colonial Courts, and the Courts of such of the United States of America as have adopted the common law of England, have invariably affirmed and supported them; so that at this day, a line of judicial decision, the current of legal opinion, and above all,

the settled practice of the colonial Governments, have con-
curred to clothe with certainty and precision what would otherwise have remained vague and unsettled. These principles
are not the creation or invention of the colonial Courts. They
flow not from what an American writer has called the "vice of
judicial legislation." They are in fact to be found among the
earliest settled principles of our law; and they are in part de-
duced from those higher principles, from charters made in
conformity with them, acquiesced in even down to the charter
of our own Colony; and from the letter of treaties with Native
tribes, wherein those principles have been asserted and acted
upon.[17]

The case was decided in 1847, at the very cusp of the positivization of
legal language. Though one can detect traces, there is on the whole little,
if any, flavor of that in this exposition of the style of judicial reasoning that
Justice Chapman proposes using in the case. When he itemizes the
sources of the common-law rule, it is not the "line of judicial decision"
that is determinative but "*above all*, the settled practice of the colonial
Governments" (emphasis added). This practice—the custom of the
colonies, as it were—conforms with "the earliest settled principles of our
law." His judgment progresses to explain that these "higher principles" to
which he has been referring are a combination of the feudal doctrine of
tenures and the wider rule from which the feudal principle came, namely,
the exclusive power of the Crown to acquire new territory.[18] The adjective
"higher" seems to be another way of saying "ancient," for later in the judgment he restates those principles:

Anciently, it seems to have been assumed, that notwithstanding
the rights of the Native race, and of course subject to such
rights, the Crown, as against its own subjects, had the full and
absolute dominion over the soil as a necessary consequence of
territorial jurisdiction. Strictly speaking, this is perhaps de-
ducible from the principle of our law.[19]

As Justice Chapman seasons his judgment with what seem somewhat
randomly selected historical examples (drawn from the North American
colonies and Port Phillip), demonstrating the application of the Crown's
"pre-emptive right," he makes it plain that he regards them as illustrative
of those principles "of the common law as applied and adopted from the
earliest times."[20] The formula that he is using to justify the application of
the rule of preemption is the classic common-law mixture of immemori-

ality and custom grounded in the situation of community demonstrated by analogous historical (but ahistoricized) examples.

Though there is this reliance on classical common-law technique (as opposed to a positivist trawl for commands), this is not to say that the judgment is free from signs of the trend toward a positivized language. For instance, Justice Chapman elsewhere provides justification for the preemption rule by reference to "our peculiar relations with the Native race, and out of our obvious duty of protecting them, to as great an extent as possible, from the evil consequences of the intercourse which we have introduced to them, or have imposed upon them." To allow the direct purchase of native land by settlers would "be virtually to confiscate the lands of the Natives in a very short time." Hence, from "the protective character of the rule, then, it is entitled to respect on moral grounds, no less than to judicial support on strictly legal grounds."[21] The sharpness of this distinction between "legal" and "moral" obligation is not so marked and carefully pronounced in common-law language of an earlier period.[22]

With *Symonds,* I suggest we are dealing with a case that sits astride two phases in common-law language, one a classical tradition formulating law in terms of immemoriality, custom, procedure, and reasoning by ahistoricized analogy, the other anticipating the modernized language's fixation with commands, "sources," and "rights." But through that change into positivist form, the common law retains elements of its classical features, namely, an incapacity to deal with temporal change except in a Whiggish and Darwinian sense of it being ever-perfecting. The procedural orientation is never removed from its logic, despite the rhetoric of "rights" as inherent and substantive.

Conclusion

The common law has been seen as a language, with its own ways of depicting the world. The common law, in its classical period, was largely a way or process of reasoning that drew on notions of immemoriality, custom, and community through procedurally oriented lenses. In its transitional phase, attempts were made to implant an external reason into its language. This was signified by rights-talk of the seventeenth century, which depicts rights as substantive and inherent rather than procedural in the classical common-law way.

The community within which the common law operated, however, was one in which tribal polities hardly qualified for membership. To the extent that the common law spoke of tribal societies, it necessarily occurred within the context of this exclusion. The tribal presence in common-law speech acts was largely a passive one. There as the "other," their role was to assist the reasoning process of the common law as it applied within its own community. Throughout the early modern period, the common law's role in relation to tribal societies lay, if anywhere, in its provision of procedural guidance: The title to lands occupied by the tribes could only be acquired through Crown agency, Crown governance could only be asserted over the tribes with their formal consent, and both propositions required the phenomenon known as "treaty-making."

But such principles of the common law were more for the guidance of settler authorities than as a means for conferring substantive rights on the tribes. It is not until what I have termed the transitional period of the common law—during one of the most active and fertile periods in the history of Western political discourse—that any suggestion of tribal rights as inherent or substantive began to appear. This is a process that continued and indeed was enhanced by the positivization of legal language through the first half of the nineteenth century.

Although I have eschewed reference to the Treaty of Waitangi in this essay, I want to finish open endedly. The vague character of both texts of the Treaty is well known. Part of that inspecificity operates at the level of "rights," the English text making no more than an extension (in the third article) to Maori of all the "Rights and privileges of British subjects." The inspecificity of what those "rights and privileges" entailed was, I suggest, a consequence of the inability of the Crown's authorities to think in the obsessive rights-based way of today. Moreover, I suggest there was also a belief that to extend the "rights and privileges" of British subjecthood to Maori was conceived as being enough in itself to bring them within the community of the common law. This is far from saying that it was intended that the common law was to supplant Maori customary law in their relations between themselves. In their relations with government, however, Maori were seen as being provided with access to the same language—the language of the common law—as that which applied within the settler community. The history of the Treaty of Waitangi, or more appropriately, its "afterlife," has been largely a tale of the settler community's failure, indeed inability, to include Maori within the community of its law. One might see Prendergast's judgment in *Wi Parata v. The Bishop of Wellington* (1877) in a context of such inability.[23]

The position taken here is not to be regarded as any recantation from subscription to any notion of "common-law aboriginal rights." Although I have stressed the point that we take too easily the collocability of "common law" with "aboriginal rights" and inject contemporaneous linguistic practice into that whole notion, the approach offered here strengthens rather than undermines the essential ingredients of the common-law doctrine. How?

First, it can absolve lawyers from responsibility for the past. Instead of rummaging through the past for a set of "principles" or commands, a task in respect of which an obligation is implicitly being assumed to extract (or to negate) coherent "presentist"-oriented doctrine, the past can be seen in terms of its own rather than our contemporary notions of legal obligation. Once that position is taken, the lawyer is relieved from the pressing intellectual necessities and agenda of contemporary linguistic practice and is able to review material in a manner less aggressively preoccupied with his own probative dictates. For instance, legal accounts of aboriginal rights have always had a somewhat apologetic attitude toward the deficient presence of case law in the early modern period. Consequently, a lot of argumentative weight tends to be placed on cases like *Calvin's Case* and cases in the U.S. Supreme Court during the 1820s and 1830s, much more reliance than the historic material suggests was made during the early modern period, and certainly much more reliance than the cases may be able to bear in terms of the doctrinal consequences extracted from them. When lawyers constructing a doctrine of aboriginal rights venture beyond the material that today would be termed the strictly legal, an element of defensiveness creeps into the account. A purpose of this essay is to suggest that such attitudes are unnecessary once explicit account is taken of the common law as a language with history. Part of that history includes the presence of common-law language in sites of utterance from which by today's linguistic practices it might be regarded as either excluded or, at least, would be more distinctively and disjunctively emplaced. In other words, law's presence in the discourse of colonization, though identifiable, is not necessarily as discrete an element of the past as we would make of it in our own discourse today. This has consequences for the type of evidence available to those wishing to provide a historical account of the common law's position with regard to tribal societies. It means that the common-law elements in the discourse of colonization can be appreciated.

A second, associated consequence results from this approach. It may seem somewhat paradoxical that a strengthened notion of a common-law doctrine of aboriginal rights emerges. The lawyer is able to range more freely through the historic material, becoming less concerned with identification of particular speech acts as "legal" (regardable) or otherwise (disregardable). Moreover, once material is freed from the obligation to submit a command or element incorporable into a twentieth-century code, it actually tenders evidence of the presence of law more freely and more plainly. The lawyer need not search for a command when none is there to be prized out. One is able, instead, to see more clearly the legal element to the relations between British settler and tribal societies, and one is able to see its pervasive presence. Relieved of a Whiggish probative method and burden, the past actually becomes more probatively fertile. This also has consequences for the way we view the presence of law in a present-day Treaty discourse where positivized legal practice has given it a disjunctive presence. At what is perhaps a simple level, to view law as a language of possibilities highlights its function as a provider of moves available to participants in Treaty discourse. It gives a heightened awareness of the rhetorical and methodological elements in the legal aspect.

The utter contemporaneity of the legal agenda coupled to the positivistic idea of law as code/command also has consequences for the way in which law might be seen to operate within New Zealand society. If the present requires recourse to the past—as it does so strongly in Treaty discourse—then the positivized present will characterize that past as one that commands. This, in turn, invests legal language with the capacity to transcend the present and make projections into the future. Law, then, has the same function as myth. Yet when one speaks of the common law as a language, it is more than one of the many languages of political discourse: It is the language for the legitimation of the exercise of state power.

NOTES

This essay is an edited version of a longer article related to work in progress.

1. P. Goodrich, *Languages of Law: From Logics of Memory to Nomadic Masks* (London: Weidenfeld and Nicolson, 1990), preface.
2. M.P.K. Sorrenson, "Towards a Radical Reinterpretation of New Zealand History: The Role of the Waitangi Tribunal," in *Waitangi: Maori and Pakeha Perspectives of the Treaty of Waitangi*, ed. I. H. Kawharu (Auckland: Oxford University Press, 1989), 159–160; M. Belgrave, "The Recognition of Aboriginal Tenure in New Zealand, 1840–1860" (paper presented to the American Historical Association, Washington D.C., 27 December 1992), 3; James Belich, "Hobson's Choice," *New Zealand Journal of History* 24 (1990): 206.
3. H. Butterfield, *The Whig Interpretation of History* (1931; New York: W. W. Norton, 1955), refers to the "pathetic fallacy" as "the result of abstracting things

from their historical context—estimating and organising the historical story by a system of direct reference to the present" (30). This "fallacy" is central to common-law method.

4. A.W.B. Simpson, "The Common Law and Legal Theory," *Legal Theory and Legal History* (London: Hambledon Press, 1986), 359.

5. The notion of an interpretive community within which a language of discourse is spoken is taken from Stanley Fish, *Doing What Comes Naturally: Change, Rhetoric, and the Practice of Theory in Literary and Legal Studies* (Oxford: Clarendon Press, 1989).

6. Michael Lobban, *Common Law and English Jurisprudence* (Oxford: Clarendon Press, 1991), 6.

7. E. P. Thompson, *Whigs and Hunters* (London: Allen Lane, 1975).

8. The Court of Exchequer Chamber was used increasingly during the sixteenth and seventeenth centuries as a forum to which difficult matters of law in any of the common-law courts might be referred for discussion by all the justices of the King's Bench and Common Pleas, together with the Barons of the Exchequer. The assembled judiciary would reach agreement by resolution recorded in a certificate referred back to the original tribunal: Sir F. Pollock, *The Expansion of the Common Law* (London: Stevens and Sons, 1924), 16–17, 134–135. *Calvin's Case* reached Exchequer Chamber on reference from King's Bench. Coke notes (7 Co. Rep. at 28a) that the five King's Bench judges adjourned the matter into Exchequer Chamber "rather . . . for weight than difficulty."

9. (1772) Lofft 1 at 2.

10. This mixture of ancient constitutionalism and rights-based argumentation is seen most notably in the "birth-right" theory talk, which emerged during the mid- to late eighteenth century, largely in connection to imperial (legislative) authority over the American colonies.

11. (1823) 8 Wheat. 543 at 572 (USSC).

12. On Locke and aboriginal rights see James Tully, *An Approach to Political Philosophy: Locke in Contexts* (Cambridge: Cambridge University Press, 1993), 137. Blackstone takes a similar position in his *Commentaries* (1765) 2:4–7.

13. (1823) 8 Wheat. 543 at 603 (USSC).

14. Ibid., 543 at 592 (USSC).

15. Ibid., 543 at 604–605 (USSC).

16. (1847–1932) NZPCC, App. 387 at 388.

17. Ibid., App. 387 at 388.

18. For were it otherwise, a subject would be able to acquire a territory and set up a monarchy in derogation of that of the Crown. The best-known example of this in British colonial history is "Rajah Brooke" of Sarawak.

19. (1847–1932) NZPCC, App. 387 at 391.

20. Ibid., App. 387 at 390.

21. Ibid., App. 387 at 391.

22. Also, it has something of an ambivalence to it: Is the distinction to be seen in a positivistic sense, where "law" and "morality" are regarded as separate codes of conduct? Or does it give an implication that the community of law from which the common-law rule is drawn is essentially Anglo-Saxon—that it is the Crown's practice in relation to its white, colonizing subjects that is central to the judicial logic?

23. (1877) 3 New Zealand Jur (OS) 72.

9

LIBERTY AND LICENSE

The Forsters' Accounts of New Zealand Sociality

Nicholas Thomas

This essay interprets the responses of two writers on Cook's second voyage to Maori societies, in the light of anthropological thought at the time. It engages with the detail of texts that may seem remote and arcane, but is motivated by reflection upon the question of how to talk and write, here and now, about histories of discovery and colonialism. In an essay reprinted not long ago, Bernard Smith suggested that it was time for the Cook voyages to be placed in a new perspective. "Amidst the collapse of the European colonial empires, amidst mounting criticism of the cultural consequences of high technology, it seems desirable that Cook and his achievements be interpreted in a less Eurocentric fashion than they have been in the past."[1] The effort, which might have both deconstructive and revisionist elements, has two dimensions, which should not be quite separate: the first is surely a fuller appreciation of the range of indigenous responses to early exploration and subsequent colonization, and a discovery of new ways of telling and retelling indigenous narratives, which might entail their appreciation rather than their appropriation by settler, as well as by indigenous, audiences. This paper belongs to the other side of the project, that is, a more critical cultural history of the European motivations, interests, responses, and conflicts around the voyages, and their subsequent representation in national histories. My sense is that an understanding of exploration that is more salient to the decaying colonial world that we inhabit might also be more adequate as an account of the emerging imperial world that Cook inhabited, than either the celebratory mythologizations of the great navigator, or the critical histories of fatal impact, which offer little more than inversions of the hagiography.

It has been widely noted, in recent discussions of colonial discourse theory, that the critique of Orientalism and related forms of imperialist representation has frequently reiterated precisely the distancing and silencing of the Other that is identified in colonialist texts.[2] The notion that the critical study of exploratory and colonial culture is a study of representations of "the Other" strikes me as especially inappropriate in colonies of white settlement, such as Aotearoa–New Zealand and Australia, given that it is the very presence and proximity of indigenous people that settler colonialism has sought to contest and deny. While I am aware that the arguments have been extended in a variety of provoking ways, the underlying implication is that Europeans were primarily concerned with the exotic, that is, with what was foreign and radically strange, and the suggestion is often that despite this preoccupation, they underestimated, or failed to recognize, some actual or absolute alterity.

The extent of actual misunderstanding may indeed be conspicuous, but an overemphasis on exoticism and otherness leaves us unprepared for the extent to which certain European writers were concerned to understand indigenous societies as neither debased nor ideal inversions of the West but rather as historically contingent forms, exhibiting analogous political predicaments and tensions—in other words, as broadly similar and related to their own societies rather than fundamentally different from them. If, for certain periods, images such as engravings represented either the noble or the ignoble savage but failed to engage with more ambiguous intermediate types, almost the reverse might be true of the late-eighteenth-century texts, in which understandings were conveyed that could be said to be more nuanced, or simply to be characterized by greater internal confusion and inconsistency. My point is not that these efforts, however flawed, anticipate a discovery of similarity that might now contradict the colonial law of segregation, nor am I concerned to say that voyagers were really not as bad or guilty as some critics have made out. Little would be gained if the notion that indigenous peoples are radically distant were merely replaced by a denial of difference; and if one is really pronouncing upon the characters, the policies, or the practices of colonists, it is surely more important to scrutinize the living than the dead. My interest arises rather from the way in which the assimilation of different societies to a common political idiom in the voyage literature exposes the heterogeneity and instability of the whole corpus. This "colonial discourse" is not relentlessly authoritative; it displays a peculiar and agitated uncertainty and oscillates between familiarization and distancing. The encounters themselves entailed moments of actual empathy and conversation, working misunderstandings as well as resistance to understanding, exchange relationships as well as simple intrusion and coercion. I have two reasons for seeing things this way. First, if the voyages are absorbed into a history of entirely one-sided colonial domination and expropriation, as they are in the fatal-impact literature, it is too easy to forget all the creative strategies of accommodation, appropriation, and resistance that *tangata whenua* employed, at the time and ever since; it is too easy to see the continuation of colonial domination as possessing the same fatal inevitability. If the voyage encounters and representations are taken to be replete with contradictions and contradictory possibilities, if their uncertainties meant that other things easily could have happened, it is perhaps easier to imagine that other things can happen now. The second reason for taking the voyages and their attendant representation to be peculiarly dispersed and unstable has nothing to do with this wishful political presentism: It is simply that that's the way it really was—which I hope now to demonstrate.

In his *History of America,* published in 1777, William Robertson dismissed the notion that a "general state of promiscuous intercourse between the sexes ever existed" and asserted rather that "even among the rudest tribes" a regular form of marriage was universal. This was not to say that conjugality took a form that would have been familiar and pleasing to refined European persons: It was well known that women were invariably degraded among savages, and marriage was accordingly less a union of equals than "the unnatural conjunction of a master with his slave."[3] Parenthood among the Native Americans, on the other hand, approximated a European sense of what was desirable and natural; Robertson noted that both parents, in savage society, were concerned to see themselves reproduced, and hoped to be cared for in their old age; they were therefore "not deficient in affection and attachment to their offspring." In no sense, however, did children reciprocate their parents' fondness, though the fault appeared to lie more in the latter's indulgence than in any constitutional peculiarity of the young in that region of the world:

> They suffer them to be absolute masters of their own actions . . . conscious of their own liberty, and impatient of restraint, the youth of America are accustomed to act as if they were totally independent, their parents are not objects of greater regard than other persons. They treat them always with neglect, and often with such harshness and indolence, as to fill those who have been witnesses of their conduct with horror.[4]

Participants in Cook's second voyage had been "witnesses," in another part of the world, to moments of violence in which children assaulted their parents. Two incidents are described in George Forster's *Voyage Round the World,* which appeared in the same year as Robertson's *America,* and of these one figured signally in the remarkable synthetic work of natural history and ethic philosophy that was published a year later, in 1778, by the naturalist on the voyage, Johann Reinhold Forster, George's father. These incidents were, of course, not typical of the many acts of violence that were recorded over the course of the voyage, most of which were either perpetrated or directly provoked by Europeans; yet the way in which they were represented marks both the content and the limitations of an interpretative, ethnographic effort that can be traced through the writings of both Forster junior and senior. What allegedly occurred during the *Resolution*'s second visit to Queen Charlotte Sound, in November 1773, does not simply exemplify the kind of fact that Robertson referred to; it was assimilated to a theoretical language, to a space of argument about the history of society, which the Forsters shared, broadly, with such writers of the Scottish enlightenment as William Robertson, Lord Kames, and John Millar.

> A boy about six or seven years old demanded a piece of broiled pinguin, which his mother held in her hands. As she did not immediately comply with his demand, he took up a large stone and threw it at her. The woman incensed at this action ran to punish him, but she had scarcely given him a single blow, when her husband came forward, beat her unmercifully, and dashed her against the ground, for attempting to correct her unnatural child. Our people who were employed in filling water, told my father they had frequently seen similar instances of cruelty among them, and particularly, that the little boys had actually struck their unhappy mother, whilst the father looked on lest she should attempt to retaliate.[5]

The other case occurred earlier, during the ship's period of refreshment in Dusky Bay in late March and April 1773. Initially, it was supposed that the area was uninhabited, but on the seventh of April, an "Indian family" was encountered, consisting of an older man, one older woman, two younger women, and several children. The older woman is distinguished by a wen or excrescence on the upper lip, which is said to render her ugly and thought to explain the man's apparent indifference to her. These people, depicted in William Hodges' *Cascade Cove* (fig. 9.1) and certain associated works, were seen from time to time over the following days, and on the nineteenth, they were to come on board the ship.

> In the mean while they had a quarrel among themselves, the man beat the two women who were supposed to be his wives; the young girl in return struck him, and then began to weep. What the cause of this disagreement was, we cannot deter-

mine; but if the young woman was really the man's daughter, which we could never clearly understand, it should seem that the filial duties are strangely confounded among them; or which is more probable, that this secluded family acted in every respect, not according to the customs and regulations of a civil society, but from the impulses of nature, which speak aloud against every degree of oppression.[6]

In one case, then, the supposed daughter strikes the father; in the other, the son assaults the mother. The superficial symmetry between these incidents is suggestive, precisely because the way in which they figure in the voyage literature is radically different. What transpired in Dusky Bay was perplexing; arguably, the whole experience of contact in that part of the South Island was pervaded by obscurity. In the passage I've quoted from George's *Voyage,* it is not clear whether the "young girl" is one of the supposed "wives" he has just beaten; that she strikes him "in return" suggests so, and she is in fact identified earlier in the text, in the section describing the first encounter with these people, as one of his wives: "He called to the two women. . . . One of the women, which we af-

Fig. 9.1   William Hodges, *[Cascade Cove], Dusky Bay,* ca. 1775–1776, oil, National Maritime Museum, Greenwich, England

terwards believed to be his daughter, was not wholly so disagreeable."[7] In Forster senior's journal, upon which George's published narrative was based, one of the wives, or presumed wives, is indeed younger than the other, but it is quite clear from his description of the actual altercation that the "young girl" was a third woman: "The old Man beat his two wives, & the young Girl beat her Father & then fell a crying. He sent the wives & Children in the Canoe out a fishing: but he & the Girl went round the Cove," and proceeded to come on board the ship.[8] The comparison between the diary and the book suggests that there was more confusion in George's publication than there was during the encounter itself, and this is less surprising than might appear, given that George's only documentary source was presumably the diary, which was hardly unambiguous, and given that his memory at the time of writing, some four years after the event, must have been complicated by a considerable number of subsequent encounters with other Polynesians, both elsewhere in New Zealand and in the tropics.

James Cook's account of these people is generally less detailed and does not mention the quarrel in which the man both dispensed and received blows. He does, however, make it clear that there were three women and not two, which incidentally is the case in Hodges' painting, though Cook also, at one point, reproduces George's conflation of the "young girl" and the younger of the two wives; the confusion may have arisen because both appear to have been singularly forthcoming and talkative.[9] The point that Cook adds, which is interesting, is that the "girl" is supposed to be the daughter not only of the man but of the woman whose countenance is disfigured by the wen. There is also, however, an emendation in Cook's manuscript journal that makes George's doubt concerning the relation between the girl and the older man categorical: "We learnt afterwards that this young Woman was not his Daughter."[10] This prejudices the very perception of the group as a family, since the woman with the wen either is not the girl's mother or not the man's wife, unless some polyandrous relationship, or illegitimate parenthood, is postulated. While the official published narrative does not reveal that the apparent daughter was not a daughter, other revisions of the journal, such as the addition of "as we supposed" in parentheses after mention of the man's two wives,[11] render identifications less, rather than more, certain, and this is still more the case in popular editions from 1780 onward, in which the relevant sentence is further altered to read, "We now saw all the man's family, as we supposed, which consisted of two wives, the young woman we mentioned before, a boy about fourteen years old, and three small children."[12]

The importance of these ambiguities is that it becomes unclear not

only whether the man was struck by his daughter, a wife, or by an otherwise related or unrelated woman, but moreover whether he had one wife
or two. Of course, the visitors were not even certain that either of the two
women who were beaten were actually the man's wives, but the fact that
an individual man, and especially an older individual, might not have
a wife presented no particular problem to European understandings of
conjugality or domesticity. In contrast, though George singled out the ab-
normality of the girl's behavior as the basis for his inference that these
people were "secluded" in a domain beyond the regulation of civil society, it is hardly necessary to emphasize that a distinction between monog-
amous and polygamous unions was so significant to the interpretation of
a people's form of civility that confusion on this point had to confound
any larger assessment of their character and situation in the history of
humanity.

Lapernière's plate in the official publication (fig. 9.2) appears less a
print after Hodges than an abstraction and repositioning of the figures in
the *Cascade Cove* painting in the National Maritime Museum. While it is
understandable that the engraver did not attempt to reproduce the dis-
orderly complexities of the waterfall and vegetation, it is notable that the
landscape is abandoned neither for the equivalent of a history painting,
although the moment of contact between Cook and the old man would

Fig. 9.2   Lapernière, *Family in Dusky Bay, New Zeland*, engraving after Hodges, from
James Cook, *A voyage towards the South Pole* (London, 1777)

have been entirely amenable to such treatment, and such foundational encounters were in fact the subject matter of many of the plates in the third voyage, nor a set of portraits, though many of the second voyage plates were, of course, the "Man of Tanna," "Woman of New Caledonia," and so on. Instead, this print claims to depict precisely what was elusive: "A Family in Dusky Bay." Not only the confusion concerning the number of the man's wives but also some uncertainty around the character of conjugal relations is suggested here, by the fact that two contrasting dyadic relations are imaged, between the man and the standing woman, on one side, and between the man and the seated woman with her baby, on the other. The woman holding the spear figures as a companion and almost as a fellow warrior, given the evident strength and weight of her weapon; the other is by no means radically bestialized but is close and conspicuously subordinate to the man, and seemingly carrying a good deal more on her back than her child.

The burden is not only a recurrent emblem of women's denigration in unrefined societies but is resonant specifically of the debased situation of women in the Western Pacific, in New Caledonia, Tanna, and especially Malekula; their condition, in the texts from the second voyage, is marked or perhaps rather constituted by the "fact" that they are treated like packhorses by their men.[13] This is no more than a visual implication, but it is significant that the woman is in shadow if not definitely dark, and that her profile clearly displays frizzy hair, which could very well have been taken by late-eighteenth-century viewers to be the "wool" supposedly characteristic of negroes, that moreover differs distinctly both from the merely wavy hair of the other two figures, and that of this woman's original in the painting and in a sketch by Hodges. This woman seems therefore to be brought into conformity, both in her physical attributes and conjugal subordination, with the typical "black" Melanesian woman, who is routinely contrasted with the lighter-skinned Polynesian and taken to be oppressed in the terms specified in Enlightenment social theory alluded to earlier, that is, because she is dissociated from the martial pursuits that men value above all else. The other figure could be seen to personify quite a different construction of barbaric womanhood, which scarcely figures in the voyage texts, in which women are imagined to be affected by the martial environment to the degree that they carry arms themselves; they perhaps therefore share the liberty and independence of their men, as this woman's poise suggests.

Cascade Cove is neither explicitly nor implicitly titled "A Family in Dusky Bay"; the relative isolation and foregrounding of the man surely renders peripheral the question of his relationship to any one or all three of the women. His rugged vigor and musculature might be taken first to echo the undomesticated strength of the rocks and the terrain, while the distinction between the seated girl and the standing adult women might imply, to any viewer concerned to speculate, that the man has two wives and a daughter, as the official narrative suggested. The engraving makes two figures of three by depriving one adult woman of her spear, reducing her to the seated position of the apparent daughter, and giving her custody not only of her child but of a burden that she lacks in the painting; this merging of one wife and the daughter is, as it happens, the same conflation that is effected at points in both James Cook's and George Forster's texts.

But the young woman herself repaid this defect of recognition with interest, in taking a common sailor, and two or three others, officers as well as mere seamen, for members of her own sex; a suggestive mistake that the Tannese among other Pacific Islanders were to repeat in the course of the same voyage. Though initially showing "a great partiality" to the young man, the woman "would never suffer him to come near her afterwards"; if this was because "he had taken some improper liberties, or whether she had any other reason to be disgusted" was unclear, in the *Voyage;*[14] in the diaries, though, it is clear, at least, that the woman discovered the sailor's true sex when she saw him urinating. The elision in George Forster's publication is motivated, of course, by delicacy, but it might be suggested that the step from a palpable circumstance to a point of ambiguity or uncertainty in the text resonates with the compounding of potential misidentifications in the matter of kinship; facts of a certain kind seem to produce here what Michael Taussig has called "epistemic murk."[15] In Cook's published text, the matter is still more obscure: "Whether it was that she before took him for one of her own sex; or that the man, in order to discover himself, had taken some liberties with her which she thus resented, I know not."[16]

I am not arguing that the fabrication of obscurity is often attested to in the Cook voyage texts, though it is perhaps a generic feature of exploratory writing, in the sense that moments of violence, and others that are peculiarly horrifying or astonishing, overwhelm the effort of apprehension and narration: "The mind is so entirely filled with its object, that it cannot entertain any other, nor by consequence reason on that object which employs it."[17] The point is rather that the Dusky Bay encounter, unlike not only those at Tahiti and in other parts of the Pacific but also those in other parts of New Zealand, was replete with aspects and ironies that were peculiarly difficult for the Europeans to comprehend; yet what was problematic tended to be paraded rather than disavowed in their texts. The want of comprehension was not, in any important way, the result simply of the fact that such knowledge of Tahitian as a few of those on board had acquired, on Cook's first voyage, scarcely enabled communication with these New Zealanders; attempts to converse proceeded mainly through gestures and mainly ineffectively. This deficiency of mutual understanding could possess its own legibility, for Forster senior wrote, "After half an hours unintelligible conversation at least as edifying as great many which are usual in the politer circles of civilized nations, & which here at least passed with a great deal more sincerity & cordiality on both sides, we took leave of our new friends."[18]

What, on the other hand, did lack legibility was the transparent fact that these few Polynesians abruptly broke off their intercourse with the visitors, much to the puzzlement of the latter, who saw the relationship as one characterized by friendliness and a degree of mutual generosity; as George Forster put it, "We never saw them again, which was the more extraordinary, as they never went away empty handed from us."[19] The sense that this was remarkable may be more directly connected than is initially apparent with a larger issue that I seek to address: the ways in which the interpretations of these events that are both implicit and explicit in what George and Johann Reinhold Forster wrote were at once enabled and deprived of coherence by an understanding of the antinomies of progress that they shared with, among others, the Scottish enlightenment writers mentioned earlier.

What is important about the incident in Queen Charlotte Sound is not that the mother is abused by her son but that the violence, and the accessory role of adult men, fathers of perpetrators and husbands of victims, is taken to be both endemic and diagnostic. George's description of the single occasion that his father witnessed is generalized on the basis of common sailors' observations (that are not mentioned in Forster senior's journal) and is followed by these remarks:

> Among all savage nations the weaker sex is ill-treated, and the law of the strongest is put in force. Their women are mere drudges, who prepare raiment and provide dwellings, who cook and frequently collect their food, and are requited by blows and all kinds of severity. At New Zeeland it seems they carry this tyranny to excess, and the males are taught from their earliest age, to hold their mothers in contempt, contrary to all our principles of morality.[20]

In Johann Reinhold Forster's *Observations,* in the first passage in his text in which these people are systematically discussed, the harsh treatment of New Zealand women by their husbands is similarly assimilated to a general condition: women "are obliged to do all the drudgery, as is common in all barbarous nations."[21] Attached to this sentence is a long footnote, which cites first Strabo and Tacitus, and a range of modern travel accounts from Africa, Asia, and America, establishing, at least to Forster's satisfaction, that both the ancient inhabitants of Europe, and contemporary barbarians, treated their women in the terms described. What I take to generate a distinctive ambivalence is not that Maori were thereby included in a capacious anthropological category, but that they were rendered similar to societies in earlier phases of European history, such as the ancient Germans,[22] whose martial condition was understood less as an uncongenial belligerence than as the basis for an uncorrupted liberty that refined nations had lost.

In the later section of Forster's book, which is dedicated to an evaluation of the state of New Zealand society, the violence against the mother is positively determined, not merely by the general truth that women are badly treated among uncivilized people but more powerfully and specifically by the effects of a certain mode of education. Forster considered and rejected the idea that the form of anthropophagy that prevailed in New Zealand—the consumption of slain enemies—was motivated by hunger, as John Hawkesworth had asserted in the official narrative of the first voyage.[23] Displaying almost exemplary anthropological relativism, Forster went to some pains to argue that the evident barbarity of the practice belied beneficial effects that it could well have, in a longer view: Warfare, conducted with such destructive effect, over a time, could only in the end impress upon victors "that a living man is more useful than one dead or roasted"; hence, conquerors would eventually enslave the people they defeated and create more extensive and cohesive social unions. This seemed not merely a hypothetical development but already a fact in the North Island, according to reports from the *Endeavour's* voyage.[24] Even if these were, in the first place, founded on the oppression of the conquered, any larger, more united society "prepares the way to a more humane and benevolent scene"; as Forster says, he "cannot help observing, that this barbarism is one of the steps, by which debased humanity, is gradually prepared for a better state of happiness."[25] This argument may appear eccentric; but Forster's contrived retreat from the immediacy of an atrocity to its historical causes and ramifications was a specifying operation, which avoided ascribing practices that happened to be repulsive to Europeans simply to a generalized want of civilization. He instead understood both this and the boy's violence as elements or effects of a warlike sociality.

In the section of *Observations* that I am drawing upon, Forster is concerned especially to distinguish the relative advancement of the New

Zealanders over a less improved population, that of Tierra del Fuego, whose inhabitants seemed striking for their apathy, misery, and indolence; in other passages of his book he was concerned similarly with accounting for the greater happiness of the Tahitians relative to the inhabitants of New Zealand, the western parts of the Pacific, and Tonga. This exercise in ranking articulated with a narrative of progress, which was animated by a grand analogy with stages in the human life cycle from infancy to maturity, but differed from nineteenth-century evolutionist arguments in several crucial respects. Although Forster did make unpleasant and invidious comparisons between the physical appearances of various Pacific Islanders, and especially Islander women, he was not concerned with intrinsic racial differences and saw stature, physiognomy, and color as effects of the mode of life, of forms of labor, of ratios of indolence and vigor, opulence and warriorhood; this comparative anthropology was thus political before it was physical.

Forster's particular arguments entered into a grand account of the effects of climate upon human happiness and progress; he imagined a general continuum between the most refined Islanders in the tropics and the more debased peoples of temperate and frigid latitudes. While the Tahitians are certainly consistently celebrated, and the Tierra del Fuegians harshly disparaged, the continuum was complicated by the differences between populations within broadly similar latitudes—notably between the Tahitians and other tropical Polynesians, and the Islanders of the Western Pacific—but Forster did not in any case advance any rigid geographical determinism. Climate was arguably so important in the anthropological thought in this period, among thinkers who had all read Montesquieu, precisely because it was conceptually flexible. If it sometimes stood for mere latitude, the earth being divided into a series of horizontal zones within which temperaments were notionally similarly determined, at other times it seemed to include the range of economic and political conditions that I mentioned, which on the one hand entailed the broad nature of particular kinds of sociality, a martial or commercial character, but on the other were recognized through, and constituted by, facts specifically related to the treatment of women and the form of the family.[26]

The animated character of the sociality of New Zealanders was certainly seen to arise from an intricate configuration of population, migration, education, and climate and was understood especially as an advance upon the debased condition of the Tierra del Fuegians. The scattered and fragmentary nature of the latter was taken to point out "the true cause of the debasement and degeneracy in savages; they can neither profit by the assistance, nor by the inventions and improvements of others, and the smallness of their numbers affords but a bad chance for a multiplicity of inventions or improvements."[27] Progress was associated with an increase in population, in part because a people's reserve of knowledge was thereby increased—in New Zealand, "their minds have acquired a larger and more liberal circle of ideas"—but more crucially because population pressure led to warfare, to efforts to extend a dominion, and to acquire superiority. "All this of course rouses their minds from that indolence and inactivity with which they were oppressed, and they in every respect conquer somewhat of that degeneracy to which they were reduced." Many cultural and technological accomplishments attested to the progress of the New Zealanders; Forster noted the elaborate decorations of tools, ornaments, dress, and arms, the "elegance and neatness" of the houses, the "easy and swift motion" of well-contrived and dexterously paddled canoes, and the elaboration of religious ideas that were not evidently merely superstitious; most significantly, perhaps, he added: "The agriculture which is so well and so carefully carried on in many parts of the Northern island, incontestably proves the superiority of the New-Zeelanders over the inhabitants of Tierra del Fuego. So that it might be superfluous in me to take up more time in multiplying the proofs of this so evident truth."[28]

It is unimportant, for Forster, that the Maori he actually encountered, at one end of the South Island and another, did not appear to practice agriculture; by implication, even if the nomadic people around Dusky Bay did not institutionalize property and law to the degree that was understood to correspond, normally, with the cultivation of the ground, they were proximate enough to the "ideas and improvements" of their settled neighbors to be ranked, quite definitively, "higher in the scale of human beings" than the Tierra del Fuegians.

Forster's arguments in favor of the "improved" state of New Zealanders, are, therefore, fairly elaborate and refer both to what might be seen as indices of improvement, such as their refined arts, and to causes of a happier and more vigorous constitution, such as the relative mildness of the climate and the extent of the population. But against this, is, of course, the "one circumstance . . . which seems to degrade them," that is, their practice of cannibalism, which is the extreme expression of a martial spirit. The point is not that a remarkable vigor coexisted contingently and inconsistently with deplorable violence, but rather that, in this conceptualization, discrepant aspects of indigenous progress and custom were rendered indissociable in a martial condition: What roused a people from indolence and led to such a range of commendable aspects of their mode of life was precisely the cause also of their custom, which Europeans could only find "horrid." Exactly what this understanding does not do is produce a coherent idea of Maori society; if the representation of Dusky Bay elevated merely perplexing facts to the level of epistemic obscurity, the understanding of sociality around Queen Charlotte Sound produced a moral and political contradiction out of what was perhaps only a discrepancy between bad characteristics and good ones.

The contradiction, however, was in no sense obscure, from the viewpoint of eighteenth-century political and historical thought. The martial condition was not so much a construction of a particular class of alien societies as a category evoked more commonly in diagnoses of the distemper of European societies. Progress tended to extinguish a military spirit and permitted men to lapse from military vigor and patriotism into indolence, vanity, and effeminacy; though property, opulence, and commerce might be conducive to refinement in the arts, and to higher forms of civility and politeness, they also prejudiced public virtue, not least because commerce entailed a specialization of labor, knowledge, and interest, which could only detract from a public and patriotic spirit. The decline of warriorhood as a general occupation and preoccupation of men also fostered licentiousness and corruption in the indirect sense that a standing army, as opposed to a civilian militia, facilitated a despotism that could not be sustained over a society of independent warriors; and despotism was understood not merely to oppress those who were subject to it but to impoverish them, and corrupt and debase both rulers and ruled in a variety of ways. All this, incidentally, is contained in the history of the word *mercenary*, which originally meant not a soldier who served a foreign power but any soldier who was paid, as opposed to the civilian who took up arms to defend his land and his country; any paid pursuit, in fact, might be stigmatized by the adjective, which retains that breadth in present usage. The tensions I am exploring turn upon the fact that if the New Zealanders were cannibals, they were, at least, not mercenaries.

I am not concerned here with the significance of these ideas in European politics, but merely point out that an ambivalent or negative evaluation of commercial society, and its attendant luxury and selfishness, may evoke or deploy rhetorically a positive or at least correspondingly mixed representation of a particular unrefined condition, which was exemplified especially by the early Germans. Preeminent among sources was, of course, Tacitus. His *Germania* was read in a singularly eighteenth-century way, which no doubt capitalized upon the critique of Roman debauchery suggested by German frugality and chastity but assimilated that moralizing geography to a distinctive political idiom. The absence of specialized occupations among the Germans is only implicit in Tacitus but assumes definite significance for Gilbert Stuart, whose history of "the progress from rudeness to refinement" in Europe appeared in the same year as Forster's *Observations:*

> The German, accordingly, being unacquainted with particu-
> lar professions, and with mercenary pursuits, was animated
> with high sentiments of pride and greatness. He was guided by
> affection and appetite; and, though fierce in the field, and ter-
> rible to an enemy, was gentle in his domestic capacity, and
> found a pleasure in acts of beneficence, magnanimity, and
> friendship.[29]

I noted earlier that Johann Forster classed the New Zealanders among "barbarous nations," and it is therefore not surprising that the last remark here resonates with evocations of a manly simplicity that precedes refined disingenuousness, which might be extracted from many accounts of travels among people classed as barbaric, and are certainly scattered through Cook voyage accounts of New Zealand. Among the most signifi-cant, perhaps, is a passage in George Forster's narrative in which the vio-lence of the Maori against Marion's party is explained and excused in terms consistent with Anne Salmond's recent reinterpretation: "The whole tenor of their behavior to Europeans, seems to acquit them of treachery and cruel malevolence. It is therefore greatly to be suspected that they took umbrage at some affront, perhaps unwittingly committed by the strangers."[30] What is not commonplace in Stuart's representation of the German is the fact that the generic male is said to be "gentle in his domestic capacity." This assertion is especially striking, given that this writer also observed that the government of "every rude community" had "a surprising affinity to that of the Germans, as described by Tacitus."[31] This contradicts the claim, which I began by citing in Robertson and have found echoed both in George's *Voyage* and his father's *Observations,* that barbarians, or savages, or both, were universally cruel to women. Stuart disputed the readings of Tacitus, and the evidence from travel writers in America that Robertson, Millar, Kames, and others had drawn upon, and put forward a variety of empirical and deductive arguments for the relatively high estimation of women among Germans and barbarians generally.[32]

Stuart's relatively unqualified idealization of barbaric society is only salient to the other material that I have discussed, because his celebratory account clearly depended upon dissent from the view that was generally subscribed to, concerning the status of women among such people; this underlines the extent to which writers such as the Forsters, who presumed that women were harshly treated by all barbarians and believed that this had been attested to by events that they had witnessed, were simply unable to produce an unequivocal estimate of society in New Zealand. This is also, incidentally, why the "noble savage," and for that matter, the "ignoble," are simply not adequate categories for the history of ideas in this period. When Forster wrote of the Maori, "Their principles of honesty, and public faith are noble," he was saying something that he was never, to my knowledge, concerned or able to say of a European nation, yet he saw the liberal manliness of the New Zealand temperament as confounded by its excess:

> Their education is the chief cause of all these enormities. The men train up their boys in a kind of liberty, which at last degenerates into licentiousness: they suffer not the mothers to strike their petulant, unruly, and wicked sons, for fear of breaking that spirit of independency, which they seem to value above all things, and as the most necessary qualification for their societies.[33]

In *The Machiavellian Moment*, J.G.A. Pocock has suggested that Scottish philosophy entailed "a theory of history which showed how virtue was built up and demolished by the growth of society itself," in which "contradiction was of the essence" and which "envisaged a future in which progress and corruption might coexist for a very long period."[34] Forster's interpretation of the societies of Queen Charlotte Sound underlines the permanent character of this contradictoriness, which belonged as much to early phases of the history of civil society as to its maturity and future; the happiness of peoples other than refined Europeans was always enhanced by certain effects of their progress, and marred or diminished by others. New Zealand and European societies, thus imagined, were not radically different but pervaded by analogous propensities and tensions; the extent to which this similarity could qualify or jostle with the historical evolution, which certainly was present in Forster's text, is suggested by the way in which liberty was seen by Millar and several other writers, as a characteristic of both early and late phases of civil society, rather than the periods in between.[35] The argument did not exactly postulate a circularity, but more the reappearance of a condition, which was as unstable as it was generally desirable. Concluding a long section on the despotic character of paternal authority in unimproved societies, and the gradual amelioration of this "excessive and arbitrary power," Millar notes that, "the tendency . . . of a commercial age is rather towards the opposite extreme, and may occasion some apprehension that the members of a family will be raised to greater independence than is consistent with good order, and with a proper domestic subordination."[36]

Because Forster shared Robertson's sense that men might oppress and degrade their wives, while their children were insufficiently restrained, it was possible to imagine something other than a long transition—instead a simultaneity of a certain despotism and a certain independence. Liberty in barbaric societies, no less than in refined ones, was consistently vitiated in its excesses; the "licentiousness" thereby generated was as much there as here, as much here as there. All this is suggestive not only of the burden of the incident in Queen Charlotte Sound in September 1773 but also, indirectly, of a further cause of the obscurity that Dusky Bay assumes in the voyage narratives, and its relative insignificance in Forster's *Observations*. George Forster's and Cook's narratives mention but do not remark upon the fact that the supposed wives are carrying spears, and as I noted, one of these is conspicuous in the engraving in the official publication. It is possible that Cook, and others on the vessel who had seen a good deal of Maori on the first voyage, understood that these were, in all likelihood, used for hunting wood pigeons,[37] but this is nowhere hinted at in the text, and readers could have seen them only as weapons. This must have been distinctly anomalous for anyone who shared the Forsters' understanding that women in barbaric societies were drudges specifically because they were strangers to the warlike pursuits that alone were valued by men; and if other understandings could no doubt accommodate the fact more easily, it is nevertheless not surprising that later engravings (figs. 9.3 and 9.4) based upon Lapernière either diminish the martial character of the woman, or further mutilate the family of Dusky Bay, by changing this warrior's sex.

Forster's identification, which I quoted earlier, of savages as those who were unable to profit from other's inventions or improvements, resonates with many observations he and others made in the course of Cook's voyages and subsequent explorations: Time and again one finds a people's civility or superiority correlated with their openness to strangers and their goods, or their standoffishness and lack of interest in cloth or iron interpreted as belligerence, as a sign of a more debased and primitive state. The positive side of this, which connected improvement with an interest in wider intercourse and foreign objects, echoed an argument of David Hume's concerning the positive effects of foreign commerce.

> In most nations, foreign trade has preceded any refinement in home manufactures, and given birth to luxury. The temptation is stronger to make use of foreign commodities, which

are ready for use, and which are entirely new to us, than to make improvements on any domestic commodity, which always advance by slow degrees, and never affect us by their novelty. . . . Thus men become acquainted with the pleasures of luxury, and the profits of commerce; and their delicacy and industry, being once awakened, carry them on to farther improvements in every branch of domestic as well as foreign trade. And this perhaps is the chief advantage which arises from a commerce with strangers. It rouses men from their indolence.[38]

While Hume was more balanced in his assessment of the effects of commerce than many of his contemporaries, and while he believed the opulence of private men might make the public more powerful,[39] the language employed is plainly ambivalent, in a sense that resonates with the debate referred to earlier. Commerce may lead to refinement, and may invigorate men, but it is evidently also feminizing and infantilizing: The restless and superficial passion for novelty, which is clearly the animating force behind commerce, is particularly an attitude of children and women.[40] Exchange between indigenous peoples and Europeans,

Fig. 9.3 *A Family in Dusk Bay, New Zealand*, engraving from George William Anderson, *A New, Genuine and Complete History of the Whole of Captain Cook's Voyages* (London, 1784–1786)

which attested to at least a limited civility on the part of the former, thus possessed an uncertain signification. On the one hand, an anxiety to acquire new things indicated a capacity for learning and improvement; on the other, it suggested that mercenary practices were not wholly alien to barbarism, even though the latter was understood as the antithesis of commercial society.

The corrupting effect of commerce was pretty evident in New Zealand, or rather in Queen Charlotte Sound, where, "the New Zeelanders went through the whole vessel, offering their daughters and sisters promiscuously to every person's embraces, in exchange for our iron tools, which they knew could not be purchased at an easier rate."[41] Here, the degeneracy of the British crew not only caused this sexual corruption but augmented the oppression of indigenous women by their menfolk; if the latter had always treated the former brutally, they only now used them as commodities, as George noted: "It may therefore be alledged, that as the New Zeelanders place no value on the continence of their unmarried women, the arrival of Europeans among them, did not injure their moral characters in this respect; but we doubt whether they ever debased themselves so much as to make a trade of their women, before we created new

Fig. 9.4 *Habitants de Mallicolo—Nouvelles Hébrides,* engraving from Domeny de Rienzi, *Océanie ou la cinquième partie du monde* (Paris, 1836–1837)

wants by shewing them iron-tools; for the possession of which they do not hesitate to commit an action that, in our eyes, deprives them of the very shadow of sensibility."[42]

In Dusky Bay, there had been no such articulation of modes of licentiousness. Exchange, certainly, took place, and the Maori were not stupidly indifferent to foreigners in the way that the Tierra del Fuegians had been; as George noted, they on the contrary possessed a singular courage: "In spight of their inferiority of force, they cannot brook the thought of hiding themselves, at least not till they have made an attempt to establish an intercourse, or prove the principles of strangers who approach them." On the other hand, the interest in novel foreign goods appeared restrained and provoked no unbounded passion for ornaments, and no subordination of virtue to trade. What George took to be extraordinary, in the unexpected departure of the group from the area, was not really inconsistent with the degree of improvement of the Dusky Bay people: They evidently were less polished, less unified, less commercial, and less corrupted than the related populations in Queen Charlotte Sound, and farther north.

The problem, I suggest, emerges also from a discrepancy between the characteristics of the people in terms of the salient anthropological language, and the essentially positive response that the Europeans had toward them. In fact, in terms of the criteria generally adduced in stadial categorizations, the Dusky Bay people were savages rather than barbarians: Their numbers were tiny, their material culture appeared rudimentary, their conjugal forms were uncertain and possibly even promiscuous; most important, they shifted from place to place and engaged in no agriculture. At two points, George goes so far as to remove them from civil society and from the regulation of custom altogether, yet these people were patently not debased into something like the indolent stupor of the Tierra del Fuegians, who were supposedly "removed but in the first degree from absolute animality." The Dusky Bay people were only at one further remove, in terms of the continuum from pole to tropic, but were clearly courageous, open, and honest.

It was the practical character of the encounter, and the responses of particular Europeans to particular Maori, that seems to have overdetermined one set of discriminations and left much indistinctness. The ambiguities were distilled, with the most delicate irony, by George, who wrote about an early stage of the encounter:

> The next morning we returned to the natives, and presented
> them with several articles which we had brought with us for
> that purpose. But so much was the judgment of the man supe-

rior to that of his countrymen, and most of the South Sea nations, that he received almost every thing with indifference, except what he immediately conceived the use of, such as hatchets and large spike-nails.[43]

The superiority of this man is not merely anomalous, from the perspective of the discourse that I have discussed. The superiority so starkly and plainly expressed in the man's indifference to trifles and baubles was in a way consistent with the uncommercial character of savagery, yet prejudiced the elaborate efforts of both Forsters, and especially the father, to specify the advancement of the Tahitians and other populations over peoples who were secluded, who were isolated from larger reserves of knowledge and education, who eked out a straggling existence in a cold climate and who left nature in a chaotic, absolutely unimproved state. At the beginning of this essay, I emphasized that I was concerned to draw attention to the contexts and ambiguities of exploratory writing, not to recuperate it. But if there is anything that we might salvage from this discourse, it is this: A natural historian could make of this little specimen of resistance a joke at the expense of his anthropology.

NOTES

This paper draws on research from 1989 to 1993 toward a new edition of J. R. Forster's *Observations Made During a Voyage round the World* (Honolulu: University of Hawai'i Press, 1996), and was written while I was a Harold White Fellow at the National Library of Australia. I owe so much to conversations with my co-editors, Harriet Guest and Michael Dettelbach, and with Margaret Jolly, that I am not sure whether particular ideas here are really mine rather than theirs, though I alone, of course, am responsible for errors or misinterpretations in this text. Earlier versions of the text were presented at the David Nichol Smith seminar in Auckland, in August 1993, and as a Harold White Lecture at the National Library of Australia in November 1993. I am grateful to Jonathan Lamb for his invitation to Auckland, and to both audiences for their responses. Somewhat different versions of this essay appeared in Chloe Chard and Helen Langdon, eds., *Transports: Travel, Pleasure, and Imaginative Geographies* (New Haven: Yale University Press, 1996), and in my book *In Oceania: Visions, Artifacts, Histories* (Duke University Press, 1997).

1. Bernard Smith, *Imagining the Pacific: In the Wake of the Cook Voyages* (Melbourne: Melbourne University Press, 1992), 240.

2. See, for example, Sara Suleri, *The Rhetoric of English India* (Chicago: University of Chicago Press, 1992), especially chap. 1. The point is developed in my book *Colonialism's Culture: Anthropology, Travel, and Government* (Cambridge: Polity Press, 1994).

3. William Robertson, *The History of America* (London: W. Strahan, 1777), 1:318–319.

4. Ibid., 323–324.

5. George Forster, *A Voyage Round the World in his Brittanic Majesty's Sloop, Resolution*, 2 vols. (London: 1777), 1:511.

6. Ibid., 1:160.

7. Ibid., 1:138.

8. *The Resolution Journal of Johann Reinhold Forster, 1772-1775*, ed. Michael E. Hoare, 4 vols. (London: Hakluyt Society, 1982), 2:258. Hereinafter cited as *"Resolution Journal."*

9. He begins by indicating that two women join the older man, whom he meets first, and says that of these the younger was singularly voluble. In the same diary entry, in accord with ship's noon-to-noon time, he explains that the whole family was encountered the next morning, "which consisted of the Man, his two wives, the young Woman before mentioned his daughter, a Boy of about 14 or 15 years of age and three small children." No young woman, in fact, is "before mentioned" except the younger of the two wives, that is, the same woman with whom George identifies the girl who strikes the man. *The Journals of Captain James Cook on his Voyages of Discovery*, ed. J. C. Beaglehole, 4 vols. (Cambridge: Cambridge University Press, 1961), 2:116–117.

10. Ibid., 2:122, n. 2.

11. James Cook, *A Voyage Towards the South Pole and Around the World*, 2 vols. (London: n.p., 1777), 1:75. There is a different account again in the Log, in which Cook refers to "a Man his Wife a Middle aged woman sister to either ye man or wife . . ." (*Journals*, 2:117, n. 3). This is likely to most approximate the actual relationships among these people.

12. John Hamilton Moore, *A New and Complete Collection of Voyages and Travels* (London: n.p., 1780), 2:1125; compare [George William Anderson], *A New, Genuine, and Complete History of the Whole of Capt. Cook's Voyages* (London, 1784–1786 [Beddie 17]), 128; Anderson, *A Collection of Voyages Round the World* (London, 1790 [Beddie 39]), 2:453. Most later editions are based on Anderson, though the wording here, and many of the plates used in first and subsequent editions of Anderson, are actually derived from Moore.

13. Cf. Margaret Jolly, "'Ill-Natured Comparisons': Racism and Relativism in European Representations of Ni-Vanuatu from Cook's Second Voyage," *History and Anthropology* 5 (1992): 331–364.

14. G. Forster, *Voyage*, 1:150.

15. With respect to narratives of extraordinary violence during the Putumayo rubber boom, Taussig writes: "The importance of this colonial work of fabu-

lation extends beyond the nightmarish quality of its contents. Its truly crucial feature lies in the way it creates an uncertain reality out of fiction, giving shape and voice to the formless form of the reality in which an unstable interplay of truth and illusion becomes a phantasmic social force" *(Shamanism, Colonialism, and the Wild Man: A Study in Terror and Healing* [Chicago: Chicago University Press, 1987], 121). It is the idea that certain encounters generate "an unstable interplay of truth and illusion" that I find especially salient; the New Zealand incidents clearly do not possess quite the same nightmarish terror as the rubber boom stories.

16. Cook, *Voyage*, 1:77.
17. Edmund Burke, *A Philosophical Enquiry into the Origin of our Ideas of the Sublime and Beautiful*, ed. James T. Boulton, rev. ed. (Oxford: n.p., 1987), 57. The salience of the category of the sublime is discussed in greater detail by Jonathan Lamb, "A Sublime Moment off Poverty Bay, 9 October 1769," in *Dirty Silence*, ed. Graham McGregor and Mark Williams (Auckland: Oxford University Press), esp. 110.
18. J. Forster, *Resolution Journal*, 2:249.
19. Compare Cook, *A Voyage Towards the South Pole*, 1:85–86. The close correspondence between the wording of parts of Cook's *Voyage* and sections of George's may be attributed to the fact that, during the protracted and abortive negotiations over who would write the official account of the voyage, Forster senior submitted a specimen based on Cook's manuscript to the Admiralty, which covered the Dusky Bay incidents (George Forster, *A Letter to the Earl of Sandwich*, London, 1778). It is possible that this is copied in BM Add. MS 27889, and was drawn upon by Cook in writing the narrative that was printed, though at the time of writing I have not had the opportunity to compare the manuscripts and publications systematically.
20. G. Forster, *Voyage*, 1:511–512. In George's *Voyage*, the terms *savage* and *barbarian* are less carefully distinguished than in his father's *Observations*.
21. John Reinold [Johann Reinhold] Forster, *Observations made during a voyage round the world, on physical geography, natural history, and ethic philosophy* (London: n.p., 1778), 237. Hereinafter cited as *Observations*.
22. The Germans are far more conspicuous in Forster's references in *Observations* than other groups, such as Hottentots and Americans.
23. John Hawkesworth, *An Account of the Voyages undertaken by the Order of His Present Majesty for Making Discoveries in the Southern Hemisphere*, 3 vols. (London: Strahan and Cadell, 1773), 3:43–44.
24. These have subsequently been considered inaccurate.
25. J. Forster, *Observations*, 330, 331 (transposed).
26. Cf. William Falconer, *Remarks of the Influence of Climate, Situation, Nature of Country, Population, Nature of Food, and Way of Life, on the Disposition and Temper, Manners and Behaviour, Intellects, Laws and Customs, Forms of Government, and Religion, of Mankind* (London: C. Dilly, 1781).

27. J. Forster, *Observations*, 318.

28. Ibid., 322–323.

29. Gilbert Stuart, *A View of Society in Europe, in its Progress from Rudeness to Refinement; or, Inquiries Concerning the History of Law, Government, and Manners*, 2d. ed. (Edinburgh, 1792), 2.

30. G. Forster, *Voyage*, 2:465; cf. Anne Salmond, *Two Worlds: First Meetings Between Maori and Europeans* (Auckland: Viking, 1991), 352–429.

31. Stuart, *View of Society in Europe*, 158.

32. Gibbon, incidentally, was far less categorical on this point that the other writers cited, and presumably his account was more influential than theirs.

33. J. Forster, *Observations*, 328.

34. J.G.A. Pocock, *The Machiavellian Moment: Florentine Political Thought and the Atlantic Republican Tradition* (Princeton: Princeton University Press, 1975), 503–504.

35. John Millar, *The Origin of the Distinction of Ranks; Or, an Inquiry into the Circumstances which give rise to Influence and Authority, in the Different Members of Society*, 4th ed. (Edinburgh, 1806), 101. Millar refers specifically to the liberty of women and free intercourse between the sexes.

36. Ibid., 138.

37. See the account of the spears known as *here*, for hunting *kereru* (wood pigeons), quoted from Tamati Ranapiri in Augustus Hamilton, *The Art Workmanship of the Maori Race in New Zealand* (Dunedin: 1896), 214–215.

38. David Hume, "Of Commerce," in *Essays, Literary, Moral, and Political* (London: A. Murray and Sons, 1870), 158.

39. Ibid., 150.

40. See especially Burke, *A Philosophical Inquiry*, 31.

41. G. Forster, *Voyage*, 1:212.

42. Ibid.

43. Ibid., 1:139–140. After "nations" is a footnote, "See Hawkesworth's Compilation."

10

EARLY CONTACT ETHNOGRAPHY AND UNDERSTANDING

An Evaluation of the Cook Expeditionary Accounts of the Grass Cove Conflict

Ian G. Barber

If anthropology and history have converged in the recent scholarship of cultural encounters in the Pacific, the same cannot be said for the studies, and students, at the heart of the enterprise. The contest of interpretations over the "apotheosis" (or otherwise) linked to Captain James Cook's violent demise in Hawai'i is the most prominent recent example of scholarly discord.[1] Debate over the representation of first contact has even accompanied Anne Salmond's largely documentary and otherwise well-received work on the earliest recorded Maori-European meetings.[2] Yet whether arguing for or against postmodernist interpretation, or the "place of cultural structures in historic events"[3] over the universality of "practical rationality,"[4] these Pacific studies all begin (and not infrequently end) mired in the problems of interpreting historic ethnography.

Despite these hermeneutic difficulties, the cross-disciplinary interface of research and interpretation in first-contact studies still offers a wealth of untapped possibilities. This potential is explored here in an approach incorporating anthropological, archaeological, and historical-ethnographic perspectives to interpret a violent English-Maori encounter. The historic event is the conflict at Grass Cove (Wharehunga Bay) on Arapana Island, near the Cook Strait entrance of Totaranui (Queen Charlotte Sound), northern South Island (see fig. 10.1). The 1773 conflict involved crew members from the *Adventure,* the sister ship to Captain Cook's *Resolution,* both of the 1772–1775 English Pacific expedition. In this incident, a grass-cutting party (to supply feed for their cattle) in the immediate charge of John Rowe, master's mate, were killed by Totaranui people, as was Rowe, while two Maori were fatally injured by gunshot. Subsequently, some of the English crew were dismembered, perhaps eaten. Given the dramatic nature of this encounter, and especially the inference of cannibalism, the event was inquired after with some vigor during the 1777 Totaranui sojourn of Cook's third Pacific expedition.

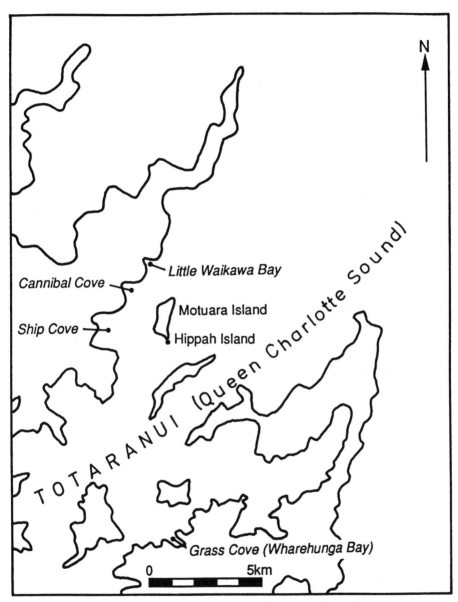

Fig. 10.1   Totaranui (Queen Charlotte Sound), showing sites of English-Maori contacts in the 1770s. Cook Strait lies immediately beyond the entrance to the Sound (north and east).

To first evaluate the problematic European refraction of the Grass Cove conflict, this study employs a comparative-textual critique of the several records of the incident. As gleaned from this analysis, the details of the conflict are then assessed in light of a broadly based, comparative-anthropological construction of local Maori society. This construction is informed by Maori history, comparative ethnography, and archaeology from the northern South Island, a synthesis contributing context and, ultimately, an independent meaning for the Grass Cove conflict. This meaning subsequently becomes a measure of the cultural agenda and interactive awareness (or lack thereof) of the European understanding.

European Records and the Grass Cove Conflict

The documentary record of the Grass Cove conflict begins with the reports of the *Adventure*'s crew in 1773, under the command of Captain Tobias Furneaux. The *Adventure* and *Resolution* had become separated off the coast of New Zealand earlier that year. In December 1773, Furneaux returned to Totaranui to replenish the ship's supplies while also hoping for some word from Cook. On 18 December, a longboat from the *Adventure* had gone in search of the ship's cutter, which had been missing since the previous day from a grass-cutting trip. According to the accounts of the longboat's crew, baskets of roasted flesh were discovered in a canoe on a beach adjacent to Grass Cove, as was a severed human hand identified by a personal tattoo to Thomas Hill, one of the cutter's crew. As the longboat's crew proceeded to Grass Cove and forced the retreat of the Maori, they found on shore human entrails, feet, a hand, and three human heads. One head was recognized as that of the cutter's "black" servant.[5]

Because Furneaux's crew had no further meetings with the Totaranui people after 18 December, the first Maori references to the *Adventure*'s December 1773 visit were recorded during the 1774 Totaranui sojourn of the *Resolution*. Cook, who had not resumed contact with Furneaux, was initially uncertain whether the *Adventure* had even returned there in December. On questioning local people in 1774, Cook received inconsistent and troubling accounts as to the *Adventure*'s December visit, including suggestions that a ship had been wrecked recently on the coast and its crew killed. "These stories made me feel very uneasy about the *Adventure*," Cook wrote. However, a few days later Cook was told unequivocally that the *Adventure* had departed "without being stranded." This eased his mind as to the safety of Furneaux and his crew, while not wholly setting aside "our doubts of some disaster having happened to some other strangers."[6]

The retrospective account of George Forster's 1774 Totaranui visit as botanist on the *Resolution* provides the earliest published reference to a Maori version of these events.[7] In assessing its content, George's account may be usefully compared with the contemporary 1774 journal entries of his father, Johann Reinhold. At the time, Johann recorded in his journal a "Native" account of a ship broken to pieces "on the coast of the northern Isle in a great Storm." He went on to note that the men of this ship, who arrived safely on shore, reportedly had "an Engagement" with, and killed, "many Natives," although the ship's crew were finally all "killed & devoured." The elder Forster added that "our people" interpreted this "to have been the fate of the *Adventure*." In keeping with Cook's 1774 observations, Johann also cautioned that "the Natives are by no means constant in their Story, so that there is little to be depended upon this Tale."[8] Yet for George, writing upon his return to Europe, those 1774 Totaranui accounts were expressed with some clarity and constancy, at least initially.

> They related, that an European vessel had put into the harbour some time ago; but that in a quarrel with the inhabitants, all her people had been killed and eaten. . . . [W]e apprehended that this vessel was most probably the Adventure. The natives were repeatedly questioned, and in every conversation we discovered some additional circumstances, by which the fact was more clearly established.[9]

As the matter was pressed further, George recalled native reticence and, finally, an assurance that the *Adventure* had left the "harbour," so that "we continued to doubt whether we had rightly understood" the initial accounts of European deaths.[10] While the relative clarity of George's 1777 narrative may be a factor more of retrospective than contemporary insight, he also provided details of the Maori version of the Grass Cove incident that went beyond those suggested in his father's 1774 Totaranui journal entries. Thus, George suggested that some of the crew may have removed their coats while cutting grass in the cove, so as to "perform their task with greater ease . . . for the accounts which we obtained from the natives at Queen Charlotte's Sound import, that one of their countrymen stole a sailor's jacket; that our people had hereupon immediately begun to fire, and continued to do so till all their ammunition was spent; that the natives had taken this opportunity to rush upon the Europeans, and had killed every one of them."[11] Of these accounts, George observed further that "we had no reason to doubt the veracity of the people at Queen Charlotte's Sound, since they accused their own countrymen of theft."[12]

By the time of Cook's 1777 return to Totaranui, during the third

Pacific expedition, the European visitors were all well aware, in Cook's terms, "of the sacrifice which the Natives made of the boats crew belonging to the Adventure in this place," as well as "the French in the Bay of Islands." (The last is a reference to the killing of Marion du Fresne and others of his French crew in 1772.) [13] Under the date 12 February 1777, Cook recorded that the expedition had reached and anchored in "our old station" in Queen Charlotte Sound. Cook noted on this day that the local people who came out in canoes could not be persuaded to come on board ship, in spite of the personal relationships and familiarity established in earlier expeditionary visits. To Cook, this appeared to be an expression of apprehension that the Europeans "were come to revenge the death of Captain Furneux's people," since "first conversation with them generally turned on that subject." [14]

On 14 February 1777, Cook made reference to "a Chief named Kahoura [Kahura] who headed the party that cut off Captain Furneaux's crew." Given what was said of him, Cook observed, "He seemed to be a man more feared than beloved by many." These "many" considered Kahura "a very bad man and importuned me to kill him" (62). On a visit to Grass Cove on 16 February, Cook took the opportunity "to enquire the reasons why our country men were killed." At this time and place, the "chief" known to the Europeans as "Pedro" [Pito?] was questioned on the matter, and answered "without reserve," since "none of these people had any hand in this unhappy affair" (63). This fact, and evidence of some animosity in Totaranui toward Kahura as indicated above, suggest that the account of the incident that Cook received at Grass Cove is unlikely to be prejudiced in favor of Kahura. "They told us that while our people were at victuals with several of the natives about them some of the latter stole or snatched from them some bread, & fish for which they were beat this being resented a quarrel insued, in which two of the Natives were shot dead" (63).

Cook was also told that Furneaux's "black" servant had been the cause of the quarrel, as he had struck "one of the Natives stealing something out of the boat . . . a heavy blow with a stick on which the fellow called out to his countrymen that he was killed." After this, "All rose and fell upon the unhappy suffer[er]s." Cook clarified that the account conveyed in Grass Cove was "confirm'd" by people "who I think, could have no interest in deceiving us," while that received "afterward" came from one of the two young Maori men who left Totaranui with the 1777 expedition (64).

Cook also recorded an account directly from Kahura himself, who visited the ship "without shewing the least sign of fear," even though Omai, the expedition's interpreter, insisted that Cook should shoot him. Cook was more interested in explanation than revenge, and through Omai, pressed insistently for the former. An initially reluctant Kahura finally "ventured to [tell] us, that on offering a stone hatchet for sale to one of the people, he kept it and would give nothing in return, on which they snatched from them some bread while they were at victuals." It seems significant that the rest of this account, as Cook put it, "differed very little from what we had been told by other people," since these "other people" apparently included some who desired Kahura's demise. Cook added, however, that "the story of the Hatchet was certainly invented by Ka-hourah to make the English appear the first aggressors" (66).

With this last remark, Cook seems to have placed the primary, or at least primal, responsibility for the Grass Cove conflict at the feet of the Maori. Thus, according to Cook, the crew of the *Adventure*'s cutter "fell a sacrifice to savage fury" (64). Yet in a 1777 reflection on Maori society in general, Cook allowed that "notwithstanding the divided and jealous state in which they live, travelling strangers who come with no ill design are well received and entertained during their stay, which is expected to be no longer than the business they came upon to transact" (72). Apparently, this observation synthesized Cook's own substantial experience of Maori hospitality with his feelings that the bounds of hospitality could still be easily broached, and "savage fury" provoked. In Grass Cove, Cook also allowed that such "fury" had been spontaneous rather than premeditated.

> All agree that the quarrel first took its rise from some thefts which they (the Natives) commited, all agree also that the thing was not premeditated, and that if these thefts had not, unfortunately, been too hastily resented no ill consequence had attended, for Kahoura's greatest enemies . . . owned that he had no intention to quarrel, much less to kill till the quarrel was actually commenced. (64)

The extensive discussion of these events in King's Log is followed almost verbatim in other February 1777 expeditionary records. King incorporates many of the same details as Cook, both of the explanation given in Grass Cove and of the personal account of Kahura. In his record of the former, King wrote that "the chief" pointed to the spot in Grass Cove where all of the English crew except one man left in the boat were sitting at dinner: "Some of the Indians snatched away part of the bread they were eating; in endeavouring to recover it the Indians made a resistance, when Mr. Rowe who commanded the party fired and killed one of them upon the spot; upon which Kaooroo called to Some Indians upon a hill to come to his assistance."[15] On seeing the muskets discharged, the local people "rushed upon them, killed some on the spot, others not directly." According to King, Rowe killed one more Maori man in the attack, while Furneaux's servant, who waited in the boat, "was the last who fell a victim to their rage." King also observed, like Cook, that other stories of the conflict were told "with trifling alterations tending to excuse themselves for first beginning by stealing the bread." King's account also confirms that Kahura, who had later been questioned at the tent, had no hesitation "in letting us know that he had the principal hand in the tragical event." According to King, Kahura explained the incident as in the account related in Grass Cove, "with the addition, that the reason of the Indian stealing the bread was, a stone hatchet had been taken from him and not paid for by one of the People."[16] Thus in narrative development and all crucial details, King agrees so closely with Cook as to suggest that the accounts may be interdependent to some extent.

A version of these events that is more independent of Cook's record appears in Bayly's Admiralty log in an entry for February 1777 headed "In Charlotte Sound." In this report, Bayly cited the testimony of Kahura, who, Bayly wrote, had "commanded the party that kill'd them."

> He said that our people were all on shore at dinner, except the Black who was in the Boat, & him & his people were set down by them & that one of his people stole a coate out of the Boat, but before he could get off with it the black (who was in the Boat) struck him across the head, which made him cry out he was kill'd, on which him and the rest of his people rose up & attacked our people.[17]

Bayly also recorded from Kahura the detail that Rowe managed to kill two men before he was secured. The other Englishmen were "knocked down" without doing any damage to "the Zealanders," and "in this rage they kill'd them All, & Eat them; & knocked the Boat in pieces & burnt it." Bayly concluded that "Kawoora said that he kill'd the Aree (or Officer) with his own hand, together with most of the people."[18] In a further log, Bayly recorded a second account from "Tabbarooa," one of the boys who accompanied the English from Totaranui. In agreement with Kahura's account, the boy remarked that "one of his country men stole one of our . . . peoples jackets on which the Seaman Knock'd him down from whence a fray ensued." The boy noted that although Rowe attempted to get to the boat, he was taken and killed, while "a great number" of men rushed in, "knocked" all of the crew "on the head & Kill'd them at once & then Knocked the Boat in pieces & burnt her." In this record, Bayly was less sure than Cook and King that the ultimate motivation for the attack was known. While it was "pretty clear" that the quarrel occurred while "our people were at dinner & consequently disarmed & off their guard . . . whether it was a premeditated scheme . . . or not we could not learn clearly."[19]

The existence and role of the stolen coat is the primary difference between the Cook-King and Bayly accounts. Cook, however, also recorded from one of the Totaranui boys with whom he left that "one of the Natives" had stolen "something" from the boat, for which he was struck a heavy blow (64). As we have already seen, George Forster's relation of the 1774 "accounts" of the conflict volunteers the detail "that one of their countrymen stole a sailor's jacket." Consistent with Forster-Bayly, "the best account" Burney could gather also allows for the theft of such an item as the coat, although (as in Cook's version) it is not identified explicitly. While "dining on the beach," a "Zealander stole something out of the Boat, and was making off with it, on which Mr. Rowe fired and killed the Thief on the spot," whereupon "the Zealanders immediately sallied out of the woods and got between our people and the boat." Burney confirmed the detail that Rowe shot and killed two men before he was overpowered. To the claim that the cutter had been destroyed, however, Burney asserted that it was "soon after taken from the Indians of Charlotte Sound" by "those of Terrawitte" (Te Rawhiti) on the north side of Cook Strait, "a strong party of whom had come over on a visit to Charlotte Sound."[20]

While this last detail seemingly disagrees with the version of the cutter's destruction and burning, it seems significant that more than one 1777 account explicitly considers the disposal of the cutter. This suggests that the English boat was the object of some interest, possibly for its metal components. The variance of items taken in Grass Cove is the only other difference of significance between any of the accounts cited above. It is possible, however (as Beaglehole acknowledged),[21] that more than one item was involved. In any case, it is generally consistent that perceptions of theft or inequity in exchange were at the heart of the matter, whether bread, a coat, or a hatchet were singularly or collectively in contention.

The most colorful if controversial account from 1777 is that of John Rickman, in the formerly anonymous *Journal of Captain Cook's Last Voyage*, published in 1781.[22] This Rickman version has been lifted almost verbatim into Ledyard's 1783 expeditionary account,[23] and is also cited (as are details from other observers) in Anderson's 1784 mélange of sources from the three Cook expeditions.[24] As it appears in its more primary form, the larger context of Rickman's account is the romantic liaison between "Ghowannahe" (in Ledyard-Anderson, "Gowannahee"), a New Zealand girl of about fourteen years, and an unnamed youth from the

Discovery. In Rickman's narrative, the ship's youth attempts to remain on shore with Ghowannahe, until Cook sends to have him forcibly removed shortly before leaving Totaranui. A dramatic interchange is also described between the youth and Ghowannahe. This follows the reluctance of the latter to discuss the Grass Cove incident, a reluctance reportedly born of the threat of death. On a declaration of devotion, however, she subsequently confides her understanding of the incident to her lover.

> She then made him to understand that one Gooboa, a very bad man, who had been often at the ship, and had stolen many things; when he came to know that it was preparing to depart went up into the hill country, to the hippah, and invited the warriors to come down and kill the strangers. . . . He told them they need not fear, for he knew where they must come before they departed, in order to get grass for their *goury* or cattle, and that on such occasions they left their *pow pow* behind them . . . while they were at work. They said they were no enemies but friends, and they must not kill men with whom they were in friendship. Gooboa said they were vile enemies, and complained of their chaining him, and beating him. . . . Gooboa undertook to conduct them in safety to the place where the strangers were to come, and shewed them where they might conceal themselves till he should come and give them notice, which he did. And when the men were busy about getting grass, and not thinking any harm, the warriors rushed out upon them, and killed them with their patapatows, and then divided their bodies among them.[25]

Ghowannahe added that "there were women as well as men concerned," of whom the former made the fires "while the warriors cut the dead men in pieces." Reportedly, the bodies were not all eaten at once, "but only their hearts and livers." In the division of the bodies, the warriors had the heads, "which were esteemed the best, and the rest of the flesh was distributed among the croud."[26]

If accurate, this explicit account is obviously invaluable to any interpretation of the Grass Cove event. In textual comparison, the proper noun "Gooboa" for the principal antagonist is within the range of variation of other recorders for Kahura. The suggestion that "Gooboa" was initially at odds with other Maori in encouraging the attack is also consistent with the contempt in which Kahura was held by at least some Totaranui people in 1777. Furthermore, the detail that Gooboa-Kahura "went up into the hill country, to the hippah," to raise an attacking force, is reminiscent of (if a variation on) King's report that after Rowe had fired, "Kaooroo called to Some Indians upon a hill to come to his assistance." The concomitant suggestion of a premeditated attack, however, is counter to Cook's assertion that "all agree" that the event was not premeditated—and Cook's "all" included Kahura's greatest enemies, who had solicited Kahura's destruction from Cook.[27] The concealment of people who rushed the Europeans also runs counter to the suggestion of a spontaneous quarrel. Certainly, other reports suggest that the longboat's crew were killed by Maori who were generally visible and known to them in Grass Cove, and that their deaths were the consequence of a disagreement, not an ambush.

In assessing these differences, one should consider that "Ghowannahe" was apparently not a participant in the events. According to Rickman, "She said she was but a child about ten years old, but she remembers the talk of it as a great achievement; and that they made songs in praise of it."[28] Furthermore, one should consider that the romantic Ghowannahe story is not confirmed by any contemporary journal or log account available, including the entries of Cook, who was supposedly concerned and responsible for returning the youth to the *Discovery*. As a consequence, Beaglehole dismissed the historical veracity of Rickman's entire Ghowannahe account. "[Rickman's] book can be taken as a source, where it is verifiable, or even likely . . . but on the whole it is a fanciful and ridiculously exaggerated production, done exclusively for the market. The romantic strain is strong in the invention of the New Zealand maiden Ghowannahe and her sailor lover."[29]

More charitably, Obeyesekere considers that Rickman's "romantic stories," such as the Ghowannahe love affair, "were probably not deliberate inventions or fabrications but a record of shipboard gossip."[30] In any case, and irrespective of the validity of the Ghowannahe story, the broad similarities between some details of Rickman's Grass Cove narrative and the 1777 reports cited above suggest that Rickman's account has an independent if distorted historical base. It is especially interesting that Rickman records the making of *waiata* (songs) in praise of the event, a unique claim that is consistent with known Maori practice. Rickman alone suggests Maori premeditation and duplicity in the conflict, as opposed to a spontaneous "savage" expression. Yet even then, Rickman's account of the relative ease with which Kahura purportedly swayed his fellows, of the seeming alacrity with which the deed was accomplished, and the sense of achievement it produced, leaves little doubt that Rickman was fundamentally aligned with a perspective of native savage fury.

Reflecting after the event, George Forster also invoked an interpretation of savage passion in his explanation of the Grass Cove incident, but allowed an explicit European component in the violence as well. Thus in a general comment on Maori-European conflict developed from a discussion of the Grass Cove incident, Forster referred to "that passionate fury which hurries on the savage into excess."[31] This point was clarified in Forster's comparison of "savage" and "civilized" societies: "The passions are wisely implanted in our breast for our preservation; and revenge in particular, guards us against the encroachments of others. Savages do not give up the right of retaliating injuries; but civilized societies confer on certain individuals the power and the duty to revenge their wrongs."[32]

If savage passions rose quickly to excess, Forster was clear that in Grass Cove, they had been provoked. Thus Forster suggested that "the whole tenor" of the New Zealander's behavior toward Europeans "seems to acquit them of treachery and cruel malevolence."[33] In explaining Grass Cove, Forster referred to Rowe as a man combining "liberal sentiments" with "the prejudices of a naval education, which induced him to look upon all the natives of the South Sea with contempt, and to assume that kind of right over them, with which the Spaniards . . . disposed of the lives of the American Indians."[34] The reported use of firearms in the cove incident came as no surprise to Forster, who remarked that Rowe "always entertained" the opinion that the New Zealanders "would never stand the fire of European musketry." This had been demonstrated in Rowe's desire to fire upon the people of the North Island east coast Tolaga Bay for taking a brandy keg, where "the judicious and humane advice of lieutenant Burney checked his impetuosity."[35] Even so, Forster identified savage passion as the critical factor immediately responsible for the deaths of the entire English crew.

The philosophical origins and place of European notions of savage violence in contemporary Enlightenment (and non-Enlightenment) thought is beyond the scope of this essay. However, the interpretative influence of a European concept of Maori savagery in the Totaranui encounters of the 1770s is apparent from several records. These include the retrospective account of George Gilbert, who was in the 1777 party sent "every day to different parts of the Sound with 8 or 10 people to cut grass for the cattle." Gilbert observed, "It was lucky for us that we never met with any of the Natives for tho we had arms with us yet they might have rushed from the woods and cut us off."[36] These suspicions were especially aroused as the party pulled into Grass Cove on one of these trips. This place, wrote Gilbert, where "the Adventure's boat crew . . . were cut off and eat upon the spot," could not be "more favourable for such intentions, as the wood was so thick that the Natives could approach close to them before they were discovered." On his own visit to the cove, Gilbert also felt personal apprehension: "We saw 4 or 5 of them, who seeing our numbers were afraid to come near us till we made them to understand we had no intentions to hurt them, we had reason to believe there were a great number of them in the woods as those with us frequently called to them."[37] Gilbert clarified these responses in his own personal characterization of the Maori—a description that has clearly been influenced by observations of the *haka*. "The savageness of their dispositions and horrid barbarity of their customs," he opined, "is fully expressed in their countenances; which is ferocious and frightful beyond imagination being much more so than any other Indians we have seen."[38] While describing the *haka*, Thomas Edgar also remarked that "there is something in them so uncommonly Savage & terrible."[39] In his extensive observations, King reinforced the perception of Maori savagery and violence in graphic detail.

> There are no people more sensible of an Injury than the New Zealanders, & none more ready to resent it, yet as they are insolent when they can be so with impunity, this argues rather a furious than a generous disposition. . . . In the summer they roam about for their food, & are then little better than wild savage beasts; using all their dexterity, to overreach and surprize one another.[40]

Context, Prejudgment, and Cultural Interaction in the Grass Cove Accounts

Several descent groups were resident in the eighteenth-century Marlborough Sounds, all with lower North Island kin connections.[41] Evidence of associated territoriality includes the relatively high archaeological concentration of defended settlements or *paa* in the Sounds region (and Totaranui especially) for a South Island area.[42] Hostilities between the peoples of Totaranui and Admiralty Bay on the northwestern margins of the Sounds are also well documented from the 1770s visits of the three Cook expeditions.[43] Group conflict even characterized the immediate region of Totaranui. King, for example, terrified a Maori companion by proceeding "rather further than ordinary" in descending beyond the tops of the hills of Totaranui, with the local man making signs "that he should be eaten by those we should meet" on the other side.[44] During 1777, in Totaranui, Cook also noted in his journal: "If I had followed the advice of all our pretended friends, I might have extirpated the whole race, for the people of each Hamlet or village by turns applyed to me to destroy the other, a very striking proof of the divided state in which they live" (62).

In this context, it is critical to understand the highly targeted, seasonal nature of the northern South Island Maori economy.[45] The matter of food production and sufficiency is complex, and there is some variance in the expeditionary accounts. Gilbert reported that the "Natives" of Totaranui were "in such a continuous state of hunger that they would eat in the most voracious manner the oil and blubber of the sea bears which we were boiling onshore, likewise candles or anything offered to them."[46] With respect to Maori cannibalism, Gilbert also added, "If any thing may be offered in favour of its practice here, [it] is that of extreme Hunger."[47] Burney similarly observed, "No Beast can be more ravenous or greedy than a New Zealander. Nothing comes amiss; but no Victuals was so highly relished by them as the rank Seal Blubber we brought from Kerguelens Land and which we boiled down here."[48] Against the scenario of constant and ravenous hunger, other writers emphasized the quantity and plenitude of fish available, which the Maori seemed ever ready to exchange. Thus, in November 1773, Cook acknowledged that the local people "were very usefull in providing us with fish which they were far more expert in catching than we."[49] Before leaving in November, Cook added, "During our stay in this place we were well supplyed with fish which we purchased of the Natives at a very easy rate."[50]

This pattern continued during Furneaux's December sojourn in Totaranui prior to the Grass Cove incident, when the inhabitants "came on board as before, and supplied us with fish and other things of their own manufa[c]ture."[51] In 1774, Clerke also recorded that in "numbers of Visits" the Totaranui people "supply us most abundantly with excellent Fish."[52] An anonymous log of the 1777 visit confirmed under a 13 February 1777 entry that fish were still purchased in "Great Numbers from the Natives at a very cheap Rate."[53] While describing the plenitude of coastal food, several of these recorders also inferred a significant storage if not seasonal component in the processing of fern root and (especially) fish. Thus, Johann Forster reported "great quantities of these [dried] provisions in their huts." He added that people were "frequently found . . . preparing both fish and fern roots, for the bad season."[54] This observation from the second expedition's Totaranui visits is also confirmed in Banks' general remarks on New Zealand prepared before *Endeavour*'s departure in March 1770. In the "Southward," Banks remarked, fern roots and fish had to serve "all the Year," adding: "Here therefore we saw that they had made vast piles of Both, especialy the latter which were dryd in the sun very well, I suppose meant for winter stock when possibly Fish is not so plentifull or the trouble of catching it greater than in Winter."[55]

Consistent with archaeological evidence from other northern South

Island localities, the geographical and seasonal subsistence focus of Totaranui Maori apparently excluded other local food resources.[56] Thus from his "Journal" of the 1777 Totaranui visit, George Gilbert remarked:

> The only sustenance that this country affords are fish and fern-root which serves the Natives for bread; I don't recollect ever seeing any of them have birds, therefore imagine they have no method of catching them; the Dog which is the only quadruped in this Country is very scarce. . . . In the most Northern parts of this Country they have a few plantations of sweet potatoes [*Ipomoea batatas*] but not one here.[57]

While Gilbert was quite wrong about the capabilities of Maori to catch birds, his remarks highlight the narrow, and perhaps ritual, focus of food procurement in Totaranui. In this regard, one should also consider that traditional Maori agriculture was not recorded in any of the 1770s expeditionary visits to Totaranui, nor in the 1820 visit of the Russians under Bellingshausen, who recorded (recently introduced) potato *(Solanum tuberosum)* cultivation only.[58] Yet the people of the Sound with their North Island connections were well aware of agricultural produce, and even possessed carved *hue* (gourd; *Lagenaria vulgaris*) containers, apparently from the North Island.[59] Furthermore, there is archaeological evidence of pre-European agriculture elsewhere in the Marlborough Sounds.[60] While taking on provisions in Totaranui, the Europeans had thus imposed upon a carefully, perhaps ritually, regulated seasonal round of fishing and food-gathering activities.

In this matter, the expeditionary record suggests that the Europeans were often either unaware of, or chose not to consider, the intrusion of their subsistence demands. Expressions of this ignorance, if not unwillingness, include Cook's 1773 claim that "[in] every part of New Zealand which I have been in, Fish have been found in such plenty that the Natives have generally caught as much as served both themselves and us."[61] From the 1777 visit, James Williamson remarked that the New Zealanders inhabited "a vast tract of Country abounding with Fish of the most delicious kinds, & great plenty of land and sea birds."[62] In both instances, the rhetorical intent of Cook and Williamson in promoting a view of plenty and abundance was to counter an argument that cannibalism was ever necessitated from want of food in New Zealand. Even Banks, who acknowledged that the vast fish stocks he saw in the "Southward" (apparently Totaranui) were meant for winter scarcity or times of more difficult capture, otherwise reported without qualification in his general summary that "Every creek and corner [in New Zealand] produces abundance of fish."[63]

Yet in spite of these sanguine interpretations, there are indications in the eighteenth-century ethnographic record that the constant English demands for fish were both difficult to meet and resented on occasion. On 3 February 1770, Cook recorded that he went to "the Hippa" on the east side of the Sound "and purchas'd of the Inhabitants a quantaty of split and half dry'd fish and such as I could get."[64] To this last rather cryptic appended remark, Cook added, "About noon we took our leave of them, which some seem'd not sorry for, for notwithstanding they sold us their fish very freely, there were some few among them who shew'd evident signs of disaprobation."[65] Banks was more forthright in his comments on this interaction, comments that also elucidate the perceived threat of such exchanges to storage requirements. "The Captn," he wrote, "wanted to buy Dry fish for sea stock, and did buy so much that at last the Old men fairly told him that he must go away or he would leave them without provisions, which they enforced by some threats; matters were however so well conducted that they parted peacably."[66] A further entry also suggests that an unwillingness to supply the Europeans with fish characterized the larger area of contact influence in Totaranui at this time. Thus on 4 February 1770, Cook reported "an excursion along shore to the Northward in order to traffick with the Natives for fish in which we had no great success."[67]

The most plausible link between these exchange difficulties and the Grass Cove incident may be the reciprocating *koha* (gift). As an institution, *koha* could cement alliances, ensure good will, distribute valuable goods and commodities, and even create a social debt. One of the most powerful categories of *koha* was and is *pounamu* (nephritic "greenstone"), which is understood to possess and cumulate high prestige and spiritual power, or *mana*.[68] The gift of *pounamu* may involve the recognition of status, the sealing of a covenant, and in some cases (especially where descent is concerned), the actual transmission of *mana*. In this light, the serious intent of exchange in Totaranui is suggested by Johann Forster's observation in 1773 that the English had "bought up all the curiosities & green Stones, the Natives in the Sound were possessed of."[69] As indicated above, in constantly and abundantly providing the Europeans with fish, Maori were also sacrificing aspects of their own important food-processing and storage activities. From the Maori perspective, the reciprocating European *koha* included nails, chisels, hatchets, cloth, biscuit, and sea mammal fat, a mix recognizing political status as well as utilitarian and subsistence needs.

In this context, *koha* recognized the legitimacy of *mana whenua* and *mana moana* (authority over the resources of land and sea) of the residents, and established good will. The sociopolitical importance of *koha* was also enhanced in a highly territorial region, such as Totaranui, where the offering had to recognize, and be commensurate with, the complexity of social and kin relationships and hierarchy. For the people of Totaranui, *pounamu* was apparently considered politically appropriate to the context of European-Maori relations. That Maori had perceptions of a like status for some European trade items is suggested in Burney's Totaranui journal entry for 24 February 1777: "Before our departure they carried [metal] Hatchets under their Cloaths instead of the [generally *pounamu*] Patow."[70]

In this potentially volatile situation in which high-level relations had to be established with several discrete social entities in Totaranui, there is evidence that some Maori groups may have felt aggrieved by, or excluded from, full participation in the European *koha*. As indicated above, there is clear evidence from the 1770 records that by the conclusion of Cook's Totaranui sojourn, some Maori at least had begun to resent the potential if not actual European impact on their provisions. At this time, Cook also recorded of some local people who visited with "stinking fish," that "trade . . . seem'd [not] to be their object, but were more inclineable to quarrel." One of the Maori was fired upon as a consequence, and "angrily threw the fish which he had sold, and for which he had been paid, into the sea."[71] A further exchange incident for 22 November 1773 underscores a Totaranui Maori perception of the sometimes inadequate European offering:

> Early in the morning we were visited by several of the Natives, some of whom were Strangers, these last offered us various curiosities in exchange for Otahiete cloth and Red Blaze &c. At first the exchanges were in our favour till an old man, who was no stranger to us, came and assisted his countrymen with his advice and in a moment turned the exchanges about a thousand per cent in their favour.[72]

The log entry of William Bayly for 15 February 1777 also describes "some little quarrel" between the *Resolution*'s Sergeant of Marines and "an old Indian."[73] Gilbert clarified that the quarrel "happen'd at the ship with the Natives when an old man came on board and told Capt Cook that some of his countrymen had a design upon our boat."[74] According to Bayly, the old man "went off in a Canoe in a terrable Rage to a little cove where was a number of Indians at dinner." These people then all launched their canoes to cross to the cove where some of the English crew were cutting grass. In Bayly's account, "Cook saw the inraged Indian & endeavoured to enquire the cause & Passify him; but he could neither do one or the other." Consequently, an armed pinnace was sent to the grass cutters for protection, "but the Indians altered their rout when they saw the Pinnis [pinnace] coming after them."[75] It is especially interesting to consider that the exchange of fish and manufactured Maori items in December 1773 immediately prior to the Grass Cove conflict was punctuated by several Maori attempts to secrete away European items under cover of dark—attempts that were met with gunshot.[76]

The latter situation highlights the reality that European-Maori interaction in Totaranui crossed not just immediate needs and desires but two quite different social and economic orders. In the laissez-faire European economy, the expectations of barter were generally made explicit and concluded within the material transaction. For Maori, however, *koha* generally incorporated less visible and potentially long-term social and political obligations as well, with due acknowledgment of *mana* always a crucial factor. With respect to Grass Cove, whether Kahura and his companions were aggrieved or believed they had certain rights of access to European trade items, one cannot ignore the common thread in all of the primary accounts that disagreement over an exchange interaction was at the heart of the incident. Because different exchange expectations and tension characterized European-Maori interaction in Totaranui throughout the 1770s, a strong circumstantial case can be made that the Grass Cove conflict was rooted in an exchange grievance or misunderstanding of a conceptual nature. Thus what was considered theft in a European view of barter may have been no more than a Maori expectation that the communal balance of exchange should account more appropriately for the social and subsistence costs of *koha*. After the shooting of Maori in the cove, the balance of exchange became a fatal ledger, and as a matter of *utu*, or deadly satisfaction, the killing of Rowe and his crew inevitable.

One should also consider that a concern for final satisfaction and protection from this event may explain the inferred cannibalism that so horrified the English. From records of the late eighteenth to the early nineteenth century, a Maori trajectory emerges from precontact times where dire consequences loomed if enemy spirits and associated *tapu* matters were not appeased or satisfied. If enemy bodies were eaten, however, any malign spiritual influences could be extinguished with the absorption of the *mana* of the consumed.[77] In Grass Cove, the potentially rogue powers of *tapu, mana,* and technology associated with the new European visitors may have been of special concern, prompting the protection of a comprehensive anthropophagy.[78]

Conclusion

The larger contextual perspective presented above could not have been anticipated, or, retrospectively, appreciated, in anything like this detail by the 1777 recorders. Yet there is evidence that certain Europeans perceived at least some of the cultural complexities of contact events in which they were participants. Thus, in response to evidence of a battle between the peoples of Totaranui and Admiralty Bay in 1773, Johann Forster made the following observation:

> I am afraid we are the innocent causes of this war. For having bought up all the Curiosities & green Stones, the Natives in the Sound were possessed of, & hearing us constantly ask for more & offering various things, which tempted their desires; They went I believe in quest of them among their neighbours . . . to possess themselves of these things which are so much coveted by the Europeans.[79]

As indicated earlier, George Forster also addressed the matter of Grass Cove with similar insight, offering Rowe's attitude of superiority as a critical cause of the conflict. Forster added, "It plainly appears . . . that the rash action of revenging this theft [of the coat at Grass Cove] with death, and most probably revenging it indiscriminately on a whole body of natives, must have provoked them to retaliate."[80] With respect to the near contemporary death of du Fresne and his crew in the Bay of Islands, Forster even went so far as to suggest that "it is . . . greatly to be suspected" that local people "took umbrage at some affront, perhaps unwittingly committed by the strangers, and revenged it,"[81] an interpretation consistent with Salmond's detailed research into this incident.[82]

Despite such cross-cultural insight, the Forsters' views are still mediated through an eighteenth-century notion of savage passion. This notion is explicitly or implicitly ubiquitous in all of the contemporary 1777 Totaranui records. Furthermore, as Hoare has commented, in spite of Johann Forster's 1773 accusation of a European influence on exchange and warfare in Totaranui, "Forster went happily on, here and elsewhere, with his own private vigorous, even aggressive, policy of collecting."[83] This more normative pattern of "vigorous" collecting, in spite of Forster's apparent reservations as expressed in a private journal entry, demonstrates the complexity and ambiguity of European behavior in early contact. It also underscores the need to evaluate the ideological and social, as well as ecological, context of these early encounters as a precondition to cultural explanation.

As descriptive historical records of later eighteenth-century Maori life, the Cook expeditionary accounts from the 1770s range between scant and nearly superb. As explanatory records of cultural interaction, however, the Cook reports appear to be seriously deficient, if judged by the standards of the 1777 Grass Cove accounts. The Europeans were capable of recognizing the cultural impact of their own intrusion, even if their behavioral responses were at best ambiguous. Yet, despite mounting evidence of cultural intrusion and consequent stress throughout the 1770s in Totaranui, including expressions of local resentment, exchange difficulties, and the exacerbation of preexisting hostilities, the conflict at Grass Cove with its accompanying report of cannibalism was ultimately ascribed by the Europeans to a savage Maori nature, and the concomitant excess of unrestrained passion outside of a civil polity. A contextual examination of the Grass Cove incident underscores the nature of the generalized European expeditionary understanding of Maori life as the partisan product of one side of a bicultural encounter, rather than the sum of the whole.

NOTES

Abbreviations

AJCP	Australian Joint Copying Project
ATL	Alexander Turnbull Library, Wellington
PRO	Public Record Office, Kew, London

The research on which this essay is based is part of a larger project on Maori-European relations in early contact. The project has received an Award in History from the New Zealand History Research Trust Fund, History Division, Department of Internal Affairs, New Zealand, for which I am extremely grateful. I should also like to acknowledge the constant assistance and professionalism of the staff of the Alexander Turnbull Library, Wellington. Their skills have facilitated my research among the Turnbull's holdings of microform and photographic copies of almost all unpublished expeditionary logs, journals, and accounts from the three Pacific Cook expeditions, as well as the

Turnbull's own relevant original manuscript holdings. In the references that follow, manuscripts are cited without accession numbers, except for Admiralty documents accessed by microform through the Australian Joint Copying Project series.

1. The authors and works central to this debate are Gannath Obeyesekere, *The Apotheosis of Captain Cook: European Mythmaking in the Pacific* (Princeton: Princeton University Press, 1992), and Marshall Sahlins, *Historical Metaphors and Mythical Realities: Structure in the Early History of the Sandwich Islands Kingdom* (Ann Arbor: University of Michigan Press, 1981); *Islands of History* (Chicago: University of Chicago Press, 1985); and *How "Natives" Think: About Captain Cook, For Example* (Chicago: University of Chicago Press, 1995). On the profile and significance of this discussion, see "A Review Symposium on the *Apotheosis of Captain Cook,*" *Social Analysis: Journal of Social and Cultural Practice* 34 (December 1993): 33–85; "Book Review Forum," *Pacific Studies* 17 (June 1994) 2: 136–155; Samuel K. Parker, "The Revenge of Practical Reason? A Review Essay on Gannath Obeyesekere's *The Apotheosis of Captain Cook,*" *Oceania* 65 (March 1995) 3: 257–267, and Obeyesekere, "Re-Weaving the Argument: A Response to Parker," 268–273; and Rick Perlstein, "Hawaii KO," *The Times Higher Educational Supplement* 1177 (26 May 1995): 21.

2. Peter Munz, "The Two Worlds of Anne Salmond in Postmodern Fancy-Dress," *New Zealand Journal of History* 28 (1994) 1: 60–75, and Anne Salmond, "Antipodean Crab Antics," commenting on Salmond, in *Two Worlds: First Meetings Between Maori and Europeans, 1642–1772* (Auckland: Viking, Penguin, 1991), 76–79. See also Salmond, "Whose God, or Not?" in *Social Analysis: Journal of Social and Cultural Practice* 34 (December 1993): 50–55, and Gannath Obeyeskere, "Anthropology and the Cook Myth: A Response to Critics," 77–78.

3. Sahlins, *How "Natives" Think,* 251.

4. Obeyesekere, *Apotheosis.*

5. See Anon. [probably J. Marra], *Journal of the Resolution's Voyage, in 1772, 1773, 1774, and 1775 . . . also a Journal of the Adventure's Voyage, in the Years 1772, 1773, and 1774* (London: Newberry, 1775), 94–97; Furneaux's narrative in John C. Beaglehole, ed., *The Journals of Captain James Cook on his Voyages of Discovery,* 4 vols. (Cambridge: Published for the Hakluyt Society at the University Press, 1961), 2:741–742; Burney's Log in B. Hooper, ed., *With Captain James Cook in the Antarctic and the Pacific: The Private Journal of James Burney Second Lieutenant of the Adventure on Cook's Second Voyage, 1772–1773* (Canberra: National Library of Australia, 1975), 96–97; and Bayly's journal account in Robert McNab, ed., *Historical Records of New Zealand,* 2 vols. (Wellington: Government Printer, 1914), 2:217.

6. Beaglehole, *Journals of Captain James Cook*, 2:572–573, 576, 577; see also Michael E. Hoare, ed., *The Resolution Journal of Johann Reinhold Forster, 1772–1775*, 4 vols. (London: Hakluyt Society, 1982) 4:675, 676.

7. George Forster, *A Voyage Round the World*, 2 vols. (London: White et al., 1777), 2:454–460.

8. Hoare, *Resolution Journal*, 4:675, 676.

9. G. Forster, *Voyage*, 2:456.

10. Ibid., 2:457.

11. Ibid., 2:458.

12. Ibid., 2:465.

13. See Salmond, *Two Worlds*, 359–429.

14. Beaglehole, *Journals of Captain James Cook* 3:59. Subsequent page references to this volume are given parenthetically in the text.

15. James King, Ship's Log, 12 February 1776–2 February 1778, holograph original (Adm 55/116, PRO; AJCP Reel 1593, ATL), 52.

16. Ibid.

17. William Bayly, "A Log & Journal Kept on Board His Majesties Sloop Discovery," 1 August 1776–3 December 1779, holograph original (Adm 55/20, PRO; AJCP Reel 1575, ATL), 48.

18. Ibid.

19. William Bayly, Log, 11 June 1776–30 April 1779 [bound with MS 1777–1778 journal], holograph (ATL) 15 February 1777, 56. Note that the unpublished text with interlinear modifications is followed here in preference to the edited account in McNab, *Historical Records of New Zealand*, 2:219–220. On the distinction between Bayly's log in ATL and his PRO Admiralty log referenced above, see Beaglehole, *Journals of Captain James Cook* 3: xxiii and clxxxix–cxc.

20. Burney's Admiralty "Journal of a Voyage in the Discovery" as cited in McNab, *Historical Records of New Zealand*, 2:197–198.

21. Beaglehole, *Journals of Captain James Cook* 3:64 n. 1.

22. Anon. [John Rickman], *Journal of Captain Cook's last Voyage to the Pacific Ocean, on Discovery; Performed in the years 1776, 1777, 1778, 1779 . . .* (London: Newberry, 1781).

23. John C. Ledyard, *A Journal of Captain Cook's Last Voyage* (1783; Chicago: Quadrangle, 1963).

24. G. W. Anderson, *A New Authentic and Complete Collection of Voyages Round the World. Captain Cook's First, Second, Third, and Last Voyages* (London: Hogg, 1784).

25. [Rickman], *Journal of Captain Cook's last Voyage*, 62–63.

26. Ibid., 63–64.

27. Beaglehole, *Journals of Captain James Cook*, 3:64.

28. [Rickman], *Journal of Captain Cook's last Voyage*, 64.

29. Beaglehole, *Journals of Captain James Cook,* 3: cv.
30. Obeyeskere, *Apotheosis,* 122, 222 n. 13.
31. G. Forster, *Voyage,* 465.
32. Ibid., 466.
33. Ibid., 465.
34. Ibid., 458.
35. Ibid., 458–459.
36. Christine Holmes, ed., *Captain Cook's Final Voyage: The Journal of Midshipman George Gilbert* (Horsham, Sussex: Caliban Books, 1982), 24.
37. Holmes, *Captain Cook's Final Voyage,* 25.
38. Ibid., 26.
39. As cited in McNab, *Historical Records of New Zealand,* 2:225.
40. King, Ship's Log, 52, 53.
41. For information on eighteenth-century Totaranui, see W. J. Elvy, *Kei Puta te Wairau: A History of Marlborough in Maori Times* (Christchurch: Whitcombe and Tombs, 1957), 60; Stephen O'Regan, "Queen Charlotte Sound: Aspects of Maori Traditional History," and David R. Simmons, "Artefacts and People: Inter-Island Trade through Queen Charlotte Sound," in *Queen Charlotte Sound: The Traditional and European Records, 1820,* ed. Glynn Barratt (Ottawa, Canada: Carleton University Press, 1987), 139–158, 159–188; S. Percy Smith, "History and Traditions of the Maoris of the West Coast North of New Zealand Prior to 1840," in *Memoirs of the Polynesian Society,* vol. 1 (New Plymouth, New Zealand, 1910), 424; S. Perry Smith, "Ngati-Kuia (or Kati-Kuia) Notes," in "Polynesian Notes Volume 1," 412 ff, holograph (ATL) 414; John White, *The Ancient History of the Maori, His Mythology and Traditions,* 6 vols. (Wellington: Government Printer, 1887) 3:316.
42. Barry Brailsford, *The Tattooed Land: The Southern Frontiers of the Pa Maori* (Wellington: Reed, 1981); see also Michael Trotter, "Settlements, Sites and Structures around Ship Cove," in Barratt, *Queen Charlotte Sound,* 105–137.
43. See Ian Barber, "Archaeology, Ethnography, and the Record of Maori Cannibalism before 1815: A Critical Review," *Journal of the Polynesian Society* 101 (September 1992) 3: 245–253.
44. King, Ship's Log, 52.
45. See Ian G. Barber, "Culture Change in Northern Te Wai Pounamu," Ph.D. diss. (University of Otago, Dunedin, 1994), chap. 4–6; Ian G. Barber, "Loss, Change, and Monumental Landscaping: Towards a New Interpretation of the 'Classic' Maaori Emergence," *Current Anthropology* 37 (December 1996) 5:870–875; David J. Butts, "Seasonality at Rotokura, Tasman Bay: A Case Study in the Use of Faunal Identifications to Establish the Season of Occupation for an Archaeological Site," B.A. (Hons.) thesis (University of Otago, 1977); David J. Butts, "Rotokura: An Archaeological Site in Tasman Bay," *Journal of the Nelson Historical Society* 3 (1978): 4–17.

46. Holmes, *Captain Cook's Final Voyage*, 25.

47. Ibid., 26–27.

48. James Burney, "Journal of the Proceedings of his Majys. Sloop Discovery . . . Febry 10th 1776 to October 11th 1777," holograph original Mitchell Library, Sydney (photographic reproduction ATL), 1/24.

49. Beaglehole, *Journals of Captain James Cook*, 2:288.

50. Beaglehole, *Journals of Captain James Cook*, 2:296.

51. Furneaux's narrative in Beaglehole, *Journals of Captain James Cook*, 2:743.

52. Charles Clerke, Logbook of the Resolution, November 1772–March 1775, holograph original, British Museum Library (microfilm copy ATL), entry for 5 November 1774.

53. "A Logg of the Proceedings of his Majestys Sloop Resolution . . . Commencing February 10th 1776 & ending November 15th 1778," holograph original (Adm.55/114, PRO; microfilm copy AJCP Reel 1592, ATL), 51.

54. Johann Reinhold Forster, *Observations Made During a Voyage Round the World* . . . (London: Robinson, 1778), 236.

55. John C. Beaglehole, ed., *The Endeavour Journal of Joseph Banks, 1768–1771*, 2 vols. (Sydney: Angus and Robertson, 1963), 2:21.

56. See Barber, "Culture Change," and "Loss, Change, and Monumental Landscaping."

57. Holmes, *Captain Cook's Final Voyage*, 25.

58. Glynn Barratt, ed., *Bellingshausen: A Visit to New Zealand, 1820* (Palmerston North: Dunmore, 1979).

59. Beaglehole, *Journals of Captain James Cook*, 2:168; G. Forster, *Voyage*, 1:220, 227, 230; J. R. Forster, *Observations*, 292; Hoare, *Resolution Journal*, 3:301.

60. Brailsford, *The Tattooed Land*, 44, 45, 59, 74, 77; Elvy, *Kei Puta te Wairau*, 22.

61. Beaglehole, *Journals of Captain James Cook*, 2:295 n. 2.

62. James Williamson, Ship's Log, 13 July 1776–17 February 1778, holograph original (Adm 55/117 PRO; microfilm copy AJCP Reel 1593, ATL), 44.

63. Beaglehole, *Endeavour Journal of Joseph Banks*, 2:6.

64. Beaglehole, *Journals of Captain James Cook*, 1:244.

65. Ibid.

66. Beaglehole, *Endeavour Journal of Joseph Banks*, 1:461.

67. Beaglehole, *Journals of Captain James Cook*, 1:244.

68. See Raymond Firth, *Economics of the New Zealand Maori*, 2d ed. (Wellington: Government Printer, 1959), 393–432; Moira White, "Greenstone and Culture Areas in New Zealand," Master's thesis (University of Auckland, 1983), 57–58 and passim.

69. Hoare, *Resolution Journal*, 3:427.

70. Cited in McNab, *Historical Records of New Zealand*, 2:198.

71. Beaglehole, *Journals of Captain James Cook*, 1:235.

72. Ibid., 2:291.

73. Cited in McNab, *Historical Records of New Zealand*, 2:220.

74. Holmes, *Captain Cook's Final Voyage*, 24.

75. McNab, *Historical Records of New Zealand*, 2:220.

76. Beaglehole, *Journals of Captain James Cook*, 2:743; McNab, *Historical Records of New Zealand*, 2: 214–216.

77. John R. Elder, ed., *The Letters and Journals of Samuel Marsden, 1765–1838* (Dunedin: A. H. Reed,1932), 220; Salmond, *Two Worlds*, 401.

78. In "'British Cannibals': Contemplation of an Event in the Death and Resurrection of James Cook, Explorer," *Critical Inquiry* 18 (1992): 643, 652–654, Gannath Obeyesekere interprets the reported Grass Cove cannibalism in terms of a historical Maori shift toward "conspicuous anthropophagy." Without contesting the reality of later, unprecedented, expanded patterns of postcontact cannibalism in New Zealand, the Grass Cove details still seem closer to the traditional concern for the mitigation of spiritual danger than to any new, "conspicuous" orientation in Maori anthropophagy. See Barber, "Archaeology," 242, 282, and passim.

79. Hoare, *Resolution Journal*, 3:427.

80. G. Forster, *Voyage*, 2:465.

81. Ibid.

82. Salmond, *Two Worlds*, 359–429.

83. Hoare, *Resolution Journal*, 3:428 n.1.

11

My Musket, My Missionary, and My *Mana*

Pat Hohepa

I preface this discussion with the remark that it is conceived from my side of the beach. I am Maori, a descendant of those Ngapuhi (my Maori nation) who owned *ahikaa, noho tuuturu,* and *mana whenua* rights of the beaches of the northern peninsula of Aotearoa–New Zealand when Europe came to the southern oceans.[1] In current terms, my ancestors were using, living on, and controlling access to the beaches and oceans and lands at the time of contact with Europe. It is my intention to give a personal Ngapuhi view of what was on the Maori side of the beach during those early years when Ngapuhi met European navigators, adventurers, castaways, missionaries, whalers, and sealers on their beaches and in the hinterland of the Bay of Islands and Hokianga. I shall present my data in accordance with Maori and Ngapuhi epistemological systems. The timespan to be covered ends with the success of Hongi Hika in gathering together a formidable fleet of war canoes with warriors armed with muskets acquired with the help of missionaries. *Mana,* missionaries, and muskets coalesced at that moment.

Some explanation of my manner of proceeding is necessary at this stage. While traditional Maori historical narratives amply answer such questions as "who" was involved, "where" it happened, and "why," Maori narration does not focus on historicity or the datelining of events. Narrative must interplay with genealogical reference to the time of the event, for genealogy links the past with the now, linking us of the present directly with ancestors. Not for Maori is the omnipresence of "when," that crossmatching of person and event, time and place (such as "Tasman discovered New Zealand in A.D. 1642"), which then becomes a truism, a given that is unquestionable. Add this formality to impersonal presentation and one becomes objective. These historical absolutes, this striving for objectivity, has no central place in Maori narrative, where the past and the future are swirling spirals of time, with events and people interacting with the presence of the narrator. Narrative coinciding with genealogy is a necessary part of Maori epistemology. In a sense, it creates a complexity of discourse more appropriate for a *marae*[2]—that is the kind of discourse presented here, not in Maori but in English. It is through this discourse that the view from the Maori side of the glass wall is given, of the voyages to the beaches of the Bay of Islands and Hokianga.

Who are these Ngapuhi? This is a question I will return to, but for the moment let me say that the name has many origins, the earliest coming from the time of the navigator Kupe.[3] His two wives were women of exceptional rank, character, and ability, and set apart; hence, they were *puhi*. They were Hineiteaparangi and Kuramarotini, the former seeing this country first. Of course, generations of students and teachers memorize that "Kupe discovered Aotearoa in A.D. 950," an Orientalized version that is wrong on all counts.[4]

The name "Ngapuhi" also comes from the time of the next major navigator to reach Northland, Nukutawhiti, whose pet esoteric oceanic minder (*taniwha*), Puhimoanaariki, was his scout.[5] The name originated with her. Another origin comes from the time of Rahiri, eight generations after Nukutawhiti. He named his group "Ngapuhi," either after his grandmother Puhikaiariki, or his grandfather, another Puhiariki, from the Mataatua canoe.[6] The ultimate origin, or the crucial event, is not important in Maori epistemology; rationalism or deductive reasoning has little to do with inductive narrative. Ngapuhi exists, and came from those origins.

Given that diversity of origins, the question can be asked as to who Ngapuhi are today. Ngapuhi is a group descended genealogically from Nukutawhiti, Puhi, and Rahiri. Their present members stubbornly retain their identity as Ngapuhi despite discovery, occupation, diseases, and other effects of colonization from Europe. There are two self-identified groups recognized. One is *Ngapuhi-nui-tonu*, Greater Ngapuhi, which includes all who descend from Nukutawhiti and other ancestors whose first navigators settled Northland. There is *Ngapuhi-tuuturu*, Real Ngapuhi, who live in the middle of Northland peninsula, bound by the harbors of Hokianga, Whangaroa, and Whangarei. The population of the latter is close to 100,000 (97,000 according to the 1990 census), while the next largest Maori nation, Ngati Porou, has half that number. Three-quarters of Ngapuhi, of whom I am but one, now live outside our subgroup territories, largely from the vicissitudes of colonization. Nevertheless, we are all descendants of those who met the first voyagers from Europe in the Bay of Islands and Hokianga.

When Maori people of the South Island discovered the ships of Abel Tasman in their bay, Ngapuhi was already a political reality and would have been the largest grouping of that time. I estimate that there were 150,000 Maori in Aotearoa at the time of Tasman, and 35,000 of that number were Ngapuhi. When Cook came in A.D. 1769, there would have been close to 50,000 Ngapuhi out of a total Maori population of 250,000. The doubling of the Ngapuhi and Maori population in the 227 years since James Cook's visits to 500,000 today cloaks the devastating reality that there was a 75 percent drop in Maori numbers in the first 127 years of contact. There were only 42,000 Maori in 1892. Comparative demographic research in Hawai'i and other Pacific countries shows parallel losses and gains, which are directly linked with colonization.

European Voyagers and Their Discoveries of the Beaches

What was the view from the Ngapuhi side of the beach concerning the coming of Europe? One can, from a Ngapuhi viewpoint, partially dismiss Tasman. No Ngapuhi saw him pass by. News of strange vessels may have flowed southward from Ngati Kurii relatives who prevented him from landing at the Three Kings Islands, but that information was not passed on to later generations.

Cook's visit was remembered. Although he returned three times in three years, he did not stay for even one year at any one time. In fact, from 1769 to 1824, which Ngapuhi would recall as the two generations of continuous visits by *pakeha* explorers, none stayed for any long length of time. Most spent their time assiduously exploring and mapping the coastline, spending various rest and recreation periods ashore, and then departing. They were all male and were all from Europe, or from European colonies and hence were *pakeha*. "Kaahore i tupu te paa harakeke" (the flax plantation never grew) is the charitable expression of Maori for them, for they left no offspring to tell their story or to mark that they had been here.

Some, but few, Maori traveled with them when they left; many of those few were coerced or kidnapped on board. Those who did travel and return transferred their information about lands and peoples they had seen to their Ngapuhi relatives.

Interspersed in the Ngapuhi narrative of navigators from the 1780s onward were other Europeans who came not to map, explore, and describe but primarily to hunt whales and seals and to trade. Their catches or cargo were soon filled, and their turnaround time, including time spent for rest and recreation, was also short in relative terms. Many more Ngapuhi men joined their expeditions and spent wretched times on inhospitable islands or scurvy- and disease-ridden boats. The establishment of a British Colony in New South Wales gave an impetus to the hunting of sea mammals. Many Ngapuhi deliberately took steerage or worked their way, and beginning in the 1790s, Sydney became a favorite port of call. The transliterated name of Poihaakena (Port Jackson) brought visions of governors, missionaries, *pakeha* slaves (convicts), muskets, and iron weapons and tools. The name itself continues in the minds of Ngapuhi even today, for Poihaakena is still its Maori name. The Bay of Islands, on the other hand, became a favorite place for replenishing food and water, as well as for rest and recreation for the whaling, sealing, and trading crews, giving ample opportunity for Ngapuhi men to pay or work their way across. As for Ngapuhi women, some went with their men, but many more were abducted. The ships sailed for foreign ports, or for other tribal areas. Cases of Ngapuhi men and women being mistreated, left to survive as best they could, or killed by other tribal groups, were reasons for later vengeance.

A small number of ship people or runaways from servitude became semipermanent beach-based entrepreneurs or traders vying for contracts for *kauri* spars, dressed flax, Maori weapons, Maori cloaks, and preserved heads. In exchange, Maori were paid with nails, iron tools and weapons, European clothing, beads and blankets, and muskets, shot, and gunpowder. Muskets were the ultimate desire. Careless or cruel actions by these temporary traders or whalers invited repercussions on them or others— as the killings of crews and passengers of the *Venus* in 1806, the *Boyd* in 1809, and the *Parramatta* in 1808 would testify, a reminder of Surville and Marion du Fresne of only a generation before. Unless one was married into a chiefly Maori family, however, and adopted as honorary Maori, or Pakeha Maori, the beaches were not safe as a permanent place. Runaway convicts, erstwhile traders, and beachcombers whose time was running out, had few choices. Some managed to survive; others decided slavery was preferable to being convicts in Australia; others became food. Up to 1814 there was no permanent European settlement.

To all this came missionaries in 1814 to trade for Maori souls. The first missionary settlement was set up by the London Missionary Society, again in the Bay of Islands. Other missions were also set up there before the Wesleyans established their first at Whangaroa. But all were still within the Ngapuhi sphere of influence. The majority of missionaries brought with them a curious assorted baggage of right-wing work ethics, Christianism, Victorianism, imperialism, and ghettoism. Samuel Marsden, if alive today, would have felt at ease in the right-wing New Zealand business roundtable of the 1990s.

But while the period from 1814 to 1840 is supposed to be the period of pacification of Ngapuhi and other Maori, muskets were absorbed much deeper and faster into Maori hegemony than missionaries. The results were disastrous. An estimated eighty thousand Maori were killed or died as a result of wars and the arms race between tribal nations. Ngapuhi itself was devastated by inter-subtribe battles, battles between four major alliance groups within its confederation, and the losses suffered even when other tribes were devastated by Ngapuhi arms. By 1835, all tribes were weary, all surviving tribes had muskets, and a stalemate was reached. A window of opportunity had opened for missionary control, and they took advantage of it. By this time there were between four or five thousand Europeans permanently or semipermanently settled in Aotearoa; Maori numbers still exceeded 150,000.

Concerning this broad-brush description, I can begin with a flat statement that right from the outset the European voyagers arrived with an inbuilt faith that they were the discoverers of Australia and Tasmania and Aotearoa–New Zealand, and many felt that they were also the purveyors of right and might and civilization. Tasman, Cook, Surville, and Marion du Fresne were prime examples. The missionaries followed their sea trails and also brought their beliefs, expectations, interpretations, and Christian morality. Those who stayed the longest with Ngapuhi had to make the greatest changes in their attitudes and lifestyles. I now return to develop "where," "who," and "what happened" before the coming of Europe.

Polynesian-Maori Voyages and Beaches

Ngapuhi has a narrative of its own voyagers who arrived at these same beaches many generations or centuries before Europeans. Ngapuhi genealogy and history trace their arriving at different times, broadly between A.D. 500 and 1200. The "when," or the accurate or reasonably approximate time of those events in Hawaiki and the departure and successive arrivals of various canoeloads of ancestors to these shores is not important. Our presence here is proof enough that Ngapuhi ancestors discovered and settled a land that was truly *terra nullius*—a land without humans. The voyages and discoveries were a deliberate search for new home islands for settlement and safety. Their own islands of Hawaiki were in turmoil, with many of the traditional accounts and ancient pre–European laments telling of wars fought over land, crops, animals, fishing grounds, *mana*, and women.[7]

There are deeper reasons for the displacement of people. My suspicion is that the tropical Pacific was subjected to the same drought conditions, perhaps El Niño induced, that caused the abandonment of civilizations in the Americas, Africa, the Near West (Asia from Malaysia to the Tigris-Euphrates) during those same centuries. Whatever the cause, people left on large, safe, double-hull voyaging catamarans, sailing old pathways and then creating new ones, searching for a land already fished up by another ancestor, or, more accurately, a fish landed by another ancestor of another time. And there it was, floating in the southern seas. That narrative will shortly be told.

For my Maori ancestors, the migration was by no means a shift from one end of the world, with its own cultural mores and histories, to another that was totally different. The voyage was not long, and was in the nature of a nomadic shift from one part of island Polynesia to another, in which they took all their oceanic cultural baggage and plants to uninhabited islands. That was what their ancestors had done in previous generations, for oceanic culture had grown and existed in these scattered tropical Pacific Islands and atolls for some ten thousand years. This time, they would travel to islands that were huge in their terms, and with a subtropical climate. But their attitude toward the undiscovered country would differ remarkably from that of the first European navigators, even if the islands were not inhabited when they arrived. The difference lies deep within the cultural beliefs carried by the migrants as a matter of faith.

That belief system began not from stories or gods brought from foreign lands by others nor from impersonal sources. It began within themselves: "Kotahi anoo te tupuna o te tangata Maori, ko Ranginui e tu nei, ko Papa-tuanuku e takoto nei, ki eenei koorero. Ki taa te Paakehaa, ki taana tikanga, na te Atua anake te tangata, me Rangi, me Papa, me nga mea katoa i hanga," wrote Te Rangikaheke, in his massive literary output for Sir George Grey in the 1850s.[8] The account means: "There is but one ancestor of the Maori people, Rangi the great Sky father who stands above here, and Papa the Earth mother lying here. To the Paakehaa or European, in accordance with their beliefs, it was God alone who created humanity, Sky, Earth and all things."

The Maori belief in what was a single ancestor who became sky and earth, from whom all things descend biologically and hence genealogically is not compatible with the European or *pakeha* belief of an independent, nonrelated god existing in splendid isolation, who, without reason or prompting, creates humans, sky, earth, and all things. If one waxes scientific and speaks of an expanding universe that continues to expand, and speaks also of an originating amoebic entity dividing into two from which all living matter began on planet earth untold millions of years ago, and from that original source came humans, that is closer to the Maori narrative of creation than it is to Christian theology of creation. The objective of this paper, however, is not theological comparisons.

That first separation is a metaphor for explaining the inexplicable, no more and no less. It is important as the starting point because from that primal origin, Maori tribal nations, including Ngapuhi, trace the creation of *mana,* and it is the lens through which they view their own voyages and beaches, as well as the lens through which they view others who arrived later.

Another early *tohunga* (ritual expert), Hikawera Mahupuku,[9] writes of Ranginui the Sky-Father lifting his arm slightly, and a chink of light came into the blackness from outer space. That brief, momentary revelation of light was held in the minds of the children of these two primal beings, becoming an obsession to the succeeding generations of one lineage, that of Taane. Many more eons were to pass before action was taken over the inherited knowledge of that minute sliver of light. The generations of many Taane (Males) came and went—Taane-tuuturi (Kneeling Male), Taane-peepeke (Crouching Male), Taane-uetika (Upright Male), and then Taane te-waiora (Male of the Waters of Life), and it was that Taane, supported by some of his brothers, and his lineage, who separated their parents to see what was beyond that sliver of light. The primeval parents were pushed far apart, with one brother of Taane, Rangihaapainga (Skylifter), carrying the wailing father away into space, remaining there forever. Rangihaapainga changed his name to Paaianuiarangi (Great Sky Barrier) and remains there forever as the Milky Way and the Magellan Clouds.

The Earth-Mother remained below, the haven for all the other children except Sky Barrier (Paaianuiarangi) and Space Twister (Taawhirimaatea). That deed of separation completed, Taane-te-waiora changed his name to Taanenuiarangi, Great Taane of the Sky-Father, taking on his father's mantle as the significant progenitor.[10]

Taane, through numerous serial marriages, became the progenitor of the moon and sun, the trees, shrubs, plants used for weaving, and various rocks and gravel. One of his progeny was the homeland, Hawaiki, and there Taane and his earthbound brothers created their house, called Moutere-rangi-ko-te-rake-pohutukawawa, and from there Taane began his search for the female element. After many fruitless couplings, he was instructed to build a female form from the sands at Kurawaka in Hawaiki, breathed life into that form, and humanity began.

She, Hinehauone (Living Earth-Woman), is the crucial link between gods and humans. She mated with Taane, and a daughter Hine-tiitama (Original Woman) was born. Taane had an incestuous relation with her, and when their daughter found out that her husband was her father, she fled screaming to the underworld in the belly of her ancestor, Mother Earth, to become Hinenuitepoo, goddess of death and keeper of all the spirits of her offspring.

The children of Taane's brothers, now departmental gods, cohabited with her offspring to create the various intertwined lineages to our human ancestors. Life continued in three worlds, the upper world of twelve skies of the Sky-Father; the middle world, the land and ocean surface of the Earth-Mother; and the lower world, the many levels within the body of the Earth-Mother. Mortal humans lived in the middle world, and when they died they simultaneously became one with the sky, earth, netherworld, and Hawaiki—as stars, as bones, as residents of the realm of Hinenuitepoo, and of Hawaiki.

This brief, truncated account, given without accompanying genealogy, contains a logical series of powerful metaphors and icons. Humans had genealogical descent from Earth and Sky, who were the origins of *mana,* which came down through demigods and superhuman beings to human ancestors. Furthermore, humans were related by genealogy to everything in Space, the Sky-Father, and on and under the earth, who is the Earth-Mother. The homeland Hawaiki was born of the gods and was therefore not merely the place of gods, superbeings, and human spirits but also the place where the ancestors set off on their voyages of discovery to the beaches of other islands. Those beaches and islands were also created by the gods. Their creation narrative was self-explanatory, internally consistent, and has reason, purpose, and inspiration to Maori.

Maori Voyagers

Te Ika a Maui, the origin of Aotearoa–New Zealand, was still a part of the ocean depths of the Earth-Mother until many generations after the creation of the first woman. Maui fished up the land after forcing his brothers to paddle far away from Hawaiki. He returned to Hawaiki to fetch a *tohunga,* an expert in rituals, to dedicate his fish, and in his absence his greedy brothers began flensing this giant fish. The writhing fish in its death throes was frozen into its present form through rigor mortis. Maui's canoe becomes the South Island. Another account states that it rests on the summit of Mount Hikurangi on the east coast. This land and its beaches, therefore, given that explanation, were crucial parts of the narration and not a passive unknown theater set waiting for a performance called "discovery." It was part of the Earth-Mother. It was also a fish, a progeny of Tangaroa, the Sea-Lord. It follows that the attitude of Maori to voyages and beaches would radically differ from that of European navigators.

Twenty generations after Maui, Kupe left Hawaiki to escape retribution for his amorous exploits.[11] He was not told to go and look for a counterbalancing southern continent, as European navigators were centuries after his voyage; he had decided to search for the fish of Maui somewhere to the south of Hawaiki, and he found it. The giant fish floated in the southern seas, its petrified body waited for discovery, and so too did its beaches. Kupe made landfall in the Hokianga harbor on the tail of the fish—*te hiku o te ika*. From there he made exploratory journeys into the harbor itself, around the tail, then along the western dorsal wing of the stingray-shaped fish, right to its head—*te upoko o te ika*, now called Wellington. He crossed over to Maui's canoe, exploring the various islands and fighting giant octopus.

There are a plethora of sources outlining his explorations of almost the whole of the North Island and the northern fiords of the South Island. This was not done in three weeks, or three months, or even three years; he stayed for more than two generations, with his two wives, his children and grandchildren, and his large crew. Eventually, he decided to return to Hawaiki, the ultimate reasons being homesickness, old age, and the suicide of one of his daughters. If he had hoped to receive the accolades that European nations normally give to their successful explorers, Kupe would have been disappointed. Even if the only outcome for him was that his navigation data would be used by others to get to these new large islands, he still would have been disappointed. Nothing happened for about half a century. Perhaps Hawaiki was a peaceful paradise, or perhaps he was ignored. We do not know.

The narrative picks up twenty-three generations after Kupe, when Nukutawhiti[12] and his nephew Ruaanui, either on separate canoes or on a double-hull canoe, decided to trace the sea path of their ancestor Kupe, to take their families and people away from the hunger and the wars over resources in a Hawaiki that was rent with droughts. That was some twenty-eight generations ago.

Nukutawhiti came to Hokianga following Kupe's directions and made landfall in Hokianga. The harbor had vast subtropical rain forests growing from the water's edge far beyond the distant uplands, teeming with birdlife, edible ferns, epiphyte bracts, and berries. The inner harbor and outer ocean were rich in shellfish, fish, birds, and sea mammals, and the rivers had their own range of fish, shellfish, and birdlife. Planting tropical crops in a subtropical environment was difficult, given the immense difficulty of clearing virgin forests. Exploring the coasts and river systems was immediate. Our traditions mention Nukutawhiti's daughter and her husband, Ruaanui, and their crew leaving Hokianga and then being canoewrecked 100 kms (62 miles) to the south, naming that area after their canoe. They later came back to Hokianga and then explored northward, establishing their hegemony over some 70 kms (44 miles) of virgin territory.

Nukutawhiti himself and his followers also explored the rivers and then the ridges, discovering the fertile volcanic plateaulands 30 kms (18 miles) into the interior. Extensive areas of forestry cover had been turned to ashes by volcanic eruptions, leaving pockets of rich, volcanic soil ready for planting. He established a permanent village there, at the same time maintaining his other villages in the Hokianga harbor. After his death, at Hokianga, and after the mortuary ceremonies, his bones were ceremonially distributed and hidden in burial caves across the territory used and claimed by his group. The bones (*iwi*) became the name of the group and their areas of distribution became the territory of the *iwi* (tribal nation). Bones became icons; the metaphor became the group name.

Reconstructions by archaeologists and other ethnoscientists tell of innovations occurring on these islands of Aotearoa–New Zealand as the population expanded. They fill in details of crops, mammals, fish, and birds eaten, the nature of village life, and the like. The style of living changed from nomadic slash-and-burn to a sedentary feudal village system, with permanent gardens and an efflorescence of artists and artisans, who created fortifications, carving styles, intricate storehouses, war canoes, and all the complex paraphernalia now subsumed under the definition of classical Maori society of the late fifteenth to the early nineteenth centuries.

The traditional evidence clearly describes who went where, what happened, and what their groups were called. Ngapuhi, as with other Maori tribal nations, kept information on discoverers, artists, priests, and political leaders male and female, on an orally transmitted genealogical ancestral database that we, their descendants, now store in Windows 95 and the like for our descendants.

At the same time, these early Ngapuhi ancestors lived in a world where the gods and other esoteric beings of the spiritual world merged with that of the human, on a land base that was also the genealogical mother of gods, spirits, and humans. This truncated account indicates that what we are dealing with goes beyond the usual classical anthropological dicta of religion per se; it was also epistemological, continuing an empirical knowledge base that had been part of the development of Oceanic peoples for millennia. While it was being nurtured and redefined in a new land that land was still part of Oceania. But there were innovations.

Five generations after Nukutawhiti's landfall, other canoes arrived in other parts of Aotearoa. The canoe *Mataatua* arrived at Whakataane, and the *mana whenua* of Ngati Awa was soon established. Barely one season was to pass when Toroa, commander of the canoe, accused his younger brother Puhi of putting a hex on his crops. The bitter argument resulted in Puhi departing in the canoe *Mataatua* with his group, sailing north and establishing themselves on the beaches north of the Bay of Islands. It was not long before the people of Puhi, also called Ngati Awa, met with the descent groups of Nukutawhiti. There were skirmishes and then agreements bound by intermarriages. Te Hauangiangi, daughter of Puhi, married Tauramoko, and their son Rahiri was born.

Another group, Ngaitaahuhu, was at the same time spreading northward from the Tamaki or Auckland isthmus area, expanding their territory and establishing themselves through agreements and intermarriage in the territory of Nukutawhiti's people. When Rahiri came of age, the peace with Ngaitaahuhu was sealed by his two serial marriages with chiefly women of Ngaitaahuhu, first with Ahuaiti, then with Whakaruru.

Ngapuhi Emerges

Rahiri established his hegemony from Hokianga to the central plateaus of the Bay of Islands, and through marriage, extended it southward to Whangarei. Rahiri became the unifier, through war and treaties, of the scattered descendants of Nukutawhiti. His group became known as Ngapuhi, after a number of grandparents called "Puhi," including the Puhi who migrated from the Bay of Plenty.

The other relatives of Rahiri, however, those of Ngati Awa, were also expanding, and skirmishes over lands, boundaries, and resources soon led to battles. The wars began with Rahiri, continued through the era of his sons, when Ngati Awa were expelled from the triangle of territory stretching from Hokianga to Whangaroa to the northern coasts and inner plateaus of the Bay of Islands. But while Ngapuhi now controlled most of the midnorth, their world was developing and changing.

These northern New Zealand subtribes were now developing sedentary lifestyles, living in permanent fortified villages, with *marae* or ceremonial plazas fronted by elaborately carved chiefs' houses. Subtribes had fleets of canoes and defined fishing areas. There were large gardens with crops stored in temperature- and moisture-controlled caves and storehouses. There were detailed agreements on waterways, trails, forests and forest products, ocean access, and shellfish and fishing grounds. There were strong intergroup trade and ceremonial relationships within and beyond the tribal nation borders. Personal trading and ceremonial visiting of Ngapuhi went as far as the Bay of Plenty and Taranaki, with an intricate movement of such prized items as greenstone eventually developing through these trading ventures to Ngapuhi villages.

These intergroup contacts served to level some of the differing cultural mores of developing Maori nations, in such areas as *tapu, muru,* and *mana* (the terms will be defined later). This also happened with various *rites de passage* of birth, initiations, marriages, and death. There were elaborate mortuary ceremonies and the secreting of important skeletal remains in caves. Ngapuhi carried it further, with the distribution of bones of important leaders to various subtribes. Personal symbols of individual *mana* took the form of permanent intricate tattoos on faces, necks, breech, buttocks, and thighs. Many tattooists were full-time specialists, traveling from one nation to another to practice their profession. The displays of preserved tattooed heads of ancestors and enemies were also formal symbols of the *mana* of individuals and groups.

After Rahiri came five generations of population growth and the creation of most of the *hapuu* (subtribes) of Ngaapuhi. Those *hapuu* were to become fiercely autonomous, though linked to other independent subtribes by a network of common ancestral lineages, shared lands, shared ocean frontages on four harbors, and shared rivers and extensive land routes.

To personalize this description, this fifth generation after Rahiri was the time of the ancestor Tupoto, who commanded the lands and subgroups of Hokianga south to the Kaipara harbor, and east to the inner Bay of Islands. He divided his territory among his six children from his two marriages. Others of his contemporaries ruled the areas south to Whangarei, the Bay of Islands, and the harbors of Whangape and Whangaroa; the coastline south of the Bay of Islands was not yet in Ngapuhi hands.

Abel Tasman came to these islands when Tupoto and his children and contemporaries were in charge of Ngapuhi. Tasman's visit in 1642 left no imprint on Maori beaches, for neither he nor his crew landed, apart from the one who was killed and taken ashore by his South Island attackers. Tasman left no impression on Ngapuhi and other tribal nations of Northland apart from the journal entries of his crew about being driven away from the Three Kings, probably by Ngatikuri occupiers. But his journals prompted visions of the possible discovery of the fabled southern continent in Europe. And he wrote of a people who attacked him and his crew, of rough voices and the Moorish trumpets of the inhabitants of this land, of giants seen striding on cliffs and hillsides. Muskets and cannons sounded for the first time off the beaches of Aotearoa. Our database does not tell us whether the news or reverberations came to Ngapuhi through the trading routes.

The five generations after the passing through of Tasman, and the time of Tupoto and his children, were times of population expansion, development of villages, fisheries, fortifications, and alliances. Prominent in the affairs of this time were the battles over land in the interior of the Bay of Islands, which were being permanently occupied by a group la-

beled Ngati Pou and said to be from Waikato, but were in fact an amal-
gam of Hokianga and Whangaroa Ngapuhi who had Waikato links. They
were expelled, retreating to their Hokianga and Whangaroa communities. The success of the interior subtribes, and their continuing arguments with the subtribes of the Bay of Islands coastlines to the south, pre-
dicted a war waiting to happen. It was precisely at this stage that Captain
James Cook came to check out Tasman's line on the map of the world.
Ngapuhi for the first time would see cannons and muskets, and hear their
sound, and know their effects. Our Ngapuhi world would never again be
the same.

Ngapuhi Meets Muskets

Cook reached Ngapuhi's women-paddling sea in 1769, some seven generations, or 127 years, after Tasman. The first meeting of Ngapuhi with
muskets was on 25 November, probably off Whananaki, where about two
hundred people from seven large war canoes sang and danced and
traded with the newcomers. One of Cook's men kept back a pair of black
breeches without trading and was fired at. When a volley of musketballs
followed, splintering a canoe, the Ngapuhi moved their canoes to a distance and began a *haka*. A cannon was fired; the shell went over their
heads, and the fleet followed it ashore.

Next morning, two small canoes arrived, then a fleet carrying trade
goods, but again a musketball was fired over the head of an errant trader.
The next day at Rakaumangamanga (Cape Brett), Cook was again met by
a cluster of canoes. Trade in fish occurred, with one incident: the gaffing
of one of the Maori crew. At Cavalli Islands that same day, several canoe
people after some time trading began to throw fish, then sticks and
stones, at the *Endeavour,* and they continued even when two musketballs
were fired through their canoe. Cook, on the poop of his ship, was show-
ered with rocks, and he shot a warrior in the face, who then fell flat into
the canoe. As more crewmen attacked, the increasing barrage of musket
fire caused the canoes to head off for land.

Cook came back into the Bay of Islands two days later, where the *Endeavour* was met by some 300 to 400 people on 37 canoes. Some, who had
probably been the recipients of shooting two days before, kept a distance
and showed wariness. Remembering that Cook had his Tahitian interpreters, whom Maori could understand perfectly, Cook invited several
chiefs on board. They included Taapua, the father of Patuone and Tari,
both of whom were there. The other brother, Taamati Waka Neenee,
was not yet born. The chiefs were presented with broadcloth, nails, and
other things, including cooked meat, in exchange for large *kahawai*.

Patuone and his sister Tari found the meat sweet and good. Other chiefs mentioned were Tuwhare and Tahapirau. The majority there with Cook were from Hokianga, including a close relative—Tuwhare, chief of Te Roroa of Waipoua.

As the day wore on, the fear of guns did not deter the men in surrounding canoes from trying to take away the buoy and anchor when Cook went below for dinner. Banks and others fired muskets at them, Banks wounding one. The cannon was fired, and the cannonball bounced to shore and was pursued there by two canoes while Tupaia, the Tahitian, invited the others back.

The Ngapuhi database enables us to access who these chiefs were. The chief Taapua, who went on board the *Endeavour*, was a *tohunga* of Ngati Rahiri, who had their villages around the Waitangi River entrance as well as the inner Bay of Islands as far inland as Pouerua Mountain and Kaikohe. His wife Te Kaweau was a chief in her own right of Ngati Hao, from the Waihou Valley of Mangamuka, an inland Hokianga valley. Tuwhare, who was both Ngati Korokoro and Te Roroa, was the young leader from the west coast of Northland who would later obtain arms for his people and die when his canoe overturned in Cook Strait on its way to attack South Islanders.

The remainder of Ngapuhi would soon know about the new weapons. Just about all the inner Bay of Islands and the Hokianga *hapuu* had canoe landings and fishing encampment sites along the eastern seaboard, which they used semipermanently, as well as during the winter months when westerly storms and rains lashed the west coast harbors and beaches. Marion du Fresne details the dismantling of an encampment and the digging of their crops in May. In South Hokianga, Tarahape and Ngao held sway, and they were closely related to Ngati Pou leaders Te Angaora and Tatua in the inner Bay of Islands, and to the Hikutu chief Te Kauri living on Moturua Island. In the inner Bay of Islands also were Te Wairua, Waikaainga, Tuutuu, Te Kiore, Hineira, Roha, Te Aokaahui, and Maru. All the above names were important in "the unfolding of the *mana* of Ngapuhi" mentioned in the Maori language narratives of Ngapuhi.

To return to the Cook narrative: The day following the buoy incident, Cook and his scientists and his marine detachment went to Motuarohia Island, leaving, they thought, the flotilla of canoes around the *Endeavour*. As soon as they landed, however, all the canoes raced to the island, and soon some five hundred to six hundred people, who had landed at various locations, moved on his party. Cook drew a line on the sand, indicating a zone not to be crossed, but there were already some Maori behind him, and intermingling. As a war dance and challenges began, some warriors went to drag Cook's boats to shore, and Cook shot the leader with smallshot. Banks and two others then fired their muskets at the warriors who were attacking the *Endeavour* party. As the warriors retreated, one tried to rally his companions; as he ran forward he was shot by Solander with smallshot and then fled. Several others were repelled in the same way. The whole encounter might have been the end for Cook, but the *Endeavour* fired a broadside from three four-pounder cannons, and cannonballs flew over the warriors' heads causing all to retreat. Cook was not to know that his own actions had incited Ngapuhi warriors, all six hundred of them, because they thought Cook and his men had hurried to Motuarohia to capture the island while all were gathered around the *Endeavour*.

The next day, Cook was told that the person he shot in the face at the Cavalli Islands had died because three small shots had penetrated his eye and entered his brain. Neither Cook nor his companions mention how this conclusion was reached. It would be logical to assume that if the person who died was of high rank his head would have been instantly removed and smoked until the skull contents could be removed as a prelude to preserving his head. One can therefore assume that the person shot was not of high rank.

Banks the next day showed a musketball to a man he shot trying to take the ship's buoy. These plus the visible evidence of smallshot and musketballs on other wounded warriors convinced Ngapuhi that muskets threw these objects farther than the stones they threw, and cannons hurled larger objects of iron much farther. They already had a cannonball that had skipped to the shore. They probably had the others that had been fired over their heads at Motuarohia. The mystique of muskets and cannons was soon dispelled, and the link between musket, powder, and shot was observed and discussed.

Was there any mystique concerning Cook and his people? There is a common stereotype in popular literature and films that indigenous peoples meeting Europeans for the first time viewed them as supernatural beings, or gods. For Maori, there are five options for how they regarded their first Europeans: (1) as gods (*atua*), (2) as goblins (*tupua*), (3) as shimmery beings who inhabit forests and glades and were pale, mischievous, and had red or multicolored hair (*tuurehu*), (4) as ocean beings coming from the deep realms of that Maori Neptune, Tangaroa (*pakepakehaa*), or (5) as normal human mortals (*tangata*). Despite the fanciful, settler European-induced accounts of some aging Maori half a century later, the facts show that Cook was immediately regarded as mortal, interesting, and dangerous. The fact that they were constantly harassed, and that they were made to flee at various times, removed them from the ranks of gods, demons, or mermen. That they were male, human, and slept with women openly also helped to remove the mystique.

Cook left and Surville arrived. Surville's rest and recreation in Doubt-less Bay within two years of Cook's departure was again a reminder of the power of muskets to northern Ngapuhi people, many of whom had not experienced Captain Cook. The actions of Surville's crew in shooting people, burning canoes and villages, and taking canoes and kidnapping Ranginui became part of the information base for all of Ngapuhi. Marion du Fresne's sojourn and his being killed confirmed once and for all for Ngapuhi that these white people were human and fallible, but they must have come from powerful nations with many muskets.

The Hiatus in Getting My Muskets

Meanwhile, in England, the years after Cook's visit were a mini–Golden Age, triggered by new manufacturing methods. James Watt had patented a steam engine in 1782, Cartwright invented the power loom in 1784, and the first steam-driven mill opened in 1785. Iron, cotton, whale oil, jute, and flax were the raw materials needed for the Industrial Revolution that was picking up momentum. The Napoleonic Wars precipitated an arms race. On the one hand, this led to a feverish hunt for raw materials glob-ally, since the building of warships required spars and flax, and this would assist Ngapuhi. On the other hand, the arms race caused the price of arms to spiral; this was not good news for Ngapuhi.

The resources of these shores drew whalers, sealers, and traders seek-ing raw material to fuel the Industrial Revolution. The Bay of Islands became an important port of call for captains of trading ships seeking to acquire native timbers and dressed flax, and to replenish their ships' sup-plies. It also became a favorite haunt for rest and recreation and restock-ing for whalers and sealers. Ngapuhi accepted all these visitors, and their goods, with enthusiasm.

Many Ngapuhi joined whaling and sealing expeditions; others were kidnapped to work on ships; and others toured the ports of Australia, Eu-rope, the Pacific, and the Americas for months or years. Many on their re-turn brought a wide range of goods, seeds, produce, and iron tools. And those who had a musket or two for their *hapuu* increased their personal *mana*. Ngapuhi *hapuu* supplied the trading ships with pork, vegetables, and women and assisted in felling, dragging, and loading *kauri* spars and in cutting and dressing flax. Their payment was mostly in cloth, blankets, iron nails, beads, axes and other implements, and potato and other seeds.

Musket prices were not within reach at this stage to any but the wealthiest *hapuu*. There was the "one ton" rule: one ton of dressed flax for two muskets plus "one ton" for sufficient powder and shot represented almost three months' hard labor for each "one ton" for those Ngapuhi *hapuu* with labor and flax plantations. The precontact alliances among *hapuu* concerning usufruct of forests, trails, beaches, and waterways were beginning to show signs of fraying as those permanently residing on the beaches asserted their *mana whenua*—their rights to land as permanent inhabitants.

The acquisition of muskets was painfully slow. Thirty-seven years after experiencing the muskets and gunpowder of Cook and Surville, and the intervening years of du Fresne, the sinking of the *Boyd,* and the whalers and sealers and traders, a grand total of five muskets were used by Ngapuhi against Ngati Whatua at Moremunui in 1807. These were said to belong to Te Morenga, who had coastal villages in the Bay of Islands, as well as an extensive hinterland of forests and flax and a sizable work force that gave him that advantage. But even with five muskets, the large Ngapuhi force was heavily defeated by Ngati Whatua at a battle in which the young Hongi Hika was a lucky participant. When the victorious chief drew a line marking no pursuit, Hongi was across that line and allowed to escape. Because of the chivalrous act of drawing that line in the sand, the chief would later fall to Hongi and his muskets, taking his regrets for loss of *mana* to the caves of his ancestors.

My *Mana*

What then is *"mana"*? The pathway to understanding is through the five key principles that maintain *tikanga,* the ruling laws, customs, and mores of the tribal nation. These principles are *"tapu"* (sacred or set apart), *"mana"* (to be explained further below), *"ihi"* (fearlessness, power, essential force), *"wehi"* (awesomeness and regard), and *"utu"* (compensation, payment, revenge) (these inadequate definitions will suffice for the moment).

Mana is the most important principle of the five; it is the driving force to ensure the happiness and good existence of the tribal nation. To describe it adequately takes time and many volumes of paper, while a summary lessens its power, potency, and enveloping nature. To begin, *mana* is a personal, nonvisible measure that all things visible or nonvisible possess in terms of ancestral or spiritual inheritance, prestige, power, recognition, efficacy, influence, authority, and other positive attributes. It is driven by power and prestige coupled with inheritance and achievement. *Mana* comes from the gods; *mana* flows through the ancestors; *mana* flows from the sea and the land, joining the personal *mana* based on physical and personal attributes and accomplishments. *Mana* can be inherited, as well as acquired. All things, whether they were visible or nonvisible, spiritual or concrete, had their own *mana,* for they were all part of the creation of the gods and descended from the gods. Because *mana* is transferred through genealogical lines, it cannot be self-imposed if one has lost *mana*.

It can be seen, therefore, that *mana* is a nonvisible changing measure; it can remain static, increase, or decrease, depending on the actions or inaction of the recipient, and it can be enhanced or diminished. It can be removed by others. Thus one can speak of the increasing or decreasing *mana* of a highly successful *tohunga* or *rangatira pakanga* (priest or war leader) facing continuing changes of fortune. One can speak of the *mana* of a warrior, the *mana* of a woman leader, the *mana* of a child prodigy. If that woman chief is captured and enslaved, however, she loses her *mana*. Her captor can make that loss permanent and absorb her acquired *mana* by killing and eating her. That acquired *mana* is retrieved by her relatives or family, who continue to hold the ancestral *mana* by successfully avenging her capture or death, in other words, achieve successful *utu*.

Muskets fit into a category where outstanding weapons or tools had much *mana*. An adze or axe used for the manufacture of canoes and houses or weapons of war had more *mana* than an adze for chopping wood or kindling. Weapons of stone, bone, wood, or iron that had wounded or killed enemies acquired *mana*. Those with a history of use by various ancestors, with awesome deaths or wounds attributed to them, had prestigious *mana* both inherited and acquired. Muskets had that potential for those layers of *mana*. Weapons, tools, artifacts, and heirlooms with *mana* are usually given names, and once they have a name and a connected narrative, they become *taonga* (things inanimate or animate that have exceptional value). Naming a musket would give it potential attributes of *mana*. If *tapu* is regarded as the "potential for power" in the Thomistic sense, then *mana* is the realization of that power.

All these aspects drove Ngapuhi feverishly to obtain muskets. Muskets meant that *utu* (revenge) for the defeat at Moremunui, especially, was a certainty. The actions of Cook, Surville, and du Fresne permanently imprinted on the minds of future leaders, who were children during the ships' visits, that muskets were the weapons that were absolutely necessary. The regaining of *mana* was the driving principle. The chosen route through normal trade was too slow.

My Missionaries and My Muskets

In the next eight years, Ngapuhi *hapuu* continued the arduous task of building up their musket supplies. That was when the importance of having missionaries entered the equation. Why missionaries instead of more traders? Accidents and incidents made Ngapuhi leaders veer toward missionaries.

From his meeting with Tuki and Huru at Norfolk Island in 1796, Samuel Marsden decided to expand his mission to Aotearoa. His chance came when he rescued Ruatara, a Ngapuhi chief, in England in 1809 and looked after him as he reached Sydney on his way home five years later. To one not knowing missionaries or Christianity, Ruatara would have likened Marsden to a powerful *tohunga*—Maori ritual experts who communed with the gods, obtained support from them in every sphere of activity, and were also privy to the chief on tactics and economics. They had *mana* in the Ngapuhi world. Marsden had *mana* in England, and also in the world of Sydney, where Marsden lived and had his own slaves and tribe.

As for Marsden, he was in a different world. His first missionaries, he felt, were to be artisans and a schoolteacher, because Marsden believed that industrial, farming, and trade skills were crucial paths to Christianity. By 1814, he had established his mission site, Rangihoua, under the protection of Ruatara. Ruatara was of another mind: He wanted traders—his own *pakeha*—who would give him an advantage over competing chiefs of the Bay of Islands. Marsden's missionaries fitted the bill perfectly. Ruatara and Hongi Hika began the battle to attract and hold missionaries, thinking they would have the kind of political power their own *tohunga* had. They would assist in obtaining guns.

"My *mana* was waiting for my missionaries to enable me to obtain my muskets so that I can regain and then enhance my *mana* I lost on the battlefields"—this would have been a constant refrain in the minds of Hongi Hika, Ruatara, and the other young Ngapuhi leaders of that era. That Thomas Kendall was chosen by Marsden to build their first mission station at Rangihoua, and that Marsden set injunctions against missionaries selling muskets, is well known. But Kendall disobeyed, and both Hongi and Ruatara were beneficiaries of his disobedience.

When Ruatara died, in 1815, Hongi became the protector of the mission and made its existence dependent on him. From such a position he became indispensable to the mission, shifting the main mission to Kerikeri, much to the visible anger of his rival leader, Te Morenga. But even up to 1818, there were not more than 120 muskets among Maori tribes, and all were in the hands of the *hapuu* of Ngapuhi, and mainly those of the Bay of Islands. Te Morenga had thirty-five when they attacked the Bay of Plenty and the East Cape in 1818. Korokoro had fifty, and Hongi was reputed to have at least thirty at that time.

Hongi and Thomas Kendall, the missionary, went to England two years later, ostensibly to finalize a Maori alphabet and a grammar. When Hongi returned to Sydney in 1820, he had sufficient funds and goods to purchase three hundred muskets and sufficient barrels of powder and shot for lengthy war campaigns. At Sydney, he told two sworn enemies, Te

Horeta and Te Hinaki of Ngati Maru, the names of his guns. His personal one was named Patuiwi—Destroyer of Tribes. The others were Te Wai Whaariki, Kaikai a Te Karoro, Waikohu, Te Ringa Huruhuru, Mahurangi, and Kaiteke, named after the battles or the incidents in those battles in which Ngapuhi had been defeated and which he intended to avenge.

Kendall also bought crates of muskets and barrels of powder in Sydney to trade for food and trade goods. Kendall rationalized his actions to Marsden by referring to muskets as "civilizing weapons" for trade and commerce. For Kendall and the other missionaries, however, the die had been cast: either they trade what Maori people wanted—and that meant muskets when they wanted them—or their food supplies were curtailed, their property in jeopardy of being subject to a *muru* raid (in which retribution for a perceived wrong would be exacted by plunder), and even their lives at risk from starvation or isolation or attack. Kendall was caught between Maori and Marsden. Kendall chose Maori until his Christian-driven shame forced his retraction and departure. But it was too late; he had become part of *my missionaries* and *my mana*, who will help me get *my muskets* and so enhance *my mana*—with *my* referring to my Ngapuhi ancestors of that era.

By the time Marsden revisited the Bay of Islands in the 1820s, and traveled to Hokianga, muskets were already in the upper river valleys and their isolated villages, and each village with muskets fired welcoming shots. He also noted that chiefly women now had their own cache of muskets. Marsden reported visiting Hongi's son, who was at home with his mother and sisters, when several naked, armed men appeared at the edge of the forests with defiant postures. Hongi's son and daughters flew to arms and loaded and fired their muskets with military precision, which also drew musket fire from the armed men. They charged their muskets only with powder, which convinced Marsden it was only a sham fight. "I could not doubt," wrote Marsden, "but they would be equally active and brave in a real battle."

But the muskets were mainly in Ngapuhi hands. During a later trip from Auckland through Kaipara to Whangarei, Marsden reported that none had muskets until he got to Whangaruru, only 6 km (about 4 miles) from the Bay of Islands, and a chief there had two.

For Ngapuhi, as more and more muskets entered the weapon arsenal of *hapuu* they were also incorporated into the culture of Ngapuhi. Carrying muskets or pistols was as natural as the carrying of the traditional weapons of wood, stone, or bone. The firing of muskets became a replacement for the blowing of warning calls or trumpets when visiting villages. It became customary to fire muskets in the air when war parties or even individuals met, partly as a sign of respect, but also to show peaceful intentions by emptying the muskets.

Those missionaries who did not participate in the trade for muskets quickly lost their value to communities. The Wesleyans or Methodists who set up their mission in Whangaroa, one of Hongi Hika's main areas of influence, survived five fruitless years teaching domestic duties, agriculture, and Victorian prudery with little success, Christianity with less, as well as intervening continuously but unsuccessfully as peacemakers between warring Ngapuhi factions. They were of no value, and the Wesleyan's first mission station in New Zealand was destroyed by Hongi's allies.

There is a more generalized moral to the story. Missionaries had their own opinions of their worth. But later, Ngapuhi realized that missionaries—apart from Kendall for a short while—had less *mana* for them than local traders. The traders lived with and among Maori, absorbed into their culture and mores as *pakeha* Maori, and sided with them in their *hapuu* skirmishes. The missionaries with their wives lived in a mission with other missionaries, usually separated from Maori community control, with ghettoism a real danger. Traders formed advantageous liaisons with Maori women of high rank for their own protection, and these women did not lose their *mana* as a result. Traders did not preach change nor did they attack Maori culture as bad and un-Christian and uncivilized. Missionaries were classified as *paakehaa tuutuaa* (European commoners), fit companions for Maori commoners or slaves if their only function was preaching the Gospel.

It was 11 July 1821 when Hongi reached the bay with his three hundred muskets and ample powder and shot. A mere two months later, on 5 September, he was exercising his fleet of more than fifty canoes off the Bay of Islands with two thousand warrior men and women, a thousand of those warriors armed with muskets drawn from Ngapuhi tribal segments from Hokianga, Whangaroa, and the Bay of Islands. More were to join him at Whangarei Harbor at the place where Ngapuhi first saw Cook some fifty years before. He had been to England with his missionary; he had managed to gather together the most formidable array of muskets to arm his warriors, and his *mana* was now at its zenith. He was at that moment the symbol of *my mana, my muskets, and my missionaries* for Ngapuhi.

NOTES

1. *Ahikaa* refers to permanent fires, *noho tuuturu* to permanent residences, and *mana whenua* to recognized authority over the land.
2. A *marae* is a ceremonial meeting ground and complex, which is the domain of the formal caller, orator, and lamenters.

3. See Aperahama Taonui, "He Pukapuka Whakapapa mo nga Tupuna Maori." MS 120, Auckland Institute and Museum Library; Himiona Kaamira, Private Collection of MS Papers, Auckland Institute and Museum Library.

4. "Orientalism" is a code word for the capturing and Westernizing of knowledge of the East, and I view Oceania as an extension of the Orient. See Edward Said, *Orientalism* (London: Penguin, 1978).

5. See Kaamira, MS Papers; also, M. Tawhai and George Graham, "Nukutawhiti," *Journal of the Polynesian Society* 49 (1940): 221–233.

6. See Taonui, Kaamira, and Tawhai.

7. See B. Biggs, P. Hohepa, and S. Mead, eds., *Selected Readings in Maori* (Auckland: Maori Studies Department, University of Auckland, 1994), where the narrative of Kupe tells of arguments over fishing, and that of Potaka Tawhiti concerns the theft of fruit from the sacred tree of the high chief, the killing and eating of Potaka-tawhiti, pet dog of two well-known ancestors, causing the migration of people. See also unpublished MSS by Kaamira, and Waitai, held in the Auckland Institute and Museum Library, Auckland, which further detail the reason for Kupe's migration.

8. Maori MSS 43, Grey Collection, Auckland Public Library.

9. "Whakapapa Tupuna," Maori MS, Hikutai Library, University of Auckland.

10. The Auckland University meetinghouse (where proceedings of the ninth David Nichol Smith Seminar began), called Taanenuiarangi, contains carved and woven and painted representations of this creation story.

11. See Himiona Kaamira, "Kupe," MSS, Auckland Institute and Museum Library.

12. See Kaamira, "Kupe," and Tawhai.

12

Enlightenment Anthropology and the Ancestral Remains of Australian Aboriginal People

Paul Turnbull

Over the past two centuries, numerous fine portraits have come to adorn the walls of the Royal College of Surgeons of England. Pride of place, however, has long been given to Sir Joshua Reynolds' portrait of the Scots-born surgeon John Hunter (see fig. 12.1). Hunter struck his surgical peers as coarse in speech and demeanor, money-hungry, and possibly irreligious. Several generations of medical students found him a diffident man but a careful and demanding teacher, whose diagnostic and surgical skills had gained him the patronage of numerous London patricians. Within two decades of his death, in 1793, John Hunter had become an almost legendary figure in British medical circles. Today, he is commonly represented as the founder of scientific surgery.[1]

This apotheosis was largely the result of astute management by London's surgical elite of Hunter's unparalleled collections of specimens of pathology and comparative anatomy. Hunter was a passionate dissector and collector. So much so that he is said to have jeopardized the financial security of family by spending much of his earnings from teaching and private consultation on assembling nearly 14,000 "rare and curious" specimens. In 1799, Hunter's "preparations," valued at £15,000, were purchased by the English parliament.[2] The following year they were entrusted to the newly constituted Royal College of Surgeons, on condition "that a course of lectures not less than twelve in number upon comparative anatomy, illustrated by the preparations, shall be given twice a year by some member of the Surgeon's Company."[3] Together with Hunter's casebooks and unpublished manuscripts, the specimens became the basis of the largest and most used repository of specimens of medical and natural history until well into the latter half of the nineteenth century. After 1814, the principal event of the college calendar was the Hunterian Oration, a lecture honoring the memory and achievements of the great man. For much of the remainder of the nineteenth century, these discourses respectfully affirmed a collegiate self-image of a company of gentlemen intent on knowing the divine mind, by scientific investigation of its expression in the economy of animate nature.

Reynolds' portrait of John Hunter is interesting on several counts, not least its calculated naturalism. Hunter is informally dressed and turned from his writing desk, quill pen still in hand. Possibly he is rehearsing the

Fig. 12.1 Joshua Reynolds, *Portrait of John Hunter* (reproduced by kind permission of the President and Council of the Royal College of Surgeons of England)

course of one of his greatly admired demonstrations, though the intensity of his gaze suggests that he has been struck by the utterance of a colleague or student. Unpowdered hair and plain dress clearly signify that the selfless pursuit of medical knowledge has banished any thought on Hunter's part of pandering to fashion or social niceties. There is a nice ambiguity here, in that the figure would have appealed to medical men of reformist temperament and also to those of a more conservative political outlook, to whom Hunter would have appeared as embodying the bluff good humor and staid paternalism of the English gentleman.[4] Indeed, it is easy to appreciate why Reynolds' portrait, from at least the 1830s, served the Royal College of Surgeons as a foundation icon, under which panels of examiners sat to assess candidates seeking admission to the college.

Viewed from the shores of Australia, the Hunterian portrait takes on a new and problematic significance. The canvas was finally completed to Reynolds' satisfaction a year or so after the establishment of the penal colony of New South Wales in 1788. Included in the final background schema of the portrait is a folio volume propped open at two pages of drawings. The historical significance of the drawings was noted by Sir Arthur Keith, arguably the most influential British evolutionary anatomist of the first half of this century, and for many years Hunterian Professor of Anatomy and Curator of the Hunterian Museum. In 1928, Keith wrote:

> The folio of drawings which stands open upon the table on which . . . [Hunter's] left elbow rests . . . has been opened to show two of Hunter's "graded series"; they give us his conception of the two structures which make man—the head and the hand. In the "head" series the skull of a European is placed at the top; then follows that of an Australian Aborigine; then a young chimpanzee's; then a monkey's—a Macaque; then a dog's; and lastly that of a crocodile.[5]

Keith tried to locate and exhibit in the Hunterian Museum the exact same skulls appearing in Hunter's folio, but he found it impossible to identify the four skulls Hunter had sketched. Nor could he locate any record shedding light on how Hunter had come by the Aboriginal skull. The folio notebook in which they appeared was one of many acquired under the terms of Hunter's will by his unscrupulous son-in-law, Sir Everard Home. After plagiarizing what he could, Home destroyed the better part of the legacy in the early 1820s.[6]

Reynolds' painting of Hunter stands as graphic evidence of a facet of Australian history since 1788 that has yet to be subjected to extended critical scrutiny. What Reynolds—or more likely one of his numerous assistants—had sought to include in Hunter's portrait as iconographic testimony to scientific genius can now be read as marking the beginnings of nearly two centuries of scientific trafficking in Aboriginal skeletal remains and soft tissue. Had he been less concerned with authenticity, Keith at the time of penning his article could have reconstructed Hunter's series using one of the hundred or so Aboriginal skulls then possessed by the College of Surgeons. For by 1928, crania from some two thousand Aboriginal people had become specimens in scientific institutions and private collections in Australia, and probably half as many again had been added to collections in Britain, Europe, America, South Africa, and India.[7]

The history of Aboriginal resistance to the procurement of skeletal remains is as old as European settlement.[8] But it has only been during the course of the past decade that controversy over the continued preservation and scientific use of skeletal remains has figured in Australian national politics, and—much to the embarrassment of national statemakers—has been the focus of international interest and concern. Aboriginal Australia speaks with many voices, which are variously inflected by localized concerns and issues. In the remains controversy, however, Aboriginal people have been heard in easy unison, condemning the continuance of uncontrolled scientific use of remains as a brutal disruption of their complex spiritual affinity to the land. The exhumation of burial places, especially, has been represented as a brutal disruption of the continuum of ancestral past, life in the land, death and return to the realm of dreaming, and, as such, indistinguishable from taking the country itself. As one prominent Tasmanian spokesperson has succinctly put it: "The remains are as important to us as land rights. It's a much more volatile issue, closer to the heart than even getting our land back."[9]

Aboriginal people see the issue as rooted in the dynamics of a colonial history, where the use, preservation, and public display of remains have been potent mechanisms of colonial oppression and terror. By displaying remains, especially within the context of lectures and exhibitions depicting the natural course of human evolution, European sciences of anatomy and anthropology objectified and dehumanized Aboriginal people in colonial eyes, justifying the often violent expropriation of Aboriginal land while drastically circumscribing the free expression of Aboriginality.[10]

Although acknowledging the legitimacy and the value of indigenous critiques of science as having been integral to colonialism, I would argue that we would do well to temper critique by scrutiny of the huge medicoscientific literature on the anatomy, morphology, and mentality of Aboriginal people that has accumulated over the past two centuries. This is not to suggest that investigation of this literature can resolve issues in contemporary cultural politics. Rather, it is to suggest that by seeking to contextualize historically the aims, assumptions, and intellectual products of late-eighteenth- and nineteenth-century "sciences of man," we might well enrich our attempts to make sense of, and work toward mutually acceptable resolutions of, the conflicting claims of Aboriginal and non-Aboriginal knowledge. In trying to make sense of the present, all we have are conceptual options that are the products of our shared history on this continent. We can try to make sense of how we think as we do by seeking to understand the conditions in which knowledge has been produced, has remained relatively stable, or has been subject to unpredictable evolution. From offering plausible accounts of discursive change, dialogue might result that in turn leads to our understanding with greater clarity past shortcomings and what appear to be good future courses of action, even though nothing guarantees that the choices we make will prove to be good.[11]

This essay is offered as a small contribution toward such a dialogue. It seeks primarily to contextualize and comment on how the skeletal remains of Aboriginal people figured in the anatomical and physiological researches of late-Enlightenment anatomists John Hunter and Johann Friedrich Blumenbach. I begin by broadly situating Hunter and Blumenbach's interests in human physiology in late-Enlightenment culture. Turning then to appraise the two anatomists' researches, the essay discusses Hunter and Blumenbach's shared conviction that organic structure and function were determined by the interaction of a subtle life force with a range of external forces, notably climate, diet, and disease. The resulting modifications in the bodily economy were seen by both men as essentially "degenerative" in the case of animals exposed to the rigors of what were deemed harsh climates by late-eighteenth-century European standards. Further, the corollary seems to have been that in domesticated animals and man in the state of civilization, life force had found its most perfect expression. I then turn to examine the use of the Aboriginal skulls by Blumenbach in his endeavor to delineate the peculiarities of difference he took to be observable among the peoples of the earth. Finally, the essay explores the key role of Sir Joseph Banks in procuring skeletal remains from the newly established New South Wales penal colony.

John Hunter and Johann Friedrich Blumenbach inhabited a mental world that for more than a century had privileged empirical investigation of animate nature. Whether students of natural history sought to apply experiential reasoning to understanding the earth's flora and fauna, or focused—as did Locke—on rational investigation of the physical and moral nature of man, animate creation was understood to be regulated by divine wisdom as expressed through moral laws. To understand the economy of nature was thus seen as a moral duty, augmenting knowledge of God's truths as revealed in Scripture. Not the least of these truths was the charge of "dominion . . . over every living thing that moveth on the earth." On examining the collecting activities of Hunter and Blumenbach, however, one cannot fail to be struck by how the attainment of scientific knowledge was in large measure understood as a challenge to make sense of an ever-increasing amount of data about difference and peculiarity among the peoples of the earth. Hunter was an avid reader of travel and exploration literature, as well as a keen collector of sketches and portraits of peoples encountered by Europeans in the remoter parts of America and the Pacific.[12] Blumenbach, as his pupil and eventual obituarist, K.F.H. Marx, recalled,

> in one branch of learning . . . had scarce his like, I mean his familiarity with voyages and travels. All the books in the library of this place he had read through over and over again, and made extracts of, and prepared a triple analysis, namely, one arranged geographically, a chronological and an alphabetical one. To this occupation, as he frequently took occasion to mention, he owed no small part of his knowledge; and for his researches in natural history and ethnography it was a most solid foundation.[13]

The fascination of both men with narratives of overseas encounters serves to remind us how profoundly colonial enterprise shaped Enlightenment culture. Since the late sixteenth century the northern European Atlantic states had embarked on colonial enterprises with varying consequences for themselves and, of course, the peoples whose resources and lands they expropriated. In the case of England, plantation regimes, first in Ireland and then North America and the Caribbean, greatly stimulated the evolution of native capitalist practices. Wealth generated through participation in various forms of colonial enterprise accelerated the domestic evolution of manufacturing and agrarian capitalism, and underpinned the rise of consumerism, all of which did much to enhance Protestant notions of individual autonomy and the importance of material advancement of the self and community. These notions facilitated the extension of market relations in communities that increasingly fell within the orbit of trade. Indeed, Hunter and Blumenbach could pursue their comparative anatomical interests because of their being in a position to supply medical knowledge and services within an emerging market for health.[14]

Colonial enterprise during the seventeenth century led to encounters with hunter-gatherer societies and small-scale garden agriculturists in Africa and America. Believing themselves providentially endowed with superior technology, traders, colonists, and their metropolitan sponsors tended to construe differences in physical appearance and social organization as signs of non-European inferiority and providential destiny to dominion over the "savage." However, the circulation of accounts of the rude peculiarities of "savage society" tended to cut both ways. In representing colonial endeavor as fulfillment of the divine will, colonial narratives tended to reinforce the truth of the Mosaic account of the single creation and its account of the dispersal of fallen humanity across the face of the earth. Difference was thus conceptualized as a historical experience. The establishment of new colonies, especially those of a decidedly Puritan caste, tended to underscore the degree to which kings, counselors, and holders of stock in colonial projects were participants in that historical process.

The subsequent pace of change in the direction of a market economy, consumerism, and technological innovation served to generate unease as much as confidence in the future. Both responses figure in the receptivity of educated Britons during the course of the late seventeenth and eighteenth centuries to texts in which the experimental methods of the new science were appropriated, to delineate regularities amid the seeming flux of human affairs through time. Philosophical discourse, especially, became focused on rendering empirically accurate descriptions of individual human understanding. For many, the task of delineation affirmed the conviction that all persons were possessed of an innate moral sense or faculty of right judgment. Whether individuals became disposed to virtuous or wicked action ultimately depended greatly on whether their moral sense or faculty had been strengthened through a careful educational regime from an early age.

By the mid-decades of the eighteenth century, British philosophical discourse gave broad assent to the Lockean premise that the human mind became truly human only on being taught "right reasoning" through carefully structured social interaction. Increasingly, moral philosophy became concerned with empirical investigation of the human mind in action, and with didactic elucidation of the personal and social consequences of action. More often than not, the results were new critical explorations of history. Indeed, by the late 1760s a new genre of moral discourse, philosophical history, had emerged to social prominence. In the works of its major practitioners, David Hume and, a little later, Edward Gibbon, philosophical history made clear its reliance on critical Protestant and Lockean habits of epistemology. Philosophical history sought particularly to demonstrate how the individual and communal benefits of "right reasoning" were enjoyable only when a society possessed a level of wealth that could nourish an elite culture of polite manners and writing.[15]

Yet the material prosperity that allowed the cultivation of virtuous politeness could also foster patrician complacency and cynicism. Should popular enthusiasm for religious and political innovation arise when the political will had been enfeebled by luxury, collapse into barbarism seemed inevitable. In the writings of Gibbon especially, the world of the Roman Empire, and the shadowy lives of the savage tribes and bands of nomadic pastoralists beyond the borders of the principate, were explored in the nervous hope of providing Britain's political elite with a unique vantage point for self-reflection on the powers and shortcomings of human reason in commercial society.

The lessons to be drawn from Gibbon's portrayal of Rome in decline, especially when the fate of empire came to rely on the judgment of the emperor and his immediate circle, were not lost on contemporaries. Through the eighteenth century, English, French, and Dutch imperial ambitions had wrought domestic turmoil and were the direct cause of international rivalry and conflicts, notably the Seven Years' War (1756–1763) and the American War of Independence (1776–1782). With the loss of the American colonies, British interests became focused on the exploitation of resources in Asia and the Pacific. Exploration and commercial voyages in the last third of the eighteenth century led to contacts with previously little-known lands and peoples in coastal Africa, Southeast Asia, and the Pacific. The writings of the philosophical historians, read against the disastrous experiences of the recent past, worked to feed uncertainty. Indeed, one suspects that there is something of the ambivalence many contemporaries felt about the materialist concerns feeding enthusiasm for colonial endeavor in utterances such as James Cook's well-known remark about the "natives" of New Holland being "far happier than we Europeans; being wholly unacquainted not only with the superfluous but with the necessary conveniences so much sought after in Europe."[16]

Given the burden placed in philosophical and historical discourse on experiential stimulation and maturation of the individual intellect, one can well appreciate the attendant evolution within medical circles of strong interest in empirical disclosure of the anatomical and physiological basis of body, brain, and mind. This is not to deny that the study of animate nature continued to draw upon an essentially Aristotelian heritage of natural history as disclosure of the signs of timeless regularity and perfection in the fabric of nature. Indeed, in the successive editions of the great systematic taxonomy of Swedish naturalist Carl von Linné, the tradition arguably found its most influential expression in the eighteenth century, and in its programmatic emphasis on discovery and classification, the tradition continued to prove far from incompatible with newer and more rigorously inductive modes of knowing. By the last third of the eighteenth century, however, the tradition was proving unable to accommodate new ideas about how life in all its variety on earth was reproduced and sustained. After the 1760s, the mixture of traditional humoralism and mechanist notions of bodily function that had generally held sway in medical curricula since the late seventeenth century gave way to concerted interest in the nervous system and reliance on new explanatory concepts, such as irritability, sensibility, and excitability. In philosophy we may detect an attendant shift in focus to experiential and often decidedly historicist modes of thought, which privileged exploration of the emotions, passion, and sensibility in moral judgment and action.

John Hunter's anatomical and physiological researches are hard to appraise. His reticence at devoting time and energy to philosophical reflection on his researches in a formal treatise, combined with his sudden death from heart failure in 1793, resulted in the bulk of Hunter's surviving writings other than his surgical lectures being largely self-contained descriptions of the structure and function of individual organs in animal and plant species. As previously mentioned, many of these texts were destroyed by Everard Home, and much of what survived are fragments, often unclear in meaning. Even so, as Stephen J. Cross' careful reconstruction of Hunter's work establishes, a coherence underlay what numerous contemporaries took to be an eccentric and costly preoccupation with procuring and dissecting exotic fauna and flora.[17]

In common with many anatomists of the later eighteenth century who embraced a medicine of sensibility, Hunter's researches were grounded in a philosophical understanding of life as a vital force or principle. Through careful observations both of normal function and pathology in a range of bodily structures, Hunter was convinced that a life principle had been necessarily "superadded" to all animate matter. Life existed as a subtle property inherent in all animal matter, even when the matter in question might at first strike the observer as so simple as to lack any sense of organization.[18] With the retreat of the power, death and decomposition occurred.[19] In this respect, Hunter was critically opposed to contemporary materialist explanations of life as simply the condition of organization within animate matter,[20] even though he was obliged to point out that the life principle was so subtle a force as not to be amenable to empirical observation.

Hunter further postulated that while the life principle permeated the bodily economy, it was responsible for peculiar powers of action inhering in specific structures. Different structures were thus rendered acutely susceptible to particular impressions, with the result that stimulation gave rise to localized actions. Hence, while guaranteeing the self-preservation of an organism, the life principle governed the complex and interdependent behavior of specific bodily structures.[21]

In this economy, growth was understood as occurring on food being turned into animal matter and imbued with the life principle within the stomach. Most of the resulting matter then became part of the blood—itself a fluid invigorated with the living principle. On arriving at specific structures via the circulatory system, matter was extruded as lymphatic fluid and became part of the structure through a process of coagulation. Similarly, decline and decay came about when animal matter was not added to structures, or coagulated at a rate less than that at which matter in structures became bereft of life. This dead matter became "as any other extraneous body" and was consequently broken down by absorbents and eventually discharged from the body. Thus, in the case of bone, "granulations arise, which push up the dead piece [of bone] against the upper sides of the cavity, and in consequence of this pressure against the newly formed bone, the absorbents are set to work to remove it and in proportion as this is absorbed, the piece is pushed out, the granulations filling the space behind it."[22] Factors such as climate, food, and disease could therefore influence bodily growth, the susceptibility of vital organs to normal stimulus or pathological reaction.

What survives of Hunter's writings give no firm indications of his views on the nature and origins of difference among the peoples of the earth, even though his small collection of rare "national skulls" and pictures of non-European peoples suggests it was clearly a topic of interest to him. Charles White, a prominent Mancunian surgeon who had known Hunter since they had studied together in the late 1740s,[23] was to lament that while Hunter possessed the most comprehensive skeletal collection in England and had clearly paid "some attention to the subject of comparison," he had not been moved to speculate publicly, or even among colleagues, on the significance of what appeared to be regularities in skull gradation between people of different nations. Nonetheless, this did not stop White invoking the authority of Hunter in a series of lectures given in 1795, and in a treatise published in 1799, to give added weight to his conviction that skull gradations were not just the most obvious signs of a natural hierarchy of physical and allied mental differences dividing the peoples of the earth, but were evidence of polygenesis.[24] The Creator had willed the appearance of different species of man at different points in time and space, ensuring that each distinct variant of man was that best adapted, physiologically and mentally, to the regions of the earth over which they had been given dominion.

Hunter, of course, employed notions of gradation in the arrangement of his anatomical specimens, as is evidenced by the series of skulls figuring in the Reynolds portrait. As the portrait makes clear, however, Hunter's use of gradation was subservient to his aim of illuminating through comparison how specific bodily structures functioned so as to sustain and reproduce life. He appears to have been inclined to modify the notion that animate nature was a continuum comprised of a finely graded chain of beings possessing in various degrees the same qualities of active powers. It was rather at the level of organic structure that gradation could be discerned,[25] and then:

> What we call "perfection" in animals does not increase in regular progression in every part, but as animals are complicated; and each complication has its degrees of perfection. These degrees do not correspond in perfection; [they are not] regularly progressive in every part from the most imperfect [animals]: although they go on in pretty regular steps of perfection among themselves.[26]

The extension of Hunter's views on the bodily economy would seem to be that the different races of mankind, irrespective of their origin, owed their peculiar physical and intellectual attributes to the interaction of the life principle with the climate and other peculiarities of the region of the earth they had come to inhabit. As Hunter tellingly was to comment when discussing the generation and regulation of heat in animals' bodies, "Men are the only animals which go to climates not congenial to themselves and consequently they are alone subject to the consequences of an unfit climate."[27]

This was certainly the view of Hunter's contemporary, Johann Friedrich Blumenbach (1752–1840), whose prestigious tenure as Professor of Medicine at the University of Göttingen lasted from 1778 to his death in 1840. Blumenbach aimed to construct a new taxonomy of the human races, which assumed the descent of mankind from one original pair and took variation among the peoples of the earth to be the consequence of the interplay of physiology with the environment. The means by which this taxonomy was to be constructed and refined was by comparison of skulls, Blumenbach having become convinced that the bones of the head and face, more than any other part of the human body, would reveal how the organic economy of the human body was affected by the interplay of physiology with the environment.

It was in his 1775 doctoral dissertation, "De generis varietate humani nativa," where Blumenbach first explored the differences apparent among the peoples of the earth, suggesting that they were the results of degeneration away from a single ancestral type. The course of degeneration had resulted in four distinct varieties of mankind, as well as peoples who were the descendants of interbreeding between two or more of the four varieties. In the course of the dissertation, Blumenbach was forced to admit that "there seems to be so great a difference between the Ethiopian, the white, and the red American, that it is not wonderful, if men even of great reputation have considered them as forming different species of mankind."[28]

Blumenbach maintained, however, that adherence to Newtonian precepts of investigation satisfactorily proved otherwise. When subjected to wide-ranging and rigorously empirical investigation, which took into account not only all significant points of anatomical similarity and difference but the sum of reliable testimony as to the demands on bodies of the typical environments in which they had lived, mankind appeared indisputably one species. The same holistic empiricism, incidentally, led Blumenbach to endorse the taxonomic principles of Linnaeus, but to do so critically, holding that the celebrated naturalist had erred in classifying humanity as a quadruped being, intellectually distinct, but anatomically indistinguishable from the ape or sloth. Blumenbach argued that dissections of apes and humans of differing ethnic origin revealed various anatomical features unique to human beings. When considered together with evidence gleaned from explorers' accounts, it made greater sense to place humanity within its own order, called "bimana," to denote man's particular ability to walk upright without employing the hands. Conversely, while impressed by the great contemporary French naturalist Buffon's attention to multiple anatomical characters in classifying organisms, Blumenbach remained unconvinced by Buffon's defining species by the capacity to produce fertile offspring in their usual environment. This simple distinction was just too simplistic, and in the case of many beings could well be overthrown by empirical test.

Through the course of the subsequent two decades, Blumenbach came increasingly to attribute the cause of variations among humanity to the hereditary transmission of changes in the bodily economy, caused by the modification of a common vital principle of life, possibly beyond empirical detection. This vital force would respond to the range of persistent forces the body met with in its natural environment. Blumenbach's schema was essentially pessimistic, in the sense that as mankind migrated away from its site of creation, most likely in the Caucasus region, they were subject over time to degeneration. Climate, food, life-styles, and endemic disease could all have subtle and transmissible effects on "bodily constitution, stature and color," which over time would result in a "nation" being easily distinguishable from those who remained closer to the original stem or type.

Since the early 1770s Blumenbach had been convinced that the most remarkable of the bodily changes resulting from the life force's modification by environmental forces were changes in head shape. In fact, Blumenbach argued, "All the diversity of the form of the head in different nations is to be attributed to the mode of life and art," and for some unspecified but doubtless "considerable" length of time, "singular shapes of the head have belonged to particular nations."[29] However, seeing the stability of head shape as highly suggestive of distinct national physiognomies being "a very vast and agreeable field" for further study, Blumenbach regretted that lack of accurate representations of different nations "forbad [him] . . . to wander in that direction."

As the years passed, the field came to prove irresistible. From the mid-1770s onward, numerous dissections and the examination of a range of "exotic" skulls served to confirm Blumenbach in the opinion that "an intimate relation [existed] between the external face and its osseous substratum." Further, "it might have been expected that a more careful anatomical investigation of genuine skulls of different nations would throw a good deal of light upon the study of mankind; because when stripped of the soft and changeable parts they exhibit the firm and stable foundation of the head, and can be conveniently handled and examined, and considered under different aspects and compared together."[30]

By the time of publishing a third and much expanded edition of "De generis . . ." in 1795, Blumenbach was convinced that comparative examination of national skulls was far more than a means of identifying the typical bodily characteristics of the people who once inhabited them. It suggested the possibility of a science that would reveal how specific skull configurations resulted from the specific experiences of peoples. On the strength of extensive clinical observations of bone physiology and pathology, Blumenbach had come to view bone as a far more plastic substance than generally imagined, and hence liable to be a prime reflection of the modification of the life-force under the demands of the environment. Examination of the physical configuration of the skull might allow one to

better understand how national custom and even character might modify bodily appearance. His first Australian skull, acquired in 1793, was to
Blumenbach's mind,

> conspicuous beyond all others for the singular smoothness of
> the upper jaw, where the upper teeth and the canines are in-
> serted. But it is now known that those barbarians have a para-
> doxical custom of perforating the septum of the nose with a
> piece of wood inserted crosswise, and of so stopping up their
> nostrils with a sort of peg that they cannot breathe except
> through the open mouth. It seems credible, therefore, that
> this smoothness may have been gradually effected by the per-
> petual pressure of this transverse insertion.[31]

By 1806, Blumenbach had come to champion comparative examination of skull configurations as a means by which general laws underlying
environmental determination of difference among the varieties of mankind might be disclosed. Indeed, such was his confidence that he was
ready to decry the length of time it had taken other naturalists to view
man as a "natural product" and the little interest shown, before his own
endeavors, in collecting skulls. He conceded that there were difficulties
in gaining such specimens, as there was an understandable reluctance on
the part of many to treat parts of bodies, especially skulls, as if they were
mere scientific specimens. But, he stressed, that the difficulties were "not
insuperable when the collector shows zeal and perseverance, and can obtain the active co-operation of men who have opportunities of helping
him in his object, is shown by the most remarkable portion of my anthropological collection, I mean the skulls of foreign nations."[32]

Blumenbach's own "zeal and perseverance" in the collecting of "national skulls" had by 1800 resulted in a collection of hitherto unknown
magnitude, consisting of some eighty-two separate specimens. The papers and lectures in which he outlined the rationale for collecting won
him the patronage of several powerful men with a keen taste for science,
including Sir Joseph Banks, through whose agency he acquired several of
his rarest skulls, including the Australian skull mentioned above. At the
time of his death, in 1840, Blumenbach had managed to acquire some
245 skulls and skull fragments. Even so, he remained of the view that the
range of skulls in his possession was insufficient to provide definitive answers to many questions raised by the existence of difference among humans. Indeed, as the pace at which European colonial involvement in
Southeast Asia and the Pacific accelerated, the resulting encounters with

many new peoples appeared to raise questions that Blumenbach felt could be answered only through possession of a much larger and more representative collection of skulls. As much is clear from Blumenbach's surviving correspondence with Sir Joseph Banks.

Blumenbach had communicated with Banks during the early 1780s, supplying the latter with the results of some experiments on freezing organic tissue and observations he had made on aspects of plant physiology. In June 1787, Blumenbach wrote to Banks, telling him of his long-standing interest in collecting national skulls, how he had recently received a skeleton and four skulls "of the Tartar nations" courtesy of Baron Asch in St. Petersburg, and of his desire to have skulls from the South Pacific. Help in obtaining skulls had been promised by a mutual acquaintance of the two men, botanist John Sibthorp, but the promise had come to nothing. Blumenbach now looked to Banks to obtain, at the very least, an accurate cranial silhouette from "la Mer du Sud."

By the end of 1787, Banks had undertaken inquiries on Blumenbach's behalf to locate interesting foreign skulls resting in anatomical collections and private cabinets across Britain. From his teens until the last years of his life, systematic identification of relations and continuities between classes of organisms—chiefly within the plant kingdom—was Banks' "ruling passion." It was a passion that depended on accurate visual depiction of new or unusual forms, and so led Banks to employ or otherwise encourage some of the most skilled natural history illustrators of the late eighteenth century. However, Banks' encounters with Polynesian, Maori, and Australian societies during the course of the *Endeavour* voyage (1768–1771) appear to have fed a curiosity about the nature and origins of difference among the peoples of the earth that the descriptive and essentially taxonomic ethnography championed by Linnaeus could not satisfy.[33]

Banks found that the interest generated in exotic skulls in Britain had led those lucky enough to come into possession of them to part with them only at exorbitant prices. Nonetheless, he informed Blumenbach that a ship was due to sail in a month and that he had persuaded the captain, and would approach the ship's surgeon when appointed, to procure for Blumenbach "good specimens" of skulls from New Holland and the South Sea Isles. The voyage was scheduled to take at least two and a half years. He would thus take up Blumenbach's suggestion and approach John Hunter with a view to supplying a silhouette or possibly even a plaster cast of a South Sea skull. The ship being readied for departure was the *Bounty*.

Banks had also written to Alexander Anderson, through his patronage superintendent of the Royal Botanic Gardens on St. Vincents, requesting that he obtain skulls of Carib Indians.[34] Anderson took some time to favor Banks, explaining the following in a letter of May 1789:

> It is a very difficult thing to get the Crania of the Yellow Carribes or aborigines the greater part of them have been extirpated by the black Carribes at present there are only two Families of them & these are in the most remote part of the island their burial places are not easily found & an attempt to disturb them is look'd upon as the greatest of crimes.[35]

Thus within the Banks-Blumenbach correspondence can be found one of the earliest examples of what was to become a commonplace ritual in European anthropological circles through the century or so to follow. An eminent patron would make clear the scientific value of indigenous skeletal remains to a client in the colonies. For any number of motives, ranging from detached scientific interest to the desire to safeguard employment, the client would dispatch the desired remains, stressing the rarity of the items forwarded, the difficulties, and the personal dangers to which he had been exposed in the course of their procurement.

In the summer of 1790, Blumenbach was mortified to learn from Banks of the *Bounty* mutiny and the loss of his long-awaited specimens. Nonetheless, Banks was keen to make good his long-standing promise, and in late December 1790, he wrote to Blumenbach that a new expedition was being sent for breadfruit, and "I hope she will bring to you Crania of the S. see Isles." A further vessel was soon "to go to New Holland so that you may expect the head of new holland also." Yet within a month Banks was to write, "I fear I shall not soon have the pleasure of sending you Crania from the South see the busy preparations for a war with Spain stop all ships bound on voyages of curiosity so that none have sail'd since the loss of the Guardian & Bounty."[36]

A fleet had to be dispatched to the penal settlement at Port Jackson, though, and with it went Bank's request. But it was not until November 1793, nearly three years later, that an Aboriginal skull was finally delivered to Göttingen, via the diplomatic pouch from London. The cause of the long delay, or so Arthur Phillip, the settlement's first governor, appears to have informed Banks, was that the Eora clans on whose land they had settled generally practiced cremation. But given Phillip's concern for peaceful coexistence, and also the clear appreciation among the officers of the First Fleet of the importance of death practices and burial sites to the Eora, one suspects that Phillip was not keen to be seen opening graves.[37] In fact, the cranium sent to England for Blumenbach in 1793 was that "of a male native of New Holland who died in our settlement of Sydney Cove" (in all probability of smallpox.) [38]

Blumenbach was especially taken on examining the skull to find an incisor knocked out, "according to the custom of those savages, even in the most distant coasts of New Holland, to pull out this tooth in their youth."[39] On comparing the skull with the representations he had to hand of mainland Aboriginal people, Tasmanians, and Papuans, new questions arose. Was the portrait of the Tasmanian man drawn by John Webber and published in the account of Cook's last voyage accurate? If so, it was a serious challenge to his whole environmentalist schema, in which marked conformity in head shape should exist among Aboriginal people, given that explorers' accounts suggested that "the inhabitants of all the known coasts of that vast continent agree so wonderful, even in the minutia of manners."[40] Blumenbach preferred to think that "Mr Webber has embellished a little his savages." Another question was more exciting. Was the full-length portrait of a "south-seas inhabitant" appearing in Cornelius de Bruin's *Travels . . . in East India* a Papuan or New Hollander?[41] De Bruin he considered an accurate draftsman. Comparison of the skull now in his possession and the print thus suggested that it was "at least not improbable" that the man was a New Hollander. But what if the man were a Papuan? This raised interesting questions concerning the place of both peoples in the history of human variation. Blumenbach had also heard that two Aborigines (Bennelong and Yemmerrawanyea Kebberah) had arrived in England with Governor Phillip.[42] Perhaps Banks had seen them and was in a position quickly to judge the accuracy or otherwise of de Bruin.

These and doubtless many related questions explain Blumenbach's pleasure when, in late 1798, Banks wrote offering a second New Holland skull, that of a young man apparently killed in a clash with a convict work party. Banks thought it might "be of service in exchange," though Blumenbach was quick to accept the offer, stressing that he had no intention of trading it, but would "keep it for Comparison with the former, & to show thereby . . . what is perhaps merely individual & accidental, & what on the contrary is truly national & characteristical."[43]

From the end of the eighteenth century until Darwinistic modes of thought revolutionized anthropological discourse after the early 1860s, monogenist environmentalism propounded by Blumenbach commanded the assent of most educated Britons in the metropolis and the Australian colonies. The varieties of mankind were the result of environmental modification of a single race. The contrary view, that physical and mental differences among the peoples of the earth were the immutable legacies of separate creations, had numerous Anglo-Saxon adherents, especially in the British sugar colonies of the Caribbean and in the proslavery American states. Polygenist writers also found a receptive audience—and gained some notable converts—especially in the aftermath of the social unrest marking the years 1848–1849.[44] Even so, most Britons in Australia favored environmentalism as it figured in such writers as John Cross and James Cowles Prichard.[45] Cross, a Scots medical practitioner, confidently asserted in 1817 that the progress of civilization in Britain had resulted in "a striking similitude among the individuals of each district." Moreover, the "vital department" had so strengthened the "animal department" in the white race that they were destined by interbreeding to supplant all other varieties of the human race: "The white man, in virtue of his superiority in all corporeal and mental powers, is lord of the world, and, in virtue of his superiority in respiration, and in structure and function of skin, is able to walk over his extensive domain."[46] Similar sentiments were expressed in the more widely read encyclopedic and reassuringly Christian writings of the Bristol physician James Cowles Prichard. A conservative Quaker, Prichard strove through his writings, and involvement with the British Association for the Advancement of Science, to reconcile the spirit of Genesis with mounting scientific reports of anatomical difference.[47] Like Blumenbach, whom he much admired, Prichard credited God with having allowed the destiny of nations to be unfurled in ways allowing environmental forces great power to mold human physique and intellectual capability with the passing of generations.

Despite the a priori assumptions or general hypotheses informing understanding of the nature and meanings of human variety,[48] there was agreement that difference was explicable only so far as careful empirical observation of the current state, or recent history, of the earth's peoples allowed the establishment of indisputable fact. For polygenists this generally meant endorsing the opinion of Charles White, that it was "an important object, in general physiology, to trace the lines of distinction" between the various species of humanity, and then describe the principal characteristics of the species so delineated. For the environmentalists, the task was to substantiate beyond question the differences that had come to exist between the principal nations or races of humanity as they had developed, and then perhaps reconstruct something of the history and pace of change that had led the natural history of man to become a history of gradual diversity.

Universal endorsement of the primacy of close empirical scrutiny of the bodily differences of non-Europeans understandably made anthropological inquiry an attractive field for naval and military surgeons in the

colonial sphere. It privileged the anatomically trained eye over that of
the philosophical travelers of earlier generations. The ambitious young
Robert Knox wrote with unmistakable delight of his South African post-
ing in 1823:

> So far as I know, none has ever viewed the savage races in-
> habiting this peninsula in an anatomical point of view, and
> hence have arisen ill-founded conjectures, and positive errors,
> too numerous to be criticised. I have endeavoured to correct
> those more immediately connected with our inquiry, but have
> carefully avoided general criticism, as leading me from the
> subject.[49]

As a result of the currency that the "anatomical point of view" had come
to enjoy by the early nineteenth century, skulls and skeletons of Aboriginal people became desirable objects. So much so that traditional moral
qualms about grave robbing or dissection were overcome, even when—
as is recorded as happening on a number of occasions—the procurement of remains involved serious risk of discovery by the deceased's
family or clan members. Indeed, in a wide range of printed and manuscript sources, one finds body snatching represented as a dangerous,
even heroic, quest in which the harsh Australian environment and its
"treacherous savages" were braved in the quest for "rare and valuable
specimens."[50]

It would be mistaken to assume, as some unsympathetic commentators have claimed over the past decade, that the preservation of remains
in European scientific collections became an issue only in the wake of
campaigns by the first nations of North America for the repatriation of remains and grave goods. Far from it. As with broad assumptions about
many aspects of Australian history, assessment of the remains controversy
has been hindered by what historian Henry Reynolds has characterized as
the "Great Australian Silence": the easy and often all-too-convenient amnesia about the dispossession of Aboriginal peoples.[51] Here I have sought
to draw attention to the fact that the procurement of the ancestral remains of Aboriginal people dates to the initial years of European settlement, and have offered a brief account of the meanings the corpses of
Aboriginal people acquired in late-Enlightenment anatomical and anthropological discourse. As we approach 2001, the year by which the
Australian federal government aims to consolidate the process of recon-
ciliation with Aboriginal Australia, we would do well to consider the procurement and use of ancestral remains in greater depth. By doing so, we
will understand how earlier biomedical knowledge served to render Ab-

original people colonial subjects. But perhaps more important, we might help greatly to give Aboriginality its rightful centrality in our historical consciousness, by showing how opposition to the desecration of burial sites is nothing new, but one important aspect of Aboriginal peoples' history of resistance to their vanquishment from ancestral country to the margins, or beyond the boundaries of white Australia.

NOTES

I would like to record my thanks to Dr. John Gascoigne, who kindly allowed me to read in manuscript several key chapters of his *Joseph Banks and the English Enlightenment: Useful Knowledge and Polite Culture* (Cambridge: Cambridge University Press, 1994). The sketch of Banksian "body snatching" draws heavily on Gascoigne's detailed and richly suggestive study in intellectual biography.

1. See, for example, the *Royal College of Surgeons of England Annual Report, 1989–1990* (London: RCSE, 1990), 15.
2. Arthur Keith, *Guide to the College of Surgeons* (London: 1910), 116.
3. Zachary Cope, *The History of the Royal College of Surgeons of England* (London: Blond, 1959), 24.
4. The political functions of English gentility are explored in Paul Langford's detailed and fascinating *Public Life and the Propertied Englishman, 1689–1798* (Oxford: Oxford University Press, 1991).
5. Arthur Keith, "A Discourse on the Portraits and Personality of John Hunter," *British Medical Journal* (1928): 205.
6. See John Hunter, *The Works of John Hunter . . .* , ed. James F. Palmer, 8 vols. (London, 1835), 1:123, 151–153.
7. Wild claims continue to be made as to the number of skulls and skeletal remains that found their way into European scientific collections. See, for example, Eve Mumewa D. Fesl's *Conned!* (Brisbane: University of Queensland Press, 1993), 30, where she speaks of thousands of Koories being decapitated. I have based my estimate on A. Hardlicka's comprehensive "Catalogue of Crania in the United States National Museum Collections," *Proceedings of the United States National Museum* 71 (1928): 1.
8. See P. Turnbull, "Ancestors and Specimens: Reflections on the Controversy over the Remains of Aboriginal People in Scientific Collections," in Ken Riddiford, Eric Wilson, and Barry Wright, eds., *Contemporary Issues in Aboriginal*

and Torres Strait Islander Studies 4 (Cairns: Cairns College of TAFE, 1993), 11–33.

9. Michael Mansell, quoted in David Langsam, "Quest for the Missing Dead," *The Independent* [London], 24 February 1990.

10. On this subject, see especially Ruby Langford, "Our Heritage—Your Playground," *Australian Archaeology* 16 (1983): 1–6; also Foundation for Aboriginal and Islander Research Action, "Aborigines, Archaeologists and the Rights of the Dead," World Archaeological Congress on Archaeological Ethics and the Treatment of the Dead, University of Southampton, 1989.

11. Richard Rorty, *Philosophy and the Mirror of Nature* (Princeton: Princeton University Press, 1979), and Charles Taylor, "Interpretation and the Sciences of Man," in *Philosophy and the Human Sciences* (Cambridge: Cambridge University Press, 1982), 15–57; and Terence Ball's *Transforming Political Discourse* (Cambridge: Cambridge University Press, 1988).

12. See Jessie Dobson, *John Hunter* (Edinburgh: E. Livingstone and S. Livingstone, 1969), 185.

13. Johann Friedrich Blumenbach, *The Anthropological Treatises . . .* , ed. Thomas Bendyshe (London: Longman, Green, Longman, Roberts, and Green, 1865), 21.

14. See especially Dorothy Porter and Roy Porter, *Patient's Progress: Doctors and Doctoring in Eighteenth-Century England* (Cambridge: Cambridge University Press, 1989).

15. J.G.A. Pocock, "Gibbon's *Decline and Fall* and the World View of the Late Enlightenment," in *Virtue, Commerce, and History* (Cambridge: Cambridge University Press, 1985), 143–156; also Nicholas Phillipson, *David Hume* (London: Weidenfeld and Nicolson, 1989).

16. Cook, cited in Alan Moorehead, *The Fatal Impact: The Invasion of the South Pacific, 1767–1840* (London: Hamish Hamilton, 1987), 142.

17. See Steven J. Cross, "John Hunter, the Animal Oeconomy, and Late Eighteenth-Century Physiological Discourse," *Studies in the History of Biology* 5 (1981): 1–110.

18. See especially Hunter's observations on the development of chick embryos, in Hunter, *Works,* 3:106.

19. Ibid., *Works,* 4:166–167.

20. Cross, "John Hunter," 36, citing Hunter, *Works,* 1:215.

21. Ibid., 44–50.

22. Hunter, *Works,* 1:526.

23. John V. Pickstone and Steven V. F. Butler, "The Politics of Medicine in Manchester, 1788–1792: Hospital Reform and Public Health Services in the Early Industrial City," *Medical History* 28 (1984): 227–249.

24. Charles White, *An Account of the Regular Gradation in Man, and in Different Ani-*

mals and Vegetables . . . Read to the Literary and Philosophical Society of Manchester, at Different Meetings, in the Year 1795 (London, 1799).

25. Cross, "John Hunter," 15–21.

26. Hunter, *Essays and Observations on Natural History . . .* , ed. Richard Owen, 2 vols. (London, 1861), 2:36–37. See also Cross, "John Hunter," 18–21.

27. Hunter, *Works*, 1:295.

28. Blumenbach, *Anthropological Treatises*, 105.

29. Ibid., 114.

30. Ibid., 238.

31. Ibid., 240.

32. Ibid., 299.

33. For one thing, there was the cannibalism of Maori. Banks was fascinated by the practice, and by the associated tradition of preserving the heads of warriors. Banks' fascination, however, was streaked with revulsion, and philosophical unease. Try as he might to explain the eating of human flesh as the result of Maori living in a perpetual state of war, Banks found it stood at odds with received conceptualizations of nature as an "admirable chain." Fish and insects might routinely prey on their own species, but in the orderly and finely graded hierarchy of nature, the utter revulsion of higher animal forms to eating their own, except "in cases of absolute necessity," provided no cogent explanation for the esteem in which Maori held the practice. See *The Endeavour Journal of Joseph Banks, 1768–1771*, ed. John C. Beaglehole, 2 vols. (Sydney: Angus and Robertson, 1962), 2:20. Likewise, similarities of language and tradition between Tahitian and Maori left Banks in "little doubt that they came originally from the same source." But the location of that source? Given what the *Endeavour* voyagers had seen of Polynesian seacraft, the prevailing winds, and the direction of currents, all that Banks felt able to commit to his journal was "no more than that I firmly believe that it is to the Westward and by no means to the East" (2:37). Yet word lists compiled from inhabitants and seamen at Batavia and Panaitan on the homeward leg of the expedition served only to complicate matters (2:241). Further, during the *Endeavour*'s passage northward along the eastern coast of Australia, the small numbers of people seen, and the distinctive material culture of those with whom they came into contact, led Banks to reflect whether the seemingly harsh environment or cultural peculiarities best explained "why mankind should not increase here as fast as in other places" (2:123).

34. See Harold B. Carter, *Sir Joseph Banks, 1743–1820* (London: British Museum [Natural History], 1988), 274–277.

35. Johann Friedrich Blumenbach, MS Blumenbach 3:30v, University of Göttingen Library. I am greatly indebted to Dr. John Gascoigne for this reference.

36. Blumenbach, MS 3, 34v–35.

37. On perceptions of Aboriginal spirituality, mortuary rites, and the concern of Phillip to maintain peace, see David Collins, *An Account of the English Colony in New South Wales,* ed. Brian Fletcher, 2 vols. (Sydney: Library of Australian History, 1975), 1:498–504.

38. In the early nineteenth century, Edinburgh University acquired the complete skeleton of a young Eora man given to Alexander Monro *tertius* by John Jamison, M.D., sole legitimate son of Thomas Jamison, who had sailed with the first fleet as naval surgeon on the *Sirius* and had served in New South Wales as surgeon general from 1801 until 1809, when ill health and his involvement in the Rum Rebellion led him to return to England. See *Australian Dictionary of Biography* entries on John Jamison and Thomas Jamison.

39. Joseph Banks, Letters, Add MSS 8098, British Library, 116.

40. Ibid., 116v.

41. *Voyage . . . par la Moscovie, en Perse, et aux Indes Orientales. Ouvrage enrichi de plus 320 tailles douces . . . ,* 2 vols. (Amsterdam; n.p., 1718) [full English translation, London: n.p., 1737].

42. For Bennelong see *Australian Dictionary of Biography.* Yemmerrawanyea Kebberah died in lodgings at Eltham, Kent, on 18 May 1794. The cause of death was most likely influenza. He was buried in Eltham churchyard. His tombstone now rests against the churchyard wall.

43. Banks, Add MSS 8098, 434.

44. See George Stocking, *Victorian Anthropology* (London: Free Press, 1987), 62–69.

45. This influence of Prichardian ethnography in colonial Australia is discussed in P. Turnbull, "A Forgotten Cosmology: William Hull's *Account . . . of the Aboriginal Natives,*" *Historical Studies* 14 (1990): 207–219.

46. John Cross, *An Attempt to Establish Physiognomy upon Scientific Principles . . .* (Glasgow, 1817), 88–89.

47. See George Stocking's introduction to his edition of James Cowles Prichard's *Researches in the Physical History of Man* (Chicago: Chicago University Press, 1973).

48. Proving compatible with both monogenist and polygenist schemas from the 1820s was a new science of mind, phrenology, which found particular favor with middle-class professionals in England and the colonies. Phrenology, with its conceptualization of mind as an economy of cerebrally localized mental powers, greatly influenced anthropological discourse until well into the latter half of the nineteenth century. P. Turnbull, "'To What Strange Uses': The Procurement and Use of Aboriginal Peoples' Bodies in Early Colonial Australia," *Voices* (Spring, 1994): 5–20.

49. Robert Knox, "Inquiry into the Origin and Characteristic Differences of the Native Races Inhabiting the Extra-Tropical Part of Southern Africa," *Memoirs of the Wernerian Natural History Society* 5 (1823–1824): 206–219.

50. On at least one occasion the quest for remains actually resulted in the death of grave robbers. This was in 1842, when the Admiralty survey vessel HMS *Fly* was at Hobart town. According to the *Fly*'s assistant surgeon, "A young gentleman of great intelligence & adventure volunteered to accompany Mr McGillivray & myself to the place of interment of the last of the aboriginal inhabitants of Tasmania who had died in their own land. I will not speak of our labours & dangers in the adventure, it was the painful occasion of the loss of two out of our three boats with their crews of nine men" (Archibald Sibbald, Owen Letters 275 [25]/h (5)/6, Royal College of Surgeons of England Library.) Having exhumed several graves on Bruny Island only to find cremated remains, they finally found a woman's corpse. The head, a leg, and an arm rested in the Royal College of Surgeons until their destruction by a German bomb in 1941.

51. Henry Reynolds, *The Breaking of the Great Australian Silence: Aborigines in Australian Historiography, 1955–1983* (London: University of London, Institute of Commonwealth Studies, 1984).

13

Missionaries on Tahiti, 1797–1840

Rod Edmond

The founders of the London Missionary Society (LMS), set up in 1795, had read Cook, spoken with Bligh, and decided that Tahiti was the most promising part of "the heathen world" for a mission.[1] Two years later, eighteen "godly mechanics" landed on Tahiti with an optimistic view of their prospects. However, the early years of the mission were a disaster. The Tahitians were unreceptive, and several missionaries either shipped out or "went native." It was only after Pomare's unexpected conversion in 1812, and his victory over his rivals at the battle of Fei Pi in 1815, that the LMS acquired the influence they sought. From then on, until the arrival of the French in the late 1830s, the LMS became a kind of established church and the Tahitian islands tiny theocracies.

During this period of ascendancy, the mission itself was split between an old guard, based on the Windward islands of Tahiti and Eimeo (Moʻorea), and a new wave of missionaries who arrived in 1817 and became established on the Leeward islands of Huahine, Raiatea, and Borabora. Among these new arrivals were William Ellis, author of *Polynesian Researches* (1829), and John Williams, author of *Narrative of Missionary Enterprises* (1837), texts that are to be the main focus of this essay.[2] They tell of the high years of the mission to Tahiti and are silent about its divisions.[3] On the other hand, correspondence from the field to LMS headquarters in London tells a different story. This chapter will make some tentative comparisons between these competing accounts.

In examining these missionary texts, it is important not to labor their prejudices nor to express moral indignation at their presumption. The published texts and the correspondence will be regarded as mutually supplementary. Neither will automatically be accorded primacy; both are equally forms of representation, constructed to achieve certain kinds of effect and aimed at particular readers. The larger task is to interpret these sources and their surrounding history in order better to understand the nature of the contact, exchange, entanglement, subordination, assimilation, adaptation, and resistance that characterized the encounter of missionaries and Tahitians in the first forty years of the nineteenth century, and the complex shifting history this inaugurated.

Ellis and Williams' texts will be analyzed as examples of "colonial discourse." Colonial discourse analysis has sometimes failed to recognize complexity and difference, reducing all its texts to the same narrative of appropriation and establishing their complicity in a monolithic project of European colonialism. The more interesting work in this field, however, has been able to identify and analyze a kind of schizophrenia in colonialist texts. *Polynesian Researches* is preeminently a work of this kind. Both the texts and the correspondence, products of a historically and geographically specific cultural encounter, will also be discussed in terms of ideas derived from postcolonial theory (a related but not identical field to colonial discourse studies). The discussion, however, will resist the totalizing tendencies of much theory of this kind. The history of cultural encounter in the Pacific is distinctive and refutes the grand generalizations postcolonial theorists are prone to make. Its great challenge to postcolonial pieties and cultural nationalists is that European colonial powers, as such, were never particularly interested in the Pacific. That said, it remains possible to use and adapt ideas from postcolonial theory without falling into the totalizing trap or becoming a proponent of "fatal impact."

Henry Louis Gates has succinctly outlined the problematic within which this chapter is situated. "You can empower discursively the native, and open yourself to charges of downplaying the epistemic (and literal) violence of colonialism," he writes, "or play up the absolute nature of colonial domination, and be open to charges of negating the subjectivity and agency of the colonized, thus textually replicating the repressive operations of colonialism.[4] There is no obvious way of escaping this impasse at the level of pure theory. It needs to be addressed in specific cultural and historical situations. It can, however, be refined. From the point of view of the colonized, we should remember Aijaz Ahmad's point that although colonialism is a key moment in the history of a colonized people, it neither constitutes nor reconstitutes the whole of their culture. There is a much longer history that has gone into its making, and there are cultural practices that remain relatively unaffected. The creation of colonial subjects according to the wish of the colonizer will always be incomplete, and sometimes quite unsuccessful.[5] And just as native points of view have frequently been elided, the colonizer has often been represented as having a single voice. There were significant differences even within the tight-knit group of LMS missionaries on Tahiti, let alone between the various agencies of colonialism in the region. Such points complicate Gates' sharp antithesis.

Ellis' *Polynesian Researches* is probably the most important source of information about Polynesian cultures in the first half of the nineteenth century. It was acknowledged as such by Darwin, and it influenced novelists as unlike as Melville and Wilkie Collins.[6] The work has some of the characteristics of what Mary-Louise Pratt has termed "anti-conquest narratives," which underwrote colonial appropriation while rejecting the rhetoric of conquest and subjugation.[7] These narratives were part of the process by which modern imperialism sought to redefine itself in civilizing and reciprocal terms. Pratt sees them as taking two apparently different but, in fact, closely related forms. First, there was the narrative of scientific neutrality, the classificatory project of eighteenth-century natural science, which became extended to ethnography. The other was that of sentimental travel writing, narratives of human reciprocity of which the transracial colonial romance was the archetype. These apparently different narratives both offered a discursive space in which Europeans could detach themselves from the unequal and exploitative nature of colonial relationships. They also complemented each other in that the language of sensibility offered an alternative, humanized way of describing colonial subjects who had already been classified and fixed in place. Together, Pratt argues, they functioned as legitimating ideologies for the harsh realities of colonial appropriation.

Polynesian Researches uses both these narrative forms. It is full of detailed ethnographic accounts rendered in an apparently neutral language of scientific observation. These passages work very much as Pratt describes. They naturalize the presence and authority of the European observer. They fix Tahitian culture in a timeless present so that particular episodes are seen not as events in time, perhaps as a response to the presence of the observer, but as expressions of inherent traits and customs. For this reason, Greg Dening has remarked there is no more untrustworthy source than the *formal* descriptions by observers of the cultures they confront.[8] *Polynesian Researches* also inscribes the human-centered, interactive narrative typical of the sentimental mode. Ellis' arrival in Tahiti is a good example, which, like most arrival scenes, represents a myth of beginnings. The first Tahitian Ellis meets comes on board for breakfast. He says grace before eating, to the amusement of the officers, whose genial scorn is regarded by the Tahitian with compassion. Ellis finds this scene "the most pleasing sight I had yet beheld."[9] In it, Ellis lines up with the converted savage against the civilized but irreligious British officers. It is an ideal tableau, a text for the sermon Ellis wishes to preach to his West ern audience, expressing the writer's desired relation with the native population he has come to convert. As with many such scenes, its historical accuracy is less important than its mythical truth. Although things will never be as perfect again, this sentimental narrative shapes Ellis' text. Structurally, the missionary is akin to the European lover of the transracial romance. He brings the love of God rather than man, but like his secular equivalent, he teaches the fickle, inconstant Polynesian the lesson of devotion, redeems him through love, and civilizes him. Or rather, this is the ideal narrative of reciprocity *Polynesian Researches* keeps trying to establish.

It is, however, a much more divided text than this. It cannot entirely allegorize away the palpable difficulties the mission confronted. And although it does employ narratives that conceal the reality of colonial relationships, it has no wish to disguise the effort to transform native culture. This would be to deny the whole purpose of the mission. On another level, then, *Polynesian Researches* is not an anticonquest narrative at all. It tells of Christian soldiers battling with the forces of Satan, of victory and conversion, and employs a much older providential narrative going back through Bunyan to the Bible. And, of course, there are many Christian readers, a potential source of funds for the mission, who want to hear this story. Telling it, however, was not straightforward, as this strangely hybrid and fissured text demonstrates.

The recurring deep structure of *Polynesian Researches* is an alternation between science and sermon, between neutral description and vehement denunciation of Tahitian lifestyles, between the Tahitians as redeemable and irredeemable, between the divinely guaranteed success of the mission and its overwhelmingly difficult task. Christopher Herbert has explained these violent alternations in terms of two competing models for understanding native life. The first is that Polynesian culture was characterized by ungoverned human desire, the absence of social control, and by an all-pervading *anomie;* that it is, in effect, "cultureless." This was the model the missionaries brought with them; their writ, he says, "was to produce allegories of natural depravity." The other, competing model derived from their slow realization that the Tahitians inhabited a world of meanings, an organized ensemble of customs and institutions; in other words, that they possessed a culture. The minutely detailed ethnographic descriptions of *Polynesian Researches* are a sign of this alternative paradigm, and an attempt to solve the interpretive riddle of Tahitian lifestyles. This alternative model of understanding was, crucially, a consequence of the missionaries learning the Tahitian language; the linguistic paradigm became a metonym for the culture as a whole.[10]

This argument is helpful in understanding the divisions found in

Ellis' text and other missionary writing, although the sequence Herbert outlines is disputable. LMS missionaries did not necessarily *arrive* with a natural depravity model in mind. The South Seas had been chosen precisely because it was thought to be different from other primitive regions. The idea of Polynesian culture as "governed by anarchic natural desire" (and this was only one of several descriptions) was also an experiential response revising more ideal preconceptions. Missionaries arriving in Tahiti frequently complained that they had been misled by LMS propaganda into expecting something altogether better. The textuality of these conflicting discourses should also be emphasized. Ellis would have been familiar with ethnographic description in the work of earlier Pacific explorers. There were home models as well in the work of early-nineteenth-century social investigators. Ellis "experienced" the South Seas in the light of these narratives as well as in terms of some putative missionary writ; hence, the competing generic models that shape his text, the clash of discourses, and their complex interaction.

It is time for an example, although no one example can quite demonstrate how the oscillation between "science" and "sermon" establishes the basic rhythm of the text. Consider Ellis' long section on tattooing. First, he explains its prohibition by the missionaries because of its connection with idolatry and other "abominable vices." He then proceeds, however, to a detailed description of its techniques, extends this into an aesthetics of tattooing (Tahitian tattoos have "greater taste and elegance" than other Polynesian forms), and even to some phrenological-type passages on tattooing as an index of character. And then suddenly it becomes an "immoral practice" again, and we are given a long account of a tattoo rebellion of young men led by the sons of local chiefs. A crusade is preached against them, and the rebels are captured, tried, and punished. The account ends with Ellis at his weekly service preaching on the rebellion of Absalom.[11] This whole section is marked by the alternation of different kinds of narration; ethnography is framed and corrected by a Christian moral discourse, and the attempt to describe something strange is overridden by something familiar. This has been prepared for earlier in the text when the death of the leader of this rebellion, who is the son of the king of Huahine, has been recounted.[12] There it was narrated as a Victorian death-bed scene with the wronged wife, grieving father, and anxious missionary all watching for signs of repentance. This familiar piece of genre painting has carried forward into the narrative, assisting it to revise the ethnographic account.

These formal dislocations express conceptual problems. Indeed, contradiction exists at the very heart of Ellis' subject, "the Polynesian." How is this recently discovered savage to be described and categorized? Existing discourses of savagery, whether from classical texts or modern accounts of the Caribbean, were not adequate to the task. In fact, the whole project of scientific classification required that they should not be; new types required new descriptions. The main discursive problem presented by the European discovery of Polynesian cultures was how to redefine existing discourses of savagery from the Mediterranean Old World and the Atlantic New World to explain this new New World.

The formal dislocations of *Polynesian Researches* are a symptom of the difficulties this entailed. It opens with Humboldt's description of the South Sea Islanders as "a mixture of perversity and meekness" living in a "state of half-civilization."[13] This is to be Ellis' text. Sometimes he uses it to draw parallels with the half-formed state of classical civilization. More commonly their state of "half-civilization" is compared to that of childhood. Volume 2 opens with a long account of "the Polynesian character." Its defining feature is inconstancy. Like children, Polynesians are quick to learn but slow to concentrate; their interest is easily roused but hard to sustain; they have enthusiasm but no stamina:

> When a boat manned with English seamen, and a canoe with natives, have started together from the shore—at their first setting out, the natives would soon leave the boat behind, but, as they became weary, they would relax their vigour; while the seamen, pulling on steadily, would . . . if the voyage occupied three or four hours . . . invariably reach their destination first.[14]

So much for a people that had spread itself many thousands of miles over the Pacific. The comparison is between adults and children. Adult character is formed; the contradictory half-formed nature of children, on the other hand, means that all their virtues are double edged. In this case, spontaneous enthusiasm quickly becomes defeated exhaustion. This reconceptualization of the savage as childlike is packed with implication. A whole developmental language that came to be applied to childhood during the nineteenth century can also be extended to savagery. Like children, savages can grow, mature, and become civilized. The "other," whether child or savage, can become like us. But there is nothing automatic about this. The analogous processes of socialization and civilization, with their associated organic metaphors, can easily go wrong. Plants can go to seed, children turn out badly, while savages can revert. Reversion, Ellis insists, is ugly; there is nothing inherently noble about the Polynesian savage. Polynesians, like all children, are tainted by original sin, but they are redeemable. Dr. Arnold was soon to talk in similar terms about his boys at Rugby. These complex transactions between the figure of the savage and the child result in the construction of "the Polynesian" as a contradictory and unstable figure who produces uneasiness at every level of Ellis' text. A correspondingly contradictory and unstable array of narratives—scientific, sentimental, punitive—are mobilized to try and contain and explain this figure.

Eventually, *Polynesian Researches* attempts to reconcile these competing narratives under an overarching domestic one in which home figures as the keystone of any culture worth the name. Ellis' text describes a thorough implantation of the domestic. On Huahine, the island where Ellis was based, houses were grouped in villages, gardens and plantations were enclosed, and women were accorded their proper place at the center of a newly privatized family. Domesticity becomes the great subject of the second volume. It is the one sure index both of Christianity and civilization, the site where these two uneasily related ideas can be perfectly married. It is the ultimate destination of Ellis' narrative reached after eleven hundred pages of vicissitude:

> Domestic happiness, though formerly unknown even in name, is now sedulously cultivated, and spreads around their abodes of order and comfort, its choicest blessings. The husband and the wife, instead of promiscuously mingling with the multitude . . . live together in the neat little cottages reared by their own industry, and find satisfaction and comfort in each other's society . . . the children grow up the objects of their mutual affection. . . . Often they appear together reading the Scriptures . . . or surrounding, not indeed the family hearth . . . which in their warm climate would be no addition to their comfort, but the family board, spread with the liberal gifts of divine bounty. The father at times may also be seen nursing his little child at the door of his cottage, and the mother sitting at needlework by his side, or engaged in other domestic employments.[15]

This passage replies to earlier set pieces deploring the absence of domestic virtues in Tahitian society. It therefore dramatizes the effects of conversion, and summarizes Ellis' narrative by rendering Tahitian culture as an ideal version of rural England, with a Pooterish explanation for the absence of a family hearth. *Polynesian Researches* ends on this note, with the Ellises looking back at Huahine from the bay as they depart for Hawai'i. They see a town of cottages, gardens, roads, schools, and a chapel. The natives are clothed and in their right mind. The production of coffee is about to begin. Christian civilization has arrived and Ellis can depart.

Of course, this is sheer melodrama, a glaring example of the imposition of British values and an expression of missionary anxieties. Generically, it is very similar to any number of Victorian novels that end with the restoration or reconstruction of family life after a lengthy narrative in which it has been threatened with disintegration, degradation, or been damagingly absent. It is therefore a version of Pratt's sentimental narrative of human reciprocity, though totally unembarrassed by the idea of "conquest." It complements the ethnographic narrative and not just by humanizing it. In bringing the sentimental to bear on the ethnographic, the latter is refashioned so that a different kind of cultural description becomes possible, one that is familiar rather than strange. For this to happen, however, the corrective narrative, a version of Herbert's depravity or Pratt's conquest narrative, must also be deployed. In the same way, discipline, and sometimes punishment, became central to the task of raising and educating children in the nineteenth century. This is the rhetoric of Ellis' second volume. It does not succeed in reconciling the competing narratives and stabilizing the text. In some ways it highlights the instabilities, drawing attention to what it tries to obscure and failing to cancel the unease that the generic promiscuity of this text expresses.

John Williams' *Narrative of Missionary Enterprises* is a different kind of text, as the title makes clear. It is a busier, more campaigning work, directly aimed at a missionary-supporting readership. It is a conversion narrative recording Williams' energetic pursuit of lost souls across the Pacific. It is more explicitly colonialist than Ellis', yet with moments of surprising cultural insight. Generically, it is a simpler text, less divided and more transparent.

Certainly, it is a conquest narrative. Williams' greatest pride was to return to his base on Raiatea surrounded by confiscated idols, as in the following description: "And as other warriors feel a pride in displaying trophies of the victories they win, we hung the rejected idols of Aitutaki to the yard-arms and other parts of the vessel, entered the harbour in triumph, sailed down to the settlement, and dropped anchor amidst the shouts and congratulations of our people."[16] Williams dispatched boxes of idols to London as regularly as a modern traveler would send postcards. *Missionary Enterprises* is also a kind of business report. Williams saw the capture and recovery of lost souls as a commercial enterprise. He complained of overmanning in the Tahitian station, and in a famous letter compared his activities to those of a merchant in search of pearls.[17] He combined the care of a double-entry bookkeeper with the ambition of a merchant whose capital was souls.

Above all, however, it is a providential narrative. Very much in the manner described by Max Weber, Williams read the world for evidence of God's favor and found it wherever he looked. After an outbreak of tattooing among young Raratongans, for example, Williams preached an angry sermon warning that "God would not now, as in the days of their

ignorance, wink at such wickedness." Soon after, the island was devastated
by a hurricane. Miraculously, Williams' ship was saved, swept inland several hundred yards, where it rested undamaged in a grove of trees.
Mrs. Williams was less fortunate, the shock of the hurricane causing her
seventh stillbirth, but "God . . . in judgement remembered mercy," and
her life was spared.[18] The workings of Providence enable Williams to
thread these events together into an intelligible narrative of punishment and redemption, and this is the pattern of the whole work. The generic forebear of this providential pattern is *The Pilgrim's Progress,* which
Williams had translated into Raratongan. *Missionary Enterprises* is like
Bunyan's text, but without the inner drama, rather as if *The Pilgrim's Progress* had been rewritten by Samuel Smiles.

The *Pilgrim's Progress* holds *Missionary Enterprises* together, providing
it with a generic coherence Ellis' text lacks. It is able to do so because
Williams' text is less curious about native ways of life, less troubled by
ethnography, and therefore gets into fewer difficulties. It even has less
overt moralizing because there is not the same need to try and shut out
the worrying implications of detailed ethnographic description; Herbert's "natural depravity" model is rarely challenged by any recognition of
the complex unity of Tahitian culture implicit in ethnographic accounts.
Paradoxically, this means that Williams' occasional moments of cultural
insight—as, for example, when he concedes that Polynesian languages
"abound in turns of peculiar nicety . . . are spoken with strict conformity
to the most precise grammatical principles," and are capable of refine-
ments beyond the scope of the English language—are left uncorrected
by any alternative narrative.[19]

Williams also uses a domestic narrative, though less strategically than
Ellis. This follows from what I have said above, and is also a consequence of the greater restlessness of *Missionary Enterprises.* Nevertheless,
Williams' description of the wholesale reorganization of Raiatean life into
villages is central to the good news he reports. It is the sentimental narrative that succeeds conquest, and was to have an important influence on
later writing about the Pacific. In Ballantyne's *The Coral Island* (1857), for
example, the description of the converted native village with neatly arranged cottages and tastefully laid out gardens, which contrast with the
random disorder and violence of unconverted native settlements, is taken
almost word for word from Williams' description of Arorangi.[20] Harriet
Martineau's novel *Dawn Island* (1845), in which a fallen Pacific is redeemed by the introduction of free trade, also highlights the absence of
domestic comforts and the low status of women before dramatizing the
domestic reorganization of native life along lines that seem to be derived
from Ellis and Williams.

The larger significance of this is quickly explained. Within colonialist texts, the absolutely "other" is often redefined as the domesticated "other" in the process of consolidating and affirming the European self. The domestic anxieties of missionary families must have made this an urgent matter. And Spivak has shown how in establishing a good society the woman has an important signifying role, often as an object of protection.[21] The Tahitian woman as centerpiece of a reconstituted Polynesian family was often represented as needing this. An interesting point of reference here is Sarah Stickney Ellis' long narrative poem *The Island Queen* (1846). Ellis, who wrote those numerous guides to the mothers, daughters, and wives of England that did much to codify middle-class domestic norms in the mid-nineteenth century, became William Ellis' second wife after his return to England. Her poem gives an idealized account of the LMS mission to Tahiti, much of it derived from *Polynesian Researches,* and includes a heroic sketch of the now-martyred Williams. The "island queen" of the title is Pomare, "a slighted wife," a victim of French aggression and duplicity, and a figure of pathos abandoned by the British. By the end of the poem another "island queen" has been invoked: Victoria, similarly "A wife—a mother—gentle queen," whose situation appears to contrast vividly with Pomare's. But the poem implies that Victoria and her island could also be threatened by their common enemy, France:

> Thou, only thou, couldst rend the eagle's breast,
> And tear the brooding mother from her nest. (Book 8)

Violation of domesticity is the common figure for this threat to the two queens, nurturing mothers of their nations. In all these other writers, however, the use of the domestic is more familiar and less interesting than in *Polynesian Researches,* where it functions to try and reconcile the deep divisions in the text. Ellis' careful particularity, unlike their sweeping generalizations, threatens the great organizing contrast of civilization and savagery on which most nineteenth-century writing on the Pacific was based.

The home correspondence from the mission tells a different story. Whereas the point of the printed text was to report good news, though without minimizing the difficulties, letters home to the LMS sought to emphasize difficulties and needs, though without undermining the mission's integrity and ultimate success. Letters, even more than diaries, freeze a moment in time rather than arrange a succession of such moments into a coherent narrative in the manner of *Polynesian Researches* and

Missionary Enterprises. An archive, however, secretes narratives, and to read the home correspondence from Tahiti is to uncover a counternarrative to that offered by Ellis and Williams. The archive is full of complaints of neglect, pleas to be repatriated, bitter mutual accusation between the Windward and Leeward groups, savage denunciations, and a paranoid resentment of the native population vividly captured in a letter from Williams: "They will watch you with *Rats Eyes*—to find little crooked places in your Conduct."[22] It is also clear from Davies' unpublished history, which in style and intention is more akin to the correspondence, that Ellis and Williams' texts stop short at the point of conversion. According to Davies, for example, the vaunted domestic revolution was short lived. Plastered houses gave insufficient ventilation, and Tahitians drifted back to former ways of building. Tables, chairs, and sofas were abandoned, and the traditional practice of sitting and eating on the ground was resumed.[23]

To what extent can these different histories, placed alongside each other, provide answers to the problem posed by Gates? Nothing could cross the beach unchanged. Ellis records how a native priest renamed his personal god Satan after it had been branded as such by a missionary, a term of damnation thereby becoming sacred.[24] What do we make of such an episode? In terms of Homi K. Bhabha's concept of mimicry, it can be read as an example of how the authority of the colonizer is subversively travestied by those it targets. Mimicry, for Bhabha, is both resemblance and menace, a sign of "spectacular resistance" in which "the words of the master become . . . the warlike, subaltern sign of the native."[25] Although a helpful corrective to the passivity of colonized cultures implicit in Said's *Orientalism,* for example, this remains limited to the colonizer's perception of the transactions of colonial encounter. It is the colonizer who experiences the partial resemblance of mimicry as menacing, and it seems to be in this that subversion consists. Colonial power, however (including that of discourse), has had ways of dealing with the threat, if such it is, of partial resemblance.

I wish to consider two examples of actual resistance, one described in *Missionary Enterprises,* the other in a letter from Williams. In the first example, recounted in *Missionary Enterprises,* mimicry goes well beyond defensive subversion to become offensive and violent. A Raiatean, part of a conspiracy of young male Islanders to kill Williams and rid themselves of Christianity, appears outside the missionary's house:

> He was dressed in a most fantastical manner, having his head decorated with leaves, and wearing a pair of trowsers as a jacket, his arms being passed through the legs; he wore also a

red shirt instead of trowsers, his legs being passed through the arms, and the band buttoned round the waist. He came, brandishing a large carving knife, and danced before the house, crying, "Turn out the hog, let us kill him; turn out the pig, let us cut his throat."[26]

The portly Williams, failing to understand that he was the pig, was only prevented by the arrival of a deacon from rushing out to confront the man and possibly being carved. Clothes, of course, are socially discursive and form part of a larger signifying system. Here, the fantastical dress vividly expresses resistance to the new order introduced by Williams, which involved the covering of native bodies with European clothing. Although Ellis had described the inconsistencies of dress adopted by Tahitian men (he thought that Tahitian women wore European clothing with more propriety), this is presented merely as an example of "the peculiar plastic, forming state of the nation."[27] Even if he has missed an element of parody, the paternalistic relation of missionary to Islander is unaffected. In the case of Williams' antagonist, however, parody has become overt challenge, a rehearsal for violent resistance, in which existing power relations are directly threatened. Discipline must follow. The conspirators were banished for four years, and the episode was used to persuade the chiefs and people of Raiatea to adopt the code of laws that Williams had drawn up.

My second example, also from Raiatea, concerns a chief's wife pregnant with a child fathered by someone other than her husband. Williams attempted to interfere with the custom of providing large quantities of food for female chiefs during confinement, telling his congregation it was inconsistent with Christianity "to pay the same respect to an adultress as to a person who had been faithful to her husband." They ignored him and countered his threat to expel any individual preparing food for the woman by threatening a mass walk-out from his church and settlement. Williams wrote defiantly to London, "A person who acts directly in opposition to his profession must be separated from us if ten thousand follow him," but he was powerless in the face of a collective refusal.[28] This incident differs from the other in that it is less a reaction to the missionary presence than an assertion of the continuity of native ways of life. In continuing to provide the food, they are insisting that they will continue to make their own history; they are not merely the objects of someone else's. It was much harder to prohibit this kind of customary practice than to resist the threat of violence, or the refusal to pay tithes, which occurred on Eimeo.[29] Introducing something new seems to have been easier than eliminating something old. The new could always be assimilated and modified. It is unsurprising, therefore, that the plot to kill Williams should figure in *Missionary Enterprises,* while the Raiateans' insistence on feeding the adulterous female chief should remain unpublished in the letters. One story tells of resistance overcome, the other of resistance unmet.

It might seem that these examples of overt resistance are too unambiguous to be worth examining. If so, it is a measure of how far the postmodern postcolonialism of Bhabha and others has turned away from agency and resistance in pursuit of its psychoanalytic shadow. In its fascination with mimicry, this school has almost lost sight of those conscious and material forms of resistance that were primarily responsible for the conflict between colonizers and native populations. The concept of mimicry subtly disturbs the passivity of colonial subjects, which colonial discourse analysis has been prone to emphasize, while ignoring both the continuity of native ways of life and the resistance to assimilation that have been among the most salient features of colonial encounter. By concentrating on how unconscious mimicry reacted in the mind of the colonizer to produce the tensions and ambiguities of colonial relationships, the passivity of so-called colonial subjects has been underwritten in a new way. The assimilation of the postcolonial to the postmodern has resulted in a dehistoricizing of colonial relationships.

An exclusive focus on colonial texts can seem to imply it is only colonialist discourse that matters, and that European descriptions unproblematically created colonial subjects. Although this essay is necessarily limited to the missionary archive, I have tried to avoid any such implication and to demonstrate that the process of subject formation was fraught with difficulty. The disorder of missionary writing, even though its agenda was unapologetically one of religious and cultural hegemony and even though the Pacific was one of the main theaters of success for nineteenth-century missions, is testimony to the vigor and adaptiveness of Tahitian culture. The tensions and contradictions within, and between, different kinds of missionary writing is clear evidence of the complex nature of the cultural encounter between Tahitians and missionaries. There was neither fatal impact nor cultural amnesia. Conversion itself occurred rapidly (as it also did in Hawai'i), and therefore fits the "politics of swift change and counterchange" characteristic of much Pacific history that the editors of this volume draw attention to. The postconversion history of Tahiti, however, suggests that discontinuity was more superficial than the missionaries, and perhaps the Tahitians themselves, first realized. Amnesia proved to be no more than concussion. But concussion there certainly was. By mid-century the LMS mission had lost much of its power, but

Christianity, like measles, was there to stay, though over time immunity could be acquired.

NOTES

This chapter has been adapted from chapter 3 of my book *Representing the South Pacific: Colonial Discourse from Cook to Gauguin* (Cambridge: Cambridge University Press, 1997).

1. Rev. Dr. Haweis in *The Evangelical Magazine,* cited in John Davies, *The History of the Tahitian Mission, 1799–1830,* ed. C. W. Newbury (Cambridge: Published for the Hakluyt Society at the University Press, 1961), xxviii–ix. Other sources for the history of the LMS mission on Tahiti are: Niel Gunson, *Messengers of Grace: Evangelical Missionaries in the South Seas, 1797–1860* (Melbourne: Oxford University Press, 1978); K. R. Howe, *Where the Waves Fall: A New South Sea Islands History from First Settlement to Colonial Rule* (Honolulu: University of Hawai'i Press, 1988); and *CWM Archives, South Seas, 1796–1840,* School of Oriental and African Studies, University of London.

2. Editions used are William Ellis, *Polynesian Researches During a Residence of Nearly Six Years in the South Sea Islands,* 2 vols. (London: Fisher, Son & Jackson, 1830), and John Williams, *A Narrative of Missionary Enterprises in the South Sea Islands* (London: J. Snow, 1838).

3. These are openly discussed in Davies. Davies landed with the second cohort of missionaries in 1801. His history was written in the late 1820s but not published until Newbury's edition. The LMS was anxious about "facts which it would be advisable to expunge." Davies resented their censorship and felt upstaged by *Polynesian Researches.* See Davies, *History of the Tahitian Mission,* 297–298, 304–309.

4. Henry Louis Gates, Jr., "Critical Fanonism," *Critical Inquiry* (Spring 1991): 462.

5. Aijaz Ahmad, *In Theory: Classes, Nations, Literatures* (London and New York: Verso, 1992), 171–172.

6. Charles Darwin, *Journal of Researches into the Geology and Natural History of the Various Countries Visited during the Voyage of H.M.S. Beagle Round the World* (London: Dent, 1908), 397–398. Ellis was an important source for Melville's Pacific works. Collins' first, still unpublished, novel, *Iolani, or Tahiti As It Was* (1846) is based mainly on *Polynesian Researches;* I owe this information to Professor Ira B. Nadel, who is editing the novel for publication.

7. Mary-Louise Pratt, *Imperial Eyes: Travel Writing and Transculturation* (London and New York: Routledge, 1992), part 1, passim.

8. Greg Dening, *Islands and Beaches: Discourse on a Silent Land* (Honolulu: University of Hawai'i Press, 1980), 43.

9. Ellis, *Polynesian Researches,* 1:59.

10. Christopher Herbert, *Culture and Anomie: Ethnographic Imagination in the Nineteenth Century* (Chicago: University of Chicago Press, 1991), chap. 3, passim.

11. Ellis, *Polynesian Researches,* 2:463–477.

12. Ibid., 1:503–509.

13. Ibid., 1:4.

14. Ibid., 2:206.

15. Ibid., 2:572–573.

16. Williams, *Missionary Enterprises,* 107–108.

17. *CWM Archive,* Box 3, Folder 2, 7 June 1820.

18. Williams, *Missionary Enterprises,* 385–401.

19. Ibid., 527.

20. R. M. Ballantyne, *The Coral Island* (London: J. M. Dent and Sons, 1913), chap. 30; Williams, *Missionary Enterprises,* 362–363.

21. Gayatri Chakravorty Spivak, "Can the Subaltern Speak?", in Patrick Williams and Laura Chrisman, eds., *Colonial Discourse and Post-Colonial Theory* (Hemel Hempstead: Harvester Wheatsheaf, 1993), 94.

22. *CWM Archive,* Box 4, Folder 1, 6 July 1823.

23. Davies, *History of the Tahitian Mission,* 330–331.

24. Ellis, *Polynesian Researches,* 1:219.

25. Homi K. Bhabha, "Of Mimicry and Man: The Ambivalence of Colonial Discourse," and "Signs Taken for Wonders: Questions of Ambivalence and Authority under a Tree outside Delhi, May 1817," in *The Location of Culture* (London and New York: Routledge, 1994), 86, 121.

26. Williams, *Missionary Enterprises,* 130–131.

27. Ellis, *Polynesian Researches,* 2:124.

28. *CWM Archive,* Box 4, Folder 5, 24 December 1824.

29. Old Orsmond MS, in Davies, *History of the Tahitian Mission,* 357–358.

14

Augustus Earle's *The Meeting of the Artist and the Wounded Chief Hongi, Bay of Islands, New Zealand, 1827*, and His Depictions of Other New Zealand Encounters

Contexts and Connections

Leonard Bell

In 1993, the Rare Book Room at the Auckland Public Library held an exhibition of late-eighteenth–early-nineteenth-century accounts of European exploration and travel in the South Pacific entitled "Raising a Curtain on a 'New' World." Such representations can be seen as stagings, as the lithograph (fig. 14.1; not in that exhibition) suggests—an image in which Samuel Brees, the principal surveyor and engineer from 1841 to 1844 of the New Zealand Company (which began organized settlement of New Zealand), appears to direct a group of Maori performing a *haka*. In fact, this group was a section of his *Panorama of New Zealand* (London 1849–1851)—a panorama, made up of a strip of continuous painted scenery unwinding from one cylinder to another before the spectators, a kind of precinematic moving picture, based on sketches made by Brees in New Zealand.[1]

Panoramas, a popular medium of visual representation in this period, could function in various ways: as a mass entertainment and spectacle; as a means by which the foreign and exotic for Europeans were made visible; and when, like Brees', depicting places where British people had colonizing interests, as advertisements for that colony.[2] The first panorama devoted to New Zealand was Robert Burford's, of the Bay of Islands, on show in London from December 1837 to February 1839—that is, before organized settlement by the New Zealand Company got under way and before New Zealand became a colony of Great Britain. Burford's panorama, in the form of a huge, static, circular, multiscene painting surrounding the spectator, of which only a description with diagrams and identification keys remains, was the first exhibition of painted representations solely of New Zealand subjects.[3] It too was based on the sketches of an artist who had been in that country—Augustus Earle (1793–1838), the first professional European artist to live there, for six months in 1827–1828, and the first to travel in the South Pacific independently, as distinct from an artist who was a member of a voyage of exploration by a European nation, a paid employee of a State.

Earle was probably the most widely traveled European artist in the first half of the nineteenth century. *The Monthly Review* noted in 1832: "His curiosity for novel scenery and manners was insatiable."[4] He spent time in North Africa and the Mediterranean (1815–1817), the United States of America (1818–1819), Peru (1820) and Brazil (1821–1824), Tristan da Cunha (1824), and Australia (1825–1827 and 1828) before arriving back in England, via India, in 1829.[5] He remained in England, except for a trip to South America in 1832 with Charles Darwin on *The*

Fig. 14.1   Samuel Brees exhibiting his *Panorama of New Zealand*, lithograph by G. B. Black, 1849

Beagle, until his death, in 1838. Earle came to New Zealand "in hopes of finding something new for my pencil," and followed the standard procedure of traveling artists—the collection of "field-notes" in the form of small drawings and watercolors, from which images for exhibition and/or publication could be made once the artist had returned to a place, like London, with an audience and market for such work.[6] Either in Sydney or, most probably, in London, Earle produced several oil paintings of New Zealand subjects. His *Sketches Illustrative of the Native Inhabitants and Islands of New Zealand,* featuring ten color lithographs after his work, with a brief letterpress by Earle, was published in 1838. Engraved reproductions of his sketches and paintings of New Zealand subjects appeared in a variety of publications—periodicals, missionary tracts, and books—most notably six in his own *Narrative of a Nine Months' Residence in New Zealand, Together with a Journal of Residence in Tristan da Cunha, an Island Situated between South America and the Cape of Good Hope* (1832). And, of course, Burford's panorama was based on Earle's sketches.

Earle's drawings and paintings and the images made from them constituted, along with those of the French artist Louis de Sainson, who traveled with the navigator Dumont D'Urville, the largest body of visual representations of New Zealand landscape and people in the immediate precolonial period from the late 1820s to the late 1830s—a period on the cusp of the colonial, when missionaries first acquired converts (after Earle's visit), when the British Government became increasingly concerned about and involved in matters New Zealand, and when projects for the colonization of New Zealand were first mooted and put into operation.[7]

In the books on Earle, his paintings and drawings have been treated as if they were primarily or exclusively "documentary." They have been regarded as topographical and quasi-ethnological descriptions of what he saw in New Zealand—basically, what the landscape and people looked like.[8] This orientation can be linked to the way pictorial representations have been used in recent books on aspects of New Zealand history, most notably in Anne Salmond's *Two Worlds: First Meetings Between Maori and Europeans, 1642–1772* (1992).[9] While it is recognized in these books that pictorial representations can provide valuable historical "evidence," there does not appear to be an accompanying realization that the nature of this evidence may be questionable; that the "reading" of visual images, both pictorial and photographic, can be at least as problematic as the interpretation of written documents. Such books seem to be sustained by an assumption that there were and are straightforward correspondences between visual images and the actualities they referred to; that such images, allowing for the occasional stylistic "conceit," classical allusion, or ethno-

logical error, were essentially mimetic—just reflecting, passively recording what was there to be seen, what actually happened, as if they offered
"windows on the world" that were fixed and certain in their effects and
meanings.

If, however, pictorial representations, whether from the colonial or
precolonial period, are located in contexts of other images, texts, and
practices, such a use of the visual appears simplistic and naïve. For instance, situated in their various contexts, Earle's depictions of precolonial
New Zealand subjects, the prime focus of attention in this essay, show
well that such representations, particularly those featuring or including
people, cannot be taken at face value, simply as a kind of reportage, but
that they could and can be read in differing, even conflicting ways, that
they are characterized by uncertainties in terms of meaning and effect.
Therein, it could be argued, primarily lies their historical and anthropological value.

Though finished and exhibitable, it is not known if Earle's *The Meeting of the Artist and the Wounded Chief, Hongi, Bay of Islands, November 1827*
(fig. 14.2) was publicly exhibited, though an 1833 article in *The Protestant
Journal* implied that Earle had exhibited his New Zealand work.[10] *The
Meeting* was used as a modello or source image for two published im-

Fig. 14.2   Augustus Earle, *The Meeting of the Artist and the Wounded Chief, Hongi, Bay of
Islands, November 1827*, ca.1833–1837, oil (Alexander Turnbull Library, Wellington)

ages—a colored lithograph in *Sketches Illustrative of the Native Inhabitants and Islands of New Zealand* (fig. 14.3), produced for the New Zealand Association, which planned to colonize New Zealand, and a crude engraving in the *Saturday Magazine* (1837), accompanying an article in which conditions in New Zealand, the impact of missionaries on Maori, and the country's prospects for colonization were described.[11] Earle's oil painting has generally been written about as if the scene and event he painted were primarily determined by an actual scene and event, as if the painting was fundamentally a report.[12] This approach no doubt primarily results from the fact that there is a four-page passage on Earle's first meeting with Hongi in his *Narrative of a Nine Months' Residence in New Zealand,* a book that has been widely, but questionably, assumed to be an account that kept close to Earle's actual experiences.[13]

The "Hongi" of the painting's title was Hongi Hika, the powerful Ngapuhi chief who had visited England in 1820 and had been a dominant figure in the internecine, intertribal warfare of the 1820s.[14] In his book, Earle described the meeting taking place in a "beautiful bay surrounded by high rocks and overhanging trees," with Hongi, seated with his wife and daughter separately from his companions, because of "his wound being taboo'd or rendered holy"; he also mentions canoes drawn up on a beach, slaves unloading them, making fires, preparing food—a scene

Fig. 14.3 *The Wounded Chief Hongi and His Family,* lithograph after Earle in *Sketches Illustrative of the Native Inhabitants and Islands of New Zealand, 1838*

generally, if not specifically, paralleling the painting's setting. Earle represented the encounter as going well for him: He was "received kindly" and "the natives were much delighted at our confidence in them, and we were equally gratified by their hospitality." He described Hongi as "emaciated," in a "new blanket," as initially "mild" but becoming "animated in conversation," as "altogether a very fine study": "With his permission, I made a sketch of him; and also one including the whole group."[15]

While there are elements in common between the visual and the verbal representations, the painting does not merely illustrate the passages in the book. There are striking differences between the visual and the verbal representations. For instance, Hongi does not look emaciated in the painting; nor are he, his wife, and daughter separate from his companions. Rather, the Maori party, spread across the near foreground of the picture from center to right, make up a unified group; the placements of the figures, many of them overlapping, implying an oval configuration, into which Earle and his European companion penetrate or "intrude." Even if the painting refers to an event that actually took place, Earle may well have invented many of the specifics of the encounter as he depicted it. The projects of traveling artists by their very nature involved constructing the worlds of the places they visited in terms of pictures to be looked at. Earle was no exception. Rather than pictorially replicating the details of the actual event, he composed his meeting with Hongi in such a way that it represented more than just the documentation of the supposed physical and visual facts of, and surrounding, that encounter. As was conventionally so in late-eighteenth–early-nineteenth-century history and narrative painting, Earle's figures are placed in a quasi-theatrical setting on a "stage," with a "backdrop" of landscape and exotic artifacts, with the prime focus of attention, the central group of Earle, Hongi, and their immediate companions, framed by three "audience" or spectator figures back to, or near back to, the viewers (of the painting) in the front plane of the picture. Such a presentation, such an organization of components for, and before, the viewer points to the operation of narrative, suggesting that there are stories to be read and that there are allegorical dimensions to the image.

Earle composed his picture in terms of a variety of source materials, including earlier images of his own and some derived from other artists. The poses of several figures, most notably the reclining "river god" left of center foreground, for instance, come from antique statuary. Many of the figures and artifacts have their origins in his New Zealand–made drawings and watercolors—at least nine disparate subjects not necessarily executed on the occasion of Earle's meeting with Hongi.[16] The figure of Hongi, for example, is based not on an earlier sketch of Hongi but on a figure in a watercolor of a group of Maori, which included a chief, Earle's protector in the Bay of Islands, whom he called "King George" (in fact, Te Whareumu).[17] Te Whareumu's relationship with Hongi in 1827 was fraught with tension, according to Earle's *Narrative*. Another figure from this watercolor also appears in *The Meeting*, seated fifth to the right of Hongi. Thus, the Hongi in *The Meeting* is not actually Hongi, either in the sense of being based on the appearance of the actual Hongi or in the sense of constituting a likeness of Hongi—a blunt demonstration that there is no essential relationship in visual representation between the image and its referent, that this relationship may be arbitrary. We, the viewers of the painting, accept the figure as Hongi because the artist has deemed him to be so, because the figure has been so labeled by the artist. The pictorial Hongi, however, was an invention of Earle's—made for the occasion of the painting and the purposes to which it was going to be put.[18]

The Meeting was a kind of assemblage of bits and pieces, put together at first instance in the interests of a good picture or spectacle—one that would be engaging for British people to look at, that would gratify viewers' taste for the exotic picturesque and indulge their curiosity about non-British "others"—primary tasks for the traveling artist producing goods for the metropolitan market.[19] The painting functions too as an inventory of exotica for Europeans; it presents a display of "savage warriors," their tattoos accentuated; idiosyncratic canoes; and strangely carved buildings and other novel artifacts, such as the *tapu* marker on the cliff above Hongi and the weaponry and an ornate canoe prow and carved panel spread across the front plane. This array of exotica could evoke a sense of the adventure experienced by the artist, and also perhaps provided a frisson of the dangerous, given the prevalent stereotype in the 1830s of Maori as warlike and violent, a stereotype of which Hongi was one of the best known personifications.[20]

But *The Meeting* offered and offers more. Earle crossed more than just geographic and cultural boundaries. In *The Meeting* he brought together elements from disparate pictorial genres. It is a hybrid piece, belonging to no single genre or image-type. So, while the painting is embedded in a field of preexisting visual representations, at the same time it differs markedly from the conventional in the various genres to which it can otherwise be related. This interplay of affinity and difference can be seen to correspond, wittingly or unwittingly on Earle's part, with his negotiations of Maori-British interactions and communications. Before pursuing the latter topic, however, the "nature" of *The Meeting*'s pictorial hybridity needs some elaboration.

The painting can be related to that image-type featuring encounters between various non-European peoples and European explorers, travelers, missionaries, and immigrants. Such images crop up with increasing frequency in European art and illustration from the later eighteenth century on, although given the huge expansion in European global exploration and travel from that period, there are not as many such representations, especially in oil painting, the most prestigious pictorial medium, as one might expect. The best-known are probably the paintings by Hodges and Webber, featuring encounters of Cook's parties with Pacific peoples and usually set on beaches, as in Earle's picture.[21] *The Meeting*, however, differs strikingly from the other paintings of this type by the inclusion of the artist as a participant, more particularly as a principal participant, in such an encounter.

It has been argued, by Edward Said and Mary-Louise Pratt, for example, that fundamental to most European verbal representations, in particular scientific and "informational" accounts, of non-European places and peoples in the eighteenth and nineteenth centuries was the separation of the observing self from the world being pictured, the exclusion or detachment of the observer from what was otherwise represented.[22] This feature or strategy was central, so it has been claimed, to the formulation and consolidation of power relations between the world of the European observer, dominating or seeking to dominate, and that of the non-European observed, subordinated or in the process of being "opened up" for subordination. This thesis has been extended to European visual representations of landscape and human subjects in colonized places, or in which Europeans had imperial designs, in the same period—notably in the "Orient" and the Americas.[23]

Certainly, in the vast majority of European paintings featuring or including non-European peoples, whether in the Middle East, Asia, Africa, the Americas, or the Pacific, at least till the end of the 1830s, the artist as the observer of and/or participant in the scene or event depicted, remained outside the picture, separate from rather than part of the encounter or event depicted, as if he was not in fact there. This is so, for example, in the works of Cook's artists, which constitute the largest body of representations of the Pacific and New Zealand up to and including the time of Earle's visit. This is so in de Sainson's work, and in the work of the numerous early- to mid-nineteenth-century "Orientalist" artists, of whom Decamps, Delacroix, Gleyre, Gérôme, J. F. Lewis, Holman-Hunt, Seddon, Wilkie, Roberts, and Lear are the best known. Earle was the notable exception to the "rule." Rather than separating himself from the subjects of his picturing projects, Earle frequently, both in his watercolors and oils in/of various parts of the globe, included himself, engaged in some activity, in the picture.[24] This procedure served at once to assert the "authenticity" of the scene and to cast the event depicted as autobiographical. Cumulatively, Earle's representations of the places he visited constitute a narrative of personal adventure, a kind of self-portraiture. Earle's assertion of copresence in *The Meeting* can also be related to that picture's allegorical operations (about which more later).

There are occasional other examples from the 1830s and early 1840s of traveling artists representing their encounters, in their capacity as artists, with the indigenous "others" they were otherwise depicting, but these are found not in oil paintings but in the lesser medium of book illustration. The American artist George Catlin, for instance, depicted himself executing an easel painting of a posed Native American.[25] The frontispiece illustration in Samuel Brees' *Pictorial Illustrations of New Zealand* (1847) shows the artist sketching his Maori subjects. And there is a sketch by Jacques Arago, the artist on French navigator Freycinet's Pacific voyage of 1817–1820, that supposedly represents Arago's encounter with a Maori chief in Sydney in 1819. This image (fig. 14.4), probably produced in the 1830s, was first published in Arago's *Souvenirs d'un Aveugle* (1839), illustrating an account of the meeting (in a text that belongs primarily to the genre of the popular adventure yarn) in which the Maori was stereotyped in the most lurid way as a wild, animalistic, cannibalistic, violent, and unredeemably savage "other"—the opposite of Maori in Earle's *The Meeting*.[26] They are represented as quietly attentive, their weapons put to one side.

The Meeting brings to mind, too, what was then probably the best-known and widely reproduced oil painting by an English-speaking artist of an encounter, also on a beach, between peoples of two very different worlds: Benjamin West's *William Penn's Treaty with the Indians* (1771, exhibited at the Royal Academy in 1772) (fig. 14.5). West's large, historical painting commemorated a crucial event in the colonization of Pennsylvania almost one hundred years earlier.[27] Despite the formal differences between the two works, most notably in the ways the figures are rendered—West's in a neoclassical manner, Earle's in that British rococo, almost faux-naïf and "clumsy" manner[28]—*The Meeting* echoes West's painting strongly. As well as the parallels in occasion and location, the paintings share a horizontal alignment of the participants in the encounter, a stagelike presentation with "audience" figures in the immediate foreground, and antique quotations in the poses and gestures of figures. Earle is believed to have known West in London, and he would have had ample opportunity to see West's image around the time he was painting *The Meeting*. Besides the numerous prints of *William Penn's Treaty with the Indians,* the painting was exhibited at the British Institution in London in 1833, while a second version, painted by West about 1809, had

Fig. 14.4   Jacques Arago, sketch of the artist encountering a Maori chief in 1819, from *Souvenirs d'un Aveugle,* 1839

been sold in London in 1829.[29] More cogently for *The Meeting*, West's painting, in which the depicted scene was the artist's invention, imaged the peaceful encounter, the desirability of peace and cooperation between different peoples occupying the same land—between two peoples previously in conflict, or whose differing modes of life contained the potential for conflict—a dimension of meaning not without its relevance both to Earle's views on the prospects of Maori-British interaction and to the lithograph of *The Meeting* produced for the New Zealand Association in 1838.

First, though, some pictorial connections. In contrast to West's historical painting, Earle's contemporary scene is small—the size of a genre painting, of a representation of a scene from everyday life. In genre painting, as in the contemporaneous work of David Wilkie and William Mulready, for instance, gesture and expression were foregrounded in the interest of a usually easily explicable narrative or anecdote.[30] In contrast, gesture and expression in *The Meeting* do not allow a single or unambiguous interpretation. Earle is holding forth, possibly seeking Hongi's permission to sketch him and his group (there is a sketchbook beside Earle),

Fig. 14.5   Benjamin West, *Penn's Treaty with the Indians*, 1771–1772, oil (The Pennsylvania Academy of the Fine Arts, Philadelphia, gift of Mrs. Sarah Harrison, The Joseph Harrison, Jr., Collection)

but it is not precisely clear what is going on, other than the meeting. The expressions of some figures, such as Earle's European companion, Hongi himself, and others in his party, suggest tentativeness and uncertainty. Perhaps this was apt for such a meeting, what one might expect in a first encounter between people of different cultures. There is a sense of mutual strangeness, while at the same time acquaintanceship is in the offing. What one does have is an image of a suspended moment—a moment in which it is far from certain how things will develop, but in which various possibilities are connoted. It is an image that begs questions.

Earle's portrayal of the gathering of a largish group of people, most of whom are kinsmen, spread informally across the foreground of a painting of this size and format, set in an outdoor location, echoes, too, a type of group portraiture common in the late eighteenth and early nineteenth centuries—the conversation piece, of which such painters as David Allan, Arthur Devis, and Johann Zoffany were leading practitioners.[31] Conversation pieces presented identifiable people, either members of the same family or people with common interests or occupations, in such a way as to demonstrate or imply their consanguinity or shared ground. They could be physically linked and/or turned toward one another in conversation. Conversation pieces were often set in environments that belonged to the depicted persons, imaging a group's property, its occupation of, or interest in, land.

The Meeting could be seen as a radical reworking of the conversation piece, in which the executive artist has inserted himself, an outsider socially, ethnically, and geographically, into the group, whose members are kinsmen, bound by common interests and purposes—a reworking that could connote, bearing in mind the painting's connection with *William Penn's Treaty with the Indians,* too, a further commonality of interest, hoped-for at least, however misconceived, between Earle and Maori. The painting, then, while not excluding other modes of operation, could function as an allegory of a desired and believed-to-be-necessary relationship between prospective colonizing British people (as represented by Earle) and Maori—allegorizing an ideal or potential, from a British viewpoint, for the future of New Zealand.[32] In such a picture Earle is the go-between. The artist is the medium for communication between two different groups, negotiating the grounds for further meetings. In this respect the gesture of the figure of Earle in *The Meeting,* and the views he articulated in *A Narrative of a Nine Months' Residence in New Zealand* on Maori potential for "civilization," are significant.

Earle's gesture, both hands extended in front of him toward Hongi and his party, the hands slightly raised, the palms sideways disposed, facing one another, may be only a small detail in the composition, but it occupies a major position in the center of Earle's staging of the en-counter—a position of centrality in terms of the possibilities of meaning relative to Maori-British relationships that the picture opens up. A single gesture or position of the hands can generate several meanings or con-notations, and indeed that is so in *The Meeting*. Yet it may be pertinent that the gesture with which Earle equipped the figure of himself in *The Meet-ing* is of a kind that has been decoded by writers on the "language" of ges-ture as the "reaching hands of the negotiator."[33] The hands are held out in a manner that suggests a desire to cross the gap between speaker and listeners, to reach their minds, to overcome or attempt to overcome the problems of difference. It has been observed too that certain gestures can play important roles in a person's attempts to make him or herself agree-able in "social space."[34] In *The Meeting*, Earle the outsider's "inclusive" gesture could connote a quest for acceptance, an attempt to negotiate a space in this "new" and different world of Maori, not just for himself (his physical body) but for what he stands for in terms of ideas about possible Maori-British relationships.

A reviewer of Earle's *Narrative* in the *Eclectic Review* claimed that Earle "as an artist naturally prefers the picturesque savagery of wild life to the tameness of civilisation."[35] *The Meeting*, at first sight, as spectacle, might seem to embody that orientation, but it also can be seen in terms of a preference for "civilization." Several of the reviews of *A Narrative* noted Earle's recommendation to the British government that it would do well to become involved in the colonization of New Zealand.[36] Certainly, Earle believed Maori would benefit from a benevolent colonization (if that is not a contradiction in terms) in which the industriousness, frugality, intelligence, and artistic skills he saw in Maori would realize their full potential in a climate of peacefulness and cooperation, provided they (Maori) listened to supposedly progressive Europeans and cast off their allegedly "barbaric" and warlike ways.[37] Note that in *The Meeting*, the type of "warlike" Maori is presented sitting quietly, heedful of Earle.

While in certain regards open-ended, what emerges strongly in this depicted meeting is an evocation of the possibilities of peaceable com-munication between different peoples, a suggestion of the discovery of common ground through engagement with the unfamiliar. Such com-munion is represented as occurring, it ought to be stressed, under the di-rection of Earle. Earle, who had lived among Maori and had begun to learn their language, wrote that he was changed by his experiences in New Zealand. Initially going there to gather material to "gratify" his and other Europeans' taste for the exotic picturesque, and equipped with stereotypical feelings of "fear and disgust" toward Maori, he left the country with very different "opinions," "in many respects, very favorable towards them."[38]

In several images, Earle represented Maori in terms of a duality, a coexistence of what might immediately seem mutually exclusive components. This takes the form of a doubleness of manifest difference and underlying affinity, with the latter suggesting the potential for future participation in the construction of a new society. Paul Carter has argued that the boundary between peoples of different cultures can be characterized as a site of communicated difference rather than as a "barrier" to knowledge.[39] Certainly *The Meeting*, as an image of a boundary encounter, could connote, from a British viewing position, a recognition of affinity in difference—a view, though, that might not have been shared by Maori he depicted.

Another of Earle's depictions of a New Zealand subject—a Maori being tattooed—reproduced in *A Narrative* (fig. 14.6)[40] and in Burford's panorama of the Bay of Islands, could also be seen as an articulation of this doubling of difference and affinity.[41] Whether this image provides ethnographically reliable information about Maori tattooing procedures, it can be related to a longstanding European fascination for, and decid-

Fig. 14.6 *New Zealand Method of Tattooing,* engraving after Earle in *A Narrative of a Nine Months' Residence in New Zealand,* 1832

edly mixed feelings about, the practice of tattooing among South Pacific peoples, as mediated by Earle's singular views (for a European in this period) about Maori tattoo, or *moko.* Tattoo, most immediately in terms of the visual, marked Maori as different from, and exotic to, Europeans. Throughout the nineteenth century, tattooing was generally represented by Europeans as a sign of barbarism, savagery, or an inferior stage of social evolution and, from a Christian perspective, of depravity and sinfulness among non-Europeans, and as a sign of criminality and moral degeneracy among Europeans.[42] Earle's evaluation of tattoo was very different. He saw it primarily in terms of the aesthetic, as a form of art and ornamentation of the highest quality. He likened the status and value of a "highly-finished face" by a Maori tattooist he met and observed at work to that of "a head from the hands of" the most prestigious portrait painter in Britain, the recently deceased (1830) Sir Thomas Lawrence.[43] So a practice that for many Europeans epitomized racial and moral difference, and social inferiority, a perhaps unbridgeable gulf, was characterized by Earle in terms of affinity.

An artist's representation of a racial and cultural "other" can indirectly be a representation of "self"—a conjunction worth pursuing in relation to *New Zealand Method of Tattooing* and *The Meeting. New Zealand Method of Tattooing* is a depiction of an artist at work in his "studio." In *A Narrative,* Earle used that term for the Maori tattooist's place of work (137). *The Meeting,* too, can be seen as an image of an artist at work in his studio, with the studio of the traveling artist being understood as the places he visited, a formulation coined by the *Westminster Review* reviewer of Earle's *A Narrative.*[44] In *New Zealand Method of Tattooing* and *The Meeting,* the two artists depicted, Maori and British, echo one another. Both are seated, facing to the right, their arms and hands positioned in front of them almost identically, by or before their sitters, in the process, although at different stages, of creating their art. The figure of Earle in *The Meeting* is not in fact sketching, but as there is a sketchbook beside him, and as in the *Narrative* he noted that he made drawings of Hongi and his party on the occasion of the encounter, Earle can be said to have pictured himself in the course of his artistic work. This reading is given added credibility by the positioning of Earle, seated, with his hands held just as they are in *The Meeting.* This configuration echoes one commonly found in another distinct image-type or subgenre (further exemplifying *The Meeting*'s pictorial hybridity or multireferential makeup), namely, self-representations of artists at work in their studios. Among English artists, Hogarth's *Self-portrait: The artist painting the comic muse* (1758, National Portrait Gallery, London) and George Morland's *The Artist in his Studio with his Man Gibbs* (ca. 1803, Castle Museum and Art Gallery of Nottingham), for instance, come to mind.[45] And there is another oil painting by Earle, *Bougainville Falls, Prince Regent's Glen, Blue Mountains, New South Wales* (ca. 1826–1827, Rex Nan Kivell Collection, National Library of Australia), in which Earle depicted himself, in the center foreground, as the traveling artist at work in his outdoor "studio," sketching a posed Aborigine. The almost identically posed (though in reverse) figure of Earle in *The Meeting* could very well, by implication or extension, have a pencil or brush in one hand, a mahlstick or palette in the other. Hongi and his companions could be seen as the drawing he is about to make, or the canvas that he will someday paint. Effectively, Earle represents himself in the executive act, engaged in the business of bringing the "other" and his self as the traveling artist into visibility—perhaps that "self" which the *Edinburgh Review* characterized "as an extraordinary phenomenon as any which he [Earle] describes."[46] So *The Meeting* tells "about," among other things, both the process and the product of the traveling artist's work.

Artistic activity, Earle could be saying, had an important role to play in cross-cultural exchange. Earle had equated Maori and British artists. He portrayed himself in a way that echoed his portrayal of a Maori artist, the Maori artist who "was delighted with my [Earle's] drawings, particularly with a portrait I made of him."[47] This was possibly the watercolor titled *A New Zealander* (Rex Nan Kivell Collection), reproduced as the frontispiece of Earle's *A Narrative* with the title *Aranghie, The Tattooer of New Zealand.* This suggests that the practice of art could allow for some degree of identification between Maori and European. It could provide a ground for meeting, for coming together. Indeed, in *The Meeting*, art making has a central role in a peaceable meeting. This reading can be linked to the notion of the artist—one can now say both Maori and European—as a medium for communication and enlightenment. Earle's evaluation of Maori tattoo has been noted. He wrote, too, "Painting and sculpture are both arts greatly admired by . . . New Zealanders."[48] Could the quiet attentiveness of depicted Maori before the artist in *The Meeting* be related to such a view? Earle also wrote of the "Great taste and ingenuity" of Maori carving and ornamentation, examples of which are prominently in the foreground of *The Meeting.*[49]

Maori carving, Earle believed, "plainly showed the dawning of the art of sculpture amongst them."[50] His use of the word "dawning" can be related to his view that Maori were at the point where they were ready and willing to participate in, and benefit from, "civilization." Most commentaries on *The Meeting* quote a passage from Earle's *A Narrative* about his first sighting of Hongi's party: "It almost seemed to realize some of the passages of Homer, where he describes the wanderer Ulysses and his gallant band of warriors."[51] This passage has routinely been cited as evidence of Earle's supposed romanticization of precolonial Maori or of his construction of them as Noble Savages. Rather than being a critic of European culture and society, however, using constructs like the "Noble Savage" to highlight its alleged defects, Earle firmly believed that an enlightened West represented the most advanced stage of social evolution. Given this, the Homeric analogy can take on quite different connotations, again correlating with Earle's view of New Zealand and Maori in the late 1820s and 1830s as standing at the "dawn" of "civilization." In Britain, from the mid-eighteenth century into the early to mid-nineteenth century, Homeric texts were generally read as representations of a "primitive" people and society in a "rude and infant state," just emerging from barbarism, at an early stage on the road to (ancient Grecian) "civilization."[52] Robert Southey, for instance, characterized the world Homer represented as "nearly as possible at the same stage of Barbarism or Civilization (call it what you will) as the South Seas Islanders when the missionaries first became acquainted with them."[53]

I have suggested that Earle's depicted meetings could be read in various ways and that such a multivalence could say something about the nature and complexities of cross-cultural interactions in the period on the cusp of the precolonial and colonial. Engraved and lithographed versions of Earle's paintings by other hands could operate in different ways again—usually in ways that narrowed the range of possibilities that Earle's imagings opened up. To take one example, the lithograph after *The Meeting* used by The New Zealand Association (see fig. 14.3) altered Earle's painting in several loaded ways. The Maori carvings in the foreground were simply deleted, and the gesture, expression, and positioning of the figure of Earle were changed so that he became the dominant figure in the exchange, as if he were commanding Hongi and his party. Most notably, perhaps, the figure of Hongi in the lithograph, described in the letterpress as "dying," is presented as if shrinking back into his blanket. Thus, the formerly all-powerful "savage" warrior is shown submitting to the new order of the future, as embodied by Earle, in a formulation perhaps designed to allay any anxieties the prospective British immigrant may have had about the prospects for peace and stability in New Zealand.

Another oil painting by Earle of a kind of meeting, *Te Rangituke, Chief of Kawakawa, Bay of Islands, with his Wife and Son* (ca. 1835, Alexander Turnbull Library, Wellington), when recontextualized as an engraved image in a missionary periodical after Earle's death, underwent a complete reversal of meaning. The painting represents a chief (and family) whom Earle had befriended in Sydney and met again in the Bay of Islands, a man whom Earle liked and admired.[54] The image is a positive celebration of good relations, with the chief posed—seated, full-bodied, frontally disposed, directly addressing the viewer, *taiaha* (long, stafflike weapon) in hand—in a way that echoes the portrayal in European art of persons, whether actual or mythological, of the highest status and eminence.[55] In the *Quarterly Papers of the Church Missionary Society* (1840) the engraved version, titled *A New Zealand Chief,* was used to illustrate a negative evaluation of non-Christian Maori as "wild . . . savages," noted for their "ferocity," while the "smiling and artless countenances of the chief's children [*sic*]" showed that they were likely to remain savage and ferocious unless converted to Christianity.[56] In *A Narrative,* Earle had directed criticisms against aspects of missionary behavior and activity in New Zealand, comments that provoked hostile responses in reviews of his book.[57] The appropriation, then, of his representation of Te Rangituke and family by the missionary periodical was ironic, perhaps an act of revenge by the Church Missionary Society, to which Earle could not reply. It also provides a particularly striking example of how images can be manipulated to take on new and very different meanings, depending on the contexts in which they are used and seen and the other texts to which they are related.

Like the New Zealand Association, the missionary periodical version of Earle's image sought to fix a single and simple meaning and in so doing closed off the potentialities and uncertainties in terms of interaction and communication between Maori and European that Earle's oil paintings allowed or connoted. I have noted that Earle's *The Meeting* represents/narrates a suspended moment, in which it is not clear how relations could develop. With the colonial era and the various ruptures it brought soon to begin in New Zealand, perhaps the moment of meeting can also be seen as a moment of parting.

NOTES

1. Brees' *Panorama of New Zealand* (in fact, Wellington) was exhibited at the Linwood Gallery, Leicester Square. See S. C. Brees, *A Guide and Description of the Panorama of New Zealand* (London: n.p., 1850), and Leonard Bell, *Colonial Constructs: European Images of Maori, 1840–1914* (Auckland: Auckland University Press, 1992), 28–29.

2. See Ralph Hyde, *Panoramania: The Art and Entertainment of the "All-Embracing" View* (London: Trefoil Publications, 1988), especially the introduction, by Scott Wilcox, "Unlimiting the Bounds of Painting."

3. R. Burford, *Description of a View of the Bay of Islands, New Zealand, and the Sur-*

rounding Country. Now Exhibiting at the Panorama, Leicester Square (London, 1838). See also *Panoramania,* and Charles Eldredge, *Pacific Parallels: Artists and the Landscape in New Zealand* (Seattle: University of Washington Press, 1991), 17–19.

4. *The Monthly Review* 38 (1832): 372.

5. For Earle's life, see the biographical sketch by E. H. McCormick in his edition of *A Narrative of a Nine Months' Residence in New Zealand in 1827, Together with a Journal of a Residence in Tristan da Cunha, An Island Situated Between South America and the Cape of Good Hope* (Oxford: Clarendon Press, 1966); Harold E. Spencer, "Augustus Earle: A Study of Early Nineteenth Century Travel Art and Its Place in English Landscape and Genre Traditions" (Ph.D. diss., Harvard University, 1967); Anthony Murray-Oliver, *Augustus Earle in New Zealand* (Christchurch: Whitcombe & Tombs, 1968); Jocelyn Hackforth-Jones, *Augustus Earle: Travel Artist* (Martinborough, N.Z.: Alister Taylor, 1980).

6. Augustus Earle, *A Narrative of a Nine Months' Residence in New Zealand in 1827* (London: Longman, 1832), 271. All subsequent page references are to this edition.

7. See, for instance, J.M.R. Owens, "New Zealand before Annexation," in *The Oxford History of New Zealand,* ed. W. H. Oliver and B. R. Williams (Wellington: Oxford University Press, 1981), 28–53.

8. For example, Spencer, Murray-Oliver, and Hackforth-Jones. The complexities of pictorial representation in respect of Earle's watercolor landscapes have been briefly addressed by some writers. See Francis Pound, *Frames on the Land: Early Landscape Painting in New Zealand* (Auckland: Collins, 1983), 12, 17, 25, 40; Marian Minson, *Encounter with Eden: New Zealand, 1770–1870: Paintings and Drawings from the Rex Nan Kivell Collection, National Library of Australia* (Wellington: National Library of New Zealand, 1990), 28–30; W.J.T. Mitchell, "Imperial Landscape," in *Landscape and Power,* ed. Mitchell (Chicago: University of Chicago Press, 1994), 24–27.

9. And, for example, E. Olssen and J. Binney, *The People and the Land—Te tangata me te Whenua: An Illustrated History of New Zealand* (Wellington: Allen and Unwin, 1990); K. Sinclair, ed., *The Oxford Illustrated History of New Zealand* (Auckland: Oxford University Press, 1990).

10. Review of Earle's *A Narrative of a Nine Months' Residence in New Zealand in 1827,* extracted from *The Protestant Journal* (Alexander Turnbull Library, P/ EARLE, 1833), 2.

11. *Saturday Magazine* 11 (353) (Supplement, December 1837): 257; titled *Interview of Mr Earle with the wounded chief Hongi and his friends.*

12. For example, Joan Kerr, ed., *Dictionary of Australian Artists up to 1870* (Melbourne: Oxford University Press, 1992), 232–236. Ian Wedde, "Talking to the 'Wounded Chief': Augustus Earle and Gordon Walters," in *Now See Hear!*

Art, Language and Translation, ed. Ian Wedde and Gregory Burke (Wellington: Victoria University Press, 1990), 39–42, provides an exception to the characterization of *The Meeting,* even if "romanticized," as a record. He sees *The Meeting* in terms of an "Augustan" "allegorisation of the British Imperial project," in which the "represented dialogue is not just between Augustus Earle and Hongi Hika; *it is also between Augustanism and the local.* . . . It is the English of Earle, and the Augustanism of his representational rhetoric, that are finally privileged in this discourse" (41).

13. For a recent instance of this, see Peter Gibbons, "Non-Fiction," in *The Oxford History of New Zealand Literature in English,* ed. Terry Sturm (Auckland: Oxford University Press, 1991), 54. Gibbons characterizes Earle's *A Narrative* as "less contrived and far closer to experience [than other accounts of travel or residence in New Zealand in this period]. . . . More than any of the other early writers he expresses his immediate emotions." That Earle's book title claims nine months' residence in New Zealand, when in fact Earle spent six months there, might in itself suggest that its reliability as an accurate factual account could be suspect. Contemporaneous reviewers had their doubts— for example: "This [*A Narrative*] is one of those mischievous publications which for a while do serious injury to the cause of truth," *Protestant Journal* 1.

14. For Hongi Hika see Ranginui Walker, *Ka Whawhai Tonu Matou: Struggle Without End* (Auckland: Penguin Books, 1990), 81–83. For Hongi's visit to England see Judith Binney, *The Legacy of Guilt: A Life of Thomas Kendall* (Auckland: Oxford University Press, 1968).

15. Earle, *A Narrative,* 64–66.

16. For instance, the *pataka* (food storehouse), the *tapu* marker, the figures of the daughter and wife of Hongi, the standing figure to the left of Earle's European companion, and several of the seated figures are close to figures in Earle's watercolor and drawings. See Murray-Oliver and Hackforth-Jones for reproductions of these.

17. Earle, *King George New Zealand Costume* (1828, Rex Nan Kivell Collection, National Library of Australia, Canberra). For "King George" see McCormick, *A Narrative,* 27, 38, and Earle, *A Narrative,* 53–56, 67–71, 87–91, 99–108.

18. See also James Barry, *The Rev. Thomas Kendall and the Maori Chiefs Hongi Hika and Waikato* (1820, oil, Alexander Turnbull Library, Wellington); unknown artist, *Hongi and Waikato* (1820, drawing, Methodist Missionary Society, London); Jules le Jeune, *Natives of New Zealand* (including Hongi) (1824, watercolor, Service Historique de la Marine, Vincennes). Without the identification of the depicted figure as Hongi in these representations, there would be no reason to recognize the figure as Hongi in a particular representation, so different do they look from one another.

19. The editor of the 1832 edition of Earle's *A Narrative* in his introduction

referred to traveling artists seeking "to gratify a refined taste for the picturesque."

20. For example, *The Protestant Journal* wrote of the "natives" of New Zealand: "Their fierce ungovernable passions; their dark treachery; their unrelenting cruelty; their horrible propensities; and their filthy and degrading habits" (1), while Burford's *Description of a View of the Bay of Islands* noted that after Cook's visits, Maori were represented as "atrocious and implacable murderers and ferocious cannibals," held in "dread" (4). In *A Narrative,* Earle noted Hongi's reputation, but observed on first meeting him, "So mild was the expression of his features that he would have been the last man I should have imagined accustomed to scenes of bloodshed and cruelty" (65).

21. For instance, Hodges, *A Cautious Landing at Tanna, New Hebrides* (1774, National Maritime Museum, Greenwich, London); Webber, *Captain Cook in Queen Charlotte Sound* (1777, National Maritime Museum), and *View in Queen Charlotte Sound* (1788, Museum of New Zealand, Wellington). See Bernard Smith and Rudiger Joppien, *The Art of Captain Cook's Voyages,* 3 vols. (Melbourne: Oxford University Press, 1985–1987).

22. See Edward Said, *Orientalism* (London: Routledge and Kegan Paul, 1978); and Mary-Louise Pratt, *Imperial Eyes: Travel Writing and Transculturation* (London: Routledge, 1992). Pratt writes, "The textual production of the other society is not explicitly anchored in either the observing self or the particular situation of contact in which the observation takes place" (64). She contrasts "informational" travel writings with "sentimental experiental" writings, in which the writer "is positioned at the center of the discursive field rather than on the periphery," but she argues that "he," too, "though he is composed of a whole body rather than a disembodied eye . . . is constructed as a non-interventionist European presence" (78).

23. For example, Linda Nochlin, "The Imaginary Orient," *Art in America* (May 1983): 179, and Timothy Mitchell, "Orientalism and the Exhibitionary Other," in *Colonialism and Culture,* ed. Nicholas B. Dirks (Ann Arbor: University of Michigan Press, 1992), 307–308.

24. See Spencer and Hackforth-Jones. As in, for example, such watercolors as *From the Summit of Cacavada* (Brazil) (ca. 1821–1824), *Solitude: Watching the horizon* (Tristan da Cunha) (1824), *Scudding before a heavy gale off the Cape* (1824), *A Bivouac, daybreak on the Ilawarra Mountains* (Australia) (1827), and *Distant View of the Bay of Islands* (New Zealand) (1827)—all in the Rex Nan Kivell Collection, National Library of Australia, Canberra. There were a few depictions of non-European landscape and/or architecture by other European traveling artists in the early nineteenth century that included, in the foreground to one side of the picture, a small figure of an artist sketching the scene otherwise depicted, from which he remains separate—for example,

William Daniell, *View of Bijaijarh* (India) (1790, watercolor, P&O Steam Navigation Company Collection). This shows Thomas Daniell sketching and William Daniell looking through a telescope at the scene before them/us. Paintings of this kind, invariably watercolors, belong to that picturesque landscape type having a small figure (not necessarily the executive artist) removed or distant from the landscape scene he is sketching, a scene laid out before him and the viewer.

25. *The Author painting a Chief in an Indian Village,* frontispiece illustration in George Catlin, *Letters and Notes on the Manners, Customs, and Conditions of the North American Indians* (London: n.p., 1841), vol. 1. Catlin later produced a small oil painting, *Catlin painting the portrait of Mah-to-toh-pa-Mandan* (1857–1869, National Gallery of Art, Washington, D.C.). Note too the aquatint after a sketch by Karl Bodmer, *The Travellers meeting with the Minatarve Indians near Fort Clark* (ca. 1834, Joslyn Art Museum, Omaha, Nebraska), which includes the figure of Bodmer with his patron, Prince Maximilien of Wied.

26. Arago's "Maori" is very close to an illustration of an Aborigine titled *Savage of New Holland Coming into Battle* in Arago's earlier *Narrative of a Voyage Round the World, in the Uranie and Physicienne Corvettes, Commanded by Captain Freycinet, During the Years 1817, 1818, 1819, and 1820, On a Scientific Expedition undertaken by Order of the French Government* (London: Treuttel and Wurtz, 1823), part 11, plate 23.

27. See Ann Uhry Abrams, "Benjamin West's Documentation of Colonial History: William Penn's *Treaty with the Indians,*" *Art Bulletin* (March 1982): 59–74; and Ann Uhry Abrams, *The Valiant Hero: Benjamin West and Grand Style History Painting* (Washington, D.C.: Smithsonian Institution Press, 1985).

28. As in the painting, for example, of Hogarth, Highmore, Hayman, David Allan, Penny, Mercier, and Devis.

29. Helmut von Erffa and Allen Staley, *The Painting of Benjamin West* (New Haven: Yale University Press, 1986), 203, 208.

30. See, for example, *Sir David Wilkie of Scotland* (Raleigh: North Carolina Museum of Art, 1982); Marcia Pointon, *Mulready* (London: Victoria and Albert Museum, 1986).

31. See Mario Praz, *Conversation Pieces: A Survey of the Informal Group Portrait: Europe and America* (London: Methuen, 1971); G. C. Williamson, *English Conversation Pieces of the Eighteenth and early Nineteenth Centuries* (New York: Hacker Art Books, 1975); Marcia Pointon, *Hanging the Head: Portraiture and the Social Formation in Eighteenth-Century England* (New Haven: Yale University Press, 1993), 159–175.

32. See n. 12 for Ian Wedde's different reading of *The Meeting* in terms of the allegorical.

33. Desmond Morris, *Manwatching: A Field Guide to Human Behaviour* (London: Jonathan Cape, 1977), 59.

34. Herman Rodenburg, "The hand of friendship," in *A Cultural History of Gesture*, ed. Jan Bremmer and Herman Rodenburg (Cambridge: Polity Press, 1991), 161.

35. *The Eclectic Review* (July–December 1832): 241.

36. For example: *The Monthly Review* (1832): 378; *Edinburgh Review* (January 1833): 346.

37. Earle, *A Narrative*, 70, 96, 122, 164–166.

38. Ibid., 271.

39. See Paul Carter, *The Road to Botany Bay* (London: Faber and Faber, 1987) 163.

40. There is an oil painting, *A Maori being Tattooed*, in the Rex Nan Kivell Collection, National Library of Australia, that was attributed to Earle (e.g., Murray–Oliver, *Augustus Earle in New Zealand*, 86; Hackforth-Jones, *Augustus Earle, Travel Artist*, 51), but is now regarded as either a copy of an original Earle painting or of the aquatint engraving after Earle in *A Narrative*, facing p. 136, titled *New Zealand Method of Tattooing*.

41. No. 27 in "Diagram of the Panorama" in R. Burford, *Description of a View of the Bay of Islands*.

42. See, for instance, Adolf Loos, "Ornament and Crime" (1908), in *Spoken into the Void: Collected Essays, 1897—1900* (Cambridge: MIT Press, 1982). Owen Jones, the English design theoretician, writing later than Earle, saw both marks of savagery and high aesthetic quality in Maori tattooing. In his *Grammar of Ornament* (London: B. Quaritch, 1856), in which a tattooed, preserved Maori head was reproduced (14), Jones wrote, "Man's earliest ambition is to create. To this feeling must be ascribed the tattooing of the human face and body, resorted to by the savage to increase the expression by which he seeks to strike terror on his enemies or rivals, or to create what appears to him a new beauty. . . . The tattooing on the head [from New Zealand] . . . is very remarkable, as showing that in this very barbarous practice the principles of the very highest ornamental art are manifest" (13).

43. Earle, *A Narrative*, 138. Earle described this tattooist, "Aranghie," as "a great natural genius" (139).

44. *The Westminster Review* (July 1832): 311.

45. Earle's style of rendering figures generally had close affinities with that of Hogarth and Morland. There are numerous similar self-imagings of artists at work. See Ludwig Goldscheider, *Five Hundred Self-Portraits from Antique Times to the Present Day* (London: Allen and Unwin, 1937).

46. *The Edinburgh Review* (January 1833): 333.

47. Earle, *A Narrative*, 138–139.

48. Ibid., 22.

49. Ibid., 21.

50. Ibid., 21–22.

51. Ibid., 65.

52. Adam Ferguson, *An Essay on the History of Civil Society* (Edinburgh: Edinburgh University Press, 1767), 113. See Donald M. Foerster, *Homer in English Criticism: The Historical Approach in the Eighteenth Century* (New Haven: Yale University Press, 1947).

53. Robert Southey cited in H. N. Fairchild, *The Noble Savage: A Study in Romantic Naturalism* (New York: Columbia University Press, 1928), 456.

54. Earle, *A Narrative,* 159–160.

55. For example (and allowing for their much larger scale and more hieratic look), Ingres, *Napoleon I on his Imperial Throne* (ca. 1806, Musée de L'Armée, Paris); Ingres, *Jupiter and Thetis* (1811, Musée Granet, Aix-en-Provence). Te Rangituke also echoes an earlier portrait in oils painted by Earle in Australia, his *The Piper Family* (1828, Vaucluse House, Sydney)—in fact, of Mrs. Piper and her children, in which Mrs. Piper is cast as a formidable-looking matriarch.

56. *Quarterly Papers of the Church Missionary Society* 97 (1840): frontispiece. There was also an engraved reproduction, titled *The New Zealanders,* of Earle's painting in Captain Robert Fitzroy, R.N., *Narrative of the Surveying Voyages of His Majesty's Ships Adventure and Beagle Between the Years 1832 and 1836* (London: Henry Colburn, 1839), facing p. 568. Earle had initially been the artist on this voyage, though he had to leave the expedition in Montevideo in August 1832 because of ill health.

57. For example, *The Protestant Journal* and *The Quarterly Review* (October 1832).

15

CATEGORICAL WEAVINGS

European Representations of the Architecture of *Hakari*

Sarah Treadwell

Sketch

Nineteenth-century colonists came to New Zealand and, perching in the unfamiliar landscape, drew the existing architecture that shaped the lives and landscapes of the indigenous inhabitants. In journals, sketchbooks, and diaries the newcomers scratched, in networks of lines, the woven and interwoven architecture of the Maori. Such small, scratchy drawings were suited, in their linear construction, to the lines of timber, the fronds of leaves, and the ropes of flax that constituted the building materials of New Zealand. They also produced vivid watercolors open to the moist air and sea of the island country. Constructed with drawings and writings, the woven architecture fabricated by the colonists serves as a critique of the European architecture to be imported. Associated with the small scale, the domestic, and the feminine, the woven architecture was not, however, confined to the *whare* (house) but was also discovered in the substantial timber *hakari* (feast) stages.

Woven Houses

An architectural object that was familiar to the colonists in early-nineteenth-century New Zealand was the "reeded hut" or *whare*, a small house built for the settlers by Maori. This form of housing, following the first European dwellings (packing cases piled on the beaches and tents strung in the bush), continued a tradition of ephemeral architecture in New Zealand that still persists. Nineteenth-century surveyor John Rochfort described such a house with a language of fabric and fabric working: "The house is what is called a *toi-toi whare;* the *toi-toi* is a reed which the natives use for the walls and roofs of their huts; these reeds are plaited together with flax; inside this is a lining of tapestry, worked entirely out of flax. The New Zealanders will build a house in this manner for a white man for five pounds."[1] The walls were plaited and lined with another fabric form, tapestry. In the writings of the settlers, houses are fabricated, like furnishings and clothing, with a terminology of lacing, weaving, and plaiting. The objects so constructed, light, permeable, and temporary, were ambivalently described by European occupants. Evocative pleasure imbues descriptions such as that by soldier Tyrone Power. Lying in such a *whare* at night, air blowing through walls and roof, points of light gleaming, Tyrone Power imagined that he lay with nature, in a structure

> built of reeds, wild flax, fern stalks, and rushes; and some of them are not only very comfortable, but are also highly ornamental. In almost any other country it would be difficult to live in such habitations without risk of colds or rheumatism; but here, where the cold is never great, and the atmosphere pure and wholesome, no one suffers, although few of our huts are quite watertight; and one has often in a night-shower to roll about the establishment with one's blankets, in search of the driest corner.[2]

Woven huts, complex timber constructions, were not, in the nineteenth century, part of European categories of architecture. Positioned as interior decoration, productive of pleasure, or conceived of as temporary, functional necessities, they were either building or furnishing. Gottfried Semper, a nineteenth-century architectural theorist, was unusual in that his consideration of the origins of architecture depended on an appreciation of weaving and cloth. Among the items in the Great Exhibition of 1851 that influenced his work were artifacts from New Zealand, "Maori plaited decorations applied to tools, ships, and houses as fetishes."[3] Semper proposed the plaited textile[4] as one of the underlying motives of architecture. He suggested that architecture was based on weaving, at first the weaving together of branches and saplings to create rough enclosures and pens, and then weaving extended into the fabrication of mats hung vertically to create an enclosure and to differentiate between internal and external space.[5]

Semper's account of architecture was at odds with traditional views, which generally saw the interior as molded by, or a reflection of, the exterior. Semper's position, acknowledging weaving and the internal, inserts, though tacitly, lightweight Pacific structures into European architectural discourse. Weaving, with its associations with the feminine and the domestic, constructs three-dimensional habitable space, the shaping of which became with the modern movement a critical architectural act. Nevertheless, in Semper's argument, weaving still "underlies" the discourse of strong structure and firm foundations. It still lies under the weight of body and foot, a traditional feminine location, forced into fabrication.

Mobile Weaving

The woven *whare* or indigenous house was generally considered rather ambivalently. Traveler Charlotte Godley disparagingly likened the *whare* to a domestic basket:

> Such huts as are in the best repair as to keeping out wind, etc., are in great request at night, and they pack in literally as *you* would put things into your little carriage basket, which I remember always much *fuller* than it could hold. It is so funny to stand at the door and see them come out, one after another, till they cover a place nearly twice as big as the house.[6]

The *whare* is associated with baskets, wickerwork, and women's work, and is represented as a container of small items of domesticity. The internal world of the *whare*/basket does not correspond, however, to its external appearance. The lack of correspondence between exterior and interior belies the amused condescension of the colonist; the surprising interior cannot be known and controlled by an external singular gaze.

As constructed by Godley, the woven house is a container that leaks. It allows for the passage of the wind; it exudes more than it properly can contain. Refusing correspondence between two worlds, the *whare* reveals an internal expansion and denies the external skin as a closed surface. The permeable container,[7] Tuccia's sieve, is recalled in a discussion of a sermon: "They might have said, as an old Maori woman long afterwards said to me, 'Mother, my heart is like an old *Kete* [a woven basket]. . . . The words go in, but they fall through.'"[8] The *kete* is associated with the accumulation of knowledge and power, allowing certain objects/ideas to lodge, while streams of water, air, and words fall through. The *kete,* a woven item that contains the valuable and the necessary, is also permeable, leaky, holding only a selection of the objects that make up the patterns of daily life. The woven designs in *kete* have a multiplicity of meanings, weaving between the contained objects and the external world.

Transportable, the woven house/basket encourages the possibility of mobility. In English society, mobility, particularly domestic and feminine

mobility, threatens the continuation of the name and property of the father.[9] Separated from public life but also the foundation of society, the
house is conceived as a strong container of property, a place for the maintenance of the father's law. It needs solid walls, strong doors, and latches
to guard against inadmissible openings. The permeable structure of the
woven house, with openings omnipresent, had the potential to lead to
dissipation, the loss of line, and the loss of property and name. The
fragility of a woven house, a leaky vessel, does not ensure the perpetua-
tion of the word and the law, thus threatening perceived prospects of authority and stability. Regarding such structures as ornamental, imperma-
nent, and promiscuous, nineteenth-century European observers tried to
control the woven, permeable architecture that was both desired and
feared.

Hakari Stage

To the colonists, the experience of the woven *whare* offered a troubling
version of an open domesticity. *Hakari* stages, located firmly in the public realm, spread the anxiety and pleasure further. These immense timber structures built for feasts were part building, part scaffolding, and
part furnishing, thus eluding categorization, collapsing the binary categories of structure/ornament, culture/nature, external/internal. Like
the *kete, hakari* stages were woven timber structures that seemed to sieve
architectural discourse. From the disjunctions and correspondences between the words and images of the colonial representations of *hakari*
stages, crucial European attitudes toward architectural persistence, consumption, and monumentality can be discerned even as they are shaken.

A number of different feast structures in the North Island of New Zealand were drawn and discussed by European travelers. The substantial
timber framelike structures were built in association with feasts, which
had, on occasion, more than three thousand people present.[10] The feast
stages varied in appearance from long lines of food stacks, lines of low
building,[11] conical or pyramidal structures,[12] and tall lines of structure.[13]
The stages are frequently characterized by extreme dimensions. There
are *hakari* stages described as ninety feet high;[14] one was recorded as two
miles long.[15]

In the Bay of Islands in the north of New Zealand, in 1849, a stage was
constructed for a substantial feast. It attracted European attention. Drawings, engravings, and written descriptions of the stage appeared in diaries, journals, and missionary publications; images of the architecture
have persisted in twentieth-century publications.[16] *The New Zealand Spec-*

tator and Cook's Strait Guardian in 1849 gave the following description of the Bay of Islands feast stage:

> It is of an oblong form, measuring 211 feet in length, and 18 feet in width at the base, and is at the top about 8 feet wide. One hundred and sixty Kauri spars, raised perpendicularly, form the framework of this singular pile, several of them are squared, and five of them from 90 to 100 feet high, to which smaller spars of from 10 to 15 feet are again added, bound firmly together with the strong vine Torotoro, making the total height of the turret in the centre from 115 to 130 feet.[17]

European descriptions of feast structures frequently utilize two words associated with architecture and building: *stage* and *scaffolding*. Colenso, for example, describing the construction of a feast stage, after discussing the positioning of poles, continues, "a series of stages were then made all round the scaffolding."[18] The terms *stage* and *scaffolding* connect the feast platform to notions of display, process, and performance—temporary phenomena, apart from the time of everyday life. To be defined as temporary has meant, usually, to be located outside the categories of architecture that assert endurance and stability. The temporary is associated with, or recalled by, ephemeral material, diminutive size, or mobility.

In the Bay of Islands stage, the confluence of terms associated with the temporary is found in conjunction with a size, monumentality, and economic power base associated with the permanent and the valorized aspects of architecture. European architecture was dependent on being well founded, materially at one with the ground, promising shelter, status, stability, and the continuation of tradition. Evidence from the early colonists indicated great anxiety on their part that architecture might blow away, crumble, burn, or shake apart.[19] And all these frequently happened. Architecture was found in New Zealand to be an unreliable buttress against the uncertainties of a new colony. Notions of permanency and transience thus became somewhat shifty in representations of *hakari* stages. This can be discerned in the workings of the idea of "scaffolding" in the representations of the Bay of Island feast stage.

According to Wigley, in Semper's explanation of architecture, the textile does not represent or give meaning to structure but rather in some way undoes it or refuses correspondence.[20] The material wall, no more than a prop, described as scaffolding, is masked by the textile. This situation, which is already a reversal for exponents of "truth to material and structure," is further complicated by the *hakari* stage. The textile, the

woven network of timber, is also the scaffolding of the stage, a scaffolding
that cannot be detached from the towers it supports, towers that are
themselves woven into the scaffolding. There is difficulty in distinguishing the condition of the wall that the stage constructs.

Captain R. A. Oliver (1811–1889), on his second visit to the Bay of Islands, accompanying Sir George Grey,[21] wrote in his journal:

> August 28th 1849. Having received a requisition from the Gov-
> ernor to proceed to the Bay of Islands where a large   of
> Natives were assembled to celebrate a Feast I started for that
> place, and found on my arrival at Kororarika that an enormous
> scaffolding had been erected it consisted of   upright poles
> of different heights supported by others on each side their
> head sloping inwards till they met the uprights whence they
> were lashed securely, at about every ten or twelve feet were
> stages or platforms on which were built up provisions and
> the natives went up and stood there adorning the poles with
> pieces of calico and blankets   their fabric was likened by
> some of our people to gothic cathedral but the best simile was
> to the Houses of Parliament with a streamer of calico on each
> weather cock.[22]

This journal entry on the *hakari* stage is dominated by the description of
scaffolding. The size, posture, and connections between the members
that make up the framework of timber are emphasized. Oliver's description of the whole as "scaffolding" has implications concerning the stage's
relationship to architecture. Scaffolding provides a space outside a building in order that work can be done on the building. It is a space outside
architecture that is also dependent on architecture. In turn, the scaffolding is necessary for the production *of* architecture. The scaffolding in
Oliver's description is not a temporary means to the construction of an
edifice; rather, it is a part of the edifice, an embedded condition of the
architecture. An attempt to contain the "enormous" structure is made by
Oliver's assessment of it as "scaffolding," a category that proves, however,
to be both marginal and necessary to architecture.

As well as on the woven structure (the mixture of scaffolding and
stage), Oliver focused on a fabric detail. He attached his words and simi-
les to the calico flags that marked the limits and possible extensions of the
structure.[23] Curiously, it is with this small detail of cloth that Oliver signified the monumental nature of the *hakari* stage, a move repeated in his
drawings.

Oliver depicts the stage, in one of his watercolors (fig. 15.1), as an immense vertical structure towering over surrounding *whare* and people. The horizontal platforms appear as substantial floors, and the vertical posts construct a light skin around the floors, creating a form reminiscent of the glass-skin high-rise buildings of this century. The technical knowledge and skill required for the construction are apparent in the image. As represented by Oliver in this watercolor, the stage is occupied and part of a vivid social situation.[24] Standing as an impressive six-story building it is undeniably a complex piece of architecture.

In his writing, Oliver connects the stage to objects of power from his own culture. The profile of the building evokes the Gothic, in that it is vertical, intricate, and substantial. Oliver, however, preferred the nonreligious simile of the Houses of Parliament, which also alludes to the Gothic but in terms of government forces, which were not always aligned with the Church. The claiming of likeness allowed an assimilation of this potentially threatening structure, which constituted evidence of a culture with a developed and refined technology. Oliver continued his written de-

Fig. 15.1 R. A. Oliver, *Feast at the Bay of Islands, September 1849,* watercolor (collection of the Museum of New Zealand Te Papa Tongarewa)

scription with a reference to the landscape in which the stage was located: "Certainly if the edifice was inferior the site chosen had very much the advantage of it[s] prototype at Westminster standing on finely raised natural terrace facing the deep blue waters of this   Bay and backed by picturesque hills that in any other Country but mountainous N.Z. might be called grand."[25] Only the "natural" landscape is allowed to flourish in Oliver's description. Terracing in the New Zealand landscape, often evidence of massive architectural constructions of Maori, is here firmly associated with nature. The architecture of the stage and land is overwhelmed by the emphasis on the pictorial qualities of the surrounding hills and mountains. Oliver's drawings of the stage, however, show the towers riding above the mountaintops, as architecture marked strongly against the background hills and a challenge to the scale of the landform. In the shifts between writing and drawing, a vacillation between delight and fear can be detected.[26]

The outline of the stage in Oliver's drawings also vacillates: Projecting pieces of timber have a tendency to unravel and also to suggest that the building could be extended or contracted in a manner very unlike the smooth-skin completion of English stone structures. The *hakari* has been given ship- or boatlike qualities, suggesting that the stage was only just kept in place through tethering and anchoring. Oliver, watching from a ship as he wrote in his journal, made apparent the guy ropes and fragile ground connections of the building.

If, for the colonist, the ship represented the possibility of venturing from, and returning to, the country of origin, then the indigenous architecture of the new land was also imbued with those possibilities.[27] Architecture in the form of the stage allowed contemplation of the possibilities of passage and avoidance of notions of founding and continuity. The building as ship suggests a new or differing relationship with the ground in New Zealand. Connections between land and architecture may be difficult to sustain, having, rather, tendencies to leap, fly, or fall apart, with purchase achievable only through a myriad of light footholds, as in the *hakari* stage.

Ornament and Excess

Cuthbert Clarke (1818–1863),[28] another observer of the *hakari* stage at the Bay of Islands, made several drawings and paintings of the structure and event. He constructs a very different object. In Clarke's watercolor (fig. 15.2), the intricacy and delicacy of the timbers and the screenlike qualities of the structure lead to formal aesthetic pleasures associated with woven and plaited domestic ornament. The composition of his watercolor weaves itself inward with strands of flax, fences, thatched roofs, and, finally, the *hakari*. The peaceful internal scene is rendered more so by the figures beyond the fence line that marshal and march.

In comparison to Oliver's depiction, the Clarke image diminishes the *hakari* stage and contains it within a pictorial and social frame. An enclosing fence separates the stage, the open ground of the *marae* space, and the adjacent *whare* from the European buildings on the hill. The stage is positioned in another world while Clarke himself draws from beyond the fence. This European representation locates the scene as picturesque, the product of an exotic Other. Figures climb up and down the platforms, hoisting bundles of food, though the destination of the food is unclear in this version of the stage. The numbers of people and the scale of the enterprise are suggested but without being overwhelming; this is a domesticated structure in an orderly, peaceful scene. The flags and colored banners, larger than life, reduce the scale of the stage timbers, as does the containment by the fence. The *hakari* stage is represented as a

Fig. 15.2   Cuthbert Charles Clarke, "The stage erected to contain the food at the feast given by the native chiefs, Bay of Islands, September 1849" (handwritten across bottom of the sheet), watercolor (Alexander Turnbull Library, Wellington)

picturesque, ornamental, and exotic artifact that can be controlled.[29] This unthreatening version of the stage formed the basis for later engravings for missionary publications.

Clarke, however, had other versions of the *hakari*. In a crayon drawing (fig. 15.3), the physical size of the *hakari* was diminished in comparison to his other versions (it depicted five rather than eight platforms). The stage is separated from its wider architectural and landscape setting. No longer operating in relationship to *whare* and *marae*, the stage is again evoked as a picturesque object. Isolated from its economic productive base, it has also become full of food, a container of abundant produce that, being detached from its producers, is rendered available. This is achieved in the drawing by causing the platforms to cast a shadow onto the solidity of the internal towers. The stage is further pictured as a container by the hanging of fabric on the outer edges of the platform. This fabric constructs an external wall and casts the woven timberwork as prop or scaffolding. The textile that for Semper underlay the construction of architectural space is internalized by another fabric wall, in a layering of

Fig. 15.3   Cuthbert Charles Clarke, [A hakari, or food stage, Bay of Islands, September 1849], crayon (Alexander Turnbull Library, Wellington)

weavings, a production to excess of the elements of architecture, wall upon wall, in a progressive interiorization.

In the Clarke crayon drawing (fig. 15.3), two parts of the stage are apparent. There are platforms, which seem to function for the movement and placement of food (although the mixture of table and stairs seems problematic in terms of Maori traditions), and towers, in which the bundles of produce are placed, and which are embedded within the framework of the platforms and supports. Within the screenlike platform system rise the towers solid with food. But even as Clarke depicts the stage as a sturdy container, he also reduces it in size and in its social power. Raymond Firth, writing on *hakari* in 1959, noted European observers' reactions to the food: "One of the outstanding points about these native feasts seems to have been the prodigious quantities of food amassed and consumed; the emotions aroused by this sight, indeed, seem to have rendered early European observers almost incapable of setting down any other information about these gatherings."[30]

The possibility of excess and in particular the evidence of surplus seemed to provoke, from the European colonists, representations that attempted to curtail the perceived impropriety of overflowing abundance. The missionaries, in particular, pared down Clarke's version of the *hakari* stage. In one such missionary publication, *The Gleaner Pictorial Album*, an engraving of the stage is accompanied by the following written description:

> STAGE ERECTED AT THE BAY OF ISLANDS. The English Government in New Zealand was firmly established in 1849. On the occasion of its Proclamation a *hakari,* or festival on a large scale, was given. Twelve months before the event, food was planted, and preparations made for it. Previously to the arrival of the guests the banquet was piled either on the ground or on wooden scaffolds. Such erections were square pyramidal towers having an elevation of fifty feet on ranges of six feet high, extending from half a mile to two miles. On these ranges were placed sweet potatoes, maize, fern-root, potted birds, dried fish, karaka berries, and other things, which were afterwards distributed among the Natives present.[31]

The passage describes the feast as a "banquet" and traces the production from planting to distribution. The food is listed, enumerated piece by piece, and the stage is described in relationship to this feast of consumables. The scale of the production and size of the stage is stressed. The passage could also be seen, however, to be indirectly concerned with the firm "establishment" of English government.[32]

As an image of celebratory architecture (commemorating the so-called establishment of government) the representation of the stage resists usual architectural notions of firm foundation. The lightweight qualities and the temporary nature of "scaffolding" were more usually associated with transitory festivals. Material such as wood was seen by the colonists as second rate and associated with animals or with temporary constructions. "Government," as announced by this architectural image, could be inferred to be theatrical, fictional, and a "mere" stage dressing.

In *The Gleaner Pictorial Album* account, the towers are separated from the "ranges" and bear the weight of foundation through a linguistic connection of "towers" to English fortifications and supervisory structures. Towers are already located within a known category of architecture, and therefore architectural difference is denied, even as the extraordinary difference of the stages to Western architecture is registered in the detailed description. The theatrical gesture of government is supported by a military and disciplinary architecture.

The passage also constructs the stage as "table" by establishing it as a structure for the placement of food. It is the weight of the food tabled in the passage that "firmly established" the government. The table, which has a head and at which bread is shared and peace cemented, is an image of government both national and domestic. The setting up of the stage as table, an item of furnishing within the house, may be a move that intends to diminish but can also be read as an acknowledgment of the stage's place within a *marae* complex. The table groaning with food that is evoked by the passage of writing is, however, picked clean in the accompanying engraving.

In the engraving (fig. 15.4),[33] there is little suggestion of a feast, just a few bundles on the ground at the base of the stage as the only traces. Small black figures climb on the many levels of the stage but few appear laden with food. Instead, the network of timbers of the stage is carefully depicted as skeletal and lacking in substance or weight. Missionary disapproval of the feast is evident in, for example, the words of R. Davis, recalled in the *Church Missionary Record:* "I told him . . . that it would be to their benefit to give up the feasts; as, in the first place, they lead to an unnecessary consumption of a great deal of food, and also to much wickedness and bad talk."[34] "Bad talk" is in contrast to the conversation, the product of missionary endeavor, engaged in by two groups of cloaked figures shown in the missionary engraving (fig. 15.4). While the stage is evidence of skill and industry, it is depicted as secondary to the conver-

sion work of the missionaries. Stripped of its "excessive" productive qualities, it is etiolated, positioned in the engraving as a backdrop to a peace
for which the missionaries presumably took credit.

This fear of sensory excess is evident in other missionary publications,
such as the *Wesleyan Juvenile Offering,* which published a pared-down version of another *hakari* stage.[35] This image also appeared in the Reverend
William Yate's account of New Zealand under the title "A Stage erected
for a New Zealand Feast" (fig. 15.5). Rev. Yate described the *hakari* as
eventually resembling a "solid mass of food" and presenting a "very imposing appearance."[36] The engraving in his account, however, does not
picture food, the solid central structure appearing to be an impervious
column, smoothly rising through regular platforms. In this missionary
representation of the *hakari* stage, the complex interlacing of timbers, apparent in the Bay of Islands stage, has been recast as simple building
geometry. The title used with the engraving in the *Wesleyan Juvenile Offering* is "Pyramid of Food"—but the food is absent. By paralleling this structure to the Egyptian pyramids, it implied that, like the pyramids, the
hakari structure is an early stage of architectural history, an impressive architecture of an era soon to be superseded.

Fig. 15.4　"Stage erected at the Bay of Islands in 1849 to celebrate peace," engraving
from *The Gleaner Pictorial Album,* 1888

Fig. 15.5   Rev. William Yate, *A Stage Erected for a New Zealand Feast*, engraving from *An Account of New Zealand; and of the Formation and Progress of the Church Missionary Society's Mission in the Northern Island* (London, 1835)

Landscape Constructions

As colonist and missionary representations mediate the relationship between *hakari* and food, they also structure its relationship to the landscape. While Clarke's crayon drawing constructs an absence of connection between the stage and its context, Clarke's watercolors, the drawings
by Oliver, and the missionary publications propose the *hakari* as contained within a fence, which is itself contained by the immediate hills of
the wider landscape. These drawings and paintings tend to constrain and
limit the influence of the stage by absorbing it within its location.

As with the engraving in *The Gleaner Pictorial Album,* in Clarke's watercolor the *hakari* stage is depicted as a backdrop or setting that imitates the
land it occupies. As a "replacement" for the land beyond, it implies that
the wider context is as containable as the enclosed space in the image.
The construction of the *hakari* stage as ornamental backdrop suggests
that the occupation of the land by Maori might be as provisional as a
world constructed with pieces of timber, a point that the later land wars
attempted to insist upon. Clarke, however, also made a drawing of the
hakari stage from a higher vantage point, which repositions the *hakari* in
terms of the landscape (fig. 15.6).

In this depiction, the stage is still framed by the immediate landform.
It is, however, angled out toward the water, thus setting up a relationship
to the beach, sea, and distant islands, with prospects of the dissemination
and ingestion of information and knowledge. The open gateway between
the stage and the long *whare* is occupied by figures moving between the
social space and the economic base that the sea and lands provide. In this
wider context, the *hakari* stage is like the ships and canoes in the distance, a signifier of connections and *mana.* The viewpoint of the drawing
(Clarke looks down on the proceedings) might tend to diminish its subject, but in revealing the position of the stage in relationship to the beach,
it shows the *marae* open to the sea and suggests that the *hakari* may have
operated as a screen rather than a wall.[37] The solidity of the other three
sides of the enclosed *marae*-type space contrasts with the open weave of
the stage.

Also shown in this drawing is a curious association between the stage,
marae space, and what appears to be a European building with pyramidal roof. The square, solid structure is pressed up against the wall of the
whare in an uncomfortable juxtaposition. The house is excluded from the
open contained space between stage and *whare.* It also overlooks or exerts pressure on the *whare,* in a relationship of awkward proximity char-

Fig. 15.6 Cuthbert Charles Clarke, *The Feast, Bay of Islands New Zealand, September 1849*, pencil drawing heightened with Chinese white (National Library of Australia, Rex Nan Kivell Collection)

acteristic of relationships between the two people. The *hakari* stage was constructed in a world of two cultures; artifacts from both formed the landscape.

Woven Fabrications

The form of the *hakari* stage appears to have vanished from twentieth-century New Zealand architecture, along with other forms of Maori architecture, such as palisades, gates, and fortifications, associated, in part, with a resistance to colonization. But a recent television advertisement for a national lottery that produces a celebratory image of New Zealand as a constant multicultural party, utilizes the architectural form of the *hakari* stage. Once again associated with a demonstration of excessive production, the *hakari* stage in the advertisement reproduces nineteenth-century anxieties and pleasures. The televised images offer both the enticement of the lightweight woven structure and the implacable grimness of scaffolding associated with the gallows of nation building.

Scaffolding, outside the realm of architecture and yet a necessary prop to the construction of the discipline, is used in the representations of *hakari* as a means of attempting to contain an architecture that exists between traditional categories. The internal fold in the word *scaffolding* mirrors the upsetting of notions of interior and exterior inherent in *hakari* stages, while the connections to textiles drawn by the European observers create an unfamiliar image of a fluid and open architecture. Reading the texts of *hakari* as fabrications, textile constructions that are located, extremely, as both originary and marginal, is to accept the scaffoldings that are constructed by the representations. These representational scaffolds also implicitly include the hangman's scaffold, a construction between life and death, and point to the provisional nature of such textual proceedings.

The reading of the *hakari* representations occurs within a network or weave that is broader than the text or its texture. To recognize threads that stretch beyond particular representations is to refuse the ubiquitous collapse into the natural associated with Maori architecture and to acknowledge *hakari* as material evidence of successful collective provisioning, gift exchange, and as part of a complex social organization.

Notes

Thanks to Dr. Mike Austin and Dr. Sue Bulmer for advice and comments on this essay.

1. John Rochfort, *Adventures of a Surveyor in New Zealand* (1853; Christchurch: Capper Press, 1974), 22.
2. W. Tyrone Power, *Sketches in New Zealand with Pen and Pencil* (1849; Christchurch: Capper Press, 1974), 80.
3. Gottfried Semper, *The Four Elements of Architecture, and Other Writings* (Cambridge: Cambridge University Press, 1989), 28.
4. The description of the plaiting as fetish prefigures Freudian analysis of plaited pubic hair fetishistically marking an absent phallus. The absence in the architecture of the plaited woven hut is indeed one of stiffening; the hut is constructed of unframed heterogeneously structured woven material. It lacks the European propriety of a solid, impermeable wall/enclosure. See discussion by Ann Bergren, "Architecture Gender Philosophy" in *Strategies in Architectural Thinking*, ed. Whiteman, Kipnis, Burdett (Cambridge: MIT Press, 1992).

5. The making of the interior enclosure was tied, by Semper, to the construction of social space for family life. The insubstantial, nonstructural mat wall was propped or held up with a supporting structure that is distinguished from the carpet/mat. As the dictates of weather and function require, the hanging mat and the wall become a single and more solid enclosing element. According to Semper, the ornamentation of the more solid wall referred, however, to the fabric "motive" that underlies it.

6. John Godley, *Letters from New Zealand by Charlotte Godley* (Christchurch: Whitcombe & Tombs, 1951), 106.

7. "Tuccia's sieve is an unsound vessel that becomes sound through a miracle, like the body of a woman, which with its open orifices, dangerous emissions and distressing aptitude for change, can yet become preternaturally sound when representing good." Marina Warner, *Monuments and Maidens: The Allegory of the Female Form* (London: Picador, 1985), 254.

8. Alison Drummond, ed., *Married and Gone to New Zealand* (Hamilton and Auckland: Paul's Book Arcade, 1960), 158.

9. See the discussion on the movement of women in Ann Bergren, "The (Re)Marriage of Penelope and Odysseus: Architecture Gender Philosophy," *Assemblage* 21 (1993): 11.

10. Raymond Firth, *Economics of the New Zealand Maori*, 2d ed. (Wellington: Government Printer, 1959), 330.

11. A 400m shed was depicted by J. J. Merrett (lithograph) at the feast at Remuera in 1884.

12. William Bambridge (1819–1879), *Journal*. Monday, March 20, 1843: "A stage . . . erected last year to commemorate a hakari or feast," pencil sketch, Alexander Turnbull Library.

13. William Bambridge [Hakari at Kerikeri, 29 March 1843], watercolor, Alexander Turnbull Library.

14. Rev. W. Yate, *An Account of New Zealand . . .* , 2d ed. (London: Seeley & Burnside, 1835), 139.

15. "Such erections . . . extending from half a mile to two miles." A. S. Thomson, *The Story of New Zealand: Past and present, savage and civilised*, 2 vols. (London: Murray, 1859), 1:189.

16. A reproduced version of Clarke's *hakari* appears as frontispiece in vol. 2 of Thomson with the title "Stage for hakari or feast given to Governor Grey in 1849 at the Bay of Islands to celebrate the peace between the two races."

17. *New Zealand Spectator and Cook's Strait Guardian*, 6 October 1849.

18. W. Colenso, *Transactions of the New Zealand Institute* 13:13.

19. Rev. R. Taylor, preaching in a church at Ihupuku on Waitotara River, 1 February 1846: "We had thunder and lightening with very heavy rain in the night, this morning very high wind. . . . Whilst I administered the Sact. the church which is a native erection of light and unsubstantial materials rocked

to and fro in a most fearful manner. I fully expected some of the rafters would come tumbling down every instant." *Journal* 3 (211/212), typescript, Alexander Turnbull Library.

20. "The textile is a mask which dissimulates rather than represents the structure. The material wall is no more than a prop, a contingent piece of "scaffolding," "foreign" to the production of the building, merely a supporting player, playing the role of support, supporting precisely because it does not play." Mark Wigley, "Architecture after Philosophy: Le Corbusier and the Emperor's New Paint," *Journal of Philosophy and the Visual Arts* 2 (1990): 86.

21. Marian Minson, *Encounter with Eden New Zealand, 1770–1870: Paintings and Drawings from the Rex Nan Kivell Collection.* . . . Catalogue of exhibition (Wellington: National Library of New Zealand/Te Puna Matauranga o Aotearoa, 1990), 43.

22. R. A. Oliver, MS, Alexander Turnbull Library, 45–47. Blank spaces in the quotation indicate words missing in the original manuscript where it was torn or otherwise illegible.

23. The flags were also said to mark the end of the holding of *hakari*, according to William Richard Wade, although they persisted past the date of his observations: "In June 1835, I was present at a hakari . . . [at] a small bay at the back of Kororareka. . . . When the baskets were all down, Heke, a well conducted chief, mounted the scaffolding to hoist a flag, significant of the termination of all hakaris in the Bay of Islands." William Richard Wade, *A Journey in the Northern Island of New Zealand* (Hobart: George Rolwegan, 1842), 119.

24. In another Oliver sketch (R. A. Oliver [Food stage erected 1849], watercolor, private collection) of the *hakari*, it is stripped of its fineness and detail. Scale removed (the smoldering fires just a trace of human occupation), it has become an object somewhere between pure structure and pure ornament, and either way improper architecture. The weaving together of the timbers, separated from the social usage and meaning, positions the stage outside architectural categories. There is no possibility of inhabitation here. The stripped object is represented as skeletal, perhaps as a remnant of an impressive past.

25. Oliver, MS, 45–47.

26. Homi Bhabha, "The Other Question" *Screen* 24 (November–December 1983): 26.

27. A drawing by C. J. Ewen, "Kororarika. Bay of Islands—N.Z." (1849), shows the stage from across water, drawing a direct parallel between the outline of a ship and the stage.

28. Minson, *Encounter with Eden New Zealand*, 47.

29. Leonard Bell, *Colonial Constructs: European Images of Maori, 1840–1914* (Auckland: Auckland University Press, 1992). "Besides recording an important political event, Clarke's depiction of the *hakari* can also be seen as an exercise in the exotic picturesque" (44).

30. Firth, *Economics of the New Zealand Maori,* 326. He also uses terms that suggest he had some problems with the *hakari:* "The best energies of the people were absorbed for long periods of time in securing food which was consumed in a few hours, often gluttonously and even wastefully" (317).

31. Church Missionary Society, *The Gleaner Pictorial Album,* vol. 3 (London: Church Missionary House, Seeley, Jackson, & Halliday [1887–1888]), 217.

32. The *hakari* given at the Bay of Islands in 1849 is described by *New Zealand Spectator and Cook's Strait Guardian* (6 October 1849) and Firth not as a feast to commemorate the establishment of English government, as claimed by *The Gleaner Pictorial Album,* but rather as being given by chiefs of Waimate to Ruhi, also of Ngapuhi tribe, in return for one given by him about two years before.

33. Also in Church *Missionary Intelligencer* (1860–1861), "Stage erected at the Bay of Islands in 1840 to celebrate peace," 217.

34. R. Davis, *Church Missionary Record* (1836; cited in Firth, *Economics of the New Zealand Maori,* 333).

35. "Pyramid for Food, Erected at a New-Zealand Feast." *Wesleyan Juvenile Offering* (1855), opposite p. 61.

36. Yate, *An Account of New Zealand,* 140.

37. See discussion of relationship between *marae* and landscape in M. R. Austin, "A Description of the Maori Marae," in *The Mutual Interaction of People and their Built Environment: A Cross-Cultural Perspective,* ed. Amos Rapoport (The Hague: Mouton Publishers, 1976).

16

PACIFIC COLONIALISM AND THE FORMATION OF LITERARY CULTURE

Simon During

Isolating Culture

Let me begin this exploratory essay on the relationship between Pacific colonialism and literature a long way from the Pacific, at Lord Pembroke's Wilton House, a monument of metropolitan taste, money, and power.

After visiting the estate around 1750, Thomas Warton reflected on the experience in sonnet form:

> From Pembroke's princely dome, where mimic Art
> Decks with a magic hand the dazzling bow'rs,
> Its living hues where the warm pencil pours,
> And breathing forms from the rude marble start,
> How to life's humbler scene can I depart!
> My breast all glowing from those gorgeous tow'rs,
> In my low cell how cheat the sullen hours!
> Vain the complaint: for Fancy can impart
> (To fate superior, and to fortune's doom)
> Whate'er adorns the stately-storied hall:
> She, mid the dungeon's solitary gloom,
> Can dress the Graces in their Attic pall:
> Bid the green landscape's vernal beauty bloom;
> And in bright trophies clothe the twilight wall.[1]

These lines are not simply locodescriptive: they are as much concerned with the poet's social relation to Wilton as with the house and garden themselves. Using a conventional idiom of mid-century, protoaesthetic writing ("magic hand," "fancy," "eternal beauty," "Graces"), they explore a way of preserving Wilton's charm and aura from a distance while, in the same stroke, they break with the patronage system. Warton does not consider Wilton's owners at all: His poetic persona has a relation to the great estate that is no longer metonymical—he is not close to, or part of, the material and political fabric of this (or, in his "humbler scene," any other) oligarchic treasure. It is a relation in which a subjective capacity, "fancy" (a mode of what will come to be construed as "creativity"), as well as a particular kind of access (something like what will later be called "tourism") substitutes for proximity and belonging. In fact, Warton is transforming the estate into what we today call a cultural, as against a social, economic, or political, monument whose value exists not so much for those who own or serve it as for a wider, more mobile, public.

The poem also articulates a psychic economy of interiorization and compensation. Fancy, with its interior power to "dress the Graces," and, magic-lantern–like, to "clothe the twilight wall" "in bright trophies," pays Warton off for the loss he feels on the road away from Wilton back to dull routine. Yet the terms in which Wilton's glory are invoked begin to undercut this economy of compensation. Warton's Wilton is a triumph of magic, animation, and mimesis: Its gardens are not grown but conjured up by art's "magic hand"; its statuary attract no contemplation or memory, rather, they are, preternaturally, "breathing forms"; its colors are not simply shaded by the sun but by an *ur*-photographic "warm pencil." The estate is dematerialized, technologized, and spiritualized: Wilton here is not embedded in any geographically particular social or economic setting and history; it shimmers, like any of fancy's productions, between this world and another more dazzling, more vital, less "real" world. As it is transformed into a theatrical, subjectivized construction it becomes not so much the real thing, which fancy can compensate for and transcend as fancy's object and plaything to begin with. And, at least in principle, its "princely domes" become as portable as Warton's own compensatory and interiorized delight in magic and visual pleasure. The fabric of English culture, represented like this, could reappear, internally or externally, anywhere on earth. To stretch this reading to its limits, we might say that Warton's sonnet is preparing for Wilton's (read "England's") cultural globalization, as well as for England's future as a center of "heritage," an international cultural tourist destination, available for memorization and imaginative recreation.

It is difficult to cast such a burden of meaning on this sonnet without becoming curious about the poem's relation to Warton's own circumstances—which, as it turns out, do lead us further into the cultural underpinning of England's global expansion. Warton was an Oxford don who became Professor of Poetry in 1757 and still later, in 1785, Poet Laureate. His scholarly fame rested on two groundbreaking books, a monograph on *The Faerie Queene* (1754) and three volumes of *The History of English Po-*

etry (1774–1781). As René Wellek pointed out in *The Rise of English Literary History,* these works marked a turning point in the study of literature.[2] They situated old vernacular poetry within a tradition that could now be mobilized by contemporary writers. But this living tradition was constructed at a price too: The structures through which poetry became literary in this new sense, that is, through which poetry became not so much a rhetorical form alongside other rhetorical forms but a form of expression within a quasi-autonomous field, also gradually shifted poetry's frame of reference back to its history and gradually restricted its appeal to readers with specialized skills and knowledges.[3] Warton's book on Spenser explicitly accepts this restriction: It is directed neither to academic scholars nor to the wider public but to those few who have a "taste" for Spenser.

Official Primitivism

Warton did not just work as a man of letters, he lived as one. Like Samuel Johnson, he was committed to literature as a profession and way of life: He chose academic life against more lucrative "preferments." He cultivated a certain donnish bohemianism, becoming well known for his love of tobacco, drink, and "low life," as early biographers put it.[4] This, like his interiorization of Wilton's aura, established a way of living at a (highly equivocal and compromised) distance from the established hierarchies, fitting for a man with a particular attraction to fancy and poetry. Indeed, to the degree that taste, creativity, and specialized knowledge came to mark a love of literature, that love implied a particular way of life. No less important, the distance between literary and the nonliterary life provided a space within which Warton could articulate a certain primitivism. Warton's Spenser, for instance, was not a canonical poet in today's sense: He was a poet attracted to the "fantastical extravagancies" characteristic of an age deemed less rational and decorous.[5] "It was his business to engage the fancy, and to interest the attention by bold and striking images, in the formation, and the disposition of which, little labour or art was applied. The various and the marvellous were the chief sources of delight."[6]

It is Spenser's wholehearted engagement with fancy and the marvelous that mark him as primitive for Warton. Yet it is not as if Warton could wholeheartedly endorse Spenser's ancient exuberance—the perceived requirements of civility and order remained too pressing for that. Warton carefully constructs a formula to balance his investment in order against the uses and pleasures of a primitivized fancy: "In reading Spenser if the critic is not satisfied, yet the reader is transported."[7] Warton styled and presented his life more as such a reader than as such a critic.

When Warton became Poet Laureate, in 1785, his will to primitivism became official and more elaborate. The odes he regularly produced on state occasions placed George III in a tradition that stretched back to a Saxon "native genius" characterized by an aggressive defense of liberty— "For oft in savage breasts the buried seeds / Of brooding virtue live, and freedom's fairest deeds!" tuned to Britain's global ambitions. The 1790 birthday ode, for instance, appealed for the king's recovery at a spa:

> Or broods the nymph with watchful wing
> O'er ancient Badon's mystic spring,
> And speeds from its sulphureous source
> The steamy torrent's secret course,
> And fans th' eternal sparks of hidden fire,
> In deep unfathom'd beds below
> By Bladud's magic taught to glow,
> Bladud, high theme of Fancy's gothic lyre? . . .
> Hail then, on this glad morn, the mighty main!
> Which lends the boon divine of lengthen'd days
> To those who wear the noblest regal bays:
> That mighty main, which on its conscious tide
> Their boundless commerce pours on every clime,
> Their dauntless banner bears sublime;
> And wafts their pomp of war, and spreads their thunder wide![8]

Here, Warton's considerable poetic skills are used to effect the transition from curative spa waters to the high seas (as the domain of commerce and martial imperialism) in a manner that enables even the irrational monarch to be presented as an emblem of British power.

These official poems (like his endorsement of fancy and primitivism more generally) reproduce the older patriot rhetoric of Walpole's opposition, now become hegemonic, if only ceremonially so.[9] At another level, Warton's official poetry smoothly integrates his literary historicism into the ideology of the state: the ancient bards hallow current Britain's global power and military preparedness. And at yet another level, Warton's official primitivism is articulated within a conceptual framework that, once again, draws directly from spectacle and drama. He conjures up martial and savage virtues with the aid of what he called his "fairy trappings," which, in turn, point to the theater—that institution most committed to retailing intense, out-of-the-world experiences, transporting its audience with charm and magic.

It should be clear that the primitivism represented by Thomas Warton is only just coherent enough to be recognized as a discrete formation. It draws together martial and imperialist aggression, theatrical spectacle, lived bohemianism, and the emergence of the literary as an autonomous and self-referential field. It also transformed English cultural geography. Thomas Warton himself was not as closely involved in this process as his brother, Joseph, a somewhat more radical figure within the Wartons' larger circle of post-Walpolian primitivizing writers (which included Thomas Gray and William Mason). Joseph Warton's literary taste could be quite directly mapped onto a preference for a particular kind of terrain:

> What are the lays of artful Addison,
> Coldly correct, to Shakespeare's warblings wild?
> Whom on the winding Avon's willowed banks
> Fair Fancy found, and bore the smiling babe
> To a close cavern (still the shepherds show
> The sacred place, whence with religious awe
> They hear, returning from the field at eve,
> Strange whisp'rings of sweet music through the air).[10]

The point of this is not simply that Avon's "winding" course reflects Shakespeare's "warblings wild" (just as, in the poem, Addison's verses are equivalent to the gardens at Versailles), but that Shakespeare, Fancy's foundling, is imagined as having been raised in isolation, tutored by that "sweet music" that shepherds still present to tourists. England's landscape is reshaped so that it mirrors the primitivist, literary imaginary. Again, theatricality is not absent in this: The Avon was chosen early on to represent the appeal of the wild just because it was the home of a theatrical "genius." Shakespeare provides a connection between theatrical "trappings" and the supposed wildness and isolation of his home landscape, his capacity to mediate between two literary institutions—the theater and poetry—and between two cultural modes—the primitive and the civil— being a ground of his preeminence.

Literary primitivism not only celebrated Britain's imperial grandeur, it prepared for a new colonialist drive. In Joseph Warton's famous "Ode to Fancy," Fancy is a "maid" who, mourning, haunts Shakespeare's tomb in Stratford, only to be exhorted:

> Like lightning, let his mighty verse
> The Bosom's inmost foldings pierce;
> With native beauties win applause
> Beyond cold critic's studied laws;

> O let each Muse's fame increase,
> O bid Britannia rival Greece.[11]

Britannia will rival Greece, that is, develop a cultural empire, when Fancy wrests the national heritage from those who champion Francophile neoclassicism ("cold critic's studied laws"). In the larger logic of the Wartons' primitivism, these lines imply that that heritage will be transmitted to those with little respect for laws who, through their asceticism and imaginative strength, possess a greater capacity to endure a hard, isolated life in "caverns" and "low cells"—not least in the colonies. I would suggest that it was against such a background that Joseph Warton could be inspired to write his casual "Lines, written extempore, on seeing some soldiers at Wickham, who were going to form a settlement near Senegambia":

> With happy omen march, ye valiant ranks,
> From Thames to Senegambia's distant banks,
> Where, beneath warmer suns and genial skies,
> May future cities and new empires rise.[12]

But a tension begins to appear here: What is the relation between these "future cities" and the primitivist impulse to isolation and wildness that legitimates colonial settlement? Joseph Warton's early "The Enthusiast" (written in 1740 in disillusion with Walpole's England) stresses colonial isolation more than empire building. It ends with the poet wishing to become a settler, joining in the life of "simple Indian swains" and, presumably, able to counter solitude with his interiorized and literary imaginative resources:

> O who will bear me then to western climes,
> (Since Virtue leaves our wretched land) to fields
> Yet unpolluted with Iberian swords:
> The isles of Innocence, from mortal view
> Deeply retir'd, beneath a plantane's shade,
> Where Happiness and Quiet sit enthron'd,
> With simple Indian swains.[13]

When these Indians came closer to view, however, Warton turned to those components of his primitivism that might help settlers most effectively

dispose of them. His popular poem "The Dying Indian" daringly condoned the Native Americans' refusal to be converted to the religion of
"those that eat their god," but, at the same time and more to the ideological point, celebrated their preparedness to die.

Eighteenth-century literary primitivism, however, had alliances and
orientations that at least appear very remote from the bloody business of
colonialism. Most crucially, it was connected in particular to the revivi-
fication of comic writing—with Thomas Warton a notable talent here
too. In his much-read light verse, especially as collected in *The Oxford
Sausage* (1764), icons of respectability and the objects of everyday life—
from newspapers to wigs, from the theater to an Oxford education—are
mocked, usually by replacing high forms by low ones. His "Prologue on
the Old Winchester Playhouse over the Butcher's Shambles," for instance, metamorphoses a theater into a butcher's shop, undercutting pretensions to civility and taste. This form of comic versifying is to be distinguished from so-called Augustan satire, which, reacting to supposed
threats to morality or civil order, could present itself as a serious contribution to social decorum by its classical antecedents. Warton's "humorous
and satirical pieces," as he called them, were a more fugitive mode, aimed
less at the greater public than at private fun. They were loosely interlaced
within primitivism because they were written as if from below: The same
motives and logic that sent Warton back from Wilton to his "low cell" and
bohemianism, from polite letters to Spenser and fancy, led him to comic
verse, where established hierarchies could also be overturned, politely
enough. The comic mode might be imbricated with primitivism, but it
avoided primitivism's paradoxes. For a figure like Thomas Warton, that
mode was engaging, no doubt, because it reconnected him to the ordinary: It was a form of writing that did not presuppose a particular education or inclination. But it was also appealing because of the difficulty of
taking seriously an official primitivism torn between celebrating oppression *and* freedom, the theatrical *and* the ascetic, the colonized *and* the
colonizer. In the comic poem, however complacently, nothing needed to
be taken seriously at all.

Literature and Early Settlement

So the loose and complex primitivism that I have been describing helped
legitimate imperial expansion and settler colonialism during the period
in which the Antipodean territories were first claimed by Britain. (Cook
first departed for the Pacific in 1768; the penal colony in New South
Wales was established exactly twenty years later.) As we have seen, the
ideal of an imaginative and solitary life in a "low cell," hallowed by a liter-

ary culture whose genealogy led back to the days of early English exuberance, even savagery, helped English men of letters boost the colonialist projects of the period. In addition, the interiorization of culture made it possible to conceive that a culturally adequate life might be lived on the borders of empire. And the transformation of the material fabric of British civility into an object of spectacle, a plaything of fancy, made it imaginable that the material fabric of the home country might be re-created, almost like a theatrical set, at the end of the earth. Of course the will to isolation contradicted the aim to build a purified version of the old society; but Pacific colonialism, with its quite specific targets and limits, needed to be able to tolerate such incoherence. For, unlike postrevolutionary America, Pacific colonialism did not claim that its new settlements represented a decisive break with old Europe, and unlike the East India Company (which administered the Indian colonies until the century's end), it was actually committed to building emigrant societies, even if often reluctantly on the British State's part.

The question remains: How was the literary culture that I have been describing transported to the new Antipodean settlements? In the broadest terms, we can say that metropolitan cultural structures and processes (and it is always a matter of structures and processes in all their contradictions and ambivalences) were adapted, reformed, or ignored according to the conditions and strategical requirements of colonial writing. More specifically, two factors were crucial in determining this transportation. First, instead of the imaginary "Indians" of official primitivism, the settlers encountered real indigenous peoples in a variety of situations. Second, until the second half of the nineteenth century, the primary institutions of a literary culture were largely absent in the new territories. In particular, there was little theater and no professional literary writers. It is no accident that the most celebrated poem about New South Wales in the early years was probably "Barrington's Prologue," which, in the spirit of comic verse as in *The Oxford Sausage,* deflated pretensions to a colonial theater by describing it as a form of criminal activity.

But perhaps the case of Barron Field is the best instance of the absence of literary institutions in the new colonies. He had connections with a new type of professional and independent "man of letters" often known as the Cockneys (of whom the best known are John Keats, William Hazlitt, Charles Lamb, Leigh Hunt, and Thomas de Quincey). These writers not only (usually) lacked the class or formal-education background, the patronage connections, or ties to the established church or political system or to a generalist bookseller that had previously been required to mount a career in letters, they also were touched by the sense that writing could radically reform society. (Immanuel Kant's fascination for many in this group needs to be read in this light, and however depoliticized the Cockneys became, they did not forget the examples of radical writers like Joseph Spence or Thomas Paine.) At the same time, they were committed to the autonomy of literature. In fact, William Hazlitt read Thomas Warton's Wilton sonnet as an expression of the opposition between the landed gentry and this specific social strata committed to culture as a self-referential sphere.[14] Because the group were relatively free-floating, it is from them that one might expect to find settler writers—and indeed one of Hazlitt and Lamb's associates did emigrate early on. Barron Field, sometimes called the first Australian man of letters, arrived in the colony in 1817 and published Sydney's first locally printed book of poetry two years later. His poems are light, if not quite humorous, treating animals like the kangaroo a little as Warton had treated a wig or a newspaper; that is, like a versified essay by Charles Lamb (pen name Elia). Field figures in Hazlitt's essay "Of Persons to have Seen," a report of a protospiritualist parlor game played by the group, and he chose David Garrick as the person he would most like to invoke from the dead, if, Faust-like, he were given the chance.[15] It is a telling choice and signals both the literary world's continuing faith in Fancy's creative powers and Field's failure as an emigrant: Sydney was no place for a Garrick fan, unless, of course, one's imagination was powerful enough to conjure up the great actor's spirit. By 1824, Field had returned to England.

So in the colonies, writing was not in the hands of professional writers committed to literature, though it referred back to the metropolitan structures and struggles that made their careers possible. This is apparent even within the official ideology of Pacific colonialism as articulated by the most effective and systematic developers of settlement: the Wakefields. Edward Gibbon Wakefield's policy documents on colonization, *A Letter from Sydney* (1829), *England and America* (1835), and *A View of the Art of Colonisation* (1849) were preeminently aimed at what Wakefield called, in the language of Benthamism, "the cure and prevention of [colonial] newness" (77), that is, the means by which the colonies could re-create British civilization rather than repeat what Wakefield regarded as the American failure to make "progress in the art of living" (68). The means that Wakefield recommended to these ends were almost wholly economic and governmental (primarily the termination of squatting through the centralized control of the distribution of so-called wastelands and the purchase from indigenous peoples of land acknowledged to be inhabited). For Wakefield, the Pacific colonies could avoid newness, could become an "extension of an old society" (85), not only by building up markets but by parceling out the new territories in blocks precisely calculated to balance isolation with community so as to encourage social cultivation and "arts of refinement."

This master idea of "systematic colonialism" required a consideration of its cultural effects. Images of what new colonial territories might become were borrowed from Georgic writings old and new. Here, for instance, is Edward Jermingham Wakefield, Edward Gibbon's son and assistant, describing New Plymouth in the mid-1840s, recontextualizing a traditional evocation of the rural by Shakespeare. Ceres' song from the masque scene in *The Tempest* promises fertile, profitable lands for emigrant smallholders:

> The abundance of the second crops in the existing native gardens, the rankness and yet softness of the grass which had sprung up in the old deserted patches, surrounded with flowering shrubs amidst which countless flocks of singing birds were chasing each other, all combined with the genial atmosphere, although it was approaching to the middle of winter, to remind me touchingly of Shakespeare's sweet picture of the perfection of agriculture. Just such a country and climate is described by him, if worked by happy and industrious farmers:

> > Earth's increase and foyson plenty,
> > Barns and garners never empty;
> > Vines with clust'ring branches growing;
> > Plants with goodly burden bowing;
> > Spring come to you at the farthest
> > In the very end of harvest!
> > Scarcity and want shall shun you,
> > Ceres' blessing so is on you! [16]

This, of course, is a long way from primitivism. Wakefield turns to Shakespeare to secure a temporal structure in which the present dissolves simultaneously into the past and future. New Plymouth reminds him of Shakespearean song but does so only because it promises the realization of a pastoral ideal "if worked by happy and industrious farmers." What is left out in this propaganda for the New Zealand Company is exactly the toughness and tolerance for isolation required of early settlers—which primitivism had begun to prepare for. In fact, Wakefield's lines pass over another transitional genre, exemplified by Joseph Banks' stanzas in praise of the agriculturist Thomas Coke, on the occasion of the Holkham Sheep Shearing of 1807, which metamorphosed the primitivist (more than pastoral) ideal of the simple life into praise of a productive and efficient agricultural labor, and whose ultimate horizon was a settler colonialism based on farming and global botanical transplantation.

The Wakefields' writings were aimed at would-be emigrants living in Britain. In his autobiography, Edward Jermingham does in fact present himself as possessing certain primitivist capabilities, but for him, literature as such signifies something else: gentility. Closer to the settler experience, such a conventional view of literature could be inadequate. Let us take as the first example William Colenso, an early New Zealand settler, missionary, and printer who, in his private journals, recorded what seem to have been the characteristic mood swings of the "pioneer," switching from excitement and joy at the prospects and peculiar beauty of new country to depression at its isolation. Colenso near Taupo wrote:

> Here, notwithstanding the pleasurable height to which my imagination had been raised whilst engaged in contemplating the magnificence and extent of the prospect before me, it soon sank below its ordinary level on finding that not a human being dwelt in all that immense tract of country on which my eager gaze then rested. The grass grew, the flowers blossomed, and the river rolled, but not for man. Solitude all! Even the very little birds, denizens of the wilds, few though they were in number, seemed (so fancy intimated) to think with me, for they flew from bush to bush around and about my path with their melancholy "twit, twit," as if wishing to have all they possibly could of the company of a passer-by. Their actions were quite in unison with my thoughts, and I feelingly exclaimed, "Oh! Solitude, where are the charms," &c.[17]

Colenso's perspective on the scene recalls the broad "prospects"— views through which the British landscape was often aestheticized and which, as John Barrell has pointed out, effaced the presence of rural labor on the land—or, in this instance, the Maori peoples.[18] Yet Colenso's response is nothing like serene appreciation: William Cowper's lines from "Verses, Supposed to be Written by Alexander Selkirk" (1782), which expressed a horror of colonial isolation, seem to pop effortlessly into his mouth, all the more so because they are so well known that they do not have to be directly cited. Cowper's half-castaway, half-colonist complained:

> Oh, solitude! where are the charms
> That sages have seen in thy face?
> Better dwell in the midst of alarms,
> Than reign in this horrible place.[19]

Colenso's panic, expressed through Cowper, implicitly anticipates its solution—the establishment of a new settler community in the very place
where, as Colenso depicts it, only birds live, themselves depressed and
sparse. The primitivist celebration of isolation cannot be expressed at this
point because it would bar the land-grab about to occur in New Zealand's
North Island.

Once that land-grab was under way, isolation did not cease. John
Logan Campbell, sometimes known as "Father of Auckland," arrived at
the Hauraki Gulf in 1840, hoping to take commercial advantage of the
town the British government was to establish. Campbell and his partner,
William Brown, acquired the uninhabited island Motu Korea (Brown's Island) from the Ngati Tamatera people, and in their loneliness the young
partners, too, turned to literature:

> We did make the best attempt we could to prevent our brains
> from getting cobwebbed over and mouldy by devoting our eve-
> nings to such literary pursuits as half-a-dozen books afforded.
> The pages of our Shakespeare were illumined dimly enough
> certainly, and by nothing half so civilised as even a farthing
> rushlight. A piece of rag on a stick planted into a pannikin of
> fat was anything but sightly to look upon, and not a little dis-
> agreeable to the olfactories, but it did brighten up the dark-
> ness of our evenings when combined with the light of the great
> poet; better this than go to bed at sunset, which would have
> been the only alternative.[20]

It is a passage that secretes its real message. Far from metropolitan civility and monuments, Campbell's response to literature seems muted
even as he dutifully genuflects in a great poet's direction. The passage's
anticlimax reveals that, for him, reading Shakespeare is barely more re-
warding than lying awake in the dark. And it is possible to place this feeling within the larger organization of metropolitan culture: Campbell's
failure to gain effective rewards from his reading is embedded in the
structure that bound culture's promise to console to its autonomization
and dematerialization. Campbell lacks the skills and the commitment
to fancy that would enable him to live in his low cell in the cultural
mode that Thomas Warton (for example) had poetically authorized, even
though he accepts Warton's values and formulations—he even seems to
assume that reading Shakespeare ought to provide a theater in the head.
What is effective for Campbell, though, at least in his telling of it, is another tactic almost as literary as his reach for the Bard, that is, his de-

ployment of comic juxtaposition with his emphasis on fat and rags as the backdrop for his "literary pursuits." What we can call "complacent comic nihilism" was often the most effective strategy offered by literature to deal with the exhaustion of cultural values at the margins of Western power and community.

The cultural structuration that prevented Campbell from realizing the solace he believed he ought to find in Shakespeare's plays also helped organize the development of a colonial tourist industry. Australasia's most famous tourist sights (until their destruction by volcanic eruption in 1886), Lake Tarawera's Pink and White Terraces, were celebrated in the theatrical vocabulary that had dematerialized the fabric of English culture. The geologist John Johnson, who saw the area in 1848 and whose reports led to its popularity, employed a trope to describe them that later occurred to others, too: "It would be an endless task to describe their varied forms. In truth the whole scene was so strangely beautiful, that it looked more like those fairy scenes which are represented on the stage, where the artist has full scope for an inventive genius, rather than a reality."[21] About twenty years later, soldier and journalist J.H.H. St. John wrote:

> At irregular intervals on the grades are pools; —pools! the word is a profanation; they are alabaster basins filled with molten silver, blue as the vault of heaven, over whose gracefully-recurved lips pours down with a gentle murmur a never ceasing flow derived from the boiling contents of the crater above. The more we gazed upon the scene, the more difficult it was to realise it, till at length one bold attempt was made at comparison, and H[enry Hunter] exclaimed that this must be the abode of the Queen of Naiads as it would be depicted by Grieve and Telbin in a transformation scene.[22]

Here nature imitates the stage scenery and machinery of the pantomimes of the period. (The Grieves and Telbins were families of London scene designers specializing in special effects; William Grieve, for instance, introduced the moving panorama to the stage in 1820.)[23] The technique that Thomas Warton had used to transport Wilton to his Oxford rooms is now applied, in a more up-to-date and direct manner (the theater is directly referred to and names named) to a phenomenon of nature. The lack of a Drury Lane or Sadler's Wells in the colonies is supplanted by turning nature itself into a form of theater; or to put it another way, the urge to create a simulacrum of the "old" world in a "new" one radically manipulates the structure of interpenetration between the natural and the theatrical that had made the Avon an early center of primitivist British cultural geography.

Literary Taste and the Colonized Peoples

Early travelers and colonial administrators could also order their encounter with indigenous peoples inside the articulation of culture that I have been describing. For example, the invention of literary history helped white settlers turn the locals into what were sometimes called "living representatives" of historical moments that Western literature had appropriated for its own genealogy. Directly in Thomas Warton's spirit, Governor George Grey compared Maori orature to Spenser's verse, for instance.[24] But again, when colonists made closer contact with the locals, less specialized literary strategies were required. In particular, both the comic voice and literature's theatricalizing power could be called upon to construct a distance between the two sides in disquieting or threatening situations. Thus, J. L. Nicholas, who accompanied Samuel Marsden in the first missionary expedition to New Zealand, in 1814, was present when the Maori *ariki* Ruatara and Korokoro staged a massive outdoor show for the visitors at Rangihoua, in what Nicholas called a "sham fight."[25] Nicholas, impressed and discomposed, found the spectacle difficult to describe, falling back on a banal concept of the sublime:

> The approach of the canoes to the ship was marked with a wild grandeur of the noblest description, and it was impossible to behold the scene without being impressed with the force of its distinctive sublimity. . . . The reader, who has never seen man in this state, can form no conception of him from the portrait I have attempted to draw, which falls infinitely short of the terrible appearance with which he presents himself.[26]

But if Maori "man" in warrior mode was simply difficult to describe, Maori woman in warrior mode required a stronger, more distancing, writerly strategy. The women also "joined in the combat with much resolution, and following the example of their queen, exposed themselves in the thickest of the fight, to mimic dangers" (200), a scene that Nicholas introduces by an appeal to literary authority, a quotation from *Macbeth:*[27]

> So wild in their attire,
> That look'd not like the inhabitants o' th' earth
> And yet were on 't. (199)

Cannily borrowed from Banquo's speech to Macbeth at the first encounter with the Weird Sisters on the heath, these words parry an affront to missionary notions of feminine propriety. They provide a line of flight away from the aggressive *wahine* back to European tradition and cultural centers; more effectively still, they reframe the Maori ceremony as a slightly comic theatrical entertainment and, in that gesture, cast the Maori women outside both civility and the sanctioned primitive.

Marsden and Nicholas belonged to the first wave of the colonizing process. They were confident of their need to secure their difference from those whose lands they helped occupy. But Shakespeare in particular remained a resource for whites who shared Maori ways of life. Frederick Maning was a pakeha Maori in the 1830s and 1840s, "married" to a Ngapuhi woman, living in the Hokianga, farming and helping his *hapu* trade with outsiders. In *Old New Zealand,* his book of reminiscences and, like Campbell's *Poenamo,* a founding text of New Zealand settler literature, he writes that he was once placed under *tapu* for accidentally handling a skull from a *urupa,* or burial ground. This meant that no Maori would have contact with him, and that he was prohibited from eating food with his hands. Hungry, he finally decides to break the *tapu,* risking death. The incident is recorded in Maning's habitual comic mode:

> I had eaten nothing since the diabolical meal of the preceding evening, and had travelled more than twenty miles. I washed my hands six or seven times, scrubbing away and muttering, with an intonation that would have been a fortune to a tragic actor, "Out, damned spot!" and so, after having washed and dried my hands, looked at them, returned, and washed again, again washed, and so on several times, I sat down and demolished two days allowance.[28]

Here something new happens: This is comic but not only comic—the compulsiveness with which Maning washes his hands signals that, for him, they really have sinned. Maning's citation from *Macbeth* cuts more deeply than does Nicholas'. It too deflates the scene by making possible a moment of self-theatricalization and self-reflection, but the quotation cannot quite contain the moment by theatricalizing it. Maning's citation also functions as a purifying incantation. This is all the more apparent when, five days later, a *tohunga* arrives to lift the *tapu* more effectively:

> He came on mumbling and grumbling a perfectly unintelligible *karakia* or incantation. I guessed at once that he was coming to disenchant me, and prepared my mind to submit to any

conditions or ceremonials he should think fit to impose. My
old friend came gravely up, and putting his hand into the little
basket, pulled out a baked *kumera,* saying *"He kai mau."* I of
course accepted the offered food, took a bite, and as I ate he
mumbled his incantation over me. I remember I felt a curious
sensation at the time, like what I fancied a man must feel who
had just sold himself, body and bones, to the devil. For a moment I asked myself the question whether I was not actually
being then and there handed over to the power of darkness.[29]

Maning's body for a moment feels the *tapu* and its dissipation. In fact, his
original recourse to Shakespeare as a conduit to a "superstitious" and
magical act returns to a source that, predating the Warton circle's literary
primitivism, retains a sense that Shakespeare's texts might communicate
the truth about supernatural regions. In 1712, Joseph Addison wrote:

That noble extravagance of fancy which he [Shakespeare] had
in so great perfection thoroughly qualified him to touch this
weak superstitious part of his reader's imagination and made
him capable of succeeding where he had nothing to support
him beside the strength of his own genius. There is something
so wild and yet so solemn in the speeches of his ghosts, fairies,
witches, and the like imaginary persons, that we cannot for-
bear thinking them natural, though we have no rule by which
to judge of them, and must confess if there are such beings in
the world it looks highly probable they should talk and act as
he has represented them.[30]

In this passage, Shakespeare's appeal to the "weak superstitious" part of
his readers' (or, we might add, spectators') imagination is transmuted
into an admission that supernatural beings and effects might, indeed,
really appear as Shakespeare imaginatively represents them. This could
come in handy at the edges of Empire, as when Maning shamefacedly attempts to lift his *tapu* by a rational white man's enfeebled magic, whose
home had become the text or the theater. Here, the elaborate structure of interiorized fancy, comic distantiation, secular transformation of
the supernatural into "trappings," and an authorized primitivism, upon
which the emerging field of the literary had been based, falls apart for a
moment.

When literature began to be produced locally, in the strong sense that
it was neither aimed at a British readership nor took for granted that
settlers lived far from the sites of the society that were culturally richest,

the relations and structures that I have been describing were transformed. Nowhere is this more obvious than in Joseph Furphy's *Such Is Life*
(1903), a text that, at least on the surface, seems to affirm literature and,
in particular, Shakespeare's capacity to provide insight into, and support
within, life at the colonial border. Here, Shakespeare seems to be, very
firmly, the culture's transcendental genius. But, importantly, this judgment is not sustained. I cannot fully elaborate my reading of the novel
here—it is enough to note that, for me, its crucial moment is when the
bullock-driver Steve Thompson tells the yarn about the death of Rory
O'Halloran's young daughter Mary—the "perfect Young Australian." For
Rory, the "two greatest thinkers and most infallible authorities our race
has produced are Solomon and Shakespeare," because of their supposed
glorification of the feminine.[31] His daughter, however, dies in the scrub
when the settlers are unable to track her and time is lost contacting an
Aborigine who can. Her death allegorizes the impossibility of her father's
faith that the home culture can simply be transported to the colonies because, at that point, the novel concedes the failure both of religion and
literature to provide sustenance for the lives of pioneering settlers.

The story is told by the nonliterary Thompson to exemplify his belief
that, in the back country, cleverness, serviceableness, and moral worth
may belong to those who are not quite "civilized": "In some cases, a person's all the better for being partially uncivilised."[32] Unknown to Furphy,
this repeats a thought that Joseph Warton had set down as a marginal
note to his Odes in 1746: "Better uncivilis'd than civilis'd," but in this context, it refers back to, and rewrites, what the narrator, in a Wakefieldian
spirit, has previously called "the disquieting theory which assumes evolution of immigrating races towards the aboriginal type," a "type" that is, in
turn, becoming demoralized and losing its identity.[33] In Furphy, Shakespeare guards against immigrant culture's supposedly regressive tendencies—except that it becomes clear that Shakespeare's works can never
form a primary source for a transplanted culture. In the bush, primitivism—rethought and inverted—may be what the future holds, but this
primitivism implies, gingerly enough, a strong sense of the limits of literary values themselves.

Of course, neither Maning nor Furphy break with the organization of the
literary, whose emergence I have described by focusing on the Wartons'
circle. Indeed, both may well stand near the head of new, postcolonial,
national literary histories. And, as I have argued, as literature developed
as an autonomous field, with its own history and readership, its own
claims to enchantment and empowerment, it more or less implicitly conceded the limits of its appeal and reach. That is inevitable once a love of

literature becomes equivalent to a private capacity for fancy, in a transformation that dematerialized culture and ambiguated its authority—not least by situating its origins in a past deemed primitive. This is particularly worth remembering, it seems to me, when we consider the fate of settler colonies' national literatures today. This is the moment when (heirs of) the colonizers and the colonized are deploying their "cultures" in the attempt to reconcile themselves to each other, as well as to a bloody and unjust colonial history. Furphy and Maning are important writers not because they broke with the literary formation that helped legitimate the injustices of that history, but because in their writing they concretely recognized, however fleetingly, literature's limits and dangers in the colonial encounter. They are canonical writers most of all when they indicate that postcolonial national cultures (which are of course not settler cultures *tout court*) are not primarily literary cultures at all.

NOTES

1. "Poems of Thomas Warton," in *The Works of the English Poets, From Chaucer to Cowper; including the Series edited, with Prefaces, Biographical and Critical, by Dr. Samuel Johnson: And the Most Approved Translations,* ed. Alexander Chalmers, 21 vols. (London: J. Johnson et al., 1810), 18:119.

2. See René Wellek, *The Rise of English Literary History* (Chapel Hill: University of North Carolina Press, 1941), 166–201.

3. These formulations refer loosely to the systems theory account of eighteenth-century literature put forward by Siegfried J. Schmidt in his *Die Selbstorganisation des Sozialsystems Literatur im 18. Jahrhundert* (Frankfurt: Suhrkampf, 1989).

4. See "Life of Thomas Warton," in Chalmers, *Works of the English Poets,* 18:34.

5. Thomas Warton, *Observations on the Fairie Queene of Spenser,* 2d ed., 2 vols. (London: R. and J. Dodsley, 1762), 1:62.

6. Ibid., 1:15.

7. Ibid., 1:16.

8. "Poems of Thomas Warton," in Chalmers, *Works of the English Poets,* 18:118.

9. See Christine Gerrard, *The Patriot Opposition to Walpole: Politics, Poetry and National Myth, 1725–1742* (Oxford: Clarendon Press, 1994), 146–147, for some insightful remarks about Warton's relation to this tradition.

10. "Poems of Joseph Warton," in Chalmers, *Works of the English Poets,* 18:161.

11. Ibid., 18:164.

12. Ibid., 18:171.

13. Ibid., 18:161.

14. William Hazlitt, "On Personal Identity," in *Winterslow: Essays and Characters Written There* (London: Grant Richards, 1902), 71.

15. Hazlitt, "On Personal Identity," 33.

16. E. Jermingham Wakefield, *Adventure in New Zealand,* ed. Joan Stevens (Christchurch: Whitcombe and Tombs, 1955), 271.

17. See William Colenso, "Excursion in the Northern Island," in *Early Travellers in New Zealand,* ed. Nancy M. Taylor (Oxford: Clarendon Press 1959), 30–31.

18. See John Barrell, *English Literature in History, 1730–1780: An Equal, Wide Survey* (London: Hutchinson, 1983), 51 ff.

19. Roger Lonsdale, ed., *The New Oxford Book of Eighteenth-Century Verse* (Oxford: Oxford University Press, 1989), 591.

20. John Logan Campbell, *Poenamo,* ed. Joan Stevens (Auckland: Viking, 1987), 206.

21. John Johnson, "Notes from a Journal," in Taylor, *Early Travellers in New Zealand,* 171.

22. J.H.H. St. John, "Pakeha Rambles through Maori Lands," in Taylor, *Early Travellers in New Zealand,* 551.

23. David Mayer, *Harlequin in his Element: The English Pantomime, 1806–1836* (Cambridge: Harvard University Press, 1969), 70–71.

24. George Grey, "On the Social Life of the Ancient Inhabitants of New Zealand, and On the National Character It Was Likely to Form," *Journal of the Ethnographical Society of London* 4.1 (January 1870): 23.

25. J. L. Nicholas, *Narrative of a Voyage to New Zealand,* 2 vols. (London: James Black, 1817), 1:193.

26. Ibid., 1:194.

27. Ibid., 1:199, 200.

28. Frederick Maning, *Old New Zealand* (Christchurch: Whitcombe and Tombs, 1906), 124.

29. Ibid., 125–126.

30. Joseph Addison, *Essays in Criticism and Literary Theory,* ed. John Loftus (Northbrooke, Ill.: AHM Publishing Corp., 1975), 172.

31. Joseph Furphy, *Such Is Life,* ed. Frances Devlin-Glass, Robin Eaden, Lois Hoffman, and G. W. Turner (Melbourne: Oxford University Press, 1991), 75.

32. Ibid., 193.

33. Ibid., 166. For the Warton note, see Gerrard, *Patriot Opposition to Walpole,* 131.

17

The Canon on the Beach

H. T. Kemp Translating *Robinson Crusoe* and *The Pilgrim's Progress*

Mark Houlahan

Who is Henry Tacy Kemp that we should speak of him? What interest does his life hold for students of Pacific voyages and beaches? I'll sketch here some answers to these seldom-posed questions. I will focus on Kemp's biography and demonstrate how his translating meshed with the rest of his life. My essay takes its origin from the typography of exile. New Zealanders who have spent any time overseas will be familiar with the sensation of feeling deprived of any news of home, saving accounts of catastrophes (earthquakes, Rainbow Warriors) here at the edge of the world. One consequence of this is that the godwit's reading eye skips obsessively to any appearance of the letters *N* and *Z* in close proximity. This way, Bill Manhire tells us, he first encountered the term *zoetrope*.[1] Similarly, I know much more than I care to about nuclear mishaps off the coast of Novaya Zemlya. While reading Christopher Hill's stalwart, pithy life of John Bunyan, this exilic eyeskip led me to the discovery that, in the 1850s, the government of New Zealand had commissioned and published translations into Maori of *Robinson Crusoe* and *The Pilgrim's Progress*.[2] It was clear that all Hill knew of these translations was the fact of their existence. Here, I want to display rather more of the Pacific lives of these two canonical texts and their translator.

I have framed Kemp by way of J.G.A. Pocock's recent proposal that the search for bicultural understanding in Aotearoa–New Zealand might usefully begin with the idea that all of this archipelago's inhabitants were originally *tangata waka*—peoples of the canoes—before any of them could have been *tangata whenua*, all peoples who live in New Zealand having traveled here at some time from somewhere else. Such peoples are compelled also by the twin tyrannies of distance and population size to keep voyaging, throughout the Pacific and beyond, for economic and cultural sustenance.[3] Because both *pakeha* and Maori, in Pocock's terms, remain voyaging peoples, they have a legitimate interest in each other's canoes—or the cultures each brought with them here—and the way those cultures have developed since arrival. The process is not simply metaphorical, of course; as Anne Salmond has documented, each of the crucial first European contacts with New Zealand begins with the local canoes paddling out to greet the *waka* hove to offshore, each party curious to see what the other had to offer in the way of material goods.[4] This process began the mingling of the materials of European culture with that of the Maori and, because the naming of parts is ever the first step to language, began also the process by which the texts from which Enlightenment Europe constructed its *mentalités* became known to the Maori. H. T. Kemp's father, James, was thus encouraged to learn three new Maori nouns a day at the Kerikeri Mission, the better to facilitate his conversions;[5] the Maori dictionary Kemp himself compiled contains an extensive "Collection of Useful Nouns," from categories of kinship, listed under the category "Of Parentage," through to "Of Government," "Of Colours," "Of Ships," and "Of Numbers."[6]

To accept the mutuality of these voyaging histories, of course, would mean that the contents of each culture's canoe were equally interesting and equally inspected by the crew of the "other" *waka;* clearly, that has not been the case historically. Since Cook's first voyage, however, there have been Europeans keen not just to offload the European canoe and (to continue the metaphor) thereby to swamp the Maori fleet but enthusiastic also about the reverse task, that of demonstrating the Maori canoe and all it holds to a European audience. Here one thinks of Cook and Banks, of Sir George Grey, and, in our time, Dr. Michael King and Professor Anne Salmond. In this company we might find a small and curious place for Henry Tacy Kemp.

Kemp was, not quite literally, *tangata waka,* his parents having arrived in New Zealand two years before Henry was born. In his teens, he made the return journey to and from England, undergoing on the way the ritual of "crossing the line." "My chin was painted then shaved with a razor . . . I had the best of the fun being the first that was shaved," and thus he became one of Neptune's people, confirming his role as a voyaging subject.[7] On his return to New Zealand, Kemp sailed extensively in coastal waters, from Otago to Northland, and made several long inland treks. This voyaging life serves as an apt background for his translation of two central English fictions of wandering, and these, in turn, confirm his interest in the translation—or moving across—of both physical and metaphysical cargo from one culture to the other. As he saw it, these translations served both cultures, or *waka*s. For if he gave Defoe and Bunyan to the Maori, he gave also Maori grammar and vocabulary to the European.

But Kemp himself was not European—he was a New Zealander, hav-

ing been born in Kerikeri in 1821. This places him in the same category
of Creole that Mary-Louise Pratt has recently described as "a descendant
of European settlers, born and naturalized in those colonies or regions,
and more or less modified in type by the climate and surroundings."[8] In
Pratt's work, these Latin Americans of European descent had a crucial
and crucially ambiguous role to play in what she calls the contact zone,
where "disparate cultures meet, clash, and grapple with each other, often
in highly asymmetrical relations of domination and subordination," in-
terpenetrating each other's ideological and material culture.[9] The Creole
(in New Zealand, the *pakeha*) finds himself figured by the metropolitan
culture as a mimic man. In turn, however, he represents that culture in
the outlying contact zone where he finds himself: hence, Kemp's zealous
beaching of the canon. Moreover, he also translates the outland and its
indigenous peoples to the metropolis, which "ongoingly calls upon the
colony to represent itself to the metropolis, in endless recording and
bureaucratic documentation."[10] Thus, the British Parliamentary papers
record Earl Grey's compliments to Kemp on the accuracy and compre-
hensiveness of his various surveys of Maori tribes.[11] A mimic man's life in
a contact zone, then, would be one way of framing Kemp. Before turning to Kemp's translations, I will fill out that frame with a chronological
sketch of his life.

Kemp was born in Kerikeri, on the North Island of New Zealand, on
18 January 1821.[12] His father, James Kemp, a blacksmith from Norfolk,
came to the Bay of Islands in 1819 as part of Samuel Marsden's mission.
James Kemp was to make and mend ploughshares, as part of the mission's
efforts to be self-sufficient, as well as to demonstrate by "example and instruction the advantages of civilisation."[13] James Kemp was not confined,
however, to advancing the purely material benefits of Christian civilization. He also took part in the Mission's evangelical effort. He had been
educated at Wymondham Grammar in Norfolk, and had received instruction on the Bible from Henry Tacy, the curate of Wymondham, after
whom the Kemps named their first son.[14] Henry never "took the cloth" of
his namesake, but we could certainly think of his translations of the pil-
grims Crusoe and Christian into Maori as an extension of the evangelical
impulse that brought his parents to New Zealand in the first place. A
sample from the practice dialogue "Of Education" in Kemp's dictionary
makes it clear that he was aware of this connection:

> Are you a Christian?
> Who taught you to read?
> *The White people.*

Is this your writing?
It is.
Do you understand the Scriptures?
Some portions only.[15]

James Kemp taught at the Mission school established in Kerikeri. Instruction was in Maori until 1842, when the influx of Europeans made it imperative to teach the Maori in English as well.[16] Kemp received his first lessons at this school, so he grew up functionally bilingual; this determined his later choice of career. In 1834, he sailed to England, where he attended the Pottersgate Academy in Norwich. He wrote a journal onboard ship; though he was only thirteen at the time, it clearly shows the beginnings of what Pratt calls "the dynamics of creole self-fashioning."[17] Kemp calls himself a native of New Zealand, using the term with latinate accuracy, to indicate his place of birth. More interestingly, he refers to it as "home" and wrote to his brother on 8 December 1835 that "I would much sooner be there [i.e., in New Zealand] than here [England]."[18] His wish was soon granted: A plan for him to train as a surgeon did not come to pass, and he returned to New Zealand in 1838. On arrival, he helped his father run the Mission Store in Kerikeri—by then housed in the Stone Store, the oldest stone building in New Zealand, and of which his father eventually became the proprietor. Kemp himself was not one for shopkeeping. Instead, he entered government service as an interpreter, and was gazetted an Officer of the Government on 6 February 1840. One of his first duties was the preparation of a full translation (later sent to London) of the Treaty of Waitangi, signed on that day.[19]

On 24 October 1842, Kemp became Protector of Aborigines for the northern province of New Ulster, graduating in 1846 to Private Secretary and then, in 1847, becoming Native Secretary and Interpreter.[20] The Department of the Protector of Aborigines was superseded in 1846 by the Office of Native Secretary. Both offices were early incarnations of what is now the Maori Affairs Department, with a wide brief to superintend the "general welfare, education [and] health" of the Maori, hence, its brief covered Kemp's translating activities.[21] All these, however, were background to the Department's main activity, up until 1862, which was the purchase of Maori land on behalf of the Crown. Kemp traveled widely as Native Secretary, writing reports on the condition of the Maori and their willingness to sell their land. He made purchases in the North, in Auckland, and in the Wairarapa. Most notoriously he purchased the bulk of the South Island—some twenty million acres—from the Ngai Tahu for £2,000, to be paid in four yearly payments of £500 per annum.[22] All these purchases involved Kemp both as negotiator and translator: The deed of sale was drawn up in Maori, and then Kemp would make his own translation of the deed. The Ngai Tahu deed still bears his name. Thus he translated—moved across—from Maori into English—while translating, or moving across—the land itself into European hands. His bureaucratic activities functioned as the material equivalent of his translations, which move European texts into Maori, the better to include the Maori in "a new nation" constructed along European lines, "in the sunny Isles of New Zealand."[23]

Kemp continued purchasing and translating until 1865, when the Land Purchase Department ceased to exist. Kemp was not relocated in a different government position, and later claimed that Walter Mantell, then Secretary for Native Affairs, had blocked further appointments because of a twenty-year-old scandal involving Mantell's relations with "native women." On this matter, Kemp accused Mantell of being a "cowardly and jesuitical liar." In 1870, he became Civil Commissioner for Auckland, a position he held until 1880. He considered that this forty years of service entitled him to a government pension as "the oldest surviving officer of the New Zealand Government," but his repeated requests were denied, on the technicality that he had worked both for the Province of Auckland and the Central Government: The two periods of employment could not be counted together. Kemp tried to rally Sir George Grey, his former patron, to the cause, and petitioned Parliament itself, but no pension was forthcoming.[24]

He lived until October of 1901, when he died of pneumonia in Onehunga. Until his final illness, he led an active and energetic life. His great-granddaughter recalls that "he was a great walker" and "when visiting my Gran at Devonport" always walked both ways—about ten miles in each direction. In the 1890s, he was also something of a dandy: "He always wore a cape and a 'bell topper' hat and a 'walking stick' so that people often asked who the French Count was."[25]

Few of these bystanders would have known that this "French Count" was the translator of *Robinson Crusoe* and *Pilgrim's Progress;* but, as we shall see, in the last year of his life, Kemp made elaborate plans to remind the nation of this fact and so to restake his modest claim to fame. In 1901, he published a memoir, first in the *New Zealand Herald,* the proprietors of which, Wilson and Horton, subsequently published as a small book, the *Revised Narrative of Incidents and Events in the Early Colonizing History of New Zealand.* In the *Narrative* Kemp recalls publishing his Defoe and his Bunyan in 1848, but here his memory misled him, and his error has misled, in turn, the Kemp family historian, as well as the *Encyclopedia of New Zealand.*[26] The first mention of this translating project comes in a letter from

Kemp dated 11 November 1851. He reports that the translation of *Crusoe* has begun and already "some considerable progress made" and requests a grant sufficient to publish one thousand copies of the book, "as it seems a Work likely to be interesting to the Natives."[27] Kemp's preface to the translation adds that the "Narrative . . . so entirely accords with the manner in which events of any importance have been related by the New Zealanders" that he trusts they will find it comprehensible and useful, as well as interesting.[28] Governor Grey endorsed Kemp's hope. When he dispatched copies of Kemp's *Crusoe* to London in June 1852, he advised Earl Grey that "by opening to the native population such instructive sources of literature, the Government will, in a very material and excellent manner, add fresh stimulus to the rapid advances the natives continue to make in the arts of civilized life."[29] He comments also that sales of *Crusoe* were expected to return a profit to the government.

Kemp's request for one thousand copies was approved, and the translation was printed in April 1852, by the press of the *Independent,* one of the two newspapers then operating in Wellington; the government did not set up its own press until 1865, so before then, all such work was contracted out.[30] In 1852, the government was also letting tenders for the publication of its Maori newspaper, *The Maori Messenger,* with a planned print run per issue of six hundred copies. A tender of £8 per issue was accepted. Throughout the 1850s, Kemp was also engaged with this Maori publication. Many of his dispatches deal with the details of such a venture, from suggestions for items to be covered through to requisitions for paper and ink.[31] *The Messenger* was only a small pamphlet, a single quarto sheet; Kemp's *Crusoe* is 170 pages—more than twenty sheets. No records of the amount paid for publication remain, but assuming similar printing costs of 3p. per sheet, somewhere around £250 seems right.

In his *Crusoe* dispatch to Earl Grey (15 June 1852), Governor Grey mentions that Kemp had already begun work on his Bunyan, which he hoped to publish in about three months, that is, in September 1852. Kemp's *Pilgrim's Progress* did not appear until March 1854; the *Independent* was again the commissioned printer. Despite the delay, his proceeding with the second and larger volume suggests Grey's continuing confidence both in the ideological efficacy of introducing the Maori to such texts and in the financial viability of both endeavors. In 1856, a "Board . . . appointed . . . to Enquire into and Report upon the State of Native Affairs" found *The Messenger* a "valuable instrument," the numbers of each run of which "might be increased with advantage," thus conferring the House of Representatives' seal of approval on these attempts to transform the Maori into a people of the book.[32]

Whether such fiscal or cultural objectives were achieved is a more difficult question. There are no records of actual sales of either volume, and the copies that have survived in public record, in the Hocken, the Turnbull, and the Auckland Public Libraries, seem originally to have been purchased by Europeans as items of New Zealandiana rather than by Maori, who were Kemp and Grey's target market. Current estimates put the population of the Maori at between seventy and ninety thousand in the 1840s; so a complete sale would have made *Crusoe* available to one Maori in every seventy.[33] Governor Grey reported that the *Crusoe* had been received "with great avidity by the native population."[34] If so, this might be attributable to the claimed similarity between Defoe's narrative and Maori narrative. Gilbert Mair told Alexander Turnbull that it was written "in the finest Maori ever printed," a strange claim to make of a work translated into rather than conceived in the Maori language.[35] This does not mean, of course, that the translation was widely read by the Maori; though there is evidence to suggest some Maori did know of Robinson Crusoe. Johannes Andersen remembers that A. F. O'Donnell had read *Crusoe* to "an old Maori, who listened attentively, and at a pause in the reading said with great conviction, 'That is no tale; that happened.'"[36] Ashley Gould, a historian in the Crown Law Office, remembers a story from the Manawatu, of a *rangatira* reluctant to part with lands at the headwaters of the Manawatu River. These, he said, were for Crusoe when he came. Both stories suggest the continuance of oracy as primary over the written record. In 1940, Sir Apirana Ngata remembered that in his childhood, "for every one who owned a copy of the Scriptures and Church Liturgy . . . there were still fifty or more content to listen to and memorize the words which were read out of printed books."[37] One reader in fifty is close enough to the one book per seventy Maori Kemp's original print run allowed for; writing *Crusoe* down may simply have enabled more people to be told the story. Kemp's project thus might not have enhanced the literacy of the Maori, but the reactions O'Donnell and Gould recollect imply, as Kemp and Grey had hoped, a comprehension of the story, even if these Maori witnesses did not make a *pakeha* distinction between fictive and factual narratives. *Crusoe*'s ideological impact would, of course, survive its conversion from textual into oral narrative.

I have found no reader responses to Kemp's *Pilgrim's Progress,* of which Andersen claimed that Maori appreciated the story at first but "lost interest in it when they learned it was no more than an allegory."[38] Andersen's dismissal of Bunyan may have more to do with his own lack of interest in allegorical modes of storytelling. Other missionaries translated portions of Bunyan for their Maori converts;[39] and the work is much closer than the *Crusoe* to the catechetical and biblical material that, in the 1830s, were the first texts printed in New Zealand for the Maori.[40] So if,

like the *Crusoe,* Kemp's *Progress* found Maori readers and/or listeners, then its rhetoric and imagery would have merged with those biblical texts that, as Donald McKenzie remarks, had "a profound effect on Maori consciousness, providing a new source of imagery in song and story and sharpening the expression of economic and political pressures on Government."[41] Through their exposure to Christian iconography and story, the Maori were translated into being a people of the Christian word as well as being a people of the Christian book. The prophet Rua Kenana, for example, even built in the vastness of the Urewera a version of the New Jerusalem that Christian and his family sought in the wilderness of this world.[42]

The 1854 *Pilgrim's Progress* was the last of Kemp's translations into Maori. Later, he published four editions of his *First Step to Maori Conversation,* pursuing the reverse task of the Pakeha Maori, that of explaining and representing the Maori to the Colonists, so that both races could operate in a European national economy.[43] His conversations tell us how to shop, for example—"I am going to Auckland. For what? To buy goods"— as well as constructing in "Dialogue 12: A departure," in another instance of Creole self-fashioning, the character of a protoliberal, *pakeha* adherent to the Treaty of Waitangi, as well as a participant in a market economy:

> They are the Queen's subjects
> They obey her Laws
> I shall promote their Welfare
> You must forsake Native Customs
> That you may be respected. And become rich.[44]

This fourth edition of his phrase book was followed twenty years later by a small flurry of publication in the last year of Kemp's life, as his memory returned to the days of his youth. His memoir recalls the great days of the colony's past and serves also to bring to the attention of his readers his own role in that past, notably his presence both at the signing of the Treaty and on board the ship when Te Rauparaha was taken captive. He also reminded the public of his activities as a translator, amending the dearth of "light literature" available to the Maori.[45] He was convinced there was still a market for these texts, and he tried to organize subscriptions to finance a new edition of both his Bunyan and his Defoe. He wrote to Thomas Hocken in Dunedin, soliciting his assistance. They had communicated before, in the early 1890s, when Hocken had enlisted Kemp's aid in searching for rare editions of early New Zealand newspapers. Kemp offered Hocken copies of his autobiography in return for the loan of copies of the first editions of his translations. It seems that Kemp had

given away all his spare copies to "European & Maori" friends, and
needed Hocken's copy to mark up in preparation for his revised editions.[46] Hocken somewhat ungraciously refused to lend his copies, and
this second edition was never published, but the Grey Collection in the
Auckland Public Library has copies of both *Robinson Crusoe* and *Pilgrim's
Progress*, with revisions in Kemp's handwriting, dated 1901; probably these
are copies borrowed from Turnbull's private collection, now on permanent informal loan to Auckland's Grey Collection.[47] In both texts, Kemp
has altered slightly his translation, adding phrases here and there and
also changing the title page and prefatory material significantly. The
dates have been changed from 1852 and 1854 to September 1901—just a
month before Kemp died. The first editions simply claimed to have been
translated "under the direction of the Government." In this last year of
his life, Kemp wanted to reaffirm his role as translator. The revised title
page of both deletes "under direction of the Government," substituting
instead "by H. T. Kemp" or "H.T.K. J.P." The publisher was to be Wilson
and Horton—who had already printed his revised narrative. Kemp asserted his authority over this revised edition: "All rights reserved," presumably to himself and his heirs. Kemp also changed the dedication of
his *Pilgrim's Progress*. Initially, he had acknowledged Zachariah Kiharoa "a
Christian Teacher and an Excellent Man," a Ngatiraukawa chief and convert who died in 1852.[48] This was to be deleted and replaced by an in-
scription "in loving memory of Her Late Majesty Victoria, Queen of the
United Kingdom Died 1901."

Below the dedication to Kiharoa, the original dedication also acknowledged the patronage of Sir George Grey, under whose command
the translation had been first prepared. This was to be entirely deleted.
Initially, I thought this must have been because Kemp was bitter at Grey's
lack of support for Kemp's pension claims, but the tone of the new dedication suggests more predictably that loyalty to his former commander in
chief was supplanted by the lugubrious demands of late-Victorian elegy
for the recently deceased queen and empress. Kemp seems finally to have
been affirming the tenor of his model dialogue "The Departure": that he
too was one of the queen's subjects and obeyed her laws; though familiar
with native customs, he had, as expected, forsaken them and followed European customs instead, and he had thereby become respected, though
not rich. That dialogue ends with a fitting conclusion to this summary of
Kemp's final, unpublished writings:

> I have nothing more to say.
> This is the end of this Book.
> It is finished.[49]

But there is more to be said about Kemp. In 1988, both the translations were republished in Palmerston North, in a photocopied facsimile edition in plastic binding, "to allow," the publisher says, "John Bunyan to recount his dream again in the *"taonga"* of the *"tangata whenua."* Meanwhile, Kemp's contributions to that *taonga* have come under attack. In the second edition of the *Oxford History of New Zealand,* Ann Parsonson claims that Kemp's translation of the Ngai Tahu deed was mischievously inaccurate;[50] recent claims have been lodged with the Waitangi Tribunal asserting that Kemp's Maori was simply wrong.[51] There will never be many Kempologists, I suspect, but Kemp's literal and fictive voyages along our beaches hold enough interest still to ensure that though his own books are indeed finished, his rest will not quite be silence.

NOTES

Research for this paper was conducted in He Kohikohinga No Aotearoa (the New Zealand Collection of the University of Waikato Library); the Grey Collection of the Auckland Public Library; the Alexander Turnbull Library; and the National Archives of New Zealand. Thanks to the informed and tireless helpfulness of the staffs at all these institutions; thanks also to Jane Wild for her enthusiastic support. Dr. Candler S. Rogers, the University of Otago's "Kempologist," graciously supplied information I should otherwise have missed.

1. See Bill Manhire's *Zoetropes: Poems, 1972–1983* (Wellington, N.Z.: Allen and Unwin); see also Debra Daley's *The Strange Letter Z* (Auckland: Penguin, 1995), where the two main characters, Nerida and Alexis, are expatriate New Zealand linguists obsessed with the letter Z.
2. Christopher Hill, *A Tinker and a Poor Man: John Bunyan and His Church, 1628– 1688* (New York: Knopf, 1989), 376–378.
3. J.G.A. Pocock, "Deconstructing Europe," *London Review of Books,* 19 December 1991, 6–10; "Tangata Whenua and Enlightenment Anthropology," *New Zealand Journal of History* 26 (1992): 28–53.
4. Anne Salmond, *Two Worlds: First Meetings Between Maori and Europeans, 1642– 1772* (Auckland: Viking, 1991).
5. "Three fresh words every day will soon furnish you with a great part of their names of things." Henry Tacy to James Kemp, 13 March 1822, cited in Joan Wilma Kemp, *The Kemp Family—A History* (1989), 49. Despite this nominalist zeal, James Kemp never acquired the fluency his son achieved; for his rel-

ative failure, see Nola Easdale, *Missionary and Maori: Kerikeri, 1819–1860* (Lincoln: Te Waihora Press, 1991), 119–120.

6. H. T. Kemp, *The First Step to Maori Conversation, Being a Collection of Some of the Most Useful Nouns, Adjectives, and Verbs, With a Series of Useful Phrases, and Elementary Sentences, Alphabetically Arranged, in Two Parts (Intended for the Use of the Colonists)* (Wellington: 1868), 5, 18.

7. Henry Tacy Kemp, "Kemp's Buffalo Journal," Friday, 10 October 1834, fol. 5, *Kemp Family Papers, 1736–1981,* Auckland Institute and Museum, MS 1212.

8. *OED* "creole": s.v. Aa. The term, of course, originates in South America, but the sense given here fits perfectly the condition of being a *pakeha* New Zealander, past and present. Giselle Byrne tells me that, in the 1890s, the term was used in this way by *pakeha* New Zealanders.

9. Mary-Louise Pratt, *Imperial Eyes: Travel Writing and Transculturation* (London: Routledge, 1992), 4.

10. Ibid., 175.

11. "The able manner in which the Report has been prepared reflects credit on Mr. Kemp, and I have to request you will convey to that gentleman the sense which I entertain of the value of the information contained in it." Dispatch from Earl Grey to Governor Sir George Grey, 1 February 1851, *British Parliamentary Papers Colonies New Zealand 7 (1851)* (Shannon: Irish University Press, 1969), 190. Parliamentary papers hereinafter cited as *BPPNZ*.

12. J. Kemp, *The Kemp Family,* 75.

13. Easdale, *Missionary and Maori,* 26.

14. J. Kemp, *The Kemp Family,* 76.

15. H. T. Kemp, *First Step,* 45.

16. Easdale, *Missionary and Maori,* 88.

17. Pratt, *Imperial Eyes,* 5.

18. H. T. Kemp, "Buffalo Journal" 29 and 30 September 1834; letter 8 December 1835, Auckland Institute and Museum MS 1212, fol. 5.

19. Kemp to Hocken, 8 July 1892, Dr. Hocken's Correspondence, Hocken Library MS 451/A.

20. *New Zealand Government Gazette,* 2 November 1842, 309; 7 May 1846, 28; 3 September 1847, 2.

21. "Maori Affairs Department History," typescript, National Archives of New Zealand, 5.

22. *BPPNZ* 8:231, 292.

23. Henry Tacy Kemp, *Revised Narrative of Incidents & Events in the Colonizing History of New Zealand, From 1840 to 1880* (Auckland: Wilson and Horton, 1901), 15.

24. Kemp's exculpatory account of these events may be found in *Papers Relative to H. T. Kemp and the Termination of His Services with the New Zealand Government,* GNZ MS 201, Auckland Public Library.

25. As Ellice Bush, Kemp's great-granddaughter recalled, Auckland Institute and Museum MS 1212, fol. 5.

26. H. T. Kemp, *Revised Narrative*, 7.

27. H. T. Kemp, 11 November 1851, National Archives of New Zealand, NM 8 51/1534.

28. H. T. Kemp, *The Life and Adventures of Robinson Crusoe, By Daniel Defoe. Translated into the New Zealand Language Under the Direction of the Government* (Wellington: n.p., 1852).

29. *BPPNZ* 9:110–111.

30. Kathleen Coleridge, "Thriving on Impressions: The Pioneer Years of Wellington Printing," in *The Making of Wellington, 1800–1914,* eds. David Hamer and Roberta Nicholls (Wellington: Victoria University Press, 1990), 99, 105.

31. National Archives of New Zealand IA 52/968a, 52/1080, 52/2950, 54/2354, 54/3371, 54/3723, 54/3836, 54/4199.

32. Report C, *Votes and Proceedings of the House of Representatives Session IV, 1856* I:appendix 4.

33. Ann Parsonson, "The Challenge to Mana Maori," in *The Oxford History of New Zealand,* ed. Geoffrey W. Rice, 2d ed. (Auckland: Oxford University Press, 1992), 169.

34. *BPPNZ* 9:110.

35. Turnbull, 21 February 1900, *Letters of A. H. Turnbull,* vol. 4, Alexander Turnbull Library, 401.

36. Johannes Andersen, in *A History of Printing in New Zealand, 1830–1940,* ed. R. A. McKay (Wellington: Richard Alexander McKay, 1940), 35.

37. Sir Apirana Ngata, "The Maori and Printed Matter," in McKay, *History of Printing in New Zealand,* 49.

38. Andersen, *A History of Printing in New Zealand,* 36.

39. Eliza White, for example, records "turning Pilgrim's Progress into Native," which she would not "dignify . . . with the Name of translation"; Eliza White "Journal 8," St. John's College, Auckland, 32. I am indebted to S. J. Goldsbury for supplying this reference. Clearly, White lacked Kemp's supreme confidence in his bilingual fluency.

40. New Zealand missionaries were not alone, of course, in thinking Bunyan might be efficacious reading for Pacific Islanders, for, as Niel Gunson reports in his *Messengers of Grace: Evangelical Missionaries in the South Seas, 1797–1860* (Melbourne: Oxford University Press, 1978), 193: "*Pilgrim's Progress* was translated into most Pacific languages." Gunson reports also that, like the Maori, other Pacific Islanders had difficulty in grasping the force of Bunyan's allegorization of the Bible.

41. D. F. McKenzie, *Oral Culture, Literacy and Print in Early New Zealand: The Treaty of Waitangi* (Wellington: Victoria University Press, 1985), 13. For a profound investigation of how that Christian imagery and rhetoric could be deployed

on behalf of Maori activism, see Judith Binney's *Redemption Songs: A Life of Te Kooti Arikirangi Te Turuki* (Auckland: Auckland University Press, Bridget Williams Books, 1995).

42. Judith Binney, Gilllian Chaplin, and Craig Wallace, *Mihaia: The Prophet Rua Kenana and his Community at Maungapohatu* (Wellington: Oxford University Press, 1979).

43. Kemp proudly described himself on the title page of the fourth edition (1876) of his *First Step to Maori Conversation*.

44. H. T. Kemp, *First Step*, 48–49.

45. H. T. Kemp, *Revised Narrative*, 11.

46. Kemp to Hocken, 1 May, 28 May, 21 June 1901, Dr. Hocken's Correspondence, MS 451, Hocken Library.

47. In his letter to Hocken of 21 June 1901, Kemp mentions the possibility of acquiring copies from Turnbull for his revising purposes. The marked copies are listed (though by no means described in bibliographic detail) in the *Auckland Public Library Catalogue of Printed Maori Literatures Contained in the Central Library, 1815–1900,* GNZM 243, 246.

48. Barbara Swabey and Helen Dempsey, "The Historic Graves of Rangiatea," *Historical Journal* (Otaki Historical Society) 2 (1979): 33–34.

49. H. T. Kemp, *First Step*, 48.

50. Parsonson, "The Challenge to Mana Maori," 179–180.

51. See Margaret Mutu's "Tuku Whenua and Land Sale in New Zealand in the Nineteenth Century," this volume.

18

Tuku Whenua and Land Sale in New Zealand in the Nineteenth Century

Margaret Mutu

For more than 150 years, the various tribes within Maoridom have been directing the Crown to return their lands (and other resources) to them. The primary authority on which such directions are issued is the Treaty of Waitangi. For a large number of cases, the Crown has been unable to defend the manner in which it acquired various lands and resources. In acknowledging that they were taken in violation of the Treaty, the Crown has agreed that they must be returned.[1] There are, however, many other instances where the tribes have directed that land be returned, and the Crown has, until very recently, refused to give any serious consideration to the matter. Included among these are the instances where very large areas of land in the Far North of the country and elsewhere were involved, and where tribes gave over the use of the land, either to individual Europeans before the Treaty was signed or to the Crown after it was signed. The Crown has claimed that when these lands were acquired, Maori lost all rights to them. The Muriwhenua tribes[2] of the Far North in particular have expressed strong disagreement with this assumption.

The Crown has claimed that the transactions carried out were "land sales." The tribes of Muriwhenua say they were *"tuku whenua."* The former is a concept belonging to the English culture, which extinguishes the seller's rights in the land. The latter is a concept belonging to Maori culture, which does not extinguish a tribe's rights in their lands.

In this article, I will discuss the land transactions that were conducted between Maori and European individuals prior to the signing of the Treaty of Waitangi and those conducted between Maori and the British Crown between 1840 and 1865 (when the Native Land Court was established). In doing so, I will describe the custom of *tuku whenua* as it was (and still is) practiced in Muriwhenua and elsewhere in the country. This section draws mainly on the oral history and traditions of the tribes of Muriwhenua as they have been handed down through the generations. I will also mention an almost identical custom that exists in other Polynesian cultures to demonstrate that the custom most certainly preceded the arrival of Maori in this country and is therefore probably well over a thousand years old.

I will then move on to consider the documentation that accompanied some of these transactions. The documents are commonly known as "land deeds" or "Crown Purchase deeds." I have taken into consideration only documents that Maori would have been able to understand, that is, those written in Maori.[3] I have examined these to ascertain the intent conveyed in them and to determine if and how that intent differs from the information recorded in the oral traditions of Muriwhenua. The conclusion I draw is that the transactions being carried out were, in fact, *tuku whenua*. Even though it is quite clear that these documents were written by Englishmen rather than Maori, I found nothing in them that is inconsistent with the oral traditions.

I then go on to consider the translations of these documents. For the pre-Treaty transactions, these were provided to the Land Claims Commissions in 1843 and 1856. For the Crown Purchases, they were drawn up at the same time as the deeds. I note that these translations contain many quite specific inaccuracies, omissions, additions, and mistranslations. As a result, the translations do not convey the same meaning as the original Maori documents. The problem, however, is that the Crown, through its land commissioners, courts, and commissions of inquiry, which have been held since 1840, has taken into consideration only documents written in English, including these inaccurate translations. The Crown has relied heavily on these documents in reaching its conclusion that the transactions were "land sales."

Tuku Whenua and the Oral Traditions

The oral traditions of Muriwhenua record that before the Treaty of Waitangi was signed, tribal lands were willingly given over under the custom of *tuku whenua* for the use of Europeans, the missionaries in particular, but on the clear understanding that such a transaction was carried out primarily to benefit the tribe and to bind the European and his descendants into the tribe's structures. There was also a clear understanding that when these Europeans and their descendants no longer needed to use the land, it would return to the tribe. There was nothing in the discussions leading to the transactions that gave the Europeans the right to sell the land, for the simple reason that the notion of selling land did not exist in Maori culture at the time. The land was given only for the use of a particular European and his descendants. The *mana whenua* (that is, very approximately,[4] the spiritual power and authority for the lands vested by the gods in a tribe, in particular, in its chief) remained always with the tribe.[5]

The fact that the tribes decided to enter into such an arrangement arose from their experiences of Europeans over several years. They had decided that their people could benefit from the knowledge, skills, and goods that Europeans could offer, and that this would greatly enhance the quality of life they already enjoyed. To incorporate these benefits into the community, however, the European would need to have the support and protection of the tribal leaders. Tribal leaders thus sought to bring individual Europeans and their families within the tribal structure, applying the custom of *tuku whenua* to those whom they chose to have living in their midst.

Under the custom of *tuku whenua*, tribal leaders who held the *mana whenua* for the tribe could allocate lands for a particular individual and his family for them to live on and use. Provided no offense was committed, which violated the terms agreed to in discussions accompanying the allocation, the family to whom the land had been allocated could remain undisturbed on the land, under the *mana* of the allocating chief, often for several generations. Should the outsider have chosen to move off the land, then rights to reallocate the land reverted to the tribe. It was common practice for a *tuku whenua* to be marked in some way, such as the passing over of a *mana tunga* (for example, a cloak, or *mere*) or composition of a *waiata* (song, chant) or *whakataukii* (proverbial saying). Such items were termed *tohu*, signs or symbols of the transaction. They symbolized not only the transaction but also the binding of the two parties in a long-term agreement. Ultimately, maybe several generations later, both the *tohu* and the land would be returned to its original owners. At no stage was the *mana whenua* of the allocating chief threatened.[6]

After the Treaty of Waitangi was signed, the nature of the land transactions changed in one essential respect. They were still *tuku whenua,* but the agreements being entered into by the tribes were no longer with individual Europeans. The tribes were now dealing with the Queen of England, the highest chief of all English chiefs, and hence, also the paramount chief of all the incoming English settlers.

Given her status in English society, and thereby the qualities of honor and integrity that she must possess, the Queen of England was a person with whom the chiefs could form very prestigious alliances. Alliances between tribes often involved land allocations, or *tuku whenua.*[7] There would have been no reason to have any misgivings about entrusting a person of such high rank with lands for her subjects for as long as she and her descendants were the kings and queens of England. After all, this was a person who would help ensure that the *mana* of both parties to an alliance was acknowledged and upheld and also that mutual on-going benefits would accrue to both parties. To fail to do so was almost unthinkable in Maori terms because of the disastrous effects that could have not only on the Queen's *mana* and her status as a *rangatira* (chief) but also on that of her descendants.

When lands were allocated as part of an intertribal alliance, responsibility for the incoming tribe was (and still is) left in the hands of the *rangatira* of that tribe. They would ensure that the members of the incoming tribe did not offend their hosts in any way, and that the resources they had been allocated were properly looked after and respected. In this practical way, the *mana* both of the incoming tribe and its *rangatira* was recognized within the territory of another tribe. Free communication between the tribes was expected through trading, marriage, and so on. Individual marriages, particularly between *rangatira* families, would help seal the alliance. Should any disputes arise in the incoming tribe, then responsibility for resolving them lay with the *rangatira* of that tribe, which with Queen Victoria was either herself, her governors as her immediate representatives, or, on matters of lesser moment, Crown agents as her servants. Throughout, there was always the clear understanding that the *mana whenua* of the host tribe remained intact and was always acknowledged.

Tuku Whenua Elsewhere in the Pacific

Evidence that the custom of *tuku whenua* is very old, established long before Maori came to Aotearoa, can be found throughout the Pacific.[8] Rasmussen reported an almost identical custom called *soʻo henua* for Tongareva in the Cook Island group.[9] Colleagues from elsewhere in the Pacific assure me that the same or similar systems apply throughout the Pacific. References to such systems can be found in the literature for Samoa, Tonga, Tahiti, Hawaiʻi, Fiji, and New Caledonia.[10] Rarotongans have frequently commented to me that when they saw what happened to the Maori of Aotearoa as a result of English "land sales" and the Maori Land Court, they were determined not to have the same thing happen to them. Thus, no land can be bought or sold in Rarotonga.

Tuku Whenua in the Literature

Until very recently, the published works of anthropologists and historians who have studied various facets of Maoridom, including land tenure systems, have had very little to say about the custom known in Muriwhenua as *tuku whenua*.[11] Then in 1991, Philippa Wyatt completed a thesis entitled "The Old Land Claims and the Concept of 'Sale': A Case Study," in which she described the custom of *tuku whenua* as it was practiced in the Bay of Islands, an area to the south of Muriwhenua.[12] Her description is derived in the main from the writings of early English settlers and observers, particularly missionaries and traders, and is remarkably close to the Muriwhenua understanding of the custom. Wyatt was then commissioned to carry out similarly detailed historical research for the Muriwhenua area, and she produced almost identical results there as well.[13] Dame Joan Metge also produced a detailed anthropological analysis of the custom in her paper entitled "Cross Cultural Communication and Land Transfer in Western Muriwhenua, 1832–1840."[14] In her work, she clearly demonstrates the misunderstandings and inherent difficulties that would have been experienced both by Maori and Europeans approaching a land transaction from two totally different cultural perspectives in the early and mid-nineteenth century.

Documents that Accompanied Early Land Transactions and Crown Purchases

Although the oral traditions of Muriwhenua are very clear about what was being negotiated and agreed to between the tribes and European individuals or the Crown, it became apparent to the tribes some time in the latter part of the nineteenth century that what they had agreed and what Europeans and the Crown were saying they had agreed were two very different things. Under the interpretation espoused by the Crown (which was the same as the European individuals), the tribes of Muriwhenua had given up their *mana whenua* over 75 percent of their lands, including all the economically productive areas, by the 1860s.

For the tribes, this was simply not possible. At one stage, when the tribes were starting to suspect all was not well, they questioned the chief Panakareao, who had played a major role in facilitating the early transactions. He was asked quite specifically about the impacts of these transactions on the *mana whenua*. His famous response was, "Horekau au i hoko i te whenua. I tukua e au i runga i te aroha, taku tuaraa ki Te Reinga" (I did not trade the land [i.e., treat it like a commodity]. I released or allocated it out of a sense of compassion, with my back to Te Reinga). This same chief, speaking before he signed the Treaty of Waitangi at Kaitaia, referred to the fact that the Treaty confirmed that it was the "shadow" of the land that would be transferred to the Queen, but that the substance, or in his words, "ko te tinana, ko te ihi, ko te mana i roto i te whenua," (the body, the essence and the power and authority derived from the gods in the land), would remain with the Maori people. He later reversed this saying when he realized that the Crown was reneging on its agreement;[15] the Crown was insisting that the tribes had effectively severed all their ties to the land when they signed the land deeds.[16]

For the tribes, the essence of the agreement was spelled out orally, and for them it was this oral agreement that was binding on the parties. For the English, it appeared that the written document was more binding. It is only in the past few years, in an attempt to persuade the Crown to look to its honor, that the tribes have started to delve into the written records of the English. Among the mountains of documents generated by these transactions are a relatively few key documents written in Maori. Included among these are many of the land deeds.

An examination of the deeds written in Maori (which are the documents Maori would have been able to understand) tells a quite different story from what the Crown had been (and still is) telling. In my papers "Cultural Misunderstanding or Deliberate Mistranslation?" and "Muriwhenua-Crown Alliances," I present very detailed descriptions and linguistic analyses of the forty-six surviving documents written in Maori that have been accepted by the Crown as being the official record of each of the transactions to which they relate. Eighteen of the documents record pre-Treaty transactions, and of these, fourteen are of almost identical format. The majority (fourteen) involve missionaries or people closely connected to the Church Missionary Society, while the chief Panakareao appears on the documents as being involved in fifteen of the eighteen transactions. It is not straightforward to calculate the amount of land involved in these transactions, because no surveys were carried out until many years after the transactions; it ended up being on the order of 49,000 acres.[17]

Of the twenty-eight posttreaty transactions, that is, Crown Purchases, all except the first five were drawn up following one of the three "standard" formats. All but two of these name H. T. Kemp as Queen Victoria's representative, and the resident magistrate W. B. White is witness to seventeen of the purchases and negotiator of seven. Although in the four earliest documents the arrangements are being made between a named chief and the queen's agent, each of the subsequent documents (except for two) refer to a tribe. Some 280,000 acres were involved in these transactions.[18]

The linguistic analysis of these documents highlights several interesting facts about the transactions. Almost all of the documents are written in the first person, using such phrases as "kua oti nei te tuku e matou"[19] (we have allocated this land) or "kua tino whakaae pu matou kua tino tukua tenei pihi whenua"[20] (we have truly agreed indeed that this piece of land be truly allocated), implying that Maori had written the documents. Yet it is clear that it was the English rather than Maori who were writing the documents. This conclusion is drawn initially from the fact that the language of all the documents, although quite comprehensible, is surprisingly clumsy. It is confirmed by the fact that sentences are unnaturally long and complicated (as are the sentences of English legal documents), there are clear grammatical errors, and there are several nonce loans from English unknown to Muriwhenua speakers today.

Another interesting point is that in only two of the documents is the Englishman involved referred to by his English name. In all the others, both pre-Treaty and Crown Purchase, the Englishmen concerned are referred by the names given to them by Maori. For Maori at least, this is a clear indication that these people accepted that the process they were involved in was a Maori process, and they were given Maori names as part of the process of fitting in with the Maori custom. This would have arisen, at the very least, as a natural consequence of the fact that the negotiations accompanying the transaction would have been conducted entirely in Maori. It is most unlikely, however, that Muriwhenua tribes would have conducted these transactions with people who were virtual strangers, and each of the Englishmen probably had his Maori name for some time before the documents were drawn up.

Then, in the Crown Purchase deeds, some phrases are so contrived that they have become nonsense. The most blatant example of this is the phrase "He pukapuka tino hoko tino hoatu tino tuku whakaoti," which is an attempt to translate the English phrase "a full and final sale conveyance and surrender." Its literal translation is something like "a truly bartering, truly giving, truly allocating forever document." The comments of present-day Muriwhenua and other Maori speakers upon hearing this phrase provide a good indication of native speaker reaction. They were quite clear that Maori is never spoken like this and never has been. They were also of the clear opinion that whoever wrote the phrase had a very poor grasp of the Maori language.[21]

In the pre-Treaty documents, interesting additions are made to the standard format of the documents as time moves on. Initially, the land was allocated for an individual forever. In 1839, the documents began to include the individual and his children. Then it moves to including "his descendants after him." The documents all specify, however, that the land is for these people, and these people only, for as long as they like. The naturally assumed implication (of the tribes) is that when these people no longer needed the land, it would revert to the tribe.

There is clear historical evidence[22] that by 1839 the English understood that the transactions they had entered into were not the same as

English land sales. Changes to the documents such as the ones given above demonstrate attempts to make them resemble something closer to the English custom. In the Maori, however, the documents all still clearly convey the transaction as a customary *tuku whenua*.

All except two of the forty-six documents refer to the transaction being carried out as a *tuku*. The word *tuku* translates as "let, allow, send, allocate, present, give freely" and so on, depending, naturally, on the context. In the context of land, it has the meaning I described at the beginning of this article (for *tuku whenua*) and can be translated approximately as "allocate."

The other two documents refer to the transaction as *hoko*. The present-day translation of *hoko* is "trade, buy, sell." But in the 1840s and 1850s, it did not carry the meanings of "buy" and "sell." Tregear in his 1891 dictionary reports "buy, sell" as modern meanings of *hoko*, while Williams' 1844 dictionary gives the translation "traffic." Anthropologists have pointed out that the notions of buying and selling were completely foreign to Polynesian cultures, where "gift exchange" was the practiced custom. Forms of trading were carried out with various commodities, such as food and goods, but land did not come into the commodity category for any Polynesian culture.[23] I have concluded that either the chiefs involved did not read these particular documents, or, more plausibly, that they did not perceive any significance in the detail of the document, having had no experience of how these pieces of paper were used. I suspect that they would have construed such an inappropriate use of the word *hoko* as consistent with the Englishmen's limited knowledge of the Maori language.

A complicating factor is that by the end of the nineteenth century, the Maori term in general use for "land sale" was *hoko whenua*. I have concluded, having considered documents in Maori written both by Maori and Englishmen of the period, that the change in the semantics of *hoko* to allow it to convey the meaning of complete alienation in respect of land is one initially introduced by Englishmen. It appears to be the term they chose to convey the English concept of "sale," a concept that was not present in the Maori culture or language until the latter part of the nineteenth century. The writings of early settlers seem to indicate that they also attempted, unsuccessfully, to have *tuku* take on the same meaning.[24]

Essential Meaning of the Land Transaction Documents

Each of the pre-Treaty documents clearly describes the allocation of lands to individuals, and later to their children and descendants as well, under the custom of *tuku whenua*. Each of the Crown Purchase deeds describes a *tuku whenua* to the Queen of England and her descendants for her subjects. Both types carry two fundamental assumptions: first, that the transaction will create a lasting relationship between the tribe and the individual or the Crown; and second, that the *mana* of the allocating tribe will always be recognized and certainly not extinguished. In the Crown Purchase deeds, this is mentioned quite specifically,[25] as is the undertaking to protect Muriwhenua customary values and rights in the land.[26]

Translations of the Deeds

The examination of the translations that accompany these documents demonstrates clearly why the Crown maintained that with each transaction the tribes severed all their ties to the land. The quality of the translations varies from good (for two documents) to careless (for several) to very misleading and essentially wrong (for the remaining majority). The most serious error in the pre-Treaty documents is that almost all of these wrongly translate *tuku* as "sell." However, they do not do so consistently. Frequently, in the same document the word will be translated both as "sell" and then "give" or "transfer" or "let go."[27] In the Crown Purchase deeds, it is translated as "transfer, convey," as well as "sell, purchase, pay." Other serious errors in the Crown Purchase deeds are that the acknowledgment of the *mana* of the chiefs is translated into payment for their "right and title over all of this land." Similarly, the undertaking to protect and preserve the customary values, rights, and relationships and connections to the land is translated as "all our right title claim and interest whatsoever thereon . . . to hold to Queen Victoria." This implies removal of the rights rather than preservation and protection.[28]

None of the translations of the Crown Purchase deeds can be described as accurate.[29] It is almost certain that the so-called translations were actually drawn up first, using complicated, quasi-legal English. Then someone attempted the virtually impossible job of translating them into Maori. I have no doubt at all that they were trying to convey the notion of complete and absolute alienation of the land. The English "translations" demonstrate that very clearly. But what they were attempting to convey were notions from English culture of English land tenure systems. The plain fact of the matter was that Maori did not possess the words or concepts to do it. Had the tribes been able to comprehend that the English were actually attempting to extinguish their *mana whenua,* they would never have agreed to any of the transactions. Furthermore, the tribes had signed a treaty with the Queen of England that guaranteed that their *mana* in their lands would always be upheld. The intentions of the English (including Crown agents) as expressed in the translations clearly were not in keeping with the Treaty. It is also quite clear, given the continuous protest of tribes that has gone on since they realized what the English intentions in fact were,[30] that the English had not been able to convey their intentions to the tribes at the time of the transactions. The documents in Maori are written proof of this fact.

The unfortunate result of these failed attempts at translation was that the Crown has maintained to date that Muriwhenua willingly and knowingly gave up 75 percent of their lands to Europeans, and hence, that the tribes effectively deprived themselves forever of their main economic base. I hope I have been able to demonstrate that the tribes of Muriwhenua did not do that.

Postscript

In March 1997 the Waitangi Tribunal, a commission of inquiry into Maori grievances, issued its findings regarding the loss of the lands of the Muriwhenua tribes. It had investigated the land transactions between Maori and the English in Muriwhenua between 1834 and 1865, drawing extensive evidence from Maori, the Crown, and many other experts in the field. Its investigations took more than seven years to complete.

The Waitangi Tribunal upheld the claims of Muriwhenua Maori and found that Maori title to all the lands transacted in the period had never been extinguished. The tribes of Muriwhenua are now moving toward settling these claims. They are seeking the return of all their lands, along with compensation for being deprived of an economic base for more than 150 years. Their primary goal is the restoration of the five tribes to prosperity, with their *mana* over their traditional territories recognized and provided for in New Zealand law.

NOTES

1. Although there has been agreement that land and other resources must be returned, only a very small amount has actually been handed over.
2. Research for this paper was conducted in the Far North among the Muriwhenua tribes, namely Ngati Kahu, Te Rarawa, Ngai Takoto, Te Aupouri, and Ngati Kuri. I have genealogical links to all these tribes, though my main affiliations are Ngati Kahu and Te Rarawa.
3. Of the sixty-one surviving documents of pre-Treaty land transactions in

Muriwhenua, forty-three were written in English. These would have been incomprehensible to Maori. It can only be assumed that they were written for English-speaking readers, such as land commissioners or Crown agents. All of the Crown Purchase deeds were written in Maori. See Margaret Mutu, "Cultural Misunderstanding or Deliberate Mistranslation? Deeds in Maori of Pre-Treaty Land Transactions in Muriwhenua and their English Translations," *Te Reo: Journal of the Linguistic Society of New Zealand* 35 (1992): 57–103, and Margaret Mutu, "Muriwhenua–Crown Alliances," Document No. H10, Muriwhenua Land Claim (WAI 45), Wellington, Waitangi Tribunal, 1993.

4. The concept of *mana* is very difficult to convey in English; likewise, *mana whenua*. The common translation of "power, authority" for *mana* and "power and authority for land" for *mana whenua* is a gross oversimplification and leaves out, among other things, the crucial component of "derived from divine powers." Possible definitions in English are discussed in Rev. Maori Marsden, "God, Man, and Universe: A Maori View," in *Te Ao Hurihuri*, ed. Michael King (Auckland: Reed, 1992), 118, and Cleve Barlow, *Tikanga Whakaaro—Key Concepts in Maori Culture* (Auckland: Oxford University Press, 1991), 61.

5. Mutu, "Cultural Misunderstanding," 60.

6. Ibid., 61. Also see pp. 62 and 64, where several examples from periods ranging from precontact times to the present are also given.

7. Raymond Firth, *The Economics of the New Zealand Maori* (1959; Wellington: R. E. Owen, Government Printer, 1973), 388.

8. It appears that this system may not necessarily be restricted to the Pacific. I am informed that the Swiss have a strikingly similar system (Maurice Alemann, personal communication).

9. Wilkie Rasmussen, "Tuku and Hoko—A Comparative Study of tuku and hoko in Muriwhenua and Tongareva Henua in the Cook Islands," term paper, Maori Studies Department, University of Auckland, 1991.

10. See, for example, Ron Crocombe, *Land Tenure in the Pacific* (Suva: University of the South Pacific, 1987), and Henry Lundsgaarde, *Land Tenure in Oceania* (Honolulu: University of Hawai'i Press, 1974).

11. Firth, *Economics of the New Zealand Maori*, 388–390; Norman Smith, *Maori Land Law* (Wellington: A. H. Reed and A. W. Reed, 1960), 102–103; and George Graham, "Whangai Tamariki," *Journal of the Polynesian Society* 57 (1948): 269–278; each mention the custom almost in passing, although Smith does attempt a definition.

12. Phillipa Wyatt, Master's thesis, University of Auckland, 1991.

13. Phillipa Wyatt, "The 'Sale' of Land in Muriwhenua: A Historical Report on Pre-1840 Land Transactions," Document No. F17, Muriwhenua Land Claim (WAI 45), Wellington, Waitangi Tribunal, 1992.

14. Joan Metge, "Cross-Cultural Communication and Land Transfer in Western

Muriwhenua, 1832–1840," Document No. F13, Muriwhenua Land Claim (WAI 45), Wellington, Waitangi Tribunal, 1992.

15. See Mutu, "Cultural Misunderstanding," 68, and Ormond Wilson, *From Hongi Hika to Hone Heke* (Dunedin: John McIndoe, 1985), 224.

16. See, for example, the reports of Land Claims Commissioners Godfrey (1843) and Bell (1857), and those of the current Crown Law Office: Walzl (1991) and Sinclair (1993).

17. Maurice Alemann, "Muriwhenua Land Claim: Pre-Treaty Purchases," Document No. F11, Muriwhenua Land Claim (WAI 45), Wellington, Waitangi Tribunal, 1992.

18. Maurice Alemann, "Mangonui, Native Reserves, and Opouturi," Document No. H8, Muriwhenua Land Claim (WAI 45), Wellington, Waitangi Tribunal, 1993.

19. From the "Kaitaia" document in Mutu, "Cultural Misunderstanding," 77.

20. From the "Muriwhenua" deed in Mutu, "Muriwhenua," A2–4.

21. The most likely author of the Crown Purchase deeds was H. T. Kemp. He is reported (by English observers) as being very proficient in the Maori language. He published a Maori grammar book, which allows a clear assessment of his ability. It is full of basic errors, not only in the description of pronunciation but also in lexical items (both spelling and translation) and grammatical explanations (see Mutu, "Muriwhenua," 24–27).

22. See Wyatt, "The Old Land Claims" and "The 'Sale' of Land" in particular, for several specific examples.

23. See Metge, Firth, and also Anne Salmond, "Submission for the Waitangi Tribunal, Muriwhenua Land Claim," Document No. D17, Wellington, Waitangi Tribunal, 1991.

24. Mutu, "Muriwhenua," 39 ff.

25. Ibid., 22–23.

26. Ibid., 30.

27. Mutu, "Cultural Misunderstanding," 91. Although the authorship of these translations is not clear, consistency of style, and types of errors, omissions, and additions seem to indicate that the Englishmen named in the documents translated them.

28. Mutu, "Muriwhenua," 24, 35.

29. Likewise, it has been clearly demonstrated that the official "translation" of the Treaty of Waitangi is very inaccurate. See Bruce Biggs, "Humpty Dumpty and the Treaty of Waitangi," in *Waitangi: Maori and Pakeha Perspectives of the Treaty of Waitangi*, ed. I. H. Kawharu (Auckland: Oxford University Press, 1991), 300–312.

30. See Claudia Geiringer, "Subsequent Maori Protest Arising from the Crown Land Purchases in Muriwhenua, 1850–1865," Document No. H7, Muriwhenua Land Claim (WAI 45), Wellington, Waitangi Tribunal, 1993.

CONTRIBUTORS

Ian G. Barber has a Ph.D. in archaeology from the University of Otago, Dunedin, New Zealand, where he also taught anthropology. He is currently acting Senior Archaeologist for the New Zealand Historic Places Trust (Pouhere Taonga), Wellington, New Zealand. His research interests include economic and environmental archaeology, the archaeology of culture change, cultural heritage management, and the interface of archaeology and historical anthropology.

Leonard Bell teaches art history at the University of Auckland. His *Colonial Constructs: European Images of Maori, 1840–1914* (1992) was published by Auckland University Press and Melbourne University Press. His current research focuses on cross-cultural representations in visual media in the South Pacific from the mid-eighteenth century to the present.

Alex Calder teaches in the English Department of the University of Auckland. He is the editor of a nonfiction anthology, *The Writing of New Zealand: Inventions and Identities* (1993) and has published many essays on American, New Zealand, and Pacific literature. His more recent writings focus on cultural theory through a study of literary and ethnographic representations of *tapu* (taboo). In 1997 he received a Marsden Award to conduct research in the area of settlement studies.

Simon During teaches English and cultural studies at the University of Melbourne. He has written widely on cultural and literary history and theory, and is the author of *Foucault and Literature* (1992) and *Patrick White* (1996), and editor of *The Cultural Studies Reader* (1993).

Rod Edmond is Senior Lecturer in English and Director of the Centre for Colonial and Postcolonial Research at the University of Kent at

Canterbury, United Kingdom. He was born in New Zealand and educated at Victoria University, Wellington and Oxford University. He is the author of *Affairs of the Hearth: Victorian Poetry and Domestic Narrative* (1988) and *Representing the South Pacific: Colonial Discourse from Cook to Gaughin* (1997). He has also published essays on Victorian literature; modernism and empire; Western writing about the Pacific, contemporary Pacific, New Zealand, and Australian writing; and literary theory. He is now beginning work on a study of disease, particularly leprosy, in colonial discourse.

'I. Futa Helu is Director of 'Atenisi University, Tonga. His writings on classical Greece and the culture and history of Tonga include *Herakleitos of Ephesus* (1995) and *Tradition and Good Governance* (1997).

Pat Hohepa is Professor of Maori Studies at the University of Auckland, where he teaches Maori language, culture, and society at undergraduate and postgraduate levels. He is the coauthor of *The Puriri Trees Are Laughing: A Political History of the Ngapuhi in the Inland Bay of Islands* (1987) and has written many other books and papers in the fields of linguistics and Maori studies.

Mark Houlahan lectures in the English Department of the University of Waikato, Hamilton, New Zealand, where he teaches and writes on the print cultures of Renaissance England and Aotearoa–New Zealand.

Jonathan Lamb was educated at the University of York and taught for many years at the University of Auckland. He is now a professor of eighteenth-century literature at Princeton University. As a fellow of the American Council of Learned Societies, in the course of the coming academic year he will be researching a new book on the culture of contact in the eighteenth century, first at the Centre for Cross-Cultural Research, and then at the Humanities Research Centre, Canberra. He is the author of *Sterne's Fiction and the Double Principle* (1989) and *The Rhetoric of Suffering* (1995), and he edited a special volume of *Eighteenth Century Life: European Voyages in the South Pacific* (1994).

David Mackay is Dean of Humanities and Social Sciences at Victoria University of Wellington. He was born in Dunedin and educated at Victoria University of Wellington and University College, London. His publications include *In the Wake of Cook* (1985) and *A Place of Exile: The European Settlement of New South Wales* (1985).

Paul G. McHugh is a lecturer at the University of Cambridge and a tutor at Sidney Sussex college. His book *The Maori Magna Carta* was published in 1991. He has published numerous articles on aboriginal land rights both in their historical and contemporary aspects. He has also advised the New Zealand, Canadian, and Norwegian governments in this field.

'Okusitino Māhina is a sociologist, anthropologist, and historian currently lecturing in social anthropology at the Tamaki campus, University of Auckland. He studied at 'Atenisi University in Tonga, the University of Auckland, and the Australian National University in Canberra, where he gained a Ph.D. in Pacific history. While on leave of absence from the University of Auckland, he will be Director of the 'Atenisi Institute in 1998 and 1999.

Malama Meleisea is an associate professor and Director of the Centre for Pacific Studies at the University of Auckland. He is the author of *The Making of Modern Samoa* (1987) and *Change and Adaptations in Western Samoa* (1992), and a contributing editor of *Lagaga: A Short History of Western Samoa* (1987) and *Land Issues in the Pacific* (1994).

Margaret Mutu, Senior Lecturer in Maori Studies at the University of Auckland, teaches Maori language and Treaty of Waitangi Issues courses. She is also the head claimant researcher for the five tribes of the Far North, whose extensive land claims against the Crown were upheld in 1997. Dr Mutu is a descendant of the Ngati Kahu, Te Rarawa, and Ngati Whatua tribes.

Bridget Orr is an assistant professor of English at Fordham University. She has published essays on Restoration and eighteenth-century literature and edited a special number of *The Eighteenth Century: Theory and Interpretation, The Pacific Eighteenth Century* (1997). She is currently completing a book on Restoration drama and colonial expansion under the later Stuarts.

J.G.A. Pocock, Professor Emeritus at Johns Hopkins University, has been Professor of Political Science at the Univeristy of Canterbury and of History and Political Science at Washington University, St. Louis. He is the author of *The Ancient Constitution and the Feudal Law* (1957), *The Machiavellian Moment* (1975), and *Virtue, Commerce, and History* (1985). He is now at work on studies of Enlightenment historiography and the political theory of historiography, which have rekindled his interest in New Zealand and Pacific history.

Nicholas Thomas studied anthropology, archaeology, and Pacific history at the Australian National University and completed a doctorate on Marquesan culture and history in 1986. He has done fieldwork in the Marquesas and Fiji, and has conducted research in many museums and archives in Europe, the United States, and the Pacific; his writing has ranged widely over Pacific history, anthropological theory, and cultural studies. His books include *Entangled Objects* (1991), *Colonialism's Culture* (1994), *Oceanic Art* (1995), and *In Oceania* (1997). He has edited scholarly republications of Johann Reinhold Forster's *Observations Made During a Voyage Round the World* (with Harriet Guest and Michael Dettelbach, 1996), George Forster's *Voyage Round the World* (with Oliver Berghof, forthcoming), and George Keate's *Account of the Pelew Islands* (with Karen Nero, forthcoming). He is Director of the Centre for Cross-Cultural Research at the Australian National University.

Sarah Treadwell is a registered architect and a senior lecturer in the Department of Architecture at the University of Auckland, where she teaches architectural drawing and design. Her main research interests involve colonial images of architecture in New Zealand and the Pacific region.

Paul Turnbull teaches history at James Cook University and is a visiting scholar at the Centre for Cross-Cultural Research, Australian National University. He has written extensively on Enlightenment historiography and early anthropology. He is currently engaged on a large, multimedia project exploring encounters between settlers and Pacific peoples, ca. 1760–1830, and is writing a book on the scientific uses of Australian ancestral remains since 1788.

Stephen Turner has taught at the University of Auckland, where he currently holds a postdoctoral fellowship in the field of settlement studies. He has published articles on European explorations of the Pacific region and is writing a book on settlement and culture in Aotearoa–New Zealand.

Index